Elizabeth's Admiral

RFrank
8 Nov 74

Elizabeth's Admiral

The Political Career of

CHARLES HOWARD

Earl of Nottingham

1536-1624

ROBERT W. KENNY

The
Johns Hopkins
Press

Baltimore
& London

The Johns Hopkins Press, Baltimore, Maryland 21218
The Johns Hopkins Press Ltd., London

Library of Congress Catalog Card Number 76-101459

ISBN-0-8018-1105-8

FRONTISPIECE: *Portrait of Charles Howard, Earl of
Nottingham, 1536–1624, by D. Mytens, courtesy of
the National Maritime Museum, Greenwich.*

To my mother and the memory of my father

Acknowledgments

I wish to express my thanks first to the Trustees of the British Museum for allowing me to work in documentary materials, particularly the Caesar Papers, which bear upon Howard's life, and to the officials of the Public Record Office and Somerset House for the help and co-operation generously given me. I am grateful, too, to the librarians and staffs of the libraries at The University of Chicago, The University of Minnesota, The Institute of Historical Research, The Library of Congress, The George Washington University, The University of Texas, and, most of all, the Folger Shakespeare Library for countless courtesies and unfailing help.

Of the many persons who helped me with advice and suggestions, I must particularly thank Professor Herbert Heaton, who first suggested the project, Professor Joel Hurstfield, Sir John Neale, and S. T. Bindoff, who guided me in the use of materials in English archives, Professor Charles Gray, Professor John Clive, and the late Professor J. Harry Bennett, who read many parts of the manuscript and recommended useful changes. I also thank Miss M. C. Cross, Miss P. M. Handover, and Mr. A. R. Batho for pointing out materials which otherwise would have been unknown to me. I wish to express my gratitude to the National Maritime Museum, Greenwich, and to the Folger Shakespeare Library for permission to reproduce illustrative material. To the Research Committee of The George Washington University I owe my thanks for financial assistance in preparing the manuscript for publication. I am deeply grateful to Mrs. Florence G. Strum for her painstaking and expert editorial assistance. Finally, my debt to my wife for her loyalty and encouragement is more than can ever be repaid.

Contents

INTRODUCTION   *1*

Howard's character and family background

I.   EARLY LIFE AND PREFERMENT   9

*Childhood and training at court; first
employment by the crown; marriage and
succession to barony; appointment as lord
chamberlain*

II.   LORD ADMIRAL   *33*

*Appointment as lord admiral; the
administration of the admiralty and the scope
of the lord admiral's powers*

III.   FRUITS OF THE SEA   *63*

*Perquisites and privileges of the lord
admiral; his droit-gathering machinery;
incomes from casualties and privateering*

IV.   IN COUNTY AND COUNCIL   88

*Appointment to the Privy Council and
participation in court politics; role as county
magnate and head of family*

V.   PREPARATIONS FOR WAR   *108*

*Howard's participation in the mobilization
against Spain*

VI.   THE COMING OF THE CRISIS   121

Howard's place in the Armada tradition; his
command of the fleet against the Armada;
the long wait for battle

VII.   HOUR OF TRIUMPH   137

Meeting and defeating the Spanish Armada;
the rewards and frustrations of victory

VIII.   THE ENGLISH ARMADA   161

Mobilization of a fleet to attack Spain; the
diversion at Calais; the offensive renewed

IX.   THE CAPTURE OF CÁDIZ   185

Rivalry between commanders; capture and
looting of the city; Essex's attempts to extend
the offensive; reception in England

X.   EARL OF NOTTINGHAM   203

Howard's growing rivalry with Essex and
alliance with Cecil; his elevation to earldom;
quarrel with Essex

XI.   LORD GENERAL   217

Mobilization against Spanish invasion in
1599

XII.   ESSEX AND ELIZABETH   233

The Essex rebellion; alliance with Cecil at the
end of Elizabeth's reign

XIII.   AN OLD MAN IN A NEW AGE   260

Nottingham's relationship with James; the
decline of wartime prosperity; second
marriage; the affair of the pirates; the wine
farm and other revenues

CONTENTS

XIV. YEARS OF DECLINE   287

*Personal misfortunes; Northampton's
hostility; the investigations into naval
corruption; surrender of the lord admiralship*

EPILOGUE   332

Retirement and death; the family descent

INDEX   339

Elizabeth's Admiral

Introduction

Charles Howard, Lord Howard of Effingham and earl of Nottingham, lord admiral of England for more than thirty years, occupies a curious place in the history of his age. Not only was he very close to the center of power for an extraordinarily long time, he had a highly visible role in most of the best-remembered events of the reigns of Elizabeth I and James I—the execution of Mary Stuart, the defeat of the Spanish Armada, the capture of Cádiz, the fall of Essex, the Spanish peace settlement, and the decline of the monarchy. Yet he remains one of the least known of the major courtiers and politicians. Born in the year of the Pilgrimage of Grace, he was a young man of promise in the early Elizabethan years, not really doing much, but evidently waiting for more significant roles. He waited a very long time, but when he finally came into his own, he held on with tenacity. In his tenure of power he outlived whole generations. Sir Francis Walsingham was not far from his own age, but Howard continued in office nearly thirty years after Walsingham's death. He outlived Burghley by twenty-six years and Burghley's son by twelve; he had been lord admiral for seven years when George Villiers, his successor in that office, was born, but Villiers outlived him by only four years. An entire generation knew him as the "old lord admiral" who had been a court presence as long as could be remembered.

But even though his longevity in politics set him apart from other men, Howard has rarely been called a statesman. He had a strong personal loyalty to his sovereign, for whom he believed he sacrificed his energies, estates, and fortunes, and he was faithful to the standards of justice and honor accepted by his class. But he was also an important monopolist at a time when it was beginning to be felt strongly that patents of privilege and political sinecures were against the public interest. Like others who were similarly placed, he used the power and perquisites of his high offices frankly and freely to augment his own income and to advance the fortunes of his followers. He was a modestly talented man whose use of authority reflected rather than helped to fashion prevailing attitudes: under Elizabeth he was a diligent, loyal, somewhat cautious administrator and commander who merited the affection of his country and carried his honors with dignity and grace; to James he was no less loyal, but his administration became flaccid and self-serving, completely blind to the corruption it was helping to create. In the life of perhaps no other man is the change in the nature of government that came with the change of dynasty so clearly reflected.

Howard owed his place in politics and office neither to his executive or diplomatic skills, which were adequate but not remarkable, nor to his charm of manner and grace of person, which were no more than he needed. He was propelled into the center of English politics by being born at the right time into the right circle. To be a Howard in the sixteenth century and to become the competent heir of one of the great officers of state was to be given an advantage over other men. Whatever gifts other men might have to demonstrate, a Charles Howard of Effingham could go very far indeed by simply being reasonably honest, respectably diligent, and unimpeachably loyal. Aristocratic government had always been a blend of rising men, men of unusual personal or public qualities, and sons of established families whose talents were almost irrelevant to the positions they held. That quality would not be quite so evident in the future, partly because of the way Charles Howard and his generation used their birthright.

As the young Howard grew up, he could have looked around the court to find a dozen or more highly placed kinsmen; he might have been pardoned for assuming that the inner circle of power was largely made up of his uncles and cousins—with, of course, his father, who became a trusted councilor to two queens. The Howards had been as successful as any noble family in building an empire in the marriage bed; if Howard blood had had a greater cementing force, Howards and their connections might well have been able to dominate the court at nearly any time in the sixteenth or early seventeenth century. The family was not old to the nobility by the standards of the time, but in the fourteenth century it had begun to rise rapidly above its origins in the lower gentry of Norfolk. A Sir John Howard at the end of the thirteenth century became a corporation counsel and finally a justice; he was followed by a line of Sir Johns and Sir Roberts who married heiresses and widows, sat in Parliament, served on commissions, presided at quarter sessions, and brawled with their neighbors in the characteristic fashion of late-medieval gentlemen. Family expectations suddenly reached a new plane when early in the fifteenth century Robert Howard married Margaret de Mowbray, daughter of the powerful duke of Norfolk, and their offspring, John, already a friend of Edward IV and a prominent Yorkist, came into line for the title. He became the close ally of Richard, duke of Gloucester, and shared as much as any man in Gloucester's rise. Richard III made him earl marshal, lord steward, lord admiral, gave him his grandfather's dukedom, and trusted him entirely, perhaps to the point of commissioning him, as lieutenant of the Tower of London, to kill the young princes in his custody. Or John might even have killed them for his own profit, since he was a principal heir of their lands.

John Howard, first duke of Norfolk in the Howard line, was faithful to his losing cause; when he died in battle, the empire he had built tottered badly. He was attainted posthumously, his titles and estates were confiscated, and his son Thomas spent three years in prison. But Lord Thomas saw nothing to be gained in futile loyalty to a dead cause; when released from prison he worked himself carefully back into the inner circle at court and earned the confidence of the new king—though not all of the confiscated inheritance. Fifteenth- and sixteenth-century Howards were usually soldiers and some won great reputations for valor, but this one was the greatest soldier of all. He put down local rebellions, he commanded

Genealogical chart (family tree)

SIR ROBERT HOWARD — MARGARET, DA. OF DUKE OF NORFOLK

SIR JOHN HOWARD, 1ST DUKE OF NORFOLK (1420-1485) — CATHERINE, DA. OF LORD MOLEYNS

ELIZABETH TILNEY — THOMAS, EARL OF SURREY, 2ND DUKE OF NORFOLK (1443-1524) — 2) AGNES TILNEY

THOMAS, 3RD DUKE OF NORFOLK (1473-1554)
ANNE, DA. OF EDWARD IV 2) ELIZABETH, DA. OF DUKE OF BUCKINGHAM
LORD EDMUND, M. JOYCE CULPEPER
SIR EDWARD, LORD ADMIRAL (1477-1513)
ELIZABETH, M. LORD ROCHFORD

HENRY, EARL OF SURREY (1517-1547)
FRANCES, DA. OF EARL OF OXFORD
THOMAS, VISCOUNT BINDON
MARY, M. DUKE OF RICHMOND
5) CATHERINE — HENRY VIII — 2) ANNE
ELIZABETH I (1533-1603)

MARY, DA. OF EARL OF ARUNDEL
2) THOMAS, 4TH DUKE OF NORFOLK (1536-1572)
MARGARET, DA. OF LORD AUDLEY
HENRY, EARL OF NORTHAMPTON (1540-1614)
JANE, M. EARL OF WESTMORELAND
CATHERINE, M. LORD BERKELEY

ANNE, DA. OF LORD DACRE
PHILIP, EARL OF ARUNDEL (1557-1595)
THOMAS, EARL OF SUFFOLK (1561-1626)
WILLIAM, OF NAWORTH (1563-1640)
MARGARET, M. EARL OF DORSET

THOMAS, 2ND EARL OF ARUNDEL (1585-1646)

KATHERINE, BROUGHTON
WILLIAM, 1ST LORD EFFINGHAM (1510?-1573)
2) MARGARET, DA. OF SIR THOMAS GAMAGE
SIR THOMAS, ATTAINTED IN 1536
ANNE, M. EARL OF OXFORD
DOROTHY, M. EARL OF DERBY
ELIZABETH, M. EARL OF SUSSEX
CATHERINE, M. SIR RHESE, AP THOMAS 2) EARL OF BRIDGEWATER

AGNES, M. WILLIAM PAULET, 3RD MARQUIS OF WINCHESTER (1535-1598)

KATHERINE, DA. OF LORD HUNSDON
CHARLES, 1ST EARL OF NOTTINGHAM (1536-1624)
2) MARGARET, DA. OF EARL OF MORAY SHE M. 2) WILLIAM MONSON, VISCOUNT CASTLEMAINE
SIR WILLIAM, OF LINGFIELD,
JOHN, LORD SHEFFIELD
MARY, M. EDWARD, LORD DUDLEY
DOUGLAS 2) (1) ROBERT, EARL OF LEICESTER 3) SIR EDWARD STAFFORD
EDMUND, EARL OF MULGRAVE (1564-1646)
SIR ROBERT DUDLEY
HENRY, 4TH EARL OF DERBY (1531-1593)
FRANCES, M. EDWARD, EARL OF HERTFORD
ELIZABETH, M. SIR GEORGE BOURCHIER
THOMAS, 3RD EARL OF SUSSEX (1526-1583)

SIR CHARLES
SIR FRANCIS
SIR EDWARD
JAMES (D. 1608)
JAMES (D. 1610)
THOMAS (D. 1616)
WILLIAM (D. 1617)

CHARLES, 3RD EARL OF NOTTINGHAM (1610-1681), M. ARABELLA, DA. OF EDWARD SMITH
CHARLES, 2ND EARL OF NOTTINGHAM (1579-1642)
CHARITY, W. OF RICHARD LECHE 2) MARY, DA. OF SIR WILLIAM COKAYNE
ELIZABETH, M. SIR ROBERT SOUTHWELL
MARGARET, M. SIR RICHARD LEVESON
HENRY, 12TH EARL OF KILDARE — FRANCES — 2) HENRY, LORD COBHAM

WILLIAM, 3RD LORD EFFINGHAM (1577-1615)
ANNE, DA. OF LORD ST. JOHN OF BLETSOE

4

fleets against pirates, he terrorized the borders—but most significantly, when he was past seventy he led his countrymen in one of the most famous exploits of their military history, the annihilation of the Scots at Flodden. The reward of victory was power; by the time of his death his hold was so firm that he was able to get his son named as successor in his offices, including the lord treasurership, as well as in his titles and lands. And he moved his family so near the throne that two of his granddaughters became wives of Henry VIII and another was married to Henry VIII's bastard son.

When he died in 1524, Thomas, the second Howard of Norfolk, left not only wealth and power but a brood of descendants by two wives who populated the Elizabethan court with their offspring. Twelve of his sixteen children reached marriageable age; of his thirty or so grandchildren, nearly all inherited, earned, or married titles.[1]

With several brief interruptions, there had been one or more Howards on the Privy Council since 1483; three Howards had been lord admiral and two had been lord treasurer. Nearly all who reached adulthood had seen military command, headed embassies, and held governorships. It was an exalted patrimony, given still greater meaning by the special place earned by William, the first Howard of Effingham. He became governor of Calais and then lord admiral and privy councilor under Edward VI and was raised to the peerage under Mary as a reward for his service at the time of Wyatt's rebellion. One tradition gives his arguments with the queen the major credit for saving the life of Princess Elizabeth after that affair. On more reliable authority he is seen as Elizabeth's principal protector in the months that followed. By the next year his loyalty to her had made him a suspected person; the imperial ambassador, one of the most reliable sources for court gossip, wrote that it was "highly probable" that Howard

---

1. The genealogical chart opposite this page shows how many of the descendants of the second duke of Norfolk were prominent at the Elizabethan court. The chart has been simplified to eliminate minor connections and children who did not survive to maturity, except for Charles Howard's own offspring.

knew of and consented to plots in which Elizabeth was believed to be involved. In April, 1555, it was he who urged in council again that her restrictions be removed and that she be brought back to court. His obvious support of the heir finally brought him the loss of his great office of lord admiral. The popularity that Elizabeth and her cause brought him, however, made him a dangerous enemy, so Mary found it expedient to mollify him with a pension and finally with appointment as lord chamberlain. Mary soon died, and for the rest of his life William Howard was a conspicuous figure at court and ranked high in the new queen's confidence. To live in the esteem of the crown was to confer an inestimable boon on his son. As long as his father lived, Charles Howard necessarily remained in his shadow, but it was a protective shadow which allowed him to accumulate the experience that would have to precede preferment, a covering under which he could find that access to the great which outsiders had to seek for long, painful, and expensive years.

As a man, Charles Howard remains more elusive than many of his contemporaries mainly because no great body of his own correspondence has survived to characterize him. From many casual and offhand references, however, one can piece together some idea of what lay behind the grave façade of his portraits. Physically he was the embodiment of nobility: tall, imposing, and—even in his old age—splendid. He was in fact a bit of a peacock; he paid close attention to the cut of the doublet and the angle of the plume, to the fullness of the cape and the fit of the hose. Even when he had passed seventy he was still appearing at court in the white satins, tawny velvets, and jeweled hats that normally might adorn gallants of twenty-five. For as long as possible he thought of himself as an athlete. Through the early years of Elizabeth's reign, he appeared at the lists with great regularity, winning prizes as often as most. When he grew too old for tilting, he redoubled his interest in hunting, both with dogs and with falcons. His dogs commanded such respect that on one occasion, when James I needed to send a gift to the king of France, he could think of nothing more acceptable than a couple of the Howard spaniels. As a hunter, among the official functions that Howard most cherished was the guardianship of the royal deer in the collection of forests for which he was keeper. Particularly when the heedless generosity of James was seriously depleting the herds, Howard seems to have worried over the selection of bucks to be given away nearly as much as over the appointment of captains to command the king's ships.

The qualities of the huntsman, the athlete, the dandy, and the soldier and mariner are not readily combined with those of the scholar, the bureaucrat, or the clerk. Howard certainly was not the man to join them with ease or grace. He had to become an administrator on a large scale, but it was always apparent that he felt more comfortable with ships and horses than with books and ledgers. This was fortunate, for he never would have gained much glory for his intellectual power or organizational genius. He was poorly and haphazardly educated; he despised lawyers and rather disdained men of letters. At the same time, he was by no means a stupid man. He had a practical common sense which was of great value as long as it did not have to be exercised with uncommon subtlety. Unfortunately, as he grew older, his common sense was no match for the growing intricacy of life and intrigue at court. His lack of courtly wit combined with a growing looseness of tongue to make him often enough sound like a fool. The Jacobean court had no great respect for his past accomplishments and set a rather low value on his present charms. In all truth, by the time James came to England, Howard, now the earl of Nottingham, must have been a bore: a vain, proud, pompous, and garrulous old man whose wealth and talents no longer matched his pretensions. But that unflattering picture must be balanced against the earlier one of a diligent adviser and careful, loyal commander of men and ships who performed ably when his country most needed him.

I: *Early Life and Preferment*

Beyond the year of his birth, 1536, almost nothing is known for certain about Charles Howard's early life. Such a situation is not surprising; children came and went in even the greatest houses without leaving much of a record. Nor is Charles's mother well known. She was Margaret, daughter of Sir Thomas Gamage of Coity, Glamorganshire, second wife to William Howard. The family was prosperous but generally undistinguished, its connections being with several Welsh and West Country families of purely local influence. This was not a brilliant match for even a younger son of the duke of Norfolk. As a child, Charles apparently was schooled in the house of his uncle, the third Howard of Norfolk, and saw some nominal service as a page to his cousin Thomas, later the fourth duke of Norfolk. What education he got can only be surmised: considerable French and some Latin, a great deal of chivalric exercise at arms, a smattering of legal traditions, and a little penmanship. Somewhere, perhaps as a complement to his schooling, he also picked up an enthusiasm for hunting and fishing which lasted the rest of his life. Charles did not stay in the Norfolk household long enough either to get much schooling or to develop any attachment for his cousin, since by 1552 he had been sent to France to the household of the vidame de Chartres. He was not treated as well as "was promised or expected," and his father went to the Privy Council to bring pressure in Paris to have him returned.[1] Presumably he had been sent to master the French language and courtly arts in a kind of sixteenth-century anticipation of

1. *Calendar of State Papers, Foreign Series, of the Reign of Edward VI, 1547–1553* (London, 1861), p. 226.

the Grand Tour, but again, since the training was cut short, the achievement was imperfect. Howard was not a well-educated nobleman even for his time, though he did plume himself on his French, nor was he ever able to think of himself as an accomplished courtier.

When William Howard began to gain preferment, the kind of training more immediately pertinent to a career at court was made possible for his son. Charles went to Calais when his father became governor and to sea when his father became lord admiral. The naval experience was not intensive —he went with the fleet to meet Philip of Spain in 1554, to take him to Flanders in 1555, and to cruise the Channel in the summer of 1557—but it did bring a growing familiarity with the handling of ships which would help him to qualify for his own great appointment years later.

The pulse of the junior Howard must have quickened even more than most Englishmen's when the perils of Mary's reign ended and the bright new age began. Despite his superficial education, he possessed all the external qualifications for a spectacular courtly career. He was three years younger than the new queen, a handsome young man with "an eminently fine person and countenance; a sweet and frank temper; and a deportment at once elegant and dignified."[2] Moreover, he was one of the handful at court who could congratulate themselves on being the queen's cousins. He was noticeable enough to be mentioned in a casual way as a possibly suitable candidate for the queen's hand if she decided to marry one of her own subjects. But not only was that prize never within reach, it was a very long time before he was able to capitalize in any significant way on the advantages of his situation.

For the next several years he continued to live as much concealed as protected by the presence of his father. Early in 1559 Lord Howard, again accompanied by his son, went as negotiator to the peace conference at Cateau-Cambrésis. When arrangements were finally concluded, Charles traveled

2. Edmund Lodge, *Portraits of Illustrious Personages of Great Britain,* 4 vols. (London, 1835), 4, no. 17.

from Brussels to give the queen first news that Philip II had confirmed the articles. It was perhaps as a reward for bringing good news that he received his first independent employment soon afterward.

Superficially, he was little more than a messenger. Henry II of France was wounded in a tourney held to celebrate the peace treaty and the marriage agreement with Spain that would guarantee it. Young Howard, now twenty-three, was appointed to carry him an expression of the queen's grief at his "inconvenience" and to wish him "speedy recovery of his hurt."[3] He left for Paris two days later but was delayed en route by an inhospitable courtier who led him astray and "evil used" him concerning his horses, so that he arrived to learn that Henry II was not recovering but dead. With Mary Stuart now queen of France and the house of Guise dominant, hostility toward England grew, making Howard's status rather uncertain. Still, he visited with the new king, Francis II, in the company of the second duc de Guise and the cardinal of Lorraine, and "the office destined for the father was performed with the son."[4] Howard waited in vain for another audience; all he got was a message from the king to take Elizabeth his commendations with the hope that she would continue "all articles between her and the late King." His lack of access to the king barred any remarkable diplomatic achievements, but while he was waiting for a second audience, Howard pressed Elizabeth's compliments on the queen of Scots and leaders of both court factions. His conduct, according to the resident ambassador, had been such as to cause the court to "conceive well of him."[5]

There are suggestions that he had a less overt mission than

3. *Calendar of State Papers, Foreign Series, of the Reign of Elizabeth, 1558–1559* (London, 1863), pp. 368–69; series hereinafter cited as *Cal. S. P. For., Eliz.*

4. *Ibid.*, 379–80.

5. *Calendar of State Papers and Manuscripts relating to English Affairs, existing in the Archives and Collections of Venice, and other Libraries in Northern Italy*, 38 vols. (London, 1864–1940), 7:394; series hereinafter cited as *Cal. S. P. Venetian.*

wishing the king well. He took with him a bill of exchange for 1,000 crowns, to be used to smuggle the earl of Arran, titular head of the Protestant lords in Scotland, from Geneva, where he had taken refuge from French custody, to England.[6] Arran, who was in line for the Scottish crown after Mary Stuart, had been mentioned as a prospective husband for Elizabeth. Safely off the Continent he might be used as a counterweight against Stuart pretensions in France; if Mary could call Elizabeth a bastard and incapable of inheriting, Elizabeth could claim that Mary had forfeited her kingdom. If this was part of Howard's mission, it at any rate was successful, for Arran was soon out of danger from his Catholic enemies.

After concluding his embassy by appearing as one of the official mourners at the memorial service for Henry II, Howard resumed his role as one of the minor ornaments of the court. He was one of the crowd of well-turned-out young gentlemen who hovered around the queen waiting to attract her notice; he performed occasional personal service, like bearing the canopy of state (with five others) when Elizabeth opened her second Parliament, and he took a regular and enthusiastic part in the jousts and tourneys with which the court amused itself. He was not completely without reward; in December, 1562, he became keeper of the queen's house and park at Oatlands at a salary of 1s. 6d. a day, and in 1564 he won a lease on the rectory at Chieveley, Berkshire, and lands at Billing and Eversholt in Northamptonshire, at an annual rent of £20 13s. 4d. But this, the only tangible evidence of his sovereign's regard in more than a decade, cannot have sated his ambition even for the moment.

As an aspiring courtier and the heir of a great lord, Howard could be expected to gain public experience by serving the crown and council in Parliament. So he did; he was a loyal but scarcely distinguished member of the House of Commons until his father died. His father had offered him first as a candidate for Surrey in 1559, but he entered late into a large

6. *Ibid.,* p. 388.

field—there were finally six candidates—and the confusion and uncertainty of the time were such that even the advice of such a man as the lord chamberlain was insufficient for the free-holders. By the time of the election in late 1562, however, when the family's influence in the county was much more settled, Charles Howard and William More of Loseley, sheriff for Surrey, were returned without opposition. Howard was elected again in 1566 and in 1572; he was regular in his attendance and presumably diligent in supporting the needs of the crown, but he did practically nothing to earn himself a place in surviving records. In 1566 he was a member of the large conference committee sent to the House of Lords to consider a joint address to urge the queen either to marry or to secure the succession; in 1572 he was one of the forty-four members who drew up the accusation of crimes against Mary Stuart after the disclosure of the Ridolfi plot. On several other occasions he appeared on committees for minor bills, but if he or his father expected him to win any kind of acclaim in Commons debates, they were disappointed.

Like most men of his station, Howard became a member of Gray's Inn (in 1564) and a Cambridge master of arts (in 1571), but the former did not mean that he undertook any serious legal study, and the latter did not suggest that he had belatedly become a scholar; neither was much more than a recognition of court prospects. In 1569, Howard for the first time received some indication of the magnitude of service that might be expected of him. With the coming of the Northern rebellion, the most serious internal disorder of Elizabeth's reign, Howard, as a completely untried soldier who had only his impressive family tradition to recommend him, was able to get an important appointment as general of the horse under the earl of Warwick, commander of the army hastily gathered in the southern counties to assist Sussex and Clinton in the north. As it happened, Howard and his three thousand horse soldiers never drew their swords; the rebels under Northumberland and Westmoreland had dispersed while the army was still in Yorkshire. The only real fighting in the episode occurred between Lord Hunsdon and Leonard Dacre, who had taken up the rebellion, after most of the troops had been disbanded and Howard had returned to London. Howard's most active role in the rebellion turned out to be his seizure of Petworth Castle and Northumberland's other properties in Sussex in the name of the queen.[7] He became the administrator of the estates and collected the revenues, perhaps keeping a share for himself, until they were re-granted by the queen.

The following summer and autumn Elizabeth again commissioned Howard for service of "a public character," a service which was half an act of diplomatic courtesy and half a protective gesture. A Spanish fleet had been created in the Netherlands to bring Anne of Austria, Philip II's new bride, to Spain. Troops and warships were necessary for a royal voyage through seas infested with French, English, and Dutch pirates and privateers, but the English feared that such an escort might be a cover for invasion to free Mary Stuart and overthrow the queen, who had now been formally condemned as a heretic. Such projects had already been discussed by Spanish and papal agents. At the end of August, when the armada on the Schelde appeared ready to sail, Elizabeth wrote Lord Admiral Clinton that she had "appointed her navy to put to sea" under Charles Howard and William Winter, a professional seaman who had blockaded the Firth of Forth to prevent the landing of French troops in 1559.[8] Howard and Winter patrolled the Channel until October, when the Spanish ships finally came; they then received the salute they felt was due and escorted the Spaniards through the "English sea." Richard Hakluyt, in the dedication to the 1598 edition of his *Principal Navigations,* made Howard's expedition a feat of great bravery in defiance of the armed might of Spain, which brought to its commander the well-earned applause of the nation: "When the Emperors sister, the spouse of Spaine, with a Fleete of an 130, sailes, stoutly and proudly passed the narow Seas, your Lordship accompanied with ten ships onely

7. State Papers, Domestic Series, Elizabeth, 66/74, Public Record Office, London; series hereinafter cited as S. P. Dom., Eliz.
8. *Calendar of State Papers, Domestic Series, Elizabeth, 1547–1580* (London, 1856), p. 390; series hereinafter cited as *Cal. S. P. Dom., Eliz.*

of her Majesties Navie Roiall, environed their Fleet in most strange and warrelike sort, enforced them to stoope gallant, and to vaile their bonets for the Queene of England." Hakluyt, of course, was writing an encomium to a powerful man he hoped to persuade to become a "munificent and bountifull Patrone" for himself and his projects in aid of navigation; the voyage actually was of far greater importance to its commander than to his country. Hakluyt exaggerated the size of the Spanish fleet grossly, for if any great fleet had attempted a landing, Howard's few ships would never have been able to prevent it. Nor could he have "enforced" the Spanish to salute his queen if the Spanish admiral had chosen to disregard the English claim that the Channel was part of their territorial waters. What is interesting about the voyage is that Howard was on it in the role of admiral. Winter certainly could have commanded the ships alone, as he had done before; Howard's presence suggests that he had perhaps been marked as a likely choice for continuing his family's long relationship with naval command.

His escort for the new Spanish queen made all his previous services seem as "nothing when put in the balance" (in the opinion of the *Biographia Britannica*[9]), and it is usually conceded that knighthood was his reward, although there are enough references to "Charles Howard, Esq." after 1570 to cast some doubt on the matter.[10] At any rate, the command was an important enlargement of Howard's public life and prospects.

In his private life, a much more important event had

9. *Biographia Britannica* (London, 1747–66), 4:2672–73.
10. A letter in the Rutland manuscripts, dated May 14, 1571, refers to Howard with no designation of knighthood when he took the role of the White Knight in a tourney, but the same letter uses "Sir" in reference to Sir Henry Lee. See Historical Manuscripts Commission, *Twelfth Report*, pt. 1: *The Manuscripts of his Grace the Duke of Rutland, K. C. B., preserved at Belvoir Castle* (London, 1888), p. 92; hereinafter cited as *Cal. Rutland MSS*. The following summer a description of the barriers at Whitehall, taken from a manuscript in the Cotton collection, follows the same pattern; see John Nichols, *The progresses and public processions of Queen Elizabeth*, new ed., 4 vols. (London, 1823), 1:276.

already occurred, one which would have lasting public impli-
cations. In July, 1563, any hope of becoming a royal consort
having withered, Howard had taken a wife of less elevated
station. But barring the queen herself, who attended as a
spectator, the age could scarcely have provided a more promising bride than Katherine Carey, eldest daughter of Lord
Hunsdon. She was probably several years younger than Howard, but she was already a maid of honor and a close personal
attendant of the queen. More important, she was Elizabeth's
closest female relative of her own generation on the safely
non-royal side and an intimate friend, insofar as Elizabeth
ever had intimate friends. After marriage she became one of
the ladies of the privy chamber, succeeding in 1572 to the
office of first lady of the chamber, an office as exalted as any
that normally could be given to a female subject. Besides
being one of her mistress's constant personal attendants, she
acted as mistress of the robes, supervising the queen's enormous and expensive wardrobe and keeping watch over the
treasures taken out of the jewel house for the queen's use. It
was Lady Howard who received and accounted for the jewels,
chains, bracelets, gold toothpicks, forks of agate and gold—
whatever could be considered jewelry or plate—that the queen
received from her courtiers at New Year's. She filled the office
creditably for fourteen years, during which time her husband
was rising from a casually employed court gallant to one of
the handful of principal officers and the primary defender of
his country's security. There is nothing to suggest that Howard's wife was in any direct way responsible for his success, but
she certainly would have been able to keep his name before
the queen and remind her, as occasion allowed, of his unflagging zeal and devotion. Nothing much is ever said of Lady
Howard's beauty or of the wealth she brought to the marriage,
but she was a wife of irreproachable conduct, exemplary
loyalty, and genuine devotion. She lived quietly and, though
bound up for many years in the affairs of the royal household,
was seldom mentioned by the vendors of gossip. There is, in
fact, no reason to think that Howard and his wife were not
entirely compatible; certainly neither of them indulged in

much of the extramarital adventure common at a sophisticated court.

But if the marriage was solidly founded in mutual esteem and high expectation, it had but a slender financial base. Lady Howard would have been given some kind of dowry—a sum like the twelve hundred marks given with Howard's elder sister, Lady Douglas Sheffield, would not have been unreasonable—but the exact amount is unknown. Howard himself got £100 a year from his father and little more than £20 from his keepership, beyond which there was precious little to support the match.

The fact is that, for all his power at court, William Howard had no great wealth with which to bless the marriage of his heir. He was one of the considerable body of Elizabethan officeholders who went to their graves complaining that they were being driven into beggary by their sacrifices to the queen's service. No doubt the complaints were uttered partly in the hope that travail would be rewarded and because their expense and responsibility stood as evidence of the queen's trust. But with Lord William the whimperings of sacrifice seem to have been justified. He received pensions and lands and had access to the crown which should have brought a shower of gifts from office-seekers. But his expenses at court were high, his large family included several daughters to be married off, and the offices in his direct gift were not many. As a result he was never able to build more than a modestly comfortable landed estate. From his father he had lands worth not quite £100 a year, but all except the manor of Little Bookham in Surrey had quickly been sold. From Henry VIII he had received Reigate Priory—which became one of the principal family residences and stayed in the hands of his descendants through the seventeenth century—Eastbrooke and Southwick manors in Sussex, West Humble in Surrey, and the priory of Barnstaple in Devon. From Edward VI, Howard got Great Bookham (an important Surrey manor), the smaller manor of Effingham from which he took his title, and a moiety of Reigate Manor. Mary gave him lands in Devonshire and Somersetshire, which he sold, and Elizabeth added the

manor of Kingswood Liberty. In 1560 Howard bought
Blechingley (valued at £45 a year), with another important
residence and influence over a parliamentary borough, and
lands at Lingfield, Hackstal, and Billeshurst. The properties,
most of them in Surrey, were worth altogether about £400 a
year. Salaries and pensions provided him with as much again,
but he found that his total income of £861 6s. 8d. was totally
inadequate to meet his needs. In a document prepared for the
queen about 1565, he said that his expenses exceeded £1,500 a
year without reckoning anything "put in to my persse for to
spend in hawkyng and hontyng & in rewards gyvyn for my
pleasiuir" or for repairs to his house or for the dowry of two
hundred marks a year for his eldest daughter. His expense for
going on progress ran to two hundred pounds a year, and gifts
and rewards at Christmas and New Year's cost another
hundred pounds. He was £2,000 in debt and saw no way to
recover himself or to provide a living for his younger children
without a substantial gift from the queen.[11]

Of course, William Howard may have been exaggerating
the disparity between income and expense in the hope of
maximizing the grant to relieve it. But certainly he thought
that he was being ruined in his service to the crown and that
the queen should lift him up from poverty. In the next few
years, he did make some kind of settlement with his creditors
without selling any more lands, but he remained relatively
poor for the rest of his life. There is a story that during his last
years he begged to be made an earl but was refused because he
lacked the means to support such a dignity.

Beyond the limited financial support which he provided, it
is difficult to assess the influence of the elder Howard on his
son in his last years. There can be little doubt that the father
was a suitor for the preferments the son did win—his small
keepership and his commands in 1569 and 1570. And Lord
William's friendship with the queen and his recognized fidelity to her interests during difficult times had created a fund of

11. S. P. Dom., Eliz., 44/143–44.

good will upon which Charles could hope to draw. But it might also be possible to argue that during his last years Lord William, by occupying one of the major offices, may have kept Charles from receiving important preferment. Not a few young lords spent their most vigorous years with nothing much better to do than display themselves at court while they waited to come into their inheritances. Charles's father, however, was evidently declining by 1570, which may have meant that Charles took over some portion of the chamberlain's duties. By the end of 1572, Lord William was no longer able to carry on and gave up his staff. But because he still needed any salary and perquisites the crown could supply him, he was made lord privy seal, an officer whose responsibilities had become insignificant. He continued to decline, and late in January, 1573, he died "full of years and honour, being of most approved fidelity and unshaken courage."[12] He was buried, in accordance with a will drawn up in 1569, in the church at Reigate.

By the terms of the will, he did not leave his son a rich man. Most of his properties had been settled by another instrument, which does not survive; the will mentions only the manor of Esher, which was to go to Charles along with his robes and collar of the Garter (a grant contrary to the statutes of the order). The younger son, William, got a small money grant, and the rest of the estate after debts were paid went to Lady Howard, who was asked to see that dowries were provided for daughters still unmarried. The language used concerning Esher implies that the manor was in Lord Howard's possession, but it had been given by Mary to the bishops of Winchester, who still held it in 1573. What Howard may have had was a promised lease, since Charles did get a lease in 1578 by threatening that if the bishop would not co-operate he would "compass his object in some other way, without any

12. Arthur Collins, *Collins's Peerage of England: genealogical, biographical, and historical . . .* , rev. Sir Samuel Egerton Brydges, 12 vols. (London, 1812), 4:267.

regard for the bishop's feelings."[13] From sources other than the will it is known that the lands at Lingfield and Great Bookham were settled on the younger son and that Reigate and its lands went to the jointure of the widow. When she died in 1581, Charles Howard paid a livery fine of £58 3s. 6d. for delivery of lands into his possession. When he inherited his title, then, he also inherited a collection of lands worth probably about £300 a year, including the manors of Blechingley, Effingham, Kingswood Liberty, Little Bookham, West Humble, Billeshurst, and Hackstal—all in Surrey—Barnstaple Priory in Devonshire, Wisshanger in Gloucestershire, and Appledram, Eastbrooke, Southwick, and perhaps Barnham in Sussex. This was slender support for a man of exalted traditions and great ambition, and, in spite of later enlargements by the queen, Howard could never call himself a really great landowner. To a greater extent than most men of his station, he had to depend on the generosity of the crown and on his good luck to supply what his patrimony had left wanting.

In some older works Howard is represented as having succeeded his father in office as well as in title and estate,[14] but the notion cannot be supported by contemporary evidence; the earl of Sussex became lord chamberlain, and apparently no new lord privy seal was appointed at all. Howard did, however, get a commission to act as deputy chamberlain in 1574 and 1575 for his cousin Sussex, whose health was so poor that he found it necessary to be away from court for months at a time. His primary responsibility as deputy must have been the co-ordination of the remarkable progress that occupied the court through the summer of 1574: after visiting Theobalds at the end of May, the court continued north and west to Northamptonshire, Warwickshire, and Staffordshire, then south into Worcester and Oxfordshire, reaching Woodstock in

13. Historical Manuscripts Commission, *Seventh Report*, pt. 1: *The Manuscripts of William More Molyneux, Esq., of Loseley Park, Guildford, co. Surrey* (London, 1879), pp. 631–32; hereinafter cited as *Cal. Loseley MSS.*

14. See *Biographia Britannica*, 4:2673; Lodge, *Personages of Great Britain*, 4, no. 17.

September. This progress was the occasion of Leicester's elaborate entertainment at Kenilworth Castle, which lasted for more than two weeks. While Elizabeth remained at Kenilworth, much of the court personnel was housed in Warwick,[15] an arrangement which complicated the responsibility of the chamberlain, who had to work with local officers in supplying housing, transportation, and messenger and food services. Sussex apparently returned to court at the end of the summer, but Howard continued to act as chamberlain through most of the next year.

Lord Howard received new evidence of the queen's esteem when on April 3, 1575, he was elected to the companionship of the Order of the Garter, filling the vacancy created by the execution of his cousin the duke of Norfolk.[16] He was installed on May 8 in ceremonies at Windsor conducted by his father-in-law, Lord Hunsdon, and Sir Henry Sidney. Howard was the nineteenth of the queen's subjects so honored since her accession; of that number, eleven were noblemen of the rank of earl or higher who became companions more or less in due course if they remained on good terms with the crown. Of the remainder, some seem to have been elected as a mark of the queen's particular favor, others to help her satisfy the needs of her preferment-hungry court.

Howard's elevation apparently came from a combination of these factors. He had not yet performed any signal service of valor for which the Garter might be a suitable reward, but he was the heir of a great house and by now a familiar face at court. No doubt he had pressed for the rewards that any nobleman needed to maintain his dignity and increase his prestige; the election might have been a mark of honor to ease the waiting for a more substantial appointment. Or if it had seemed by the time of the Garter election that Sussex would be able to return to court as chamberlain, Howard's appointment might have been designed to compensate him for the

15. Nichols, *Progresses and public processions,* 1:318.
16. George Frederick Beltz, *Memorials of the Most Noble Order of the Garter* (London, 1841), p. clxxxi.

loss of his staff. At any rate, his selection was more a reward for his prospects than for past services; only with the future in mind could he be considered one of the twenty-five most illustrious knights of the realm.

During the next eight years, among the most critical of the reign for determining the direction of basic English policy, Howard remained relatively inconspicuous, though diligent in attendance at court and pressing, whenever he could, for a chance to prove his fidelity and ability in some position of trust. He ranked in this period as one of the lesser nobles about the court, the husband of one of the queen's confidential friends. With no permanent employment, he took precedence as fifteenth among the barons when the Parliaments of 1575 and 1580 met.[17] Such a subordinate role cannot have been to his liking; by 1580 he was forty-four years old, and despite all his claims on the queen's favor, he possessed little tangible evidence that those claims were recognized or would be rewarded. As he approached middle age, the brilliance of his prospects remained unfulfilled.[18]

Howard is, however, first seen during these years as a gentleman of influence in local affairs, a kind of logical continuation of his earlier experience as knight of the shire for Surrey and as his father's deputy lieutenant. Beginning in

17. Sir Symonds D'Ewes, *A Compleat Journal of the Notes, Speeches and Debates, both of the House of Lords and House of Commons throughout the whole Reign of Queen Elizabeth, Of Glorious Memory* (London, 1693), pp. 227, 267.

18. There is some possibility that he may have seen further sea duty on occasion during these years. One of the Fugger correspondents wrote on June 28, 1578, that Lord Howard had arrived as ambassador to the archduke and had been given a splendid welcome in Antwerp (Victor von Klarwill, ed., *The Fugger News-Letters,* 2d ser. [London, 1926], p. 23). This is obviously an error; the ambassadors on that occasion were Sir Francis Walsingham and Lord Cobham. Howard may, however, have escorted the ambassadors by sea and then joined their company during the negotiations. The embassy was a large one, including more than 180 persons; it would have required several ships to carry it with suitable dignity, and it is not unlikely that a man of Howard's standing and availability would have been assigned to take it.

1576, his name appears near the top of lists of gentlemen and property owners appointed to perform some of the numerous duties expected of all members of their class. In a letter and warrant of March 21, he received instructions as a commissioner of muster, along with Lord Admiral Lincoln, the earls of Arundel and Leicester, Viscount Montague, and others, to levy a hundred and fifty able men from the muster of the previous year and to train them as soldiers. The letter dates their appointment from 1574.[19] By 1580, Howard had displaced the other noblemen and appeared at the head of a muster commission, joined by Sir William More, Sir Thomas Browne, Sir Francis Carewe, and Thomas Lyfield.

In 1580 Howard's name appears for the first time on the commissions of the peace for Surrey and for Middlesex. The commissions were made up of two score or so of the principal landowners in each county, headed by some of the chief officers of state. The appearance of names like Bromley, Burghley, Lincoln, and Sussex on Middlesex and Surrey commissions of the peace did not mean that they took active part in the enforcement of peace and law in the counties; the essential members were the county magnates who were in touch with the Privy Council and the court, who sat on the quarter sessions, and who acted as lines of communication between local and central levels of government. Howard and others of his rank would not normally busy themselves with the multiplying details of the justices' administrative tasks, but from the viewpoint of the court he would be, from this time on, one of the officers chiefly accountable for preservation of order in the two counties where the queen would most often be found.

At court he took a conspicuous place in the ceremonials of 1581 associated with the visit of the duc d'Anjou to make a last effort to win the queen's heart and hand. In the fall, after his troops were put in winter quarters, Anjou came to England in person, since long negotiations through regular channels had produced no settlement. He was received by the queen

19. *Cal. Loseley MSS*, p. 628.

with every show of affection and stayed for three months, somewhat to the discomfiture of the English court. After a month, word came of the fall of Tournai to the Spanish army, and Anjou resolved to return to his duties in the Netherlands. Lord Admiral Lincoln left court to prepare a fleet to take him across the Channel, and Lord Howard, who had as much experience in dealing with the French as most, was appointed to command it. On December 18 one of the earl of Rutland's correspondents wrote that it was likely that Anjou would take his leave the next day. But he was easily persuaded to postpone his departure and did not leave until February, 1582. Elizabeth showered him with promises and prepared an elaborate retinue to escort him to Antwerp. She probably did not seriously consider accompanying him farther than the coast, but may have planned to see him off at Dover, since on February 4 Howard, who had left court earlier to assemble the fleet, wrote Walsingham that the town lacked sufficient accommodation for both "Monsieur" and the queen and warned that six houses had been visited by plague. He suggested that the queen should take her leave at Canterbury instead, and so she did.[20] After readying the fleet, Howard rejoined the court and was able to take his due place with Leicester and Hunsdon as one of Anjou's companions at the head of the elaborate procession. When Howard convoyed the queen's suitor and the company of England's "prime knights" to Antwerp with his fleet of fifteen ships, he was undertaking his second naval command of any importance, a command which gave him some further limited sea experience. The company was met at Flushing by the prince of Orange and elaborately entertained at Middleburg and Antwerp; the festivities are described in great detail by Nichols.[21]

In the summer of the same year, Howard again took to sea, although the nature of his mission is not clear. A letter of the merchants of Rouen to the French ambassador complained that in June a privateer of Wight whom they had arrested had

20. *Cal. S. P. Dom., Eliz., 1581–1590* (London, 1865), p. 45.
21. Nichols, *Progresses and public processions,* 2:347–85.

been released by Howard, who had promised to turn him over to admiralty court jurisdiction after his return from the sea but had not done so. The letter indicates that Howard was on his way to Ireland, so he may have been convoying troops.[22]

Howard had now been at court long enough to be considered one of the leading gentlemen and was sometimes ranked among the figures nearest the queen; in a letter of October, 1582, Seigneur de Lanssac, a French nobleman of some standing who was one of Walsingham's contacts in Paris, listed Howard—along with Burghley, Lincoln, Sussex, Leicester, and Walsingham—among those to whom he wanted to be remembered at court.[23] Howard's long attendance on the queen was now to find a reward. Although he had held only minor appointments, he was by 1580 the leading member of a great noble family that had furnished councilors and commanders to every sovereign for a century and that looked upon the patronage and wealth at the disposal of the crown as its rightful reward. Attendance on the queen, command of her armies and navies, and custody of the seals and staffs of office were the rights and duties of Howard's class, and grants of land, gifts of office, privileges, and perquisites were its normal rewards. Even though positions of trust were no longer the monopoly of the aristocracy, Elizabeth had a marked respect for lineage and gave substance to noble pretensions whenever she conveniently could in granting offices and favors. Such a tendency could only favor a Howard; as long as he avoided the disgrace that overtook the Norfolk line, he would get his preferment.

Charles Howard's preparation would qualify him for either of the great offices his father had held, and it can probably be assumed that he was ready to accept whichever became available. As it happened, the chamberlainship fell vacant first. But court gossip did not consider him as the leading candidate for the succession when Sussex seemed to be dying in June, 1583. On June 2 Roger Manners wrote the earl of Rutland: ". . .

22. *Cal. S. P. For., Eliz., May–December, 1582* (London, 1909), p. 130.
23. *Ibid.,* p. 365.

My Lord Chamberlain groweth towards an end. God comfort him and send him grace to contynue faythfull till the end. Som think my Lord of Hundesdon shall be Lord Chamberlayn, my Lord of Bedford, justice of Ayre, my Lord of Warwick, capytain of the pentioners; but I think her Majestie woll not in hast mak a Lord Chamberlain, and so do som others wiser than I."[24] Hunsdon, Howard's father-in-law, had been deputy chamberlain in 1582. Twelve years older than Howard, he had been warden of the East Marches and governor of Berwick since 1568 and had higher claims on the queen's affections. Another likely candidate was Hatton, the vicechamberlain, though his lack of noble ancestry might have proved a serious handicap in running the aristocratic household.

Roger Manners and those wiser than he were right in predicting that the queen would not hurry in making her choice. Sussex died on June 9, and months passed while the queen hesitated and the would-be chamberlains presumably pressed for a decision. Finally, on New Year's Day, 1584, Howard was appointed chamberlain and Hunsdon captain of the pensioners. "This was don all at ons when it was lest loked for," wrote Manners. "Mr. Vizchamberlain bereth all things with great patiens and strangely well contented."[25] There is no contemporary evidence to support such a conclusion, but one is tempted to speculate whether the outcome was a compromise in which each got something now and the hope of something more later on—Howard was advanced to the admiralty and Hunsdon to the chamberlainship when the earl of Lincoln died, and Hatton got the more prestigious lord chancellorship in 1587. Offices were sometimes disposed of in such a manner in an effort to satisfy everyone.

There were two Tudor officers commonly called lords chamberlain, but the distinction between them is easy to make. The lord great chamberlain of England, recognized by the statute of 1539 as fifth in precedence among the great

24. *Cal. Rutland MSS*, p. 151.
25. *Ibid.*, p. 157.

officers of state, no longer had practical functions, and his ceremonial duties were recognized as hereditary in the earls of Oxford. Howard became chamberlain of the household, lower in formal rank—eleventh in parliamentary precedence by the same statute—but of much greater practical importance. He, rather than the hereditary great chamberlain, was the chief officer of the court in its normal routine, and as chamberlain, Howard experienced a great accretion of dignity and gained a seat on the Privy Council, an official salary, and a chance at influence over patronage and gifts which made even lesser offices worth competing for. The chamberlain's fee was £133 6s. 8d., plus a table at court and other allowances, including a livery from the wardrobe.[26] His direct powers of patronage were not great, since a great many of the officers under his supervision—such as ladies of the privy chamber, carvers, cup bearers and servers, clerks of the closet, and gentlemen ushers—performed services directly for the queen, and their selection received her personal attention. But the chamberlain's close daily association with the queen gave him a greater opportunity than even the favorites had to recommend candidates for vacancies throughout the government; what use Howard made of the opportunity is unknown, for none of his letters from the period survive, but no Elizabethan magnate in his right mind would have neglected it.

The responsibilities of the chamberlain were various and trying. Although the queen was the very real head of the court and household, it was the chamberlain who ran them for most ordinary purposes. He directed the twenty household departments that supplied the queen and her house with meat and dress—the wardrobe, the jewel house for which Lady Howard had a special responsibility, the kitchen, bakery, spicery, and so on. Distribution of lodgings in the palace was a particular responsibility, as was order in the banqueting hall, over which he presided with his white staff. He exercised some supervision of the royal chaplains, chapel, and vestry, and

26. Powers and perquisites of the chamberlain are described in E. K. Chambers, *The Elizabethan Stage,* 4 vols. (Oxford, 1923), 1:32–48.

controlled the various surgeons, apothecaries, painters, astronomers, mole-takers, and masters of hounds whose services were required by the court. The players who performed before the queen came under his direct authority, and he planned the revels and entertainments for the court. His supervision of the summer progresses has already been noted. A number of "standing offices" financed separately from the household, such as the ordnance, mint, works, and tents, were usually at least partly under his control. Finally, he was, at least in theory, responsible for the foreign ambassadors at court, for arranging their reception and audiences with the queen, even though in practice Elizabeth's relations with ambassadors often required few formalities.[27]

But possibly the most significant commission received by Howard while lord chamberlain, at least in terms of his future, had nothing to do with the household. In the autumn of 1583, the council appointed the lord treasurer, the principal secretary, the lord admiral, the lord chamberlain, and the chancellor of the exchequer to inquire into the state of the navy and to examine in particular the charges made against John Hawkins, treasurer of the navy. The chamberlain presided over the investigation, later known as the "Lord Chamberlain's survey." Williamson places Hunsdon on the commission rather than Howard,[28] but it was Howard who was chamberlain in the fall of 1583—Hunsdon's appointment did not come until 1585, when Howard was promoted to admiral. The fact is of some significance; since it was Howard who was appointed and since he played such a primary role, he must have been recognized at that time as having a special relationship to the navy, special interest in it, and particular qualifications for judging the performance of its officers. The appointment supports the idea that he may have been promised the office of lord admiral on Lincoln's death, or was at least being

27. F. M. G. Evans, *The Principal Secretary of State* (Manchester, 1923), pp. 305–6.
28. J. A. Williamson, *Hawkins of Plymouth* (London, 1949), p. 266.

considered for it, and had been given the chamberlainship as an interim job to satisfy his ambitions temporarily.

Three of the commissioners, including the lord admiral, were empowered to act in the commission's name; Burghley and Walsingham, as the most overburdened of the queen's advisers, were relieved of the duty of constant attendance but could keep their hands in if they chose to. The commissioners were joined by a jury of experts named from the best-known sea captains to hear testimony and decide upon Hawkins' guilt. The treasurer of the navy had become the center of bitter dispute; earlier he had accused the officers of the navy, particularly Sir William Winter, of gross mismanagement of the queen's funds and had convinced Burghley to entrust him with a contract for the upkeep of the fleet. Now Winter and his associates were bringing the same complaints against him; he had, they said, enriched himself while allowing the queen's ships to become rotten and worthless. The commissioners were first instructed merely to investigate Hawkins' administration of the navy to judge the specific complaints against him. Later, in order to contrast his record with that of his accusers, the instructions were broadened; the commissioners were to examine the ships for evidence of decay and to look for signs of embezzling and corruption since the beginning of Elizabeth's reign. The commission ended its hearings by vindicating Hawkins entirely and by apparently impressing Howard with his administrative ability.[29] The experience was a valuable one for the future lord admiral; it required him to make a close study of the administrative history of the navy for the previous twenty years and thus it improved his qualifications for the position he was to take. It is a curious quirk, though, that Howard, whose association with the navy became so corroded by peculation and intrigue, should have begun by investigating the corruption of his predecessor.

A chamberlain did not automatically gain a seat on the Privy Council, as did the chief secretary or the lord treasurer, but he had become a figure of such importance that his

29. *Ibid.,* pp. 265–68.

presence was necessary and he soon became a member if he was not so already. Howard must have been named a member of the council at the time he received his appointment as lord chamberlain, or within a few days, since he was participating in council meetings by January 9, 1584. On that date Bernardino de Mendoza, the Spanish ambassador, was summoned to the house of Lord Chancellor Bromley, where Leicester, Howard, Hunsdon, Walsingham, and Bromley were in session, and was informed that he had fifteen days within which to leave the country; diplomatic relations with Spain were not resumed before the actual outbreak of war. This momentous meeting may have been Howard's first formal participation in the council, but from that time on, through the rest of Elizabeth's reign and most of James I's, he was one of its most diligent members, except on the half-dozen or so occasions when other duties required long absences from court.

Howard was chamberlain for only a year and a half. His brief tenure was preoccupied once again—apart from the routine government of the daily life of the court—with the summer's visits. The elaborate and extended progresses of the early part of the reign had been discontinued, but Elizabeth still made a number of short excursions in the late summer, visiting houses in Surrey, Berkshire, and Hampshire. The spring and summer of 1585 were also spent in and near London, so Howard did not meet the difficulties of moving the court about the countryside that he had ten years earlier.

Among the duties of the lord chamberlain were the supervision and control of the plays and other entertainments presented for the court especially during the Christmas season; during his short term in the office he was not himself a patron of players, but he had been before and was again later, possibly because of relationships formed at this time. A company of players called Lord Howard's men appeared at court the year after he had been Sussex's deputy; they performed one play in December, 1576, and another in February, 1577, and played again the following Christmas. Soon after Howard's promotion in 1585, a company called the Lord Admiral's men played at Dover and was seen frequently at court and in the provinces until late 1587, when a fatal accident forced it into temporary retirement.[30] The group reappeared at Christmas, 1588, and was active until 1606, when the leading members of the company came under the patronage of Prince Henry.

Howard's companies did not achieve immortality by employing Shakespeare, but the second company was one of the most popular of the time. Richard Burbage, the most famous of the Elizabethan actors, performed with the company at Dulwich in 1590 in a play called *Dead Man's Fortune;* its leading actor during most of the period was Edward Allyn, who may originally have played the title role in Marlowe's *Tamburlane.*[31] The business manager and impresario was Philip Henslowe, author of a famous diary, a London man of business who became Allyn's father-in-law; their link with Howard was apparently Allyn's elder brother, John, who had been a servant of Howard's nephew, Lord Sheffield, in 1580, and was the lord admiral's servant in 1589.[32]

Howard's relationship to his companies was apparently rather a formal one. The queen enjoyed play-acting, so patronage of players, which meant enrolling them as domestic servants and allowing them to wear livery so that they could avoid arrest as vagabonds, was another device for paying compliment to her. There is no real evidence that Howard was seriously interested in theatrical arts or had any motive other than to flatter his sovereign. He did, however, help his players get exemptions from the restrictions the council repeatedly placed on playhouses as "occasion of the ydle, ryoutous and dissolute living of great numbers of people" who sought escape from "all such honest and painefull course of life as they should folloe."[33] In 1584 he and Hatton were alone in opposing a request from the city that the two theaters then

30. Chambers, *The Elizabethan Stage,* 2:135.
31. *Ibid.,* p. 136; Sir Walter Besant, *London in the time of the Tudors* (London, 1904), p. 350.
32. Chambers, *The Elizabethan Stage,* 2:136–39.
33. J. R. Dasent, ed., *Acts of the Privy Council of England,* new ser. (London, 1890–), 30:395–98.

operating be suppressed, and late in the reign his company was able to secure a semi-monopoly on productions in and about London. To restrain the trafficking of the idle, it became a general practice to allow two companies to operate at theaters on the outskirts of the city under the regulation of the master of the revels, but to suppress all others. Almost invariably, the Lord Admiral's men were one of the favored groups, the Lord Chamberlain's men usually being the other. In January, 1600, Howard interceded with the Middlesex justices of the peace to help Allyn and his men move from the Bankside in Surrey, where they had operated for years, to a new theater, the Fortune; he cited the queen's favor toward Allyn and hoped they would let him proceed "without anie your lett or molestation." Neighbors complained to the council and got a restraining order, but in June the council reversed itself and allowed the Fortune to stand as the only theater in Middlesex.[34] In other seasons, however, Howard had been present when the council voted to suspend all play-acting around the city, so his patronage was not consistently successful.

34. *Ibid.*, pp. 495–98.

II: *Lord Admiral*

After a year and a half as lord chamberlain, Howard gave up his staff to take the office he was to keep for the rest of his political life and on which his considerable political power rested, that of lord admiral. The old lord admiral, Edward Clinton, elevated to the earldom of Lincoln in 1572, had held the office since the accession of Edward VI, except for the four years during Mary's reign when it was given to the first Howard of Effingham. However, he had not gone to sea for years when he died on January 16, 1585, even though he had kept his seat on the Privy Council and took part in court and local functions. After his death, the queen, as was her habit, did not immediately announce her choice of a successor. By spring, however, it was clear that Howard would get the office. William Chaderton, the bishop of Chester, wrote to Lord Derby on May 23: ". . . Being most joy-full of my dear good frend the Lord Chamberlayne his advancement to that place of trust and servyce wyshynge with all my harte and dayly prayinge God to move her Maiestie your lordship may succede hym. . . ."[1]

The news of the appointment must have been spread abroad at about the same time, for by June 3 the congratulations of the French king had returned to England. In a letter to Walsingham, the French ambassador fretted over the delay in making the appointment effective, as a matter of concern to himself:

. . . I have always been very slow to complain of anything, either to the Queen or her Council, always trying to use gentle

1. John H. Pollen, ed., *Unpublished Documents relating to the English Martyrs* (London, 1908), p. 110.

33

means and to keep France and England in perfect amity; but for God's sake, tell her Majesty to give me the means of doing right, and to bethink herself of the good choice which she assured me of at Croydon, of M. de Hawart, her great Chamberlain, to be made her Grand Admiral, a choice worthy of her virtue and prudence and very necessary for the Admiralty. I pray you tell her that the King has written to me by an express to thank her for having elected so good an admiral, from whom he hopes great things for the peace of his subjects.[2]

The delight of the French came not out of personal regard for Howard but, as the king hinted, from their hopes of "great things for the peace of his subjects." Both the French and the Dutch were suffering from English privateering, which would cause complaints throughout the Spanish war; no doubt the French hoped that by cultivating the good will of the new admiral from the first a favorable solution to the problem of seizures could be reached.

Howard was the one obvious choice for the office, even more than he had been a logical candidate for lord chamberlain in 1538. He had commanded royal fleets in 1570, perhaps in 1578, and twice in 1582, and had seen some inferior service earlier while his father was at sea. And again, the Howard tradition was a factor in his favor. Three of his relatives other than his father had held the office in the past century, although two of them served only short terms. The first duke of Norfolk was appointed in July, 1483, but was killed two years later; Sir Edward Howard became lord admiral in 1512 but was drowned in a fight with the French the next year. He was succeeded by his elder brother Thomas, later the third duke of Norfolk, who held the office until it was transferred to the duke of Richmond in 1525. A much more potent reason for the selection of Howard was that scarcely anyone else was eligible. Experienced seamen were available in numbers, but none of suitable rank. There was no precedent for appointing a mere captain, no matter how remarkable his exploits or how obvious his abilities; since the

2. *Cal. S. P. For., Eliz., 1584–1585* (London, 1916), p. 522.

fifteenth century, when the lord admiral became a permanent officer, he had always been a nobleman or at least the son of a titled family. So Drake, Hawkins, Winter, Holstock, Grenville, and their colleagues were barred by their birth. Of the aristocrats who later achieved naval notoriety, both the earl of Cumberland and Lord Thomas Howard were still too young to have much naval experience, and Thomas Howard's right to title had not yet been restored.

There is some evidence, too, that Howard of Effingham had been considered the naval commander second in rank to Lord Admiral Lincoln as early as 1574. An unsigned document in the State Papers Domestic, entitled "The names of Sundrie gentlemen and Captens for the Sea" and dated May, 1574, groups noblemen and gentlemen into two classes, those who "have served" and those "that have not served." The lord admiral and Lord Howard are bracketed together as the only noblemen who "have served"; Lord Henry Seymour, who later commanded a squadron in the Armada battle, Lord Talbot, and Lord Russell are the noblemen who had apparently offered themselves for service at sea but had not yet seen duty. Neither Drake nor the Gilberts are given at that time among the gentlemen with service, but the list does include such names as Sir Arthur Champernowne, Sir William Winter, Nicholas Gorges, William Holstock, John Hawkins, Anthony Jenkinson, Henry Palmer, Christopher Baker, and Thomas Fenner; the gentlemen who have not yet served are mainly sons of court figures, including a Carey, a Hastings, a Manners, a Stafford, and a St. John.[3] The list seems to include only those officers who had commanded the queen's ships; certainly there were many others, both gentlemen and aristocrats, who had gone to sea with their own ships or with merchant fleets in search of private gain. At any rate, it does suggest that within naval circles Howard was thought of as being clearly in line for the highest command. His status of expectancy had been recognized by naval writers as well: both William Bourne, whose *Inventions or Devises,* a tract on ships

3. S. P. Dom., Eliz., 96/257.

and "Martiall affayres by Sea," appeared in 1578, and Robert Norman, one of the most important students of navigation of his age and the translator of two Dutch guides to North Sea coastlines (1584), dedicated their books to the admiralty's heir apparent.

Possession of the admiralty conclusively made Howard one of the greatest officers of the crown in prestige, dignity, influence, and—very soon—income. When he attained it he was just under fifty, no longer a young man but not yet an old one, even by Tudor standards. By this time he had begun to assume the look familiar from his portraits, almost all of which were painted in his old age—imposing, dignified, and impressive in spite of the elegant courtier's dress he affected even in his advanced years. He was, said Fuller, "an hearty Gentleman, and cordial to his Sovereign; and of a most proper person."[4] Sir Robert Naunton called him "as goodly a gentleman as the times had any, if Nature had not been more intentive to compleat his person, than Fortune to make him rich. . . ."[5] Throughout his life he had a taste for show and ceremonial and a keen sensitivity for the privileges of his place; now he had an office which enabled him to cut a great figure at court and would furnish him with the means for extravagant display. It would be grossly unfair to represent him as being interested only in the wealth and prestige of his position; he was genuinely devoted to the queen and her service and undoubtedly would have performed to the best of his abilities wherever he had been placed. But neither can there be any doubt that the trappings of glory were attractive to him or that he enjoyed the deference that was his due as chamberlain and even more so as lord admiral. As he grew older, he tended to give more importance to the trappings than to the substance of his responsibilities.

The office he now possessed, says a contemporary document, probably prepared for Sir Julius Caesar and bearing

4. Thomas Fuller, *The Worthies of England*, new ed., 2 vols. (London, 1811), 2:361.
5. Sir Robert Naunton, *Fragmentia Regalia* (London, 1797), p. 124.

notations in his hand, "is one of the cheifeste and most honorable" of the realm, "but of greater power and co-maundement then any of the rest." His great power, the document continues, has two parts: "Ffirst in that he is the cheefe ordinarie Judge of all causes foraine and maritime; next in that he hath th'orderinge of the Navie Royall and of all the seamen of her Mats dominions next unto her highnes."[6] The writer may justly be suspected of trying to flatter the lord admiral, since his purpose was to induce him to give away a quarter of his income, but he did not exaggerate seriously. Howard was the only one of the crown officers who was, by the same patent, a principal administrator and the commander of a fighting force—the only permanent fighting force at the queen's immediate disposal. His powers had evolved and the department he headed had, like the other Elizabethan offices, grown during the past two centuries from a temporary function exercised as needed by one of the king's friends to a complex and unwieldy organism with its own bureaucracy, methods of procedure, and customary law. The growth of overseas commerce, let alone the demands of national security, meant that the navy's chief officer must be a man of "power and comaundment" equal to any, but he was also a vested interest—the admiralty had begun as and remained a private franchise, a vast domain of public responsibility, which was designed to yield a profit to the holder.

The admiral's specific areas of authority were summarized in notes by Sir Julius Caesar in 1611; probably his powers had been largely stable since the time of Howard's appointment. First of all, said Caesar, he may examine "all Treasons & all oth'r inferiour crimes" committed within the admiralty's jurisdiction, which included not only the high seas but also bays, harbors, and fresh-water streams as far inland as the first bridge. Further, he judged the validity of contracts between Englishmen and foreigners, among foreigners in his jurisdiction, and among Englishmen overseas. He exercised martial law in wartime in his own domain and could fine, outlaw, or

6. Additional MSS, 12,505/274–76, British Museum, London.

banish "contemners & resisters of his Jurisdiction." He might seize any merchant ship at any time for the service of the crown, and he could commit any person to prison on his own warrant, "wthout rendring a reason, unlesse the person be holpen by an habeas corpus" from the King's Bench; if the commitment was for piracy, not even habeas corpus brought relief. He issued passports and safe-conducts to English merchants and others traveling overseas, both in time of war and in peacetime; he could cause the royal fleet to be rigged out and sent to sea, and none could contravene his orders except the sovereign or the Privy Council. His officers could seize and search any ship for prohibited, contraband, or pirate goods. His hand, said Caesar, was "the voucher to all Admiral reckonings & allowances," and he was empowered to impress mariners for the king's ships or for any ships in the king's service. His judgments, issued by the admiralty court, were good against "the bodies goods & chatels of all men without exception." Finally, "Hee is simply the officer of the greatest powr & strength in the kingdome, having at his command all the shipping, marines, seamen, fisshermen, & as many more, as hee will presse at any time. . . ."[7] The emphasis here, as might be expected from the judge of the admiralty court, is on his judicial functions rather than his command duties, but he was still the principal naval officer who personally commanded the royal fleet in major engagements and took it to sea on other occasions on the word of the crown or the Privy Council. The queen's ships and men were entirely at his command, and he could and did use them for any purpose he chose, even to the extent of putting them at the disposal of the wife of the governor of Flushing when she and her children crossed the Channel. In August, 1588, when the fate of the Armada was still unknown and it might be assumed that every available ship was needed for defense, Howard detached one of the queen's ships on a similar errand, bringing his sister Lady Stafford home from France. He was at the same time a military officer of extensive power on land; he had the "rule"

7. Lansdowne MSS, 145/5, British Museum, London.

of the queen's forts lying on the seacoasts, whose principal function was to guard against surprise attack from the sea, and he was intimately involved with problems of their administration and supply.

The judicial functions had always been exercised through a deputy, the administrative duties by a clerk of the ships, and since some of the early admirals never went to sea, the office was sometimes merely a title of honor held by courtiers or soldiers who had no special knowledge of naval affairs. All the admirals, however, learned to draw incomes from perquisites, which were stated ever more generously as time passed. Moreover, the ambitious foreign policy and frequent wars of Henry VIII insured that his admirals—except his son, the duke of Richmond, who was given the office at the age of nine —acquire experience in the actual command of ships at sea. Not until the last years of Henry's reign, however, did the lord admiral have anything like continuous administrative duties, and these required his time and power of decision even in peacetime. In 1546 the general direction of the navy was vested in an executive committee, later to become the Navy Board, which included five officers—a lieutenant of the admiralty, a treasurer, a comptroller, a surveyor, and a master of ordnance. Two others then appointed were soon discontinued, but in 1550 a surveyor of victuals was added. The lord admiral sat as the head of the board, which met frequently, often at his house, and furnished the navy with a continuity of policy unknown before.

The office of lieutenant had long been vacant and would remain so until Howard revived it for his son-in-law; John Hawkins, as treasurer for marine causes under a patent dating from 1578, was the most important member of the naval committee. The aging Captain William Holstock was comptroller of ships; Captain William Winter was both surveyor of ships and master of naval ordnance. Edward Baeshe, son-in-law of Sir Ralph Sadler, had been surveyor of victuals since 1550, and Captain William Borough was clerk of the ships. All were professionals of long experience, and, since their patents were held directly from the queen, they were not

replaced by incoming admirals. These were the officers responsible for the day-to-day management of the queen's ships,
sailors, and docks, for enforcing policies laid down by the
Navy Board under the supervision of the lord admiral and,
ultimately, the queen.

Each one of the officers, assisted by a growing number of
clerks, operated independently in what were actually separate
spheres of activity.[8] By far the greatest responsibility lay with
the treasurer, Hawkins, who at this time received £4,000 a
year, out of which he contracted to meet the ordinary costs of
maintaining the navy; what remained was his own salary. He
was charged with maintaining detailed supervision of the
work of the dockyards, with building, equipping, and repairing the ships, supplying sufficient stores of suitable quality,
and all other administrative matters except those dealing with
ordnance, food supply, and impressing men. Although he was
responsible to the commissioners of the navy and to the lord
admiral, Hawkins dealt directly with the lord treasurer much
of the time, a fact which tended to make Burghley as much
the responsible officer for naval causes as the lord admiral.
Such a tendency, however, was not disruptive of naval operations as long as the lord admiral and the lord treasurer could
work together closely and amicably, and Howard never
seemed to resent the probable loss of authority involved.

When Howard received his patent as admiral, Edward
Baeshe was almost at the end of his long tenure as naval
victualer, and in May, 1586, he gave six months' notice to
terminate his contracts. He, like the treasurer, was essentially a
capitalist. He agreed to furnish each mariner with a daily
pound of biscuit and gallon of beer, plus two pounds of salt
beef four days a week and stockfish, butter, and cheese the
other three days. In return he was paid fivepence halfpenny
per day for men in harbor and sixpence a day for those at sea,
paid not by Hawkins but by the exchequer. Therefore he, like
the treasurer, felt himself primarily responsible to the lord
treasurer and Privy Council. Baeshe struggled to make a

8. S. P. Dom., Eliz., 221/12.

LORD ADMIRAL

profit on his contracts, but by his own report he failed; in
1576 he wrote that he had lost £500 a year for four years. In
1586 when he resigned he anticipated an even greater loss.
James Quarles, who had been granted the succession in 1582,
was given somewhat more favorable terms for his supplies.
However, his efforts to supply the fleet at the time of the
Armada proved altogether inadequate to the navy's needs and
thus provoked repeated complaints from Howard about bad
beer, shortages, and spoiled food.

The victualer was essentially a civilian holding a crown
contract; after the treasurer, the principal professional seaman
was Winter, the surveyor and master of ordnance, especially
charged with supervising the goods delivered for navy use and
keeping watch over the maintenance and good repair of ships
and dockyards. He was a captain of long experience who died
shortly after the Armada fight. All the commissioners except
the victualer retained their status as captains and were able to
go to sea from time to time despite their official duties;
Hawkins, Winter, and Borough commanded ships in the admiral's squadron in 1588. Owing allegiance to the commissioners and the lord admiral, most of them through the treasurer, were installations at Chatham, Portsmouth, Woolwich,
and Deptford, with numerous subordinate officers such as
master shipwrights, master gunners, keepers of stores, pilots,
clerks of cheque, and, of course, the personnel of the ships. In
each of the maritime counties, too, vice-admirals deputed to
look after admiralty affairs and the admiral's interests maintained staffs of their own.[9]

The lord admiral's judicial functions were performed, under
his direct supervision and with his continual interference, by
the High Court of Admiralty, presided over in 1585 and
through the rest of the reign by Julius Caesar, later knighted
and made master of the Court of Wards and finally chancellor
of the exchequer. The relationship between Howard and Caesar was a close and interesting, if not always harmonious, one,
and their correspondence, beginning in 1585 and continuing

9. See pp. 69–70 below.

for more than twenty years, is a treasure house for any student of the admiralty. Caesar and judges in the maritime counties not only settled disputes in civil controversies over maritime matters but tried criminal cases arising on the high seas or elsewhere within the lord admiral's jurisdiction, ruled on the legality of prizes brought into English ports, and issued warrants for reprisals and for the stay of goods in dispute and passports to merchants and others trading beyond the seas. County admiralty judges also existed, but not for all maritime counties or at all times.

The departments of the admiralty were all largely self-sufficient and at least partly self-serving, having been created in periods when the lord admirals were, at most, fleet commanders and continuing to function on a semicontractual basis. But Howard and his immediate predecessors became virtually full-time administrators—or at least gave their duties almost all the time that could be spared from the demands of Privy Council and court. Howard for some twenty years by no means allowed the commissioners to run the navy without him, even though his attentions were somewhat scattered and selective. Without full records of the sittings of the officers of the navy, it cannot be known whose was the decisive voice in determination of policy—if indeed it was not the queen's. But Howard can be seen outside the meetings, injecting himself into the normal operations of the offices and personally performing a multitude of functions.

From the available evidence, one may suppose that Howard took a greater interest in the operation of the High Court of Admiralty than in the other offices under his jurisdiction. The greater part of his correspondence with Caesar deals with matters currently before the court, and his personal concern with its work is clear. Some of this concern, especially later in the reign, would by modern standards be called interference with the due course of law. In January, 1603, for example, Howard wrote in behalf of the masters of Trinity House, who, as owners of a ship called the *Katherine*, had petitioned him to have a case removed from the admiralty docket:

. . . I . . . doe fynde their request to bee so reasonable and
honest, as I must needes recomende it unto you, Prayinge yow
to take present order for the referringe of the hearinge of the
matters they complayne of to the Mrs of the Trynitie Howse,
unto whom in right they doe espetiallye belonge, And as I
formerlie entreated yor good favor unto them in this busines,
Soe doe I nowe hartelie againe praie the same bothe in regarde
of the reasonablenes thereof, and that they are parsons whom
I desire maye receave favor.[10]

The following March he wrote again that he "would be gladd
out of the good conceipte and opinion" he holds of a certain
Captain Griffith, being held for illegally capturing a flyboat,
"to doe him any good favor I maie for his libertie." Therefore
Caesar is instructed, "if yor opinion concurre wth myne and
the Lord Cheife Justices wch is that his cause is bayleable," to
accept whatever bail Griffith offers and release him. Howard
concludes, "Herein lett me praye yow to doe the gentleman all
the lawefull favor yow maie, wch I knowe bothe himself and
his freindes will verie thanckfullie acknowledge unto yow."[11]
In September he wrote again to ask for favor, this time for
John Newman and Elizabeth Lewis, who had been arrested on
an admiralty-court warrant. "The weight of the cause I am
unacquaynted wthall," he said,

and likewise what proceedinge there is had against them.
Neverthelesse by cause the poore widdowe hath bene an earnest petitioner unto me to be bayled, wch in my conceipte is a
request verie reasonable. I doe verie hartely praie you that if
the cause be bayable [sic] you will afford unto them such favor
as the lawe will permitt, if not then that you will yeald unto
them the best expedition you maie in determininge of the suyte
comensed against them, so as they maie be eased of the great
charge and trouble they endure by imprisonmt. Herein Lett me
entreat yor good and kynde favor unto them for my sake, wch
I will thanckfullie acknowledg unto you on their behalfe. . . .[12]

10. Additional MSS, 12,505/66.
11. *Ibid.*, 12,505/48.
12. *Ibid.*, 12,505/72.

Howard hesitated even less to interpose himself in the judicial process when his own profit or that of his followers or retainers was involved. In such situations he looked on Caesar not as a disinterested jurist but as the defender of admiralty interests, which were identical with his own; in a letter of November 7, 1599, he opened with an admonition "to have a good care of such thinges as doe concerne me" and closed with "once againe myndinge yow to be carefull of my buyssines."[13] What he meant by being careful of his business is illustrated in a letter written earlier that year. The flyboat *Dragon* of Bristol and the *Concord* and *Amity* of London were captured as pirates, and if condemned as such would have become the property of the lord admiral. His counsel brought charges against the vessels and their owners, but for some reason Caesar halted the proceedings, producing, in effect, a command from the admiral not to interfere: ". . . I must therefore praie and requyre yow not onelie to suffer them to goe forwarde wth the confiscation of those shippes but to yeald unto them all yor best aide and furtheraunce therein, wch I am perswaded yow will doe for that they are matters that speciallie concerne my profit. . . ."[14] One of the clearest cases of his interference in behalf of a follower is seen in the 1590 capture by a man identified as "my servante Coverte," perhaps a member of the well-known Sussex family, of a prize disputed by Sir Walter Raleigh. Howard wrote:

> . . . this bearer my servante Coverte hathe of late broughte home a prise wherunto Sr Walter Rawlye as I am enformed wthout reason makethe clayme and hathe by commission oute of the highe courte of the Admiralty made stay and areste of the same good [sic] prise And for that Covert is one whom I favoure and wold not have overborne wth the mighte of anie theise shalbe to praie you to graunte him sup sadies [writ of supersedeas] uppon indifferent surtyes or any other course or beneficiall order of lawe that you can for his behoof beste devise. . . .[15]

13. *Ibid.*, 15,208/476.
14. *Ibid.*, 15,208/442.
15. *Ibid.*, 15,208/162.

44

To reassure his judge that the steps he asked for would not be inequitable, he added a postscript in his own hand: "for if it be trew that Cowerte dowthe Informe me ther is no question in it but it standethe very cleer."

In October, 1594, Howard wrote to ask for dismissal of a case against another servant, named Gassone, for title to some wrecked goods: ". . . for that he is my servaunte I will see that he shall doe noe wronge and therfore doe pray you to forbeare him and not to suffer him to be further troubled before you. And som ten or twelve dayes hence I shalbe at London and shall have convenient leasure to heare and end that cause. . . ."[16]

Howard's attempts to bring pressure to bear on Caesar in favor of a party in a suit were not frequent enough to become part of the ordinary routine of the court. And, as in these examples, he did not ask Caesar to disregard the merits of a case; he always asked for such favor as the law would allow —which in most Elizabethan courts was considerable. Still, pressure on the judge from his superior officer must have been of particular weight, especially since Caesar repeatedly petitioned the lord admiral to press his own suits with the queen and had repeatedly pleaded with him for a greater share of his prizes and prerogatives.[17]

On other occasions Howard wrote to Caesar in the hope of expediting particular cases, which was in substance another form of interfering with the impartial course of justice. One such case occurred in March, 1603, after Caesar had granted a delay in hearing a case involving prize goods captured in a vessel of Stavanger, a Norwegian port under Danish rule. "I knowe yow are wise and wyll not delaye theise thinges wthout iust grounds," he said, since failure to get a quick award would be "a great discoraging to such as goe fourth in this nature, to attempt the like. . . . Therefore I praie yow either lett there be sentence geaven for the same (yf alreadye it be not) or

16. *Ibid.*, 15,208/329.
17. See *ibid.*, 11,406/100, 12,505/274–76; Lansdowne MSS, 157/430, 432, 436, 438.

else lett me understand from yow the causes of staye, that I maye be hable to satisfye such as have and wyll conferr wth me therein."[18]

It is possible that Howard would not have admitted that considerations of ethics or honor were involved in his efforts to channel the flow of justice. He was extremely sensitive to shadows cast on his honor, as he made clear to Caesar early in his term of office, and at least at this time recognized that honor demanded an impartial administration. Caesar, in some of his own early letters, apparently had hinted that Howard's justice was malleable, but he received a hot rejoinder:

> . . . how often I have charged you befor the M[ajesty] of God to dow Justes to all men wt all Indyferenc and that I wolde have the Jugment of Causes betwyne parte and parte unto you. I pray Mr Caesar when did I ether wryghte or speke to you to dow otherwyse then ryght Just I protest it befor the fase of Almyghtie God I never in my lyfe thowght to do it and I besyke God I lyve not to dow it therfor I pray wryght unto me in what thynge I ever moved you ether by worde or deed or wrytyng to hynder procedynge of Justes. Truly I look to be satysfyed in it. And I Charge you agayne and so have I ever as you wyll auncer befor God for it That you dow trew Justes is as muche as in you lyethe. . . .[19]

The letter, written in Howard's own orthographically uncertain hand, exhibits an unmistakable indignant sincerity. In this early period, at any rate, he was keenly conscious of an ideal of just proceedings which he believed he maintained; as he grew older he lost his hold on these earlier ideas of justice, or, more likely, he did not believe his standards jeopardized by changes in scheduling of cases and requests for "all lawful favor." The court was, after all, his own court, and he ruled it as a baron ruled his manorial jurisdiction—to his own taste.

Soon after the two were settled in their offices, Caesar adopted a practice of acquainting the lord admiral with "any weightie matter" before taking any kind of action, a course

18. Additional MSS, 12,505/50.
19. *Ibid.*, 15,208, September 28, 1586.

which Howard expressly approved in a letter of December 28, 1585.[20] The practice seems to have been followed as long as Caesar remained judge, and it placed in Howard's hands the responsibility for making all important decisions. Their mutual acceptance of Caesar's function in executing the policies set by the lord admiral is seen in Caesar's several letters requesting instructions for proceeding in matters before him. A famous case in 1602, for example, involved Sir Thomas Shirley, who had captured a Dutch ship bearing, he claimed, Spanish goods; the Dutch disputed the legality of the prize and made representations through their ambassador. The case was a complex one, since many persons had shares in ownership and the goods captured were of several kinds, including some that were not legal prize, and so it dragged on for months without reaching a settlement. While some parties sought further delays, the cargo, which was in the custody of the admiralty court and included a quantity of sugar, deteriorated. Finally, on September 2, Caesar wrote the lord admiral that the cause "has been so much delayed, that it must on Monday next receive an end." Therefore, he said, "I would know your pleasure" as to how to satisfy the owners, including an Englishman, of the goods not legal prize,

> . . . whose satisfaction being first had out of the goods to be adjudged good prize, the residue will not be worth their travail who labour for the same. The sugars run out upon the ground, where they lie, and the spoil made of the merchants' goods, which are not prize, is so great that, if good order be not taken, the good prize will not satisfy half the same; so that I am the more desirous to end the cause lest the little which is left to the merchant should by further delay come to nothing.[21]

Not surprisingly, Howard seemed most concerned with the work of the court when his own jurisdiction and prerogatives

20. *Ibid.*, 15,208/31.
21. Historical Manuscripts Commission, *Calendar of the Manuscripts of the Most Hon. the Marquess of Salisbury, &c. preserved at Hatfield House, Hertfordshire* (London, 1883–), 10:302; hereinafter cited as *Cal. Hatfield MSS.*

were called into question. In February, 1591, he wrote to Judges Aubrey, Ford, and Lloyd that the King's [sic] Bench must stop infringing upon admiralty jurisdiction by granting prohibitions and other processes in naval matters, which, he said, had grown into a daily custom and hindered the course of justice; they were asked to join him and Caesar to consider the lord admiral's patent and authority in order to decide what steps should be taken to remedy the abuse.[22] In 1595 a challenge to his authority arose at Lynn, where local officers claimed independent admiralty jurisdiction, "by what graunt," Howard said, "I knowe not." So he asked Caesar to appoint a time for the mayor and his colleagues to appear to produce whatever proof they had, praying his judge at the same time to "use yer beste care and meanes to overthrowe their claymed lyberty." He also used Caesar to investigate and, if possible, quash the attempts that were occasionally made to dispute or to divert a share of his prerogatives, such as the claim made by Lord Rich in 1592 for possession of goods wrecked on his lands on the Essex shore, or the question raised by a book published in 1593 concerning his right to a share of goods taken by privateers.[23]

At times Howard assumed directly some of the functions which traditionally had been performed in his name by the admiralty court, and in so doing he did not fail to provoke a protest from Caesar. One such function was the issuance of passports, letters of reprisal, warrants for seizure of goods, or the like, for each of which the judge received a fee. Caesar supported his request that Howard stop issuing warrants with an elaborate justification:

> The L. Admiralls honour and $p$fit groweth from the reverence and obedience given to the warrants awarded out of his Courts and especiallie from his lyeutenante or cheife Judge. Wch being crossed or cleane displaced by private warrants or letters (things in truth not warranted by the lawe; and soe blunted and disgraced in th' opinion of the people, that they

22. Additional MSS, 15,208/239.
23. *Ibid.*, 15,208/275, 277, 374.

being freed from the sharpe warrants of the lawe, doe become careless of the Judge and of the L. Admirall, whose place he representeth; and use those private warrants as they list and when they liste, rather as propper to theire disordered affections, then as meanes for the furtherance or execution of Justice. Knowinge that when the L. Admirall hath blunted his lawfull sword that it can noe more cutt, his unwarranted warrents may safelie be disobeyed.[24]

In a letter of 1588 concerning passports, Caesar cut more directly to the heart of the matter. First, he said, it was advantageous to maintain a consolidated record of all who received passports, which he believed should be kept by the court. Then, for entering each in the record and for fixing the lord admiral's seal to the signed documents, the judge and register of the admiralty should "have for every pasport a noble a piece (wch is theire due, and hath bene alwaies, as the records of th' office doe testifie). . . ."[25] An additional advantage would accrue from the convenience of having bonds taken at the same time for the return of ships to the place of discharge specified in the passport. But to Caesar the central issue was the fee, not efficient record-keeping, and he ended his letter with a plea that the lord admiral, for their mutual benefit, support his officers as they deserved.

Howard's supervision of ships, men, and stores was perhaps not as close as that of the admiralty court, which had an intimate connection with his personal revenues. But there is ample evidence of his exercise of authority and his direct participation in a wide variety of matters. The collected state papers and the admiralty records are heavily sprinkled with letters, memorials, estimates, orders, and warrants in his hand, bearing his signature, or addressed to him, and they indicate a close attention to all levels of naval operation. However, they also show that lines dividing spheres of authority and jurisdiction were almost non-existent, and that the lord admiral shared his wide powers—or exercised them in co-operation

24. *Ibid.*, 12,505/275.
25. Lansdowne MSS, 157/452.

with other officers and agencies, especially the lord treasurer and the Privy Council. While he lived, Burghley was probably more responsible than Howard for the fundamental policies of the navy. Both sat on the Privy Council, and it too, omnicompetent and omnipresent, frequently was the voice of authority in naval matters as it was in the affairs of every other department of government.

The mechanics of naval administration have been carefully studied by M. Oppenheim and others and do not need to be repeated at length. But the lord admiral's relation to the details of administration may be shown by looking briefly at a single representative year, 1591. The lord admiral can be seen to have been continually occupied with the immediate problems of setting fleets to sea, seeing the ships properly manned, maintained, and repaired, and carrying out the general orders and plans that he no doubt had a hand in preparing but that probably were not ultimately his own.

The primary English naval effort of the year was Lord Thomas Howard's Azores expedition, which is famous for bringing the death of Sir Richard Grenville and the loss of his *Revenge*, the only royal ship captured during the entire Spanish war while sailing under the queen's commission. The goal of the expedition, like that of so many other fleets, was the capture of Spanish treasure as it came from the West Indies. The year before, the activities of Hawkins and Frobisher in the Atlantic had caused Philip II to cancel the sailing of the bullion ships, so the 1591 shipment, desperately needed by the Spanish crown to finance both domestic government and military operations, promised to be great, "such as in no yeare hearetofore the like hath bene," according to a Privy Council letter.[26] Necessarily, it would be unusually well guarded, a fact which called for careful English preparations in response. To rig the ships, on January 16 Hawkins and James Quarles received a warrant to pay and victual a hundred men for a month, and the work of preparing the ships for the sea was begun under Hawkins' supervision. Ten days later he prepared

26. Dasent, *Acts of the Privy Council*, 21:186–87.

an estimate of the cost of fitting out five ships carrying six hundred men which would be the queen's share of the proposed voyage. He calculated a total of twenty ships and pinnaces under Howard's command, which the lord admiral, Lord Thomas, and Sir Walter Raleigh would share with the queen in supporting. The relative shares of cost, which would in theory govern the distribution of expected prize money, had not yet been entirely worked out; on February 13 Hawkins wrote to Henry Maynard, Burghley's secretary, that he had conferred with the lord admiral, who agreed to underwrite the cost of the *Bonadventure,* one of the queen's principal ships. They also decided that the *Garland,* originally appointed to go with Lord Thomas, would be sent instead on a concurrent expedition under the earl of Cumberland, largely a private enterprise, and that the *Revenge,* paid for by Raleigh, would be substituted; the charge for the other ships would be borne by the queen or the lord admiral.[27]

This is Admiral Howard's first entry into the planning in any guise other than that of a private adventurer in hope of gain; the decision to send Sir Richard Grenville and the *Revenge* with Thomas Howard rather than with Cumberland came out of his February meeting with Hawkins. The previous preparations, largely concerned with fitting out the ships, levying men, laying in food supplies, and apportioning the costs, had been carried out under the supervision of Hawkins with the lord treasurer and the council. By the first of March the relative shares of the charge had been worked out and the lord admiral had agreed to set out seven of the ships, including the *Bonadventure.* But when Lord Thomas left, he had fewer ships than planned—fourteen—of which the lord admiral had outfitted only three.

Lord Thomas was able to get away in April, his destination the Azores. Cumberland, after he left Plymouth in May, headed for the coast of Spain; a squadron of the queen's ships under Sir Henry Palmer was left behind to keep watch in the

27. *Cal. S. P. Dom., Eliz., 1591–1594* (London, 1867), pp. 2, 6, 9.

Channel. In May, word came to England of a Spanish fleet about the Scilly Isles and another between Cape Santa Maria and Point Marroquí, so the lord admiral sent fresh instructions: his cousin should be careful to keep his fleet and any prizes he took together so that stragglers would not fall into the hands of the Scilly fleet. He left it to Lord Thomas' own judgment whether to wait for the treasure fleet at the Azores or at Cape Santa Maria, near Cádiz, but advised the latter. The instructions were worked out by the lord admiral and a draft was drawn up in his handwriting on May 15; the Privy Council then issued them on May 18, adding an article allowing Lord Thomas, if he missed the India fleet, to go to Newfoundland and seek prizes among the fishing fleets of Spain and the Catholic League.[28]

By June the lord admiral was personally involved in the preparation of the revictualing ships, to be convoyed by two of the royal warships; by his own estimate, the mission, involving four ships and a flyboat, would raise the cost of the voyage by £715. It may be indicative of the close co-operation between lord admiral and lord treasurer that with Howard's estimate appears a list in Burghley's hand of the names of four other ships, possibly being considered as alternatives to those designated as supply vessels. Also indicative of the joint nature of the responsibility is the letter sent on June 21, under both signatures, informing Lord Thomas of the preparation of the supply ships and instructing him to send two fast ships to Havana to discover and keep watch on the treasure fleet. Just a month later the two again acted together in instructing Sir Henry Palmer to meet the supply squadron and escort it safely past the Spanish fleet, reported to contain thirty or forty sail, that still lurked about the Scilly Isles.

The reinforcements and victuals were sent in July, but contrary winds held them at Plymouth until August 17. They did not reach the Azores until after the *Revenge* was lost to a strong fleet that had put out from El Ferrol. Spanish intelligence was apparently very accurate; Philip II knew, according

28. *Ibid.*, p. 37; Dasent, *Acts of the Privy Council*, 22:140–42.

to prisoners who escaped the next year, not only the English design, but also the size of Lord Thomas' fleet, the name of each ship and its captain, and the number of soldiers aboard. So he was able to postpone the sailing of the treasure fleet until winter, when the sea would be free of the English, and to arm a strong squadron to repulse Howard. After extricating the main part of the fleet at Flores, Lord Thomas may have hung about the coast of Portugal for a time, but then returned home without attempting any prizes on the Newfoundland fishing banks. He had, however, captured a ship out of Lübeck, loaded with masts and other naval stores valued at £10,000, and five lesser vessels. Captain Flicke, commander of the revictualing squadron, took several prizes before his return in October, which, according to Monson, "defrayed the better part of the whole action."[29]

The prizes, contrary to the lord admiral's instructions to keep the fleet together, began to drift into English harbors in August. Ordinarily, prizes taken by privateers or vessels operating under letters of marque and reprisal would have been placed in safe custody by the vice-admiral of the county or by local admiralty officers until judgment could be received from the admiralty court. But since this expedition was sailing under the queen's commission, its plunder became the concern of the Privy Council. On August 10 the council, with both Burghley and Howard in attendance, wrote in haste to the mayor of Bridgwater, where Captain Robert Cross of the *Bonadventure* had brought a prize loaded with sugars and sold it, the council feared, for his private profit. The mayor was told to have the goods assessed, since it was understood that Cross had sold them at too low a price, and to take bonds of the buyer for double their value, to be answerable for the true value to the queen and the adventurers in the voyage.

In the latter part of September, the ships of the main fleet began to return. Since the supply squadron under Captain Flicke was supposed to have furnished them with an addi-

29. Michael Oppenheim, ed., *The Naval Tracts of Sir William Monson,* 5 vols. (London, 1902–14), 1:256, 260, 265–67.

tional two months' ration, they were expected to be bringing home extra food. Marmaduke Darrell went to meet the ships and take custody of the remaining victuals, to help reduce the queen's charge. However, since Flicke never established contact with Lord Thomas and his ships, he apparently returned with little or no food to spare. Again, such steps would ordinarily have been taken on the authority of the admiralty officers themselves, but in major expeditions they were superseded even in such relatively unimportant details by higher organs of government.

The whole voyage cost £21,991, of which the lord admiral had ventured £4,906 and Sir Walter Raleigh £1,500; the prizes captured were not exceptionally rich, but the queen was anxious to make what she could of them. When the council was informed that the London ships in Flicke's squadron had taken prizes, Sir Thomas Gorges and Richard Carmarthen (the London customs collector) were told to hurry to Plymouth to keep the sailors from embezzling the goods; before they arrived, the council warned Sir Francis Drake to be on hand to see that no one went ashore and that cargoes were not broken until the queen's commissioners came. In another letter to the local admiralty officers on Drake's behalf, Howard cloaked himself with the authority of the council to pray that they also give due assistance to the commissioner who would be sent to safeguard his personal interests.[30]

The Azores expedition, despite all the attention it received from the queen and council, as well as from admiralty officers, was, after all, only one of the concerns of naval administrators, even though the most important one. Another problem on which much time and care was expended in 1591, as throughout the latter part of Elizabeth's reign, was the transportation of troops. After they were levied, armed, and collected at the ports, the soldiers that were sent to Ireland, the Netherlands, and France had to be convoyed under the authority of the lord admiral. The arrangements were carried out

30. *Cal. S. P. Dom., Eliz.,* 1591–1594, p. 118; Dasent, *Acts of the Privy Council,* 22:37–38.

under his personal direction, often reinforced and supplemented by the power of the Privy Council. The customary procedure for transportation of soldiers, a service of only a few weeks that did not justify the employment of the royal fleet, began with an embargo on shipping in the port where the soldiers were to embark. Admiralty personnel would unload the vessels seized and negotiate with the owners a reasonable price for their use. After employment by the queen, the borrowed ships returned to port and to their normal occupations. However, the difference between what the admiralty considered a fair price for ship hire and what the owners believed a fair return for their time and risks sometimes produced conflict. On April 1, for example, the principal officers of the navy—Hawkins, Borough, and Benjamin Gonson—wrote to the lord admiral about difficulties in negotiating with Thames shipowners for the vessels that were to take men and horses to Sir John Norris in the Netherlands. The merchants, they said, demanded pay not by the man but according to their usual tonnage, and they had asked the help of the commissioners in obtaining crews. The officers also needed authority for spending extra money to hire three more ships for horses; when that was allowed, they promised they would lose no time in furthering the service. On a similar occasion in July the merchants tried to strengthen their hand in the negotiations by declining to unload their ships, but such tactics were not to be allowed; Admiral Howard, writing under the seal of the Privy Council, informed the lord mayor that if the ships were not "presently" unloaded and readied for service, ". . . I, the Lord Admirall, will geve order to the officers of the Admiraltie for the taking forthe of the said goods, because her Majesty's service is not to be disapointed or to receave any hindrance or delaie. . . ."[31]

The phrase, "I, the Lord Admirall," is frequently encountered in the letters nominally sent by the lords of the council on maritime subjects. The usage suggests that the authority of the lord admiral alone was not always enough for the speedy

31. Dasent, *Acts of the Privy Council,* 21:294.

execution of instructions and that the additional dignity and command of the Privy Council were freely borrowed. Also during July of 1591—and probably for the same service—the full weight of the council was employed for a stay of shipping at Hull. The mayor had written that there were too few ships in the harbor to carry the soldiers appointed to be collected there, so, in a letter signed by the lord treasurer, lord chamberlain, Lord Cobham, and Treasurer Fortescue, as well as by the lord admiral, he was told to continue arresting all ships that entered the harbor until the soldiers arrived, and also to stay any vessels in the creeks and harbors to either side of Hull.

The lord admiral also involved himself directly, though not to the exclusion of other crown officers, in overseeing construction of new ships by both private individuals and the master shipwrights of the crown. Ships, like gold, horses, and guns, were considered to be irreplaceable assets, and careful precautions were taken to keep foreigners from getting them. Builders of new ships were rewarded by the queen—the master shipwright Richard Chapman got five shillings for each of the two hundred tons his new ship, the *Dainty,* would hold, "in consideration of his charges"—but at the same time the admiralty court was required to take "caution," usually in the form of a bond, to see that ships were not sold abroad. Still, the urge to maximize profits was as strong among shipbuilders as among other men, and a report reached the Privy Council that Italians and Scots were buying ships in the Thames. A letter of October 18, 1591, directed Hawkins and Borough to conduct an inquiry and to "certifie me the Lord Admirale" of appropriate action.[32]

Meanwhile, the routine work of the navy had to be carried on. The commissioners of the navy met at least monthly, with the lord admiral usually in attendance since he signed all but a few of the certificates of monthly cost for maintaining ships and dockyards. A memorial in the lord admiral's handwriting, dated May 24, provides a sampling of the subjects that were probably introduced at the meetings of the commissioners. It

32. *Ibid.,* 22:30–31.

deals with several unrelated matters, indicating for each what steps need to be taken: Sir Henry Palmer's ships should be victualed at Plymouth; the two prizes taken by Martin Frobisher are useless and should be sold so that two "nimble vessels" can be made with the money; ten specified ships should be sent to Portsmouth to be ready for sudden service; a storekeeper and assistant should be appointed, apparently at Chatham, to replace the one person who had held both places before.

In the fall the lord admiral decided to winter the queen's ships at Portsmouth rather than bring them back to Chatham and the Thames, a decision which evoked a lengthy protest from Hawkins and Borough. The number of shipkeepers, they said, would have to be doubled and more ground tackle provided; the harbor was so exposed it would be dangerous in winter storms, and a few enemy ships could sail in and set fire to the whole fleet without much risk. They urged that the ships be sent to Chatham to be put in order, then carried to the Isle of Wight the following April, where they might stay ready for service all summer. They understood, Hawkins and Borough continued, that his lordship had been to Portsmouth and inspected the place, and they did not doubt that "when he has consulted men of experience there, he will be of their opinion." The language bears a note of condescension, though Howard could hardly be considered inexperienced at this time; at any rate, Howard evidently took their advice, since there are references in the next few months to the cost of bringing at least two of the queen's ships from Portsmouth back to Chatham.[33]

The documents for 1591 may not be entirely accurate in the general impression they leave of the lord admiral's relation to the administration and command of the navy. Since he did not go to sea himself that year, he is not seen in his primary role as a commander of ships and men. Nevertheless, at least for this year he was by no means just a titleholder; he concerned himself actively with the problems of maintaining

33. *Cal. S. P. Dom., Eliz., 1591–1594*, pp. 116, 197.

the naval establishment and directing its employment. But at the same time he was not absolutely the master of his own house; the lord treasurer was just as deeply involved as he in most matters and seemed to override him in some—and of course the lord admiral yielded his authority whenever the Privy Council or the queen cared to intervene. There is no evidence, however, of mutual jealousy or competition between officers of the crown or organs of government; from all appearances Burghley and Howard worked together in harmony and in recognition of the fact that it was impossible to segregate one area of the queen's interest from another. Maintenance of the navy was one of the queen's greatest annual expenses, and it was inevitable in the somewhat informal pattern of Tudor government that the chief financial officer be drawn into any important decisions concerning it, especially when that officer was the closest of all to the sovereign's mind and will.

Within the framework of their co-operation, though, there can be no doubt but that Burghley was the senior partner, even in matters which pertained strictly to the admiralty. In March, 1591, a new form of the bond required of all mariners who obtained letters of marque and reprisal against Spain and Portugal was prepared, pledging the signer not to attack French or Scottish ships or those of any country friendly with England, not to break bulk until a captured cargo had been declared prize by the admiralty court, to have inventories and appraisals made, and to pay the lord admiral his share within six weeks. Here was a matter which had intimate bearing on the authority of the admiralty court and the prerogatives of the admiral, but the form evidently was drawn up under Burghley's orders and was corrected in his hand. Under the date August 2, 1591, there is a draft of a letter from the council to the commander of one of the queen's pinnaces which was to be sent to sea again, ordering that his men should be paid for three months rather than one, as previously arranged, "lest they go away and more have to be pressed."[34]

34. *Ibid.*, p. 80.

The draft is by the lord admiral but shows Lord Burghley's corrections. Such documents are not confined to 1591 but are scattered through the state papers and the Cecil manuscripts dealing with the whole course of the Howard-Burghley relationship. The closeness of their professional relationship is also shown by the fact that on the two occasions when Howard was absent from England for extended periods—when he was at sea with the fleet in 1588 and when he commanded the expedition to Cádiz in 1596—he formally deputized Burghley to act as lord admiral. In addition there are a great many letters on naval matters written jointly to Burghley and Howard, or to Burghley alone, by persons qualified to know to whom such matters appertained.

There were, though, some rough divisions of authority between Burghley and Howard. As a finance minister Burghley had an unquestioned ascendency in matters relating to providing and maintaining the fleets; he corresponded directly with the responsible officers and he received the periodic estimates of navy charges which were signed by the lord admiral as well as the treasurer and comptroller. His hand had been a controlling one in naval government even before he became treasurer and long before Howard had any significant association with the navy. As the queen's secretary he had spent some time as early as 1559 reorganizing the admiralty and studying the state of the royal ships. Through the next twenty years he had labored to bring economy and order to the navy,[35] and there was no likelihood that he would give up his interest in the appointment of a new lord admiral, just at a time of imminent national peril when economy and order were more necessary than ever. There is little chance that Howard disputed the interference of the lord treasurer; he was not the kind of man who would object to sharing his more tedious duties with an able and devoted servant of the crown as long as he could keep his privileges and rewards. So he worked with Burghley without much complaint, allowing

35. See Conyers Read, *Lord Burghley and Queen Elizabeth* (New Haven, Conn., 1960), p. 410.

himself to be overridden or bypassed when he had to, and blaming Burghley for any deficiencies in the service that resulted.

The actual command of the ships was not Burghley's sphere, and he did not often interfere in it directly. The orders were usually given to the captains by the lord admiral or directly by the Privy Council but it was the Privy Council or the queen that decided what the orders would contain. As seen in 1591, it was the Privy Council that despatched the final orders to Lord Thomas Howard on May 18 which gave directions to Sir Henry Palmer for escorting the victual ships and instructed Sir Francis Drake to secure the prizes. The same exercise of command is to be seen throughout the period. Any matter regarding the policy of the navy was settled in the council; then directions were translated into specific terms by the council's own staff or through the lord admiral. Council supervision applied not only to the instructions sent to captains but even to the exercise of the lord admiral's own special prerogatives. On July 9, 1585, immediately after he received his patent, Lord Admiral Howard got instructions from the council for issuing letters of reprisal which set out in detail to whom the letters might be given, what the procedure for granting them would be, and how the prizes would be handled.[36] In later years the council was involved in nearly every admiralty action—giving orders to captains, arresting ships, hearing complaints from wronged shipowners, sending out commissioners to make investigations, directing payment of warrants, authorizing expenditures, and so on.

The council's constant and close control of naval matters did not make the lord admiral a sinecurist. As one of the highest officers within the Privy Council, he inevitably took a principal part in discussion of all matters affecting the navy. In the case of the final orders given to Lord Thomas Howard in 1591, the draft of the instructions in the lord admiral's handwriting predated the council letter embodying largely the same articles. It is probable that Howard prepared the orders and submitted them to the council; then, after more discus-

36. Lansdowne MSS, 143/309–13.

sion, the orders were approved with the addition of the paragraphs concerning Newfoundland. The council maintained a like control over all the agencies of Elizabethan government; without it there could have been little unity of policy and no united action. The lord admiral was the medium of communication and co-ordination with the navy and was the council member with special knowledge and experience particularly fitted to advise on maritime matters.

One duty remained the lord admiral's special province. He was the representative of England, English merchants and sailors, and English commerce in the eyes of foreign countries, and representatives of these countries sought him out when they had grievances against English ships and mariners. Such grievances were frequent, causing Howard to spend much time with ambassadors who were offended by the piratical tendencies of Englishmen. The rules governing the capture of enemy goods left ample room for dispute with neutral nations. English privateers could, without forfeiting their admiralty bonds, not only prey on Spanish ships and ships of the Catholic League but also could make prize of any goods which were owned by Spanish citizens or any war matériel under shipment to Spain. In their zeal to capitalize on enemy commerce, the English privateers captured a great many Dutch, Danish, German, and Italian ships in the hope that part of their cargoes might be proved in a friendly court to belong to the queen's enemies. Privateers sometimes found technicalities of ownership beyond their ken and became outright pirates, attacking whatever ships offered themselves. The aggrieved merchants were quick to make representations for restitution, and it was to the lord admiral (except in some special cases) that they were referred. These complaints were clamorous even before the war with Spain had become a recognized fact. There is some evidence that in 1584, as heir apparent to the old lord admiral, Howard had already become involved in disputes over prize goods. Letters of Sir Edward Stafford, English ambassador in Paris, indicate that before December, 1584, two Englishmen who had been imprisoned and sentenced to pay £4,000 in damages for illegal prizes had been set free on Howard's authority. A year later the French council was still seeking satisfaction of the judgment before issuing letters of reprisal against England. The French ambassador, however, was not concerned with these cases alone; on December 2, 1585, he advised Howard and Walsingham that he was receiving daily complaints of the depredations of the English on French merchants, and he warned that if some action were not taken "great dissatisfaction" would result. Within two weeks the lord admiral, besides endeavoring to satisfy the French, had to write apologetically to Scotland for the "manifold and great robberies" committed daily against Scottish vessels, promising justice whenever the offenders were caught and restitution of goods identified as Scottish. But at the same time he countered with a complaint that Scots abused the passes given them to cross England by smuggling bolts of cloth over the border in their trunks. At the same time that the French and Scots demanded justice, the Dutch were offended. On January 3, 1586, the Dutch representative wrote to Walsingham to complain of "the great and daily increasing wrongs done to us at sea." Walsingham directed him to the new lord admiral, and in a "long discourse" on the 13th they agreed that there were grounds for negotiation of a general commercial policy to help prevent the recurrent conflicts. Thus, within less than two months the lord admiral had been drawn into discussions of maritime depredations with France, Scotland, and the Netherlands. The pattern seen in these two months can be traced throughout the entire Spanish war. Despite treaty arrangements, common interests, and mutual good will, conflicts between England and neutral or allied states continued to occur and continued to preoccupy the admiral. Most cases were handled by the ordinary processes of the admiralty court, with the lord admiral acting as an agent of communications and settlement between the court and the ambassadors. In a similar fashion, he presented grievances of English merchants against foreign privateers to the respective ambassadors. This role as a buffer between the English crown and foreign states was sometimes assumed by the council, but over the years it remained one of Howard's most persistent problems.

III: *Fruits of the Sea*

The lord admiral not only was one of the highest officers around the queen, expected to be able to influence her about a variety of matters, naval and non-naval, and able to advance the private fortunes of his dependants as few others could, but he also ruled over a financial empire of his own. This empire was a wide but somewhat shadowy one, its limits ill-defined and somewhat flexible; in the hands of vigorous persons it was capable of great expansion. As a capitalist seeking a profit in the maintenance of public safety, the admiral possessed a variety of perquisites and privileges that few could hope to match, a collection of opportunities which, if sufficiently pressed, would give him an income little short of princely. They were designed to give the admiral an adequate revenue for the support of his office in time of peace; in time of war, because of the peculiar kind of war England fought against Spain, they yielded dazzling profits.

The admiral's incomes were largely at the making of the admiralty judge, the manager of his franchise, who passed sentence on prizes, confiscated the goods forfeited to the admiral, and kept watch over his droits. If the judge were a diligent and efficient servant, protected and encouraged by his patron, as Caesar reminded Howard again and again, then the admiral would become rich; but if the servant had to employ himself in looking after his own interests, then the master would suffer. Caesar was ambitious of his own advancement, constantly pressing the queen for grants and offices and ceaselessly reminding the great men at court of the suits which they had, he said, promised to further. In order to gain the important support of the lord admiral for his own causes, Caesar promised early in his tenure to unlock vast treasures for him—but the treasures were contingent upon concrete evidence that Howard was busying himself on Caesar's behalf.

A long series of letters suggests that the learned judge did practice a kind of blackmail upon his patron. If Howard would agree to his conditions and further his suits, Caesar would milk the admiralty cow with such diligence and ingenuity that they both would become rich. If he did not, Howard would see his income dwindle, as he said it had recently; very few of the ships being brought back to England were proving to be legal prize—prize, that is, whose legality was acceptable to the judge of the admiralty and of which the lord admiral would receive a share.[1] Here indeed is a case of the use of the court for private purposes, a use that reinforces K. R. Andrews' view that it had "the character of a great feudal franchise."[2] It was possible at least for the judge to administer the court for his own and not his lord's ends, using it against the interests of the franchise-holder.

In the Caesar letters that survive there is no clear statement of his plans for making the lord admiral, as he said he would, "the richest and greatest that ever was in England." One letter does mention that the judge had four inventions up his sleeve, the poorest of which would be richer than the tenths.[3] There are, however, compilations of the rights and perquisites of the lord admiral, most of which depended on sentence, condemnation, or decree from the admiralty court. From these lists it seems likely that Caesar planned to increase his patron's income at least partly through a vigorous collection of those droits which clearly belonged to the lord admiral by law or custom or to which claim had been made with some success in the past. Whether Howard could have been losing £10,000 in three months by not getting his rights, as Caesar once indicated,[4] is questionable. At the same time, the prerequisites listed are many, and in the hands of a vigilant and determined

1. Lansdowne MSS, 157/434.
2. K. R. Andrews, *English Privateering Voyages to the West Indies, 1588–1595* (Cambridge, 1959), p. 3.
3. Lansdowne MSS, 157/432.
4. *Ibid.*, 157/438.

officer they might have produced large sums. The admiralty court did, in fact, try to extend the admiral's claims as far as it could in as many directions as possible; there are references in the Howard-Caesar letters to most of the different kinds of perquisites mentioned in Caesar's lists. The attempt to interpret in the broadest possible sense the terms of the admiral's patent, according to Marsden, led the court to make claims that were "wholly unfounded in law" and brought it into popular discredit.[5]

The most complete single list of admiralty droits is one in the Sloane Manuscripts entitled "Of the Office of the Admyraltie of England, together with the Articles concerninge the same office."[6] The document enumerates rights held at some time in the past, but all of them and others were still claimed in Howard's time. It and similar lists may have guided Caesar and the Elizabethan and Jacobean admiralty courts in their efforts to aggrandize the admiral and, through him, the judges themselves. A few of the rights probably never were seriously pressed or never could be strictly enforced, but the great majority either were held without challenge or at least were claimed for him with occasional success. The document contains fifty articles, of which half pertain to the lord admiral's income:

Persons taking prisoners of lower degree than royalty had to "satisfie the Admyrall for his shares aswell for suche a prisoner, as for all other goods taken upon the sea." Presumably this would mean a tenth of the ransom.

The lord admiral was to receive half of all wreckage found in the sea, goods cast overboard from distressed vessels, or goods sunk in the sea with a buoy attached that they may be found again (flotsam, jetsam, and lagan); persons finding such goods without sharing with the admiral lost the entire find by way of penalty.

He could keep fines laid upon persons convicted of setting

5. R. G. Marsden, ed., *Select Pleas in the Court of Admiralty*, 2 vols. (London, 1892–97), 2:xviii.
6. Sloane MSS, 1605/3–15.

mines or obstructions that may be "noyous or hurtfull to the saylers or shippes"; those arrested for royal service who break arrest; fishermen and others who destroy young salmon or other fish; persons convicted of forestalling or engrossing naval victuals; persons who cut or stole buoys and brought injury to shipping; persons who hired foreign ships when English were available; carpenters and other workmen in his jurisdiction guilty of taking excessive wages; those who threw ballast, lastage, or filth into a harbor or haven; those convicted of striking or beating another person, of drawing blood or causing "any fraye" within his jurisdiction; those who regrated grain, fish, or other goods to raise the price; and persons within admiralty jurisdiction who used false measures or balances.

In a number of situations goods or equivalent sums were to be forfeited to the lord admiral: goods, especially jewels, found on the body of a dead man; goods exported without proper license, against statutory prohibitions, or without payment of customs; equipment, such as cables, lines, or anchors, which had caused a death at sea—even a ship, if its movement caused the accidental death of a crew member; the goods of traitors, pirates, felons, and outlaws found within the admiral's jurisdiction and any property of those committing treason, piracy, or felony within his jurisdiction. He could demand the value of the cargoes of ships used to transport felons and banished men, or the ship if it carried no other cargo. And he received a share of the value of "royal fish"—whales, porpoises, and sturgeons—and part of wreckage washed ashore, except where royal grants or long-established custom interfered.

All these privileges were associated with the admiral's responsibility for keeping peace and good order on the seas and for protecting the interests of the crown in areas where law enforcement through normal channels was impossible. Most were essentially punitive powers, granted so that the lord admiral would have a direct and personal concern in enforcing the law. Income from such sources could have been uncertain and erratic but would necessarily have increased with a greater effort and stimulated activity in the admiralty court.

To these fines and rewards must be added other sources of revenue arising from the issue of passports and warrants, from customary rights, and from the issue of letters of marque and reprisal. Lords admirals of the sixteenth century inferred from the terms of their patents other privileges—the right to supply ballast, to appoint measurers of coal and grain, to license water mills and fishgarths and to collect the profits from those erected without license, to cut and gather kelp, etc.—rights concerning which the power of the crown itself was doubtful and which involved the admirals in continuous litigation. As long as the cases were heard by the admiralty court itself, the admiral's claims were fairly sure of a sympathetic hearing, but sometimes he had reason to complain that cases were being taken out of his jurisdiction.[7]

The greatest of all the lord admiral's perquisites were those derived from privateering. The lord admiral, through the High Court of Admiralty, issued commissions allowing the owners of private ships to capture, bring home, and sell for their own profit goods belonging to the Spanish king or Spanish subjects, in return for which the admiral received for his own use a share of the cargo. His portion had once been a third,[8] but during Howard's tenure it was a tenth. If a ship sailed to capture prizes without receiving the admiral's commission, it became his property upon confiscation in the admiralty court. The usual form of commission, at least after 1589, was the letter of reprisal, which was given theoretically to allow a shipowner to recompense himself for losses sustained from the warships or privateers of other countries. Letters of reprisal allowed a ship to commit acts that ordinarily would be considered piracy; the distinction between piracy and privateering was sometimes lost to the mariners themselves, as the

7. *Cal. S. P. Dom., Eliz., 1581–1590*, p. 384; Additional MSS, 15,208/239.
8. Marsden, *Select Pleas*, 2:xviii.

many complaints by neutrals of the depredations by Englishmen testify.

In order to obtain a letter of reprisal the prospective privateer was required to make a formal pleading in the High Court of Admiralty, supported by witnesses, to prove that he had suffered losses at the hands of the Spanish, and to pay a fee of 13s. 4d., which was one of the judge's perquisites.[9] But formal pleadings and sentences became unnecessary after 1585. No one who applied for a commission and paid the fee was refused, and almost never was a letter of reprisal withdrawn because the recipient recovered more than he lost. Any Englishman who could outfit a ship could have a go at Spanish commerce; among other results, the litigation over doubtful prizes in the Court of Admiralty grew in volume as the war progressed. But under sympathetic administration the number of prizes accepted as lawful also grew, swelling the revenues of the lord admiral and his judge. It is not known how many letters of reprisal were issued; one fragmentary list, probably compiled soon after Howard became admiral, contains the names of fifty persons who were given reprisal letters to recover losses totaling £139,764. Of the fifty, all but five were to set out ships against Spain, the others against the Dunkirk privateers.[10]

Before they got commissions, privateers were obliged to post sufficient bonds to the lord admiral, usually £3,000 for each ship, promising they would not attack the queen's allies and would follow the procedures defined by the admiralty in returning and reporting their catches. Bonds could be waived at the discretion of the lord admiral: in the case of his brother-in-law, Sir George Carey, who set out three ships in 1586, Howard wrote to Caesar, "My brother Sir George is a man sufficient to aunsweare for anythinge that his ships may commit, and therefore it shall not nede to take bonds of him, and his losses are commonly knowne."[11] However, since the

9. Additional MSS, 12,505/216.
10. Lansdowne MSS, 115/196.
11. Quoted in David Beers Quinn, ed., *The Roanoke Voyages, 1584–1590*, 2 vols. (London, 1955), 2:512.

bonds themselves were a source of income, Howard did not often make exceptions. When the conditions of the bond were violated, the privateers could be prosecuted and the amount of the bond collected for the lord admiral's use.[12]

The enforcement of the privateering regulations and the collection of his due rights required a rather elaborate machinery which spread throughout the coastal areas. In most of the maritime counties vice-admirals were appointed, with patents from the lord admiral, to watch over his interests. The vice-admirals themselves often were great noblemen—a list for 1587 includes the earl of Leicester for North Wales, the earl of Pembroke for South Wales, and the earl of Derby for Chester and Lancashire. Others, and the deputies who acted for such court figures as Leicester and Pembroke, were prominent local landowners, often connected with the lord admiral, like Sir William More in Sussex and Sir Robert Southwell in Norfolk; or they were sea captains and members of great seafaring families, like Sir William Winter in Somersetshire and the Killigrews, Raleighs, Gilberts, Harrises, and Vivians, who acted at various times for Devonshire and Cornwall. For each port in his county, the vice-admiral chose a "fit person" to board each vessel brought in as prize, make an appraisal and inventory, arrange to seal up the cargo or sell it if perishable and hold the money in safekeeping, and return the tenth to the lord admiral. Presumably the same officer also would be responsible for executing the orders of the admiralty and for collecting the lord admiral's occasional dues, such as wreck, flotsam and jetsam, and deodand. The vice-admirals themselves were under bonds to "make a true, just, and perfect account" of all pirates' goods, concealments, and casualties twice a year to the lord admiral, but few of these reports survive.[13] Probably they found it possible to keep most of what they collected. Howard complained in 1591 that most of

12. Additional MSS, 15,208/225.
13. Lansdowne MSS, 194/23–24. The rules for the conduct of the waiters and searchers given here are for a later period, but they seem to have been generally operative in Elizabethan times as well.

his vice-admirals "seldom or never" rendered up what was due.[14]

In some areas the lord admiral also employed collectors of tenths, who were responsible only to him and who presumably also maintained representatives in the port towns to gather his share of prizes. The division of authority between these personal financial agents and the waiters and searchers responsible to the vice-admirals is now rather uncertain and may not have been clear at the time; Caesar sometimes referred to a state of confusion which had resulted in the delay or denial of his own share of the prizes.

The income that the lord admiral received through the efforts of his judge, his vice-admirals and their searchers and waiters, and his collectors is nowhere fully summarized. There are enough fragments of evidence, though, to indicate that, while it fluctuated considerably, the revenue from prizes and perquisites was always great, sometimes enormous. From the gross total, however, had to come funds for maintaining the machinery of collection. Grants to servants and sometimes grants for charitable purposes also reduced the sum remaining to the admiral. The vice-admirals got half the value of the pirates' goods that were confiscated within their counties, all the salvage that owners of shipwrecked goods could be induced to pay to regain possession of their property, and half the value of casual dues arising within their jurisdictions. Out of their profits the vice-admirals were expected to satisfy the finders of the shipwreck and probably pay their local port officers as well. The right to the remaining half of pirate goods was farmed before 1607 to Humphrey Jobson, one of the lord admiral's secretaries, for an unknown amount. The terms of the farm seem to have been ambiguous, since Jobson became involved in a dispute with the earl of Southampton, vice-admiral for Hampshire, over the ship and cargo of a

14. High Court of Admiralty Records, 14/28, #65, Public Record Office, London. See K. R. Andrews, *Elizabethan Privateering* (Cambridge, 1964), p. 29.

French pirate brought into Portsmouth, both men apparently claiming rights to the whole prize.[15]

The collectors of tenths in at least one case received a percentage of their takes; the writer of Harleian Manuscript 598, one of the fullest surviving records, kept a twentieth of the prize goods. Another percentage went to the judge of the admiralty, which helped to make Caesar, on paper at least, the most liberally rewarded of all the admiralty officers, in spite of his unceasing pleas of poverty. By a grant of October 14, 1589, Caesar received, in addition to salaries and fees, a twentieth of Howard's share of prize goods, a tenth of the money received from Flemish merchants for passports and safe-conducts, a quarter of the goods forfeited as prohibited exports, a quarter of fines, penalties, and forfeitures of bonds, and a quarter of all other casual dues.[16] Apparently Caesar's share of the casual dues was paid without demur since he did not complain about not receiving it, but he had repeated difficulties in getting his share of the prize tenths.

In October, 1588, Howard surrendered to Trinity House, a guild of Thames pilots and watermen, all his rights concerning the management of beacons in the Thames and a life-long lease of his privilege to supply anchors. Later the grant was enlarged to include the management of beacons and buoys on all coasts and the right to supply ballast to ships in the Thames. These grants made Howard the first lord admiral to give away any of his privileges, but the rights transferred were among those to which Marsden said Howard's title was doubtful, if not usurped.[17]

In some cases the lord admiral's title to wreckage also was given away and frequently was challenged by owners of property on which the goods were found. The bishop of Chichester

---

15. Historical Manuscripts Commission, *Calendar of the Manuscripts of Major-General Lord Sackville, preserved at Knole, Sevenoaks, Kent*, vol. 1: *Cranfield Papers, 1551–1612* (London, 1940), pp. 137–38; hereinafter cited as *Cranfield Papers*.

16. Additional MSS, 12,505/296.

17. Marsden, *Select Pleas*, 2:xviii.

in 1591 was given a renewed grant of the profits from all wrecks within his diocese, which he had held since 1573. It would seem, too, that rights concerning wreck were also, at least in some cases, given to the vice-admirals. In several instances the lord of a manor claimed the right to wreckage on his shores, either by royal grant or by long-standing custom. In such instances litigation almost invariably resulted, with Lord Rich in Essex, Sir Drue Drury at Eccles, Norfolk, and the earl of Huntingdon at Stokeham, Devonshire, among others. The Cinque Ports and their warden also claimed right of wreck and other droits in the Downs and on the Goodwins, a claim of long standing which came to a head in 1619, shortly after Nottingham's retirement. It was not settled until 1624, when Lord Admiral Buckingham agreed to pay Zouche, the lord warden, £1,000 in cash and £500 a year for life in return for a surrender of the wreckage rights.[18]

The admiral's revenue potential was diminished still more by claims of local admiralty powers which were sometimes exerted successfully. Like the claims of wreckage, these supposed jurisdictions were given close scrutiny by Howard and Caesar, and all means at hand were used in the effort to have them overturned. In January, 1589, the lord admiral had the mayor and aldermen of Southampton summoned before the Privy Council for "contemptuously" disobeying and resisting orders to restore a ship and cargo which town and admiral each claimed. The town was sternly warned ". . . to beare a more respective regard to their Lordships' requeste hereafter, and not upon everie vain presumpcion to delude themselves and deferre the execucion of justice by their frivolous aunswers and delaies."[19] Traditional jurisdiction rights at Newcastle, Tynemouth, and Scarborough were repudiated, but the claims of Colchester, Harwich, Dartmouth, and the Cinque Ports were not settled until after 1618. Bristol had been expressly exempted from the lord admiral's jurisdiction by charter as early as 1403, an exemption confirmed by Henry VI

18. *Ibid.*, pp. xxi–xxiii.
19. Dasent, *Acts of the Privy Council*, 17:17–18, 51.

and Edward IV, so the best that Lord Howard could do was to recognize its privileged status, with the provision that criminal causes would not be tried by the city and that the admiral would enjoy his traditional forfeitures.[20] These ports were among the most important in the realm, and as long as they could resist the admiral's authority, they could take for themselves the profits which his collectors and officers demanded. Local jurisdictions, however, no matter how strenuously maintained, usually affected only casual dues and not tenths.

Only scattered indications now exist as to precisely what income remained from casualties after special jurisdictions had been excepted and allowance had been made for grants to officers and servants. From the available fragments, however, the impression of great affluence emerges. One extremely important account prepared for Caesar shows his income from naval causes, thereby shedding some light on his patron's revenues.[21] It covers the period from October 14, 1589, when the lord admiral's grant became effective, to the end of November, 1595. During this time Caesar shared in casualties worth a total of £4,132 0s. 9d., of which he took £1,033 0s. 2d. Far the greater part came from forfeitures of bonds, capture of pirate goods, and seizure of ships that had sailed without reprisal letters. Only one pirate ship is listed among the seizures, a Spanish capture brought home by "Stratford the pirate" in July, 1591, but it alone was worth £225. One other ship was forfeited during the six-year period—the *Minion* of Bristol, for which the lord admiral got £300—but in other cases heavy fines were paid to gain release of ships that had spoiled the commerce of neutral countries. These payments amounted to £1,842, together with ordnance and other goods seized as illegal exports, which in the account are not always separated from the discharge of ships. Other fines and forfeited bonds in the admiralty court totaled £631 8s. The remaining £344 0s. 9d. came from a variety of sources: a forfeited anchor, worth £3 15s., some small finds of wrecked

20. Marsden, *Select Pleas*, 2:xx.
21. Lansdowne MSS, 133/21–26.

goods, and the like. A few entries refer to the accounts rendered by the county vice-admirals, but the amounts are never significant, suggesting again that the vice-admirals did not pay what was due.

There is no comparable evidence for Howard's later years as lord admiral, although there are scattered reports of particular forfeitures and dues. If the years covered by the Caesar account were representative, Howard received something like £700–£800 a year from confiscations, forfeitures, fines, and other occasional sources. Such a revenue alone would not make him rich, but in Elizabethan England it was a large sum.

A document in the Lansdowne Manuscripts[22] entitled "Seasures made of things forfeited to the L Admirall" indicates that at times Howard may have received far more than £800 a year from casualties. It lists five seizures of goods loaded on foreign vessels for transshipment around the English coast, mostly from Rye to London, in violation of the navigation act passed during the fifth year of Elizabeth's reign. The document covers only a four-month period in 1585, but the goods taken were worth £220 to the lord admiral. If such activity continued on a year-round basis, which cannot be assumed from this single document, then forfeited goods in the port of London alone might have grossed £800 a year, without reckoning incomes from other forms of casualties.

Some few surviving letters would indicate that particular value was attached to what might be considered one of the admiral's minor perquisites, his right to half the value of whales, sturgeons, and porpoises—the so-called royal fish. They were valued as delicacies apart from any monetary equivalent, and Howard preferred to be given the fish itself rather than its cash value. Once in 1587, when he was brought two sturgeons as his share of a catch, he directed Caesar to send them as presents to the earl of Leicester and Lord Chancellor Hatton. Howard seems to have taken personal notice of receiving royal fish, since on one occasion when he received none he called it to Caesar's attention. "I

22. *Ibid.*, 145/420.

mervaile," he wrote on May 9, 1593, "that all of this yeare I can heare of no sturgeons that have bin taken in the river. . . ." He asked Caesar to make a "diligent serche . . . and enquirye" into the matter and "if you understand of anie taken and not prsented hertofore or herafter to let me heare thereof to the end I my self maie see them punished."[23]

The lord admiral had the right to seize pirate goods for his own uses, which gave him a personal stake in clearing the seas and seeing the law obeyed, but Howard's attempts to suppress piracy met with little success. According to Oppenheim, piracy in Elizabeth's reign "almost attained the dignity of a recognized profession."[24] Some of the most conspicuous western families, including the Champernounes, Killigrews, Careys, Horseys, and Oglanders, had begun as pirates. Oppenheim found that many were captured but few executed, principally because English pirates caused far more injury to Spanish and French shipping than to domestic traffic. When James I came to England and began to try to make peace with Spain, he discontinued the use of commissions of marque and reprisal against Spanish commerce, and as a result some who had been privateers became pirates. By 1604 piracy was so widespread that it became a serious concern of the king and Privy Council, and—officially—the lord admiral despaired of seeing it controlled. But the fact was that if piracy were completely crushed, his own interests would suffer. The admiralty court was not inactive; cases regarding spoil and piracy made up a great part of its business. A summary list prepared by Caesar in 1600 indicates that as many as eighty-nine persons were indicted for piracy in a single year.[25] But the great majority of these were civil cases, in which the goods in question were awarded to the successful party, and they had little effect in reducing the frequency of forced seizures. Finally, in 1616, the government commissioned two London merchants to seek out

23. Additional MSS, 15,208/293.

24. Michael Oppenheim, *A History of the Administration of the Royal Navy and of Merchant Shipping in Relation to the Navy,* new ed. (London, 1961), p. 177.

25. Lansdowne MSS, 134/86–96.

the pirates, promising them three-quarters of the goods they took.

One of the reasons for the royal navy's failure to suppress piracy was the lord admiral's financial interest in it. Clearly he tended to see the subject in terms of personal revenues; several times he wrote to Caesar asking for speedy sentence of captured pirate goods and ships so that they might be converted to his own use, but when steps were taken for suppression of corsairs, they were usually taken at the instance of the Privy Council. The fact that the lord admiral farmed his interest in pirate goods to his secretary, just as he farmed his grant for wine licenses, is another indication of the nature of his concern; he was willing to let his servant do what was necessary to make a profit out of piracy while he enjoyed a settled revenue. Finally, there is evidence that the lord admiral accepted gifts from pirates at least once without troubling himself about any ethical problems involved.[26]

There is a great deal more evidence concerning the lord admiral's income from ships captured as prizes than from piracy, although in many respects it remains tantalizingly incomplete. From the fragments that survive, it is clear that Howard's tenth of prize goods was far and away his most important source of revenue, great enough, while it lasted, to make him enormously rich by the standards of the day and to give real substance to his pose of splendor at court.

It might be pointed out, however, that the lord admiral did not receive a tenth of all the prizes that were captured by English ships, but only of those which were sailing under commissions of marque and reprisal. Of the prizes brought home by fleets sailing under the queen's commission, which included all the large-scale expeditions into Spanish waters, he got no guaranteed part. He was often a shareholder in such voyages and was rewarded in proportion to his venture, but that usually meant less than a tenth of the gross. The two biggest prizes of Elizabethan times were taken by ships under the queen's commission, so the lord admiral missed getting

26. See below, pp. 267-71.

both tenths; he was, however, a shareholder in at least one of
the two expeditions. In 1587 Sir Francis Drake took the
carrack *San Felipe,* with a cargo—a major part of the year's
pepper supply—valued at nearly £115,000 even after much
plundering. In the division of spoil, Howard got £4,338 in
return for his contribution of two ships, the *White Lion* and
the *Cygnet,* a handsome reward, certainly, and enough to
leave him a profit after his expenses in outfitting the two ships
had been paid, but it was not what he could have expected if
the ship had been taken by a private adventurer. The greatest
share, £46,672, was taken by the queen, and Drake got
£18,235.[27]

The *Madre de Dios,* taken in 1592 by a fleet under the
command of Sir John Burroughs, was an even richer haul, but
Howard's share in it, nowhere specifically set down, probably
was much smaller. This carrack, whose cargo was valued
officially at £141,000 even after "indiscriminate looting,"[28]
carried quantities of pepper, cloves, cinnamon, cochineal, and
thousands of diamonds and other stones. Howard, along with
the earl of Cumberland, Sir Walter Raleigh, Sir John Hawkins, and many others, was a shareholder—according to Monson, he ventured one small ship, the *Lion's Whelp,* a 100-ton
pinnace.[29] He is not mentioned, however, in the various lists of
those who took part in the division of the profits. The queen
had taken the major part of the spoil before any division took
place, even though she had contributed to the fleet of ten only
one ship, whose service had been of questionable value in the
capture. Most of the goods other than the pepper, which the
queen took for herself, were finally divided into six parts, of
which Cumberland received three (worth £36,000), Raleigh
two, and the city of London one.

The pepper, which made up the greater part of the cargo's
worth, was sold to a London syndicate after a great deal of

27. S. P. Dom., Eliz., 204/467; Oppenheim, *Administration of
the Royal Navy,* p. 165; *idem, Sir William Monson,* 1:139.
28. Lawrence Stone, *An Elizabethan: Sir Horatio Palavicino* (Oxford, 1956), pp. 213–14.
29. Oppenheim, *Sir William Monson,* 1:281.

negotiation and unsuccessful market manipulation by the crown. The syndicate had spent more than £1,300 on gratuities and rewards to persons at court in the effort to get the contract, and if Howard got only a minor share of the prize itself, he had further cause for complaint in the distribution of gifts. Such payoffs were far from unusual; in this case the arrangement was so matter-of-fact that a list of the recipients was sent to Lord Buckhurst for his inspection. But after the money had been distributed, it was discovered that somehow the lord admiral had been left off the list. Robert Cecil wrote to Thomas Myddelton, one of the commissioners for the sale, that as a result of the omission there was "some unkindness taken." "Rather than his lordship should be offended," Myddelton replied, he would "provide new angels, 100 in a bag," to which he would add, if necessary, £50 from his own pocket in order to make £100; he would also send a note to the lord admiral stating that "I have a remembrance for him, though not so good as I could wish." The syndicate apparently grumbled about supplying the "new angels," and a month later, when the lord admiral still was unsatisfied, Myddelton offered to pay the whole amount himself rather than risk offending him.[30] Such gifts had become so customary that Howard felt himself publicly slighted in not receiving one, and the situation was a legitimate matter of concern among other officers of state. There remain, however, few references to these goodwill gifts. It may be inferred from situations like these that gratuities of considerable size were part of the revenues of the great figures around the queen; it is impossible even to guess at their frequency or the amounts that might have been involved.

Caesar's papers contain hundreds of references to prize ships and goods and are a valuable source for the study of every aspect of privateering. Caesar enjoyed a twentieth of the lord admiral's tenth, a fact to which he frequently alluded. Thus his records ought, if complete, to provide an accurate basis for calculating his patron's income from reprisals. Unfor-

30. *Cal. Hatfield MSS,* 4:358, 375.

78

tunately they are not complete, and those which do remain serve mainly to substantiate Caesar's own cry that he was not getting his due. Nevertheless, his receipts were considerable. In October, 1589, when he began to receive his twentieth, Sir John Hawkins and William Dudson seemed to be the principal tenth collectors, and were charged with delivering to Caesar his share; by the following January, Hawkins had been replaced, probably because of the demands of his other naval appointments. But at the end of the month, he paid Caesar £211 15s. as his share of the prizes collected since October 14, 1589.[31] Caesar's account of the payment listed fifteen prizes, but it might easily be that Caesar received a major part or all of enough prizes to make up what was due him as a twentieth of a far larger number. Most of the sums listed, as a twentieth of a tenth, are quite small, but for one prize, identified by the name "Somers," Caesar got £96 13s. 6d. and for another, beside which the name Sir Walter Raleigh appears, he received £42 15s.

The prize identified in Caesar's receipt as "somers" was probably the one brought into Dartmouth by Captain George Somers in December, 1589. And a rich prize it was—four Spanish barks bearing quantities of Spanish money, bullion, cochineal, and hides. For marketable commodities like the cochineal and hides, the collector of tenths usually made arrangements for sale and then made regular accountings to the lord admiral for profits, but gold or silver in any form was delivered directly to him, with a certificate from the port officer who had received it. In this case, Francis Burnell, later vice-admiral for Essex but in 1589 admiralty officer in the port of Dartmouth, testified that he "received to the use of my Lorde Admirall in part of his Lo[rdshi]ps tentes" £767 in money, plus forty-four pounds by weight in bullion, one pound of gold, and four pounds of musk—in all, goods worth about £1,000. A tenth of the cochineal came to £1,650, and the hides were worth £283 10s., so the four ships of Captain Somers should have been worth £2,700 to the admiral, even

31. Lansdowne MSS, 144/36.

without the bullion, gold, and musk. A few such prizes every year would have made the lord admiral a rich man indeed.

Another of Caesar's accounts purports to contain "all such receipts of sumes of money wch I have received for my L Admirall" from October 14, 1589, to November 30, 1595.[32] If it were complete, it would be most valuable as a guide to the lord admiral's naval revenues, but clearly it lists only a fraction of the prizes actually brought into English ports. No legitimate prize is mentioned after February 28, 1592, though the record continues for nearly three years longer, and between October, 1589, and February, 1592, only twenty-six prizes are named. Andrews counted no fewer than 299 prizes during almost exactly the same period.[33] The twenty-six captures listed in Caesar's record include only three of those listed on the receipts from Sir John Hawkins. Nevertheless, while the handful of prizes cannot be taken to represent all of Howard's revenue from that source, they did produce a sizable sum—£2,719 8s., not including the judge's and the collector's shares. As seemed to be the usual case, a great part of the total came from a few rich catches: an East Indiaman loaded with spices, wines, and precious stones brought to London by John Bird in February, 1591, worth £543 to the lord admiral; a prize of gold and grain taken to Harwich the same month, which paid £407 in tenths; a sugar cargo brought to Bristol in October, 1589, with tenths worth £378; and two prizes of silk and block wood captured by Captains Somers and Buckley and brought to Dartmouth, which brought the lord admiral £535. After February, 1592, the account seems only to include the fines and fees arising in the admiralty court itself and some of the casualties collected by vice-admirals. Probably after that time some other bookkeeping arrangement was worked out and prizes were listed in a separate record which does not survive. But if Caesar shared in only twenty-six prizes during the twenty-eight months after October, 1589, his bitterness toward the tenth collectors and Howard was amply justified.

32. *Ibid.,* 133/21–26.
33. Andrews, *Elizabethan Privateering,* p. 125.

Far more important than Caesar's own prize records is a single surviving account book of one of Howard's tenth collectors,[34] probably either William Dudson or Edward Fenner, both of whom are known to have been collectors during the period covered by the document. Whoever the collector, he was charged with receiving the lord admiral's share of prize goods and converting them into cash, which was delivered periodically to his employer at court. The account includes 273 prizes brought into Hampshire, Dorsetshire, Bristol, and Bridgwater between May 2, 1587, and November, 1598, plus four others, one sent to London, one to Dartmouth, and two with no port designated. Of the total, all but twenty-four went either to Weymouth, Bristol, Southampton, or Portsmouth, with Weymouth being the most active of the group. Why the record would have included a single prize delivered to London and another to Dartmouth is difficult to say, but clearly, excluding Devonshire and Cornwall, the area of the collector's authority was restricted to the western counties.

By far the most valuable product reflected in the collector's record was sugar; sugar prizes were easily the most frequently caught and were sometimes worth hundreds of pounds to the lord admiral. Almost all the big prizes were either partly or exclusively sugar. Prizes of spices were far more rare, but, particularly when pepper was involved, spice ships tended to yield large sums. The most valuable single prize listed, an East Indiaman brought to Weymouth on November 20, 1590, by John Randall's bark *Randall,* was loaded with pepper, sugar, ivory, Pernambuco wood, and raw silk and paid Howard a total of £1,137 7s. 2d. But it was almost matched by the four West Indiamen captured by the earl of Cumberland and brought to Portsmouth in May, 1594. Sugar was the most important part in that cargo, which also included pearls, hides, indigo, oils, block wood, and mustard, worth £1,035 14s. in tenths. No other prizes approached these in importance, although a considerable number paid from £300 to £500.

In a great many cases, particularly when sugar was in-

34. Harleian MSS, 598, British Museum, London.

volved, Howard himself made arrangements for sales; for a time he had a standing arrangement with Thomas Heton, a Southampton merchant, to buy the tenths of sugar at a flat rate of £7 per chest, regardless of the type or quality of the sugar, with Heton assuming all expenses and customs charges. Heton sometimes accepted other products such as hides, nails, fish, wines, cotton, and woods at similar flat rates. On other occasions the collector bargained with the shipowner for the value of the tenth or received the goods themselves and sold them to other merchants for whatever he could get. The arrangement with Heton does not seem to have been continued after 1595, and it is noticeable that the collector was usually able to get a higher price for sugar when he handled it himself. Refined sugar, referred to as "white powder sugar," sometimes fetched as much as £15 a chest, thereby more than balancing the lower prices paid for muscovado and the unrefined type usually called "pannales," particularly since the greater weight was usually in the white. Of course, when the goods were sold by the collector, the tenth had to bear the queen's custom and the cost of handling, but these were never great. So it is possible that the lord admiral had been required to come to a contractual agreement with Thomas Heton (and sometimes others) at somewhat unfavorable terms because of the pressure of debts, and that after the obligations were paid he could make more profitable arrangements.

By custom and admiralty law, the lord admiral had a right not only to a tenth of the cargo but also to 10 per cent of the value of ships captured bearing enemy goods. The receiver's account, however, indicates that this was never a major source of income and also that it was often given away. Until 1590 many of the entries noted that the tenth of the ship was sold for a pound or two, never for more than £4; for several years after February 10, 1590, a notation regularly appeared at the bottom of most entries—"tenths of the prize ship delivered to Mr. Souch and Mr. Gastrell, by your Lordship's warrant." Gastrell is not known in any other connection, but "Souch" was probably Nicholas Zouche, one of Howard's officers and a man frequently named to investigating commissions and the like. So it seems probable that this small source of revenue was assigned to two retainers to supplement a nominal salary. The prize ships were valued so low on arrival at English ports, however, that a tenth of their worth would never have amounted to more than a few score pounds a year; it would not be surprising, then, if Zouche and Gastrell were able to made a tidy profit from resale or by breaking up the old vessels and reusing materials.

Even after the tenth of the ships had been given away and after 10 per cent had been taken out to pay the admiralty judge and the collector, Howard's receipts from Dorsetshire, Gloucestershire, and Hampshire ports were impressive. Between May 2, 1587, and November 30, 1598, the account listed tenths totaling £24,357 14s. 11d. after landing expenses, customs, and costs of handling and transportation. The salaries of Caesar and the collector would subtract £2,435 15s. 5d., leaving the admiral £21,921 19s. 6d. free of all known charges, or an average of slightly more than £1,800 a year from reprisals in these three counties. Actually, this record itself is not complete, so the total would have been higher. During the last several years covered, a number of prizes were received and the tenth was paid in goods, but the goods were not immediately converted into cash, so no figure appeared in the record. For some of them—goods of types commonly received, for which the price was fairly stable—it is possible even now to calculate what they should have brought on the market; by my own figures, these goods would have added about £1,080 free of charges to the total.

Another kind of prize is harder to calculate. Several of the ships captured contained gold or silver in some form or another, pearls and other precious stones, sometimes mounted in jewelry. Commodities of this kind were not entered by value in the collector's records; he received his tenth, often—but not always—recording the weight, then took them at the earliest opportunity to the lord admiral. On no occasion did he place a monetary value on such goods, and, of course, it is totally impossible to do so now. It can be said only that there were enough such prizes to make a significant difference in the final total. One such prize, for instance, brought to Weymouth in May, 1595, by Peter Neale's *Little Katherine,* sent to Howard, besides other goods, twenty "round orient pearls of the best sort," ten smaller pearls, an ounce and a quarter of small bored pearls, sixteen "great ragged pearls," a quarter of an ounce of seed pearls, ten uncut emeralds, half an ounce of white uncut opals, twelve uncut purple stones, seven "various cut stones," seventeen pieces of bullion containing ten and a quarter ounces, a chain of gold with two extra links, three pieces of silver plate weighing fourteen ounces, and £77 15s. in what was termed "royalls of plate." Another such prize, taken by Philip Bell's ship, the *Exchange,* paid, besides other goods, almost thirty-six ounces of pearls, nearly ninety-six ounces of plate, and more than twenty-seven ounces of bullion; from the bark *Band* in October, 1593, came eighty-eight orient pearls and unspecified quantities of diamonds and rubies. There were eight such gem prizes in all, bringing goods that should have added materially to the value of reprisals as a source of wealth.

Yet another group of prize goods not included in the collector's figures, though not so important as the bullion and pearls, would still have raised the final total by a few hundred pounds. Several times a year, a ship carrying exotic table delicacies or wines or grain—goods that would be immediately useful to a noble household—was taken. In such cases, part of the tenth was frequently taken in kind and shipped to one of the lord admiral's houses for his own use. The items were never of great value, although on one occasion wheat that would have sold for about £88 was sent to Chelsea, and on another, sugar, pepper, and cloves worth more than £30 (besides cinnamon, sugar candy, almonds, and succades) were shipped off "for your Lordships provision." Still, the steady stream of tropical foodstuffs and other luxury goods—a barrel of figs, a butt of Madeira, a bale of velvets and taffetas, boxes of marmalade, or barrels of olives—undoubtedly represented a significant sum of money over a long period of years.

And there is reason to think that the record does not list all the prizes brought in during the entire twelve-year period.

There is not a single entry for 1588, for example, and while it was certainly true that a large part of the English commercial fleet had been taken over for the great national effort against Spain, most of those ships that were taken were released by August, with time enough left to reoutfit for a few privateering forays by the end of the year. So prizes in the Armada year, though they would have been few, may have been recorded in separate documents.

For 1596 the volume of prizes again was so low as to suggest that the account must be incomplete. For every other year covered except 1588, the total value of tenths was well over £1,000, reaching £3,864 in 1593 and £4,021 in 1590. But for 1596, only eleven captures are listed, with the tenths —not including those that were sent directly to the lord admiral—worth only £285 12s. 1d. No prizes are listed between March and October, 1596, and a blank is left in the account book as though the collector expected to make other entries. This was the year of the great expedition to Cádiz led by the earl of Essex and the lord admiral himself. But again, the entire privateering fleet would not have taken part in the voyage, nor would all enemy commerce have remained off the seas for fear of the English. The incompleteness of the record for the two years Howard was at sea suggests the possibility that he might have directed his prize revenues into some abnormal channel to help meet his own extraordinary expenses at those times.

In spite of its possible incompleteness, "Harleian 598" is still extremely important as an indication of the kind of income that the lord admiral must have received from prizes. Although revenues obviously would have fluctuated a great deal from year to year, it is evident that during the years of greatest activity in the Spanish war, Howard should have averaged at least £2,500 a year from these three counties alone. Evidence concerning other areas is hopelessly scattered, even though admiralty records contain countless references to individual prizes at a variety of ports. But if the other districts served by tenth collectors—Devonshire and Cornwall, London and the Thames, East Anglia, and the area of the Cinque Ports

—were as active in privateering as Hampshire, Dorsetshire, and Bristol, prizes might have yielded as much as £10,000 a year, a princely figure in the sixteenth century and an income that any nobleman might envy. The ports of Kent and Sussex, however, no longer had the commercial importance they enjoyed in the late Middle Ages, so the Cinque Ports could not be expected to send out as many ships or bring home as many prizes as the more prosperous maritime counties farther west. Nor could the ports north and east of London. Towns like Harwich and Lynn were important in most commercial activities, and their ships were frequently among those making captures. But since the great bulk of ships and cargoes seized were Spanish and Portuguese, engaged in transport to and from America and the Far East, they were usually taken in the Atlantic southwest of England and returned to the nearest English port. A ship of Harwich, bringing home a captive after a hunt of several months, would most likely take it into Plymouth or Bristol or Weymouth, the most convenient English ports, rather than spend more days at sea. So it is probable that instead of a fifth of the value of prizes, the area covered by the collector's account would constitute a third, in which case the average annual income from prizes might be about £7,500—still an impressive reward for the cares and labors of the lord admiral's office.

The most complete modern study of the value of prize goods, however, indicates that even £10,000 might not be an exaggerated figure. From various sources, K. R. Andrews compiled a listing of all known prizes brought into English ports for the years 1589, 1590, and 1591.[35] He found evidence of 299 prizes, of which 71 were taken to London, 41 to ports in Devonshire and Cornwall, 43 to Bristol and Bridgwater, 35 to Dorset, 34 to Hampshire, and 73 to other ports. For these years Dorset, Hampshire, and Bristol accounted for slightly more than a third of the whole number. Of the total, there is no record of the value of just over half. The value of the remaining 145 prizes, however, was estimated at nearly £280,000, of which just over a third was accounted for by the

35. Andrews, *Elizabethan Privateering,* pp. 243–65.

71 ships brought to London. Prizes returned to Dorsetshire ports were worth £71,226, the Devonshire and Cornwall prizes £34,330, and the Bristol and Bridgwater prizes £31,148. If it may be assumed that those whose value is not recorded—half the total number—were worth at least half as much as those whose value is known, the privateers probably brought to England goods worth as much as £420,000. The lord admiral's tenth, if it was collected on all the known prizes, would have come to as much as £42,000, or an average of £14,000 a year for the three-year period. This figure does not allow for Caesar's twentieth or the collector's twentieth, which would have reduced the yearly total by £1,400. But even allowing for these grants and others, the tenth, if assiduously collected, should have come to as much as £12,000 a year during the three war years. Some captains were able to slip their prizes home without paying the lord admiral his due; in another work Andrews indicates that there was a great deal of evasion of payment.[36] But the whole admiralty machinery was aimed at making such activity difficult or impossible, and it is likely that most of these prizes on which Andrews' calculations were based were legal prizes that paid the due charges; it should be remembered that anyone who was caught trying to avoid payment of the tenth would quite likely find his whole ship and cargo confiscated.

In summary, the lord admiral's sources of income from the sea were many, but they were also variable, and on surviving evidence it is very hard to reach reliable estimates. About all that can be said is that the incomes must have been enormous for the time. There were the many thousands of pounds from privateering, far greater than all his other incomes combined; maybe a thousand pounds a year from casual fines, dues, and penalties; and a few hundred pounds as salary. The total, added to his small non-maritime resources, may have been £12,000 a year; it may even have been £15,000 or more, but it must always have been impressive as long as raiding Spanish commerce remained a favorite avocation of Englishmen.

36. Andrews, *Privateering Voyages to the West Indies*, p. 5.

IV: *In County and Council*

When Howard received his patent as lord admiral, he was also commissioned as the queen's lord lieutenant for Surrey and Sussex, another mark of the ascendancy he had finally achieved at court. The office was one of great local prestige and was always given to one of the most important local landholders, who could then regard himself as the natural leader of the gentry in matters of local administration as well as defense. Lords lieutenants were usually men of standing both at court and in the countryside and were often privy councilors or holders of high preferment. Elizabeth usually picked men of some military pretensions, since the first duties of the office dealt with the command of local levies; sometimes officers like Burghley, who lacked military background, had some difficulty getting themselves appointed, despite their great power.[1] Howard, like most of those who inherited titles, had received early experience that equipped him at least nominally to command troops, though he had never led men into battle, and there is no indication that he had to use Burghley's stratagems to win his patents. But more important than his training was the fact that there were no greater magnates who might challenge his leadership in Surrey and Sussex.

The office had in the past been a temporary appointment for the needs of a particular crisis, but with the Spanish war, the need to keep local forces in some kind of readiness and the need for ways to summon the defenses of the country quickly made the lords lieutenants permanent officers. Howard kept his lieutenancies until his death, even though in his last years his authority was shared with his son and though for the

1. Read, *Lord Burghley and Elizabeth*, p. 413.

entire time he had a co-lieutenant in Sussex. (Thomas Lord Buckhurst, later earl of Dorset, was Howard's partner in Sussex until his death in 1608.)

Howard's patents of lieutenancy, dated July 3, 1585, are in the form that had by this time become standard. The queen gave him full authority to levy and assemble all such subjects as were "meete and Apt for the warrs," to array them and put them in readiness with arms and training, and to muster them from time to time. He was also commissioned to lead the levies against the queen's enemies within his counties as occasion required, "And with the said Enemyes traytors & Rebells to fight & them to invade, resyst, represse & subdue, slay kill & put to execution of death by all wayes and meanes by your good discretion." He was to execute all other things required for the "Levyinge and government" of the queen's subjects and for the conservation of her person and her peace. He had the power to declare martial law and was expected to suppress disturbances with his own person. His deputies, as was often the case, were specified in the patent: in Surrey, his younger brother, William Howard, Sir Thomas Browne, and Sir William More were nominated; in Sussex, Sir Thomas Shirley, Sir Thomas Palmer, and Walter Covert were named.[2] The wording is almost exactly the same as was used in other appointments; Howard received no extraordinary duties or rights.

In practice, however, the duties and services expected of Howard and other lieutenants were not limited to those specified in their patents. Almost anything before the council which could be defined as a local concern or which would be effected by local action was made the responsibility of the lords lieutenants. Since many of the lieutenants were, like Howard, required to be at court constantly, the directions of the council were left to be performed by the deputies, to whom the office must have been trying, despite the command and prestige it brought. One deputy in a letter to Cecil voiced what many of them must have thought: "If aught were well done the Lieutenant has the praise and thanks, although all the charge and travail is borne by us, but if any business has ill

2. Harleian MSS, 703/33.

success the blame is laid upon us."[3] This is a complaint that Howard's deputies may well have echoed. He was for the council the officer responsible for Surrey and Sussex, but it was Sir William More and his colleagues who bore the burden of enforcing upon their neighbors compliance with council directives.

The years immediately following Howard's appointment were those in which the defenses of the country were raised against the expected Spanish attack; lieutenants and their deputies could not expect to take their obligations lightly. Companies had to be mustered, soldiers armed and trained, ordnance provided, and machinery for control and communication established. Within two weeks after his commissioning, and even before his deputies were notified, Howard had instructions to levy 250 men in his counties,[4] and more instructions soon followed. Since his and Buckhurst's lieutenancy included part of the southern coast, which was most vulnerable to Spanish attack, additional precautions had to be taken. The coastline had to be examined for possible landing places, coastal defenses inspected and improved, castles furnished with ordnance, and beacons kept in readiness. These steps were repeated during each of the invasion scares, and men from Surrey and Sussex took arms for each mobilization effort. The levying of soldiers was a continuing responsibility, not simply to meet anticipated invasions, but to furnish support for the wars in the Netherlands, France, and Ireland. Raising troops other than militiamen went beyond the specific power of the lieutenancy, but the council had no other convenient mechanism for creating an army, and the procedure was not challenged. The cost of providing men and fortifications was left to the counties, so deputy lieutenants often found themselves turned into revenue collectors.[5] Occasionally, labor

3. *Cal. Hatfield MSS,* 8:486, quoted in Gladys Scott Thomson, *Lords Lieutenants in the Sixteenth Century* (London, 1923), p. 69.
4. Harleian MSS, 703/34.
5. Lieutenants and their deputies were also required to collect such non-parliamentary levies as the forced loan to help fund the fight against the Armada.

forces as well as soldiers had to be recruited, to help provide for the defense of primary targets like Portsmouth.[6] From the first a major responsibility was the preservation of good order, which would prevent the riots and rebellions that would require lieutenants to bring out their forces. Preservation of peace was given a broad meaning which covered almost any unusual occurrence—suppression of public panic in the days when the Spanish army was expected; prevention of landings by Jesuits and other subversives or their capture upon landing; control of vagrants, including discharged soldiers; enforcement of Lenten observations; and precautions against the spread of plague. The iron forges and furnaces in Sussex and Surrey constituted the greater part of those in the country equipped to cast ordnance, and the council was anxious that they be guarded as an important strategic asset. Watching the activity of gun founders created an added responsibility for Howard and Buckhurst.[7]

Howard's role as a lord lieutenant was as a vehicle for communicating the wishes of the council to the lower officers who would carry them out. Except when he was at sea, communications to the deputy lieutenants were almost always transmitted through him, and he reported their work to the council. His standing and his place may have expedited the work of his deputies, but his direct role in it was limited. Characteristically, when he did involve himself, it would be over a matter of patronage. Soon after his appointment, he began to quarrel with the city of Chichester over the appointment of militia captains; he finally overrode their claims of privilege and saw his own candidate installed.[8] A few months later he insisted on the selection of one of his own servants as clerk of the peace for Surrey.[9] Control of patronage was an area of responsibility which no court figure with a following

6. Dasent, *Acts of the Privy Council*, 14:340–42, 345; 15:269, 282.

7. *Cal. Loseley MSS* furnishes a good idea of the range of responsibility of the lieutenancy for Surrey.

8. Harleian MSS, 703/41*b*, 43*b*.

9. *Cal. Loseley MSS*, pp. 641, 651–52.

to satisfy would allow to slip out of his grasp; otherwise, Howard's was a lieutenancy exercised almost entirely *in absentia.*

Since his first great preferments, Howard had necessarily spent little time in the country; as chamberlain, and even more as admiral, he was constantly needed by queen and council—there was not much leisure to be spent hunting and gossiping with his deputies and neighbors in Surrey. He was more fortunate than some, though, in that his properties were not far from Westminster—he could easily ride down to Reigate to be with his family if a respite of only a few days offered itself. For the most part he had to stay near the court, which meant the expense of another household. Probably soon after he inherited his title he acquired a house on King Street in Westminster, which at that time ran from Charing Cross past Whitehall to St. James's Palace. The street was a narrow one, but the location could scarcely have been more convenient. He entertained the queen for two days in 1585 and on two occasions in 1587; the council met there often until 1591, when Howard set up a more prestigious establishment at Chelsea.

Elizabethan grandees did not like to keep their young children in the contagious atmosphere of the city, so, since both Howard and his lady were in attendance on the queen, their children rarely saw them. Direct parental supervision was not, of course, necessary in a noble household well supplied with tutors, chaplains, physicians, and servants, but the lack of any more personal contact tended to formalize family relationships. It can only be guessed that Howard missed the company of his two young sons, for there is no body of fond fatherly letters, and he seldom mentioned "my boys" in other correspondence, usually only when they were sick. He was diligent, though, in fulfilling his obligations to provide academic and spiritual instruction: Edmund Hakluyt, youngest brother of the learned geographer, was tutor in Howard's house for four years; household chaplains included Stephen Chatfield, who was named by the bishop of Winchester to be master of a new school in Surrey which he and the lord

admiral would sponsor, and Dr. Richard Webster, later arch-
deacon of Middlesex.[10]

The sons—William, born in 1577, and Charles, born in
1579—were as yet too young to need much of the courtly
atmosphere that would prepare them to take their father's
place, which in fact neither of them ever did. Howard's three
daughters, however, were older and exacted obligations of a
different sort: suitable marriages would have to be arranged
and suitable dowries provided. It is perhaps conclusive testimony to the slenderness of Howard's estates during his rising
years that he was not able to give his daughters what had been
provided for his own sisters; their marriages were all beneath
what might have been expected for a man of Howard's station
and influence.

The eldest, Elizabeth, was married in 1583 to Robert
Southwell, heir of a wealthy Norfolk family with strongly
recusant associations. But having been brought up as a ward
of the queen, Southwell was not himself a Catholic. His
father-in-law gave him a ship to command in 1588, knighthood, the vice-admiralship for Norfolk and Suffolk, and a seat
in the House of Commons in 1597, and he became a respected
figure in county affairs, but not much more. After his death in
1598, his widow apparently became one of the occasional
mistresses of the earl of Essex, which must have caused her
father enormous chagrin.[11]

10. The Anglican orthodoxy of these chaplains is as conclusive
evidence as exists to disprove the old story that the lord admiral was
a Roman Catholic. For a fuller account of the matter of his religion,
see *Notes and Queries,* December, 1969.

11. Walter Devereux in his *Lives and Letters of the Devereux,
Earls of Essex* (2 vols. [London, 1853], 1:475) decided that the
Elizabeth Southwell who bore Essex a son was the lord admiral's
granddaughter who later ran away to Italy with Robert Dudley.
The reason for this conclusion was that since the mother had been
married in 1583, she would have been too old to be Essex's mistress.
The elder Elizabeth Southwell, however, could not have been born
earlier than 1564, and Essex was born in 1566, so she was not much
older than he, if at all, and she did have a young son, for whom she
sought Salisbury's influence in 1612.

The marriage of the next daughter, Margaret, to Richard Leveson of Lilleshall, Shropshire, in 1587 was one that was plagued by family difficulties. The son-in-law himself became very close to Howard; he was, like Southwell, knighted in 1588, became one of the most experienced naval commanders of Queen Elizabeth's last decade, and finally was appointed vice-admiral of England. But his father, Sir Walter, was a tempestuous man, a naval adventurer who had already been accused of piracy when the marriage was arranged. Sir Walter was a wastrel who refused to pay his debts and finally died in prison, but before his death he was accused of trying to kill both his son and daughter-in-law.[12] For years Howard interceded for him, but by the late 1590's the relationship had become a source of embarrassment and annoyance, and he joined the numerous ranks of Sir Walter's enemies. Margaret lost her only child and then, because of "her bad father-in-law's dealing with her, whom God forgive for it," lost her senses, so that when Sir Richard died in 1605, her father had to apply to the master of the wards to have her committed to his custody.[13]

The third daughter, Frances, was married about 1589 to Henry Fitzgerald, twelfth earl of Kildare, who had been left impecunious by the treasons and attainders of his ancestors. His remaining lands were spoiled by rebels when he took the government's part against Tyrone, so that after his death in 1598, his widow had to seek pensions to replace her jointure.

Howard, of course, could not have predicted the outcome of any of these marriages, but it seems odd that all three of them were from the beginning so far out of his own political circle —unless he was unable to provide his daughters with the dowries that better-placed families would expect.

First as chamberlain and then as admiral, Howard finally began to be seen within the inner circle of the queen's advisers as a member of the Privy Council. And it was at a critical

12. Additional MSS, 11,406/214, 389; *Cal. S. P. For., Eliz., January-July 1589* (London, 1950), p. 149; *Cal. S. P. Dom., Eliz., 1598–1601* (London, 1869), pp. 400–402.

13. *Cal. Hatfield MSS,* 17:347.

moment in the history of his country that he appeared in such a role. It was years before he became one of the three or four upon whom the queen relied most heavily and who carried the burdens of the ordinary administration of the country. But at least he was a member of that restricted group, and if he was not immediately a dominant figure, he was a conspicuous follower.

Queen Elizabeth's Privy Council was her arm of administration and policy, a collection of from twelve to twenty of the holders of high office or high rank, men who by birth or demonstrated ability were capable of making the queen's plans and ruling in her name. Nothing was outside its competence and practically nothing escaped its notice. By its own prestige and that of its members it could demand almost any act or exact almost any penalty without fear of stay. Of course, like everything else in the state, it was subject to the queen's will; she could accept or reject its advice or contradict its action, but disagreement between queen and council in matters of ordinary government was rare. Her will was made known to the council through her secretaries or through another officer; then its task was to translate that will into political deed. On matters of the highest importance, the council supplied the queen with information and gave her advice and suggestions; she was entirely free to reject such advice without attempting to justify herself, but, in matters of practice, policy was formed by a subtle kind of negotiation between the mistress and her servants, who were completely devoted to her but also anxious to set the state on a particular course.

The council itself could not have a single answer to the problems of the realm. Its members reflected many shades of political opinion and aim; every member was ambitious of his own advancement and each pressed to get favors for a swarm of followers—a post given to someone else was one denied to him and his friends. Each would have liked to become the paramount adviser and the accepted channel through whom wealth and power flowed, so the council inevitably tended to divide into competing groups and the groups fell into line behind two or three of those who seemed closest to the queen's ear and heart. By 1585 the factions had crystallized somewhat, as differences over policy coincided with differences over interest, and it became possible to speak of two feuding parties in the council, one dominated by Burghley the minister, the other by Leicester the favorite. It is possible, however, to carry the split too far; the two groups could and did co-operate. Burghley and Leicester were not sworn enemies and on occasion supported each other warmly. And the same was true of their followers; the line between them was not so sharply drawn that it could not be crossed and recrossed with relative ease. The council, then, was not paralyzed by a continual power struggle between exclusive groups; rather, its members met and debated informally, each deciding for himself on the basis of interest and conviction but finding that sympathies tended to follow traditional patterns. Howard's position is an example of the lack of precise definitions in the party divisions.

Howard's appearance on the council and his promotion to lord admiral has been generally interpreted as an advancement of Leicester's faction in the highest circle of the queen's advisers and an increment of strength to the "war party" in the council. Conyers Read so regarded Howard in his study of factionalism in the council,[14] and later observations usually agree. This classification seems generally correct, but Howard was certainly able to keep a foot in more than one camp.

It is true that, at the time, he was taken for one of Leicester's friends, and with good reason. In the early months of 1583, the Spanish ambassador, Mendoza, heard that Howard had even then been promised the office of lord admiral upon the death of the old earl of Lincoln, but that Howard had arranged with Leicester to exchange it, when it became his, for Leicester's mastership of the horse. The deal, according to Mendoza, would give Leicester control of the ports of entry when the queen died, so that he could seize the crown for

14. Conyers Read, "Factions in the English Privy Council under Elizabeth," *Annual Report of the American Historical Association* (New York, 1911), 1:117.

Arabella Stuart, to whom he was trying to marry his son.[15] It is doubtful that such a deal was ever even considered; the Spanish ambassador tended to magnify Leicester's machinations, if not his ambitions. And the queen would no doubt have put a stop to any such trafficking in her highest offices. But the fact that Mendoza would credit such a story suggests that Howard was the kind of individual who could be expected to abet Leicester's plans.

Sussex's death came before Lincoln's, so Howard got a patent as lord chamberlain to satisfy his claims on the queen. He was, then, chamberlain of the household when the scandalous *Leter Wryten by a Master of Arte* was published; enlarging upon Leicester's pre-eminence, the author noticed that "twoe or three of the wisest, gravest, and most experienced" councilors who opposed the favorite were dead, "and their places supplied to Leycesters good liking."[16] Howard and Sir Thomas Bromley are referred to as successors to Sussex and Sir Nicholas Bacon, and they are called Leicester's followers without any apparent strain on the readers' credulity. When Lincoln died and Howard got his post, Bernardino de Mendoza again linked Howard's advancement to Leicester's ambitions. He wrote to his master on May 12 that the queen had "suspended" the appointment of Howard as admiral and that of Derby as chamberlain to replace him, which had been known eight days earlier, because Leicester would not give up his mastership of the horse when he became lord steward.[17] It was Hunsdon who succeeded Howard, not Derby, but the context is significant. The delay of Howard's patent, if this

15. *Calendar of Letters and State Papers relating to English Affairs, preserved principally in the Archives of Simancas, Elizabeth,* 4 vols. (London, 1892–99), 3:451–52; hereinafter cited as *Cal. S. P. Simancas.*

16. [Robert Parsons?], *The Copie of a Leter, Wryten by a Master of Arte of Cambridge to his friend in London, concerning some talke past of late between two worshipful and grave men about the present state, and some procedinges of the Erle of Leycester and his friendes in England* (Antwerp, 1584), p. 54.

17. *Cal. S. P. Simancas,* 3:537–38.

actually happened, was thought by onlookers to be a retaliatory step against Leicester.

Walsingham, Leicester's most important ally on the council, indicated late in 1585 that Leicester could consider Howard his man. When Leicester left for the Low Countries, Howard hoped to become his deputy as justice in eyre while he was gone. No doubt he approached Leicester about the matter himself, but he also enlisted Walsingham, who wrote on December 20 that "he has always showed himself forward to further all good causes, and seems particularly to wish well to your lordship; therefore it may please you to do him this pleasure."[18] A year later, Howard was reminding Leicester of his constancy in friendship. One of Leicester's agents, he wrote, had taken goods in Flushing belonging to London merchants, goods bound for London under pass from the admiralty; without his own intervention for Leicester's sake, the merchants would have made supplication to the queen "in most extreme sort." Nevertheless, Howard feared that some unfavorable story might return to Leicester, and he prayed that "no base person may put into your hed any concet of me other then I shall gyve you cause, wyche I wyll never mor then unto my most derest frend."[19] He did not feel so secure in Leicester's esteem that he could not be shaken by malicious misrepresentation of acts meant for Leicester's benefit.

But if they were not then as close as Howard would have liked, within less than a year he had little cause for complaint. When Leicester returned to the Low Countries, in June, 1587, Howard made the crossing with him. They landed at Flushing amid "fyres of joye" and other demonstrations of good will, then proceeded to Middelburg; by the next week they were inspecting the defenses at Bergen op Zoom. Howard's purpose was to gather information on the state of the queen's investment in the Dutch war, and all matters, it was reported back

18. *Cal. S. P. For., Eliz., 1585–1586* (London, 1921), p. 227.
19. P. J. Blok, ed., *Correspondance Inédite de Robert Dudley, Compte de Leycester, et de François et Jean Hotman* (Haarlem, the Netherlands, 1911), pp. 72–73.

to England, "have been familiar to his eye and ear," since he went with Leicester "everywhere."[20] On July 4, Leicester, whose position at that time was not an easy one, wrote to Walsingham that he "could not for ten thousand pounds have spared" the lord admiral's company. The trip had been a quick one; Howard left apparently that same day, with Leicester mourning that now he would "feel the want" of him. But they saw each other again in July when Howard brought back intercepted newsletters of the Jesuits and the full story of the "impediments" that were causing Leicester so much toil. These visits were the high point of their relationship; testimony to the intimacy it produced is offered by the fact that in September, when Leicester threatened to resign, he recommended Howard to Burghley as his successor, if the queen wanted to maintain the existing level of commitment. A few days later, Leicester added a codicil to his will, naming Howard, with Warwick and Hatton, as one of the overseers, thus strengthening the impression that late in his life he had come to consider Howard a cherished friend and ally.[21]

At the same time, Howard's connections were by no means altogether in Leicester's camp. The earl of Sussex, Leicester's most passionate enemy, was Howard's first cousin; Howard had served under Sussex in the Northern rebellion and had acted as his deputy chamberlain. More significantly, Howard's closest formal tie at court was with another conspicuous enemy of Leicester, his father-in-law, Lord Hunsdon, whose illness at the time of the Armada caused Howard to grieve, as he said, "wonderfully."[22] And regardless of any differences on political issues, the lord admiral, as suggested earlier, co-operated very closely with the lord treasurer, even while he was thought to belong to a hostile group. Sir Edward Stafford, who pledged himself as Burghley's man and who recommended that Leicester be left in the Netherlands long enough to undo

20. *Cal. S. P. For., Eliz., 1587* (London, 1929), pp. 145–46.
21. Harris Nicolas, *Memoirs of the Life and Times of Sir Christopher Hatton* (London, 1847), p. 481.
22. Read, "Factions," p. 115.

himself,[23] also was a tie between Howard and Burghley. He had married Howard's sister, the widowed Lady Sheffield, after Leicester repudiated her and left her with a child he branded a bastard.

Further, Howard's temperament and his essential political sympathies were more in line with Burghley's than with Leicester's and Walsingham's. He was a conservative and cautious man, hesitant to commit himself or the queen, anxious to avoid unnecessary risks. These tendencies became more pronounced as he grew older, until he became one of the most conservative of James I's advisers. In 1585 he was a promoter of war with Spain; his stand on this great issue alone would have forced him into the company of Leicester and Walsingham, but their daring in other matters must have caused him some uncomfortable moments. The position of his allies on the matter of religion, which Read believed to be at the root of most sixteenth-century issues, added to his discomfort. Walsingham was a zealot, a Marian exile, who would have liked to equate his duty to God—and therefore to advanced Protestantism—with his political loyalty. Leicester, whatever his private convictions, was one of the most important patrons and protectors of the radical clergy.[24] But to Howard, religion was the affair of theologians. His father had conformed to all the vicissitudes of the established church in the middle years of the century, and Howard had lived through the astringent Protestantism of Edward and the determined Catholicism of Mary, apparently without any convictions that might have bedeviled his conscience. Forms were a matter of no concern; he probably could have followed the formulas of Calvin or of Pius V with equal ease. He was a humane and kindly man but not a religious man; he never discussed or even alluded to doctrinal matters in his letters—God is invoked in them only in the form of occasional manly swearing during exasperated moments. So the insistent religious bent of Walsingham's

23. *Cal. S. P. For., Eliz., 1586–1588* (London, 1927), p. 1, pp. 130–31.
24. Patrick Collinson, *The Elizabethan Puritan Movement* (Berkeley, 1967), p. 53.

policy must have presented a sizable obstacle to his sympathies. In political terms, the deaths of Walsingham and Leicester and the submergence of a Puritan party after 1588 probably brought the lord admiral a sense of secret relief. Now he could withdraw with dignity into the more congenial if less bracing atmosphere of conservatism.

During Howard's early years on the council, though, the war was the great issue, and on that subject he could second the Puritans with genuine enthusiasm. He was, in the larger sense of the term, a military man, the product of one of the strongest military traditions in England; one after another of his ancestors had gained favor as warriors, and he was inclined to follow the same avenue to glory. He was now a middle-aged man, old enough, perhaps, to rid himself of dreams of military grandeur. But like most of Elizabeth's favorites he was vain, and he coveted the honors of war as long as the war lasted.

A taste for heroism was justified and reinforced with selfless and patriotic arguments. The Netherlands was in desperate danger; its leaders had been killed, its cities taken one after another, and its strength drained away. Without massive support, the vigorous Alexander of Parma would inevitably reduce the Dutch to absolute obedience. France was more distracted than ever; the danger was very real that unless England intervened the country would become a client of Spain, which had just finished absorbing the Portuguese empire. Both French and Dutch Protestants had clamored for years for Elizabeth to become their champion; in 1583–85 it seemed once again that, if she didn't, England might be reduced to a state of vulnerable isolation. At home, Mary Stuart's long captivity was proving to be a source of constant danger to the safety of queen and country. So it had begun to seem even to the moderate that unless some vigorous initiative were taken, the continued existence of the realm would be in doubt.

Then, too, the indignities suffered by English merchants were an affront to Howard as admiral, and those injured looked to him for the means of recovering their losses. No damages had been felt so keenly as the seizure of English ships along with those of other hostile states in May, 1585, a few days after Howard's appointment as admiral became known. English ships, of course, had been spoiling other commerce, but any country tends to feel the outrages against it much more keenly than the outrages it commits. Naval officers were showing that the legalized piracy that war could bring might make fighting the king of Spain a profitable pastime. From his voyage of 1585–86, Drake brought back a load of Spanish plunder and pragmatic argument which could not fail to impress. The English could fight Spain on peculiarly advantageous terms: Spain could not hurt England directly except by an expensive and dangerous invasion, but England could cut the sinews of the Spanish empire and enrich itself in the process by capturing Spanish commerce. In addition, the idea must have occurred to the lord admiral that war would be particularly rewarding to him, since it was sure to be a stimulus to privateering, with each returning ship paying him a due share of the take.

Self-interest and consciousness of the gravity of England's international position combined to make immediate offensive action seem to be sound policy. In January, 1585, Philip II had promised Spanish help to the Holy League's war of exclusion against Henry of Navarre in the Treaty of Joinville. The treaty was secret, but it was not long before Spain's role in it was revealed. In May came the confiscation of English commerce which provoked Drake's retaliatory expedition; neither the seizure nor England's response was an act of open war under the conventions of the time, but both brought war nearer. In June, just as Howard was getting his patent as lord admiral and as the queen began to negotiate a new subsidy treaty with the Dutch, Philip's ambassador in Rome suggested a crusade to bring England back to the holy faith, to give Mary Stuart her rights, and to extend Spanish influence over the country. To English ministers, an attack on England could best be avoided by keeping the Spanish occupied in the Netherlands. Thus the terms upon which English aid would be given to the Dutch were worked out in July and August,

1585. The assassination of William of Orange, the withdrawal of French support, and the successes of Alexander of Parma and now his seige of Antwerp made the situation of the Dutch rebels almost hopeless. Elizabeth was not anxious to come to their assistance; she abhorred rebellion and hated religious fanaticism, and the Dutch were rebels for the cause of religion. But it was argued that if the Dutch were overpowered, the might of Spain would turn on England. Even if war did not come immediately, great Spanish fleets in Flemish and Dutch ports would pose a constant and paralyzing threat to English commerce. The Netherlands States-General sent over a formal commission to press for support on almost any terms, and Elizabeth named most of the principal members of the council—Burghley, Leicester, Howard, Hunsdon, Sir Francis Knollys, Sir Christopher Hatton, and Sir Francis Walsingham —to meet with them.[25] In such company, Howard's voice did not yet carry far; Leicester, Burghley, and Walsingham were the major negotiators, and the shadow of the queen herself was always in the background. For some days the commissioners haggled. Meanwhile the city of Antwerp, from all reports, had reached the point of surrender. Its needs were so pressing that a separate treaty had to be drawn up; on August 2, 1585, despite her reluctance to commit herself to open aid, Elizabeth agreed to send Sir John Norris with 4,000 men as immediate relief. A few days later there came a premature report that the city had fallen. The shock was great, and under its stimulus a general treaty was hastily completed by the commissioners. According to Professor Read, Elizabeth did not believe that Antwerp was in the immediate danger that the Dutch claimed; when it did fall, she raised her offer of support to 4,000 foot and 1,000 horse under the command of a nobleman.[26] The treaty of August, 1585, coinciding as it did with the preparations for Drake's predatory voyage, was the beginning of open warfare. As soon as Leicester led his army over

25. *Cal. S. P. For., Eliz., 1586–1588*, pt. 1, p. 708.
26. Conyers Read, *Mr. Secretary Walsingham and the Policy of Queen Elizabeth*, 3 vols. (Cambridge, Mass., 1925), 3:109–12.

with elaborate display, English soldiers and seamen under the orders of the queen were fighting the king of Spain.

Meanwhile the possibility that the queen might be killed in an attempt to free Mary Stuart and put her on the throne was becoming paralyzingly apparent. As long as Mary lived, she would be cause for conspiracy among her friends and panic among her enemies and a pretext for foreign invasion. This was a fact that Howard no less than Walsingham and Burghley recognized, and Howard played an important secondary role in bringing about her death.

In the unfolding of the Babington plot Howard had no direct part, although Ballard, the Jesuit who had been its driving force, was arrested on his warrant. The lord admiral was in constant attendance on the Privy Council as it dealt with the waves of anxiety which followed the disclosure of the plot and helped to prepare coastal defenses in case of invasion. Trained bands were placed in readiness on the southern coast, and John Hawkins, then at sea, and Sir William Winter, at the Medway, were ordered to keep on the lookout for signs of a French landing party; new efforts were made to search out Jesuits and seminarians; lords lieutenants were warned to be on their guard in case Spanish ships should appear off the English coast.[27]

Howard was also named to the commission to try Mary, but he is not listed among those who actually sat. He was with the court when the commission met at Westminster, and presumably he stayed there while the commissioners went on to attend to their duties. With the archbishop of Canterbury, Hunsdon, Cobham, Buckhurst, Davison, and Wolley, he attended to routine council affairs throughout October.[28]

Within a few days after the commission had completed its work, the subject of the queen of Scotland was taken up in Parliament. The two houses, both led by council members, adopted a petition pleading with the queen to put Mary to death lest they be brought "in utter despair." On November

27. Dasent, *Acts of the Privy Council*, 15:212–14.
28. *Ibid.*, pp. 236–45.

12 a joint committee, heavily weighted with council members and officers of state, waited on the queen to present her the wish of the nation. Howard had a place on the committee, as did most of the conspicuous patent-holders among the nobility. But Elizabeth hesitated; hers was the final responsibility for putting to death a sister sovereign and a blood relative, an act which might create as many problems as it would solve. And apart from her convictions, the queen needed to maintain a pose of reluctance as long as she could in order to appease the anger of the Scots and the French. So the sentence was delayed until early December, after Parliament had been adjourned until February.

The council then pressed Elizabeth to give immediate effect to the sentence by signing a warrant of execution. Late in December, Burghley was finally allowed to draw up a warrant, which was placed in the keeping of Secretary Davison. But the queen declined to sign it, and weeks passed while she wrestled with her problem, under tremendous pressure from those around her. According to the explanation of Davison, written after the event, it was Howard who finally brought her the decisive argument. On February 1, after the ambassadors from Scotland and France had gone home, he spoke with her "of the great danger she continually lived in"; there were stories current of new plots against her life, and rumors were circulating that Mary had escaped from prison. The queen, said Davison, was "moved by his lordship to have some more regard to the surety of herself and the state than she seemed to take," and she made up her mind at last. She told Howard to send for Davison and his warrant; Howard sent a messenger, then met Davison at his coming and told him that the queen was now "fully resolved" and had commanded him expressly to bring the warrant to be signed, "that it might be forthwith despatched and deferred no longer." Before the day was over it was signed and passed under the Great Seal.

Elizabeth later blamed Davison for breaking her commandment to tell no one what had been done, but if, as he claimed, Howard had called for the warrant, the news would have gotten out anyway. This was the word the council had been waiting weeks to hear, and Howard, who tended to be garrulous, could not have been expected to keep it to himself. At any rate, when the queen appeared to be losing her resolution, Davison became alarmed and went to Hatton for advice. Hatton took him to Burghley, and the three decided to call a meeting of the council. The next day, joined by Howard and the other principal members, they decided to take the responsibility for the execution upon themselves. It was unanimously agreed that the council send letters to the earls of Kent and Shrewsbury advising them to see the warrant executed.[29] They saw to their duties promptly, and the queen of Scots met her death in a scene as full of melodrama as the life she had lived. When Elizabeth learned that the deed was done, she claimed that her ministers had exceeded their authority and terrified them with a storm of grief and rage, real or assumed, such as few had witnessed. The council was summoned and sternly rebuked; Burghley was banned from her presence and Davison was sent to the Tower. Howard, however, was not singled out for any show of special displeasure.

Mary's death was the final symbolic break with the Catholic world and with peace. The kings of Scotland and France found it possible to avoid a clash over the tragic affair, but as Professor Mattingly has demonstrated, Mary's death confirmed Philip of Spain's resolution to seek an answer through the use of massive force.[30] Charles Howard's place in achieving the break was that of a coincidental catalyst at most. The arguments Davison credited him with using cannot have shattered the queen's resolution to avoid bloodshed; her mind was changed by the simple political imperative which her ministers had constantly kept before her. In conversation with Howard she finally faced the necessity. Like most of the council and most Englishmen, Howard could rejoice that Mary was dead, that the threat of subversion was reduced, and

29. Harris Nicolas, *Life of William Davison* (London, 1823), app. A, pp. 231–55.
30. See Garrett Mattingly, *The Armada* (Boston, 1959), pp. 69–81.

that the needs of war might be dealt with openly. As the only major officer of the state whose sole responsibility was the security of the realm from foreign enemies, the needs of the war would absorb all his energies for the most productive part of his life.

V: *Preparations for War*

While the Babington plot and its consequences, which were entirely out of proportion to the danger from the conspiracy itself, were occupying the council and exciting the nation, Howard was exploring his new realm. He had become lord admiral at that one point in time most propitious to the service of his own fame. War with Spain was at hand; it would necessarily be a naval war, and he would necessarily preside over it. Any success the nation achieved would cast its warming glow on him; in honoring him England could remember and congratulate its own heroism.

More immediately, however, his office promised to be more troublesome than rewarding, not only because of the demands of wartime preparedness, but also because of the untidy incidental product of the privateering war. He had time only to accustom himself to his new dignity before he was immersed in controversy over the violation of shipping rights. There were few universally accepted principles governing international maritime relations, especially in the areas of privateering, piracy, and neutral rights in wartime, and English and other seafarers tended to interpret trade privileges broadly for themselves, narrowly for others. The result was an endless series of quarrels during which ambassadors turned to the admiral for settlement. Admiralty procedures and the lord admiral's justice were slow, however, and it is indicative of the distribution of power in Elizabethan government that diplomats often turned to Walsingham and Burghley for help. As English hostilities toward Spain were expressed more openly, collisions became still more frequent, especially with the Dutch, who saw no ethical or strategic difficulty in maintaining their rebellion by trading with the enemy. Trade was

confined to nonessential materials, but it was predictably difficult to define what was nonessential. Dutch ships stopping off
in England found themselves stayed and their cargoes confiscated, despite protests from the merchants, who claimed that
they were carrying no war matériel. The States-General was in
no position to be unduly sensitive, so in November, word was
sent to its deputies to approach the lord admiral to be "informed of her Majesty's intentions in regard to the traffic with
France, Spain &c." Did she mean to forbid all transactions
with Spain, and what kinds of traffic would she permit with
Calais and other French ports? "If her Majesty will declare
her views," the States-General would "conform to her will as
nearly as is anyway possible; and will advertise all men
publicly thereof, so that none may be injured unless they are
at fault." Howard's authority over the matter was clear, but he
did not attempt to solve it alone; he deferred any answer until
he had been to court and consulted with Walsingham.[1] Even
then, although the particular ships being held were released,
no statement of principle was made, so that a month later the
deputy of the States-General complained again of the "great
and daily increasing wrongs" committed. Some who entered
English ports found that they had to pay a full third of their
goods to obtain release; others could not get free even then,
but were sent from one person to another, as though the
admiralty were trying to "make [them] lose heart, courage
and patience, and by such means to weary them in their just
pursuit."[2] The French shared the problem. Later during the
same winter the French ambassador addressed himself to
Howard and Walsingham to complain that "his master daily
receives complaints from the subjects of the King, robbed and
despoiled by the English not only at sea, but in the ports."
Immediate restoration of the goods was demanded but was not
to be forthcoming.[3]

Outrages committed by the English against foreigners
proved to be a theme on which the ambassadors played again

1. *Cal. S. P. For., Eliz., 1585–1586*, pp. 181.
2. *Ibid.*, p. 280.
3. *Ibid.*, p. 412.

and again throughout the reign; dealing with them was a constant source of annoyance to the admiral. He and the other admiralty officers were quite willing to see justice done, including justice to themselves, but in due course; pressures through diplomatic channels only aroused resentment. The main troubles lay in distinguishing neutral goods from war matériel and in the pace of admiralty procedures. English captains were always willing to bring home prizes; if they encountered a French ship, it might be one of the Holy League; if its crew spoke German or Dutch it might be a Lubecker trading with Spain. So any ship either on the high seas or in English ports was apt to have its papers and cargo closely scrutinized for evidence of dealings with the enemy. If it resisted search, an eager English captain and crew might see prima facie evidence of guilt and bring it home. Once in harbor, the ship had to be inspected by an admiralty officer, any goods suspected as contraband impounded, and the ship held until a decision could be reached in the High Court of Admiralty. The crew might or might not be given money to go home. Admiralty dockets were crowded, and often months or even a year or so passed before a judgment became final. Shipowners were understandably upset about the deterioration of cargo and the enforced inactivity of the ship; the officers and crew sometimes had to live in an alien land without means of supporting themselves or even without means of communicating with their homeland.[4] Ambassadors found it difficult to understand why such cases could not be expedited and were quick to demand damages and to write threateningly to the admiral or to the Privy Council itself. But no simplified procedure was ever worked out, and complaints lasted as long as the war.

Of course, complaints were not always against the English. Prize procedures everywhere were clumsy and poorly worked out, and English mariners found themselves the victims as well as the aggressors, although perhaps the latter more fre-

4. One such case is described in detail in *Cal. S. P. Dom., Eliz., 1591–1594*, pp. 230–31, 248–51.

quently. Thus the lord admiral, when approached by angry diplomats, could counter claim with claim and grievance with grievance. Early in 1598, when the French ambassador obtained the ear of Privy Council members through reports of pillage and spoil, the lord admiral wrote hastily to Caesar "to cause a collection presentlie to be made of all complayntes and grevaunces of anye of or nation against the frenche for spoyles done by them of late yeares" so that he could be prepared for debate if the matter came before the council. As an afterthought he told Caesar to summon all those who had complaints to follow the French ambassador about town and "suffer him never to lie in quyet, for I dow assur you he hath an unquyet spryte." It would not do, of course, for the man to know that his sleep was being interrupted on the lord admiral's orders, so Caesar "shall not seme to know it, but let him be persecuted with suters."[5]

There were, however, in Howard's first years as lord admiral, matters at hand which were much more important than the settlement of disputes over privateering. Waging the Spanish war was peculiarly the business of the navy, so these were necessarily times of great activity for the head of the navy, who would profit from the war more than any other Englishman. His presence at court was required almost continually. He made repeated visits to the dockyards and works. And when the occasion was sufficient he went to sea himself to command the queen's fleets. It is in connection with the war that Howard appears at his most attractive, although his role was perhaps not all that it might have been.

During the first years after 1585, the problems of the navy were at least threefold. First of all, the fleet had to be strengthened and expanded if it was to be able to make a great effort against Spain or to defend the country against the "English enterprise" known to be in preparation. In 1578 the queen's entire combat fleet had consisted of five large ships, of about 600 tons burden or greater; five smaller ones, in sizes from 450 tons; and twelve vessels of less than 400 tons, some

5. Additional MSS, 15,208/460.

of them quite small. A few vessels, mostly of the type known as pinnaces, had been added since that time, but a list prepared in 1585 still showed twenty-three ships above fifty tons and ten smaller pinnaces. It was a dangerously small force upon which to place the burden of defense from foreign invasion. Secondly, it would be necessary to take steps to make Spain unable to wage an effective war against England. Fleets would be sent out to capture or destroy the treasure fleets and to interrupt and frustrate Spanish naval preparations. Finally, it would be necessary to maintain a fleet in the seas about England to be on guard for invaders, to patrol for pirates and raiders, to supply the queen's armies across the Channel, and to perform courier and diplomatic duties between England and the Continent. All these areas of activity came under the lord admiral's purview, although in some of them his direct participation was slight.

Work toward strengthening the fleet was already well underway, and as it continued it involved the new lord admiral less frequently. His office had originally been one of command: an admiral was appointed for a particular campaign, and the appointment ended with the completion of that service. His functions had expanded enormously since the beginning of the century, but they still had something of the same character; he was first of all a martial officer and almost incidentally the administrator of a governmental department. The day-to-day supervision of the ships and yards, especially those ships not in use, had passed to the treasurer of the navy, Sir John Hawkins. Hawkins had been highly critical of earlier administration, accusing Sir William Winter in particular of lining his own pockets while the queen's ships fell apart for lack of repair. He convinced Burghley of the justness of his attack, and in 1579 the lord treasurer and the treasurer of the navy concluded what was called the First Bargain. The terms of the bargain provided that Hawkins should maintain the ships in good repair, under the supervision of his critics, and pay himself for his trouble for a flat yearly sum smaller than what had been expended in the past. In the years that followed, Hawkins himself was accused of every kind of misdealing, but Burghley was satisfied and Hawkins' honesty was vindicated by the "Chamberlain's report." About April, 1585, during the interim between Lincoln's death and Howard's appointment, Hawkins negotiated a Second Bargain, which set forth even greater powers. Afterward, until the scope of the war made the bargain impractical, the upkeep of the ships was substantially a commercial franchise, subject to the supervision of the admiral and the officers of the navy, but ultimately directed by the lord treasurer.

New ships were constructed through similar arrangements. Contracts were drawn up between the crown and the master shipwrights, who promised to deliver a vessel built to specification, lacking only rigging and fittings, for an agreed sum. Presumably Hawkins was responsible for the terms of the contract, but the plans for at least three ships, and probably others as well, were drawn up by a special committee of experts headed by the lord admiral, Drake, Hawkins, Sir William Winter, William Borough, Edward Fenton, and shipwrights Richard Chapman and Matthew and Christopher Baker.[6] It was this committee, then, that was responsible for the changes in naval design—principally the longer and narrower hull, lower silhouette, and improved firepower—which gave the queen's ships a critical advantage when their test came. Hawkins' biographers insist that the revolution in design was his idea, and it may have been, but the earliest new-model ships, the *Foresight* and the *Revenge,* were built before his long administration of the navy began.[7] At any rate, the lord admiral was an officer progressive enough to see the advantages of the new pattern, and the ships built or rebuilt during his tenure incorporated it. During the first two years he was in office, the navy built three major ships, bought a fourth, the *Ark Royal,* "the pride of the fleet" and Howard's flagship in 1588, added new pinnaces, and rebuilt and enlarged some of the older ones. So by the first days of the Armada year the queen had twenty-five ships above a hundred

6. Oppenheim, *Administration of the Royal Navy*, p. 129.
7. Williamson, *Hawkins of Plymouth*, p. 250.

tons and eighteen pinnaces capable of extended service. The increase in the number of vessels had not been great—from thirty-one to forty-three—but the increase in tonnage was greater. And the effort, considering the financial demands made upon the queen, was considerable.

Hawkins, then, was chiefly responsible for the preparedness of the fleet; Howard's most important function was creating an atmosphere in which Hawkins and his fellow officers could work together. Before 1585 Hawkins had been bitterly estranged from Winter, the comptroller of ships and master of ordnance, and from Borough, clerk of the ships. He had been responsible for their loss of profitable contracts and had dealt serious blows to their reputations and usefulness. After he had replaced them, he had become their target, and their attacks were vindictive and unrestrained. Here matters stood when the old lord admiral died. In April, after opposing Hawkins' Second Bargain with all his resources, Winter indicated that he was tired of the fight, but the two would not be reconciled. Their co-operation, however, was essential: Hawkins was responsible for building the ships, Winter for arming them. By the end of 1585 they were working together in harmony. Borough, also an enemy of Hawkins, sailed with him as vice-admiral in 1586 and was thereafter one of his firm supporters. Williamson believes that it was Howard who brought the factions together;[8] this view is given strong support by an anonymous attack on Hawkins in 1587 which quotes the lord admiral as saying that he had made Hawkins and Winter "as fast as buckle and girdle."[9] If the boast was justified, then Howard should be given much credit as an administrator. The officers of the navy were often a jealous and suspicious lot; there were wounded feelings and outraged dignities and unfulfilled ambitions during Howard's tenure of office, but at least they remained subordinated to larger purposes during the critical years of the war.

8. *Ibid.*, p. 296.
9. Lansdowne MSS, 52/43; Julian S. Corbett, ed., *Papers Relating to the Navy During the Spanish War 1585–1587* (London, 1898), p. 251.

England's naval offensive against Spain in the first years of the war—made possible at least in part by Hawkins' successful "bargains"—took the form of the joint expeditions that became so familiar to the age. A small core of the queen's ships, usually fewer than ten, strengthened by armed merchant vessels and ships belonging to court figures, would sail under royal commission but as a private venture, hoping to interrupt American or Indian trade or to raid Spanish harbors. Every commander expected to stagger home under a load of stolen riches, but rarely did. The silver fleet was never captured, despite the best efforts and the highest hopes of the English nation; but there were some notable captures of individual vessels, especially East Indian carracks carrying spices and jewels, and enough other prizes to excite the imagination of a luxury-loving court. Many of the joint enterprises and most of the private ventures spent more money than they took, as did Drake's voyage of 1585–86. Nevertheless, even though this kind of warfare brought very limited direct success for the English, its nuisance value was great. Several times word of English activities caused postponement of the silver fleet's departure for as much as a year; the capture of spice ships was a material blow to merchants of the Spanish empire and an unsettling factor in the European pepper market; and the occasional destruction of fleets was a source of great expense and trouble to Philip II, who sometimes was required to revise his plans and seek new loans. The uncertainty of the treasure shipments so injured Philip's credit that he consistently had to pay far higher rates of interest on loans than did Elizabeth, whose resources were much smaller.

Drake's voyage ended in late July, 1586, after skirting the Spanish coast and attacking some of the strongest cities in the West Indies. His was an exploit which won him the reputation of a genius throughout Western Europe. By the time he returned home, a small fleet under Hawkins had been sent out, but it suffered from bad weather, inflicted no real damages on Spain, and returned in need of extensive repairs. Nor were there prizes to offset the cost of this trip, a matter of "great annoyance" in England, as Mendoza heard from Paris.

But within a few weeks there was talk of a third expedition, perhaps inspired at least in part by Hawkins' plan for maintaining a continuing blockade of Spanish harbors. At first the council leaned toward invasion of Portugal. Dom Antônio, bastard son of the last king's brother, had been promised support if he would lead a rebellion, suggesting an opportunity that to many seemed too good to miss. Elizabeth promised Antônio money and ships but could not be pushed into immediate grants of large-scale support on the basis of uncertain intelligence. By February it was known that a fleet would be sent, but every effort was made to keep details, including the name of the commander, in secret.[10] Mendoza heard that a "great fleet" was being readied to go to sea under the lord admiral; he could learn nothing as to its schedule or destination, but he speculated that it was intended to meet the Armada, about whose purpose, he said, the English knew.[11]

Mendoza's source of information was his "new friend," either Sir Edward Stafford, Howard's brother-in-law and English ambassador in Paris, or a member of his household.[12] It was, then, a source close to the lord admiral, which gives some weight to the report that he may have intended to command the marauding fleet himself. But before preparations were in hand, Drake, an incomparably more experienced commander, was substituted. When ready, Howard's instructions made no reference to Dom Antônio, whose ambitions were deferred, but directed Drake to "seek by all the best means you can to impeach" the preparations for the Armada and to prevent the union of the squadrons in Lisbon; details were to be left to his discretion. Drake left Plymouth on April 2 with a well-armed fleet, including one ship and a pinnace belonging to the lord admiral. Never had an Elizabethan commander been given such a broad grant of authority, a circumstance which argues

10. Corbett, *Papers Relating to the Navy*, p. xvii–xviii.
11. *Cal. S. P. Simancas*, 4:17.
12. Professor John Neale concluded that the "friend" was not Stafford himself but someone in his household; see "The Fame of Sir Edward Stafford," in Neale's *Essays in Elizabethan History* (London, 1958), pp. 146–69.

the ascendancy of the "war party" at the time he left. Soon afterward, however, the queen evidently experienced misgivings and sent amended orders after him, requiring him to confine his efforts to capturing prizes at sea, "avoiding as much as may lie in you the effusion of Christian blood."[13] Drake's haste in leaving insured that he never got the changed orders. According to the later testimony of Captain William Borough, Howard had told Drake that, despite the latitude of his first orders, he was not to land on Spanish soil. If this were true, it would make Howard appear to have been cautious about Drake's purposes all along and would suggest that he had brought the queen to share his misgivings. But Borough's word is unsupported by other evidence and was given when he was being charged with treason against his commander because of his own hesitancy.

Tight security was maintained about the real purposes of the trip; Mendoza's friend assured him that "no living soul," except the queen and Burghley, knew what the fleet's destination was. Elizabeth, he said, had forbidden even the lord admiral to know, "as she considers him a frank-spoken man."[14] It seems most unlikely that the lord admiral, whose personal efforts had to be involved in the preparation of the ships—including two of his own—was denied the knowledge of where those ships were going. The story is interesting, though, in that it is the first suggestion of what may have been an important limitation of Howard's usefulness. He was indeed a "frank-spoken man"; the notion that he was so garrulous that he could not be trusted with an important state secret recurs several times—an innuendo here, a hint, a witticism there.[15] If this was the case, then it would certainly explain why he always seemed to be found slightly at a distance from most of the critical events and decisions of his time—always involved, but usually on the periphery.

Drake's voyage was one of the most notable successes of

13. Corbett, *Papers Relating to the Navy,* pp. 52–69.
14. *Cal. S. P. Simancas,* 4:69.
15. See below, pp. 249–50. The suggestion of garrulity here becomes quite explicit.

Elizabethan naval history; if the admiral had wanted to lead it himself, he must have greeted Drake on his return with twinges of jealousy. Drake destroyed valuable shipping in the harbor of Cádiz and "singed the King of Spain's beard"; he made an audacious demonstration before Lisbon; he seized the fort at Cape Saint Vincent and used it as a base for destroying supplies, such as salt fish and barrel staves, that were being collected for the Armada; and on his way home he captured the carrack *San Felipe* with a cargo worth more than a hundred thousand pounds, one of the biggest prizes of the war. His already glittering reputation was enhanced, the queen and her adventurers, including Howard, had substantial profits, and Spain had been humiliated, though not substantially injured.

The queen could never spare more than a fraction of her strength—five ships in 1586 and four in 1587—for these glorified privateering expeditions. Most vessels had to be kept nearer at hand, in the Medway, at Portsmouth or Plymouth, or cruising in the Channel and North Sea to guard against surprise raids and to support English efforts on the Continent with new victuals, troops, and arms. In this routine but essential duty the lord admiral was frequently found during the first years of his appointment, and it sometimes kept him away from court for weeks at a time.

Howard's first command of ships as lord admiral was a commission to take Leicester with his showy retinue and his army to the graveyard of his reputation in the Low Countries. It was a service that any captain in the queen's pay might have performed, but the presence of the lord admiral added to the glamour of the crossing and heightened the grandness of the queen's gesture and her viceroy's regality. Leicester crossed in September; later in the fall Howard made another crossing, this time to Oostende, whose English garrison was preparing for a siege. Its detachment was reinforced by Leicester's troops and by a few high-ranking volunteers from court, among whom were two Careys, brothers of Lady Howard. In his *Memoirs,* Sir Robert Carey recalled that, as "reports increased daily more and more of the enemy's approach," his brother-in-law "that was our admiral" brought munitions and victuals and spent two or three days in the town, leaving Sir William Read behind to command the defense. The Careys stayed a fortnight longer, until word came from Leicester's headquarters that Parma would not attempt a siege before winter.[16]

In the following year, Howard presumably did not go to sea; his absences from the meetings of the Privy Council were not long enough to permit more than an occasional trip to Deptford or Chatham or a few days in Surrey. He was gone for two weeks in April and somewhat less than two weeks in May, but the rest of the time his attendance at court was notably regular. The Channel fleet that summer was commanded by Sir William Winter, strengthened by Hawkins' expeditionary force, and the lord admiral did not need to go out. In 1587 he was far more peripatetic. In March he spent several days at Rochester looking after the fitting of eight of the queen's ships, four for Drake and four for Channel duty against Dunkirkers. In the middle of June he took perhaps the same four Channel ships with impressed merchantmen and hoys to Flushing to escort the earl of Leicester and his troops. This congenial chore occupied nearly a month; the lord governor and the lord admiral were entertained and feasted by the States-General, then with a distinguished escort they made a leisurely tour of the Dutch fortifications, ending with an appearance at besieged Sluis. Howard recrossed to take his place at court by July 7, but before the end of the month he was aboard ship again. Probably on July 25, he left the court at Theobalds to confer with Leicester in the vicinity of Flushing, returning again before August 5. It is barely possible that he witnessed the fall of the citadel at Sluis, which had held out against Parma's forces for many months while Leicester and the Dutch tried ineffectually to relieve it. The town surrendered on July 26; on the 31st, Leicester wrote to Burghley that he had acquainted the lord admiral "with all our proceedings" so that he could impress upon Burghley, the lords of the

16. Robert Carey, earl of Monmouth, *Memoirs of Robert Carey, baron of Lippington and earl of Monmouth* (Edinburgh, 1808), pp. 9–11.

council, and the queen the "daily greater impediments" the royal service was receiving.[17] To obtain such reports from Leicester was probably the lord admiral's reason for going to Sluis, though it was later reported that he had tried to persuade Count Hohenlohe, one of the principal commanders in the Netherlands who had been carrying on a running feud with Leicester, to come to England for talks with Elizabeth.

17. Professor Garrett Mattingly listed Howard among those present at Sluis on July 25, New Style (*The Armada,* p. 139); he implied that Howard, with a squadron of English ships, abetted Leicester's efforts during the next fortnight. The queen's ships undoubtedly were present, but the admiral does not seem to have been in command himself. He is listed as being present when the Privy Council met at Theobalds on July 14 and July 16, Old Style (or July 24–26 New Style), and he apparently remained constantly at court for another week; he was present when Buckhurst, Norris, and Wilkes were examined by the council on their stewardship of the queen's affairs in the Low Countries, and he signed a council letter to Leicester about the examination, dated July 25. This letter refers to Howard's imminent departure: the council would examine Buckhurst again, "but having the opportunity by my Lord Admiral . . . we thought good to refer you to his report for the circumstances of our round dealing with them" (*Cal. S. P. For., Eliz., 1587,* p. 197). So it seems probable that Howard left Theobalds sometime on the 25th; it would take a day's ride to get to Chatham, even longer to Margate, so if Howard saw Sir Roger Williams and the other defenders of Sluis give up their swords on the 26th, English Style, he arrived barely in time. More likely, allowing for some reasonable delays, he reached Leicester on the 27th.

VI: *The Coming of the Crisis*

The lord admiral's return from his brief mission to the Netherlands soon after August 1, 1587, can be considered the beginning of the most remarkable period of his life, or of the lives of most of his contemporaries. The events of the next thirteen months made him one of the most honored men of his time. By the happy outcome of those events, he became the saviour of his country's liberty and independence, the defender of his queen against the wicked design of the international Catholic conspiracy and the "lewd Ambition and Av'rice" of the Spanish king.[1] In later years the memory of his services "of so great desert" was sufficiently potent that he escaped blameless from a situation that would have destroyed almost anyone else. He had earned his nation's gratitude and could do nothing to forfeit it.

Despite some criticism by men who considered themselves qualified judges of naval strategy, Howard's own age was generally willing to give him ample credit for the defeat of the Spanish Armada. He was the personification of the English fleet—narratives of the fight were written in terms of a combat between two individuals, Howard and "the Spaniard" —and the victory of the fleet, however accomplished, was his victory. He was the "Admiral with Lion on his Crest," compared with Alcides on the strand of Troy, able to command the seas themselves.[2] To the Elizabethan world, as to Edmund Spenser, he was

1. The phrase is from Beza's congratulatory poem to Elizabeth. Theodore Beza, "Poem on the defeat of the Armada, translated by T. H.," *The Harleian Miscellany,* ed. William Oldys, 12 vols. (London, 1808–11), 2:150.
2. J. L. [John Lily?], "An answer to the untruths published and printed in Spain in glory of their supposed victory achieved against

. . . brave Lord, whose goodly personage
And noble deeds, each other garnishing,
Make you ensample to the present age
Of th' old Heroes, whose famous ofspring
The antique Poets wont so much to sing . . .
 Sith those huge castles of Castilian King
 That vainly threatned Kingdomes to displace,
Like flying doves ye did before you chace;
 And that proud people, waxen insolent
 Through many victories, didst first deface. . . .[3]

Spenser's verse was designed as flattery, but his sentiment was the verdict of the time. Later naval historians, particularly the great generation at the end of the nineteenth century, sharply revised Howard's reputation. They made him a noble figurehead, a nominal commander who deferred to the greater experience and abilities of the "seadogs" and whose rank obscured the fact that the glory ought to have gone to Hawkins and Winter and Seymour and, far above the rest, Drake, the paragon of the century. The official praise given to Howard in his own time may indeed have overshadowed Drake unfairly, but the waxing Drake legend more than corrected the score. Now a more balanced appraisal, such as Williamson's, is possible.[4] The victory certainly was not all Howard's, nor was it Drake's or Hawkins'; it was the vindication, partly through shrewd judgment and the loyalty of the nation, partly through lucky gambles and a happy set of circumstances, of the policy of the council and queen. The story of the Armada fight, the most celebrated hour in English history, has been told many times, most recently and most vividly by Professor Garrett Mattingly. The political setting and the chronicle of the victory have been sufficiently explored, but it might not be

our English Navy," quoted in B. M. Ward, *The Seventeenth Earl of Oxford, 1550–1604* (London, 1928), p. 291.

 3. Edmund Spenser, "Verses to various noblemen," *Complete Works,* Globe ed. (London, 1890), p. 8.

 4. J. A. Williamson, *The Age of Drake,* 3d ed. (London, 1952), pp. 305–10.

superfluous to trace the role in these great events of the man who benefited most from them.

The efforts of the Privy Council with Howard in almost constant attendance, were much given during the fall of 1587 to preparations against the time of invasion. Drake's exploits on the coast of Spain had "bred a marvellous grief" to the enemy, but had only postponed the assault. Indeed, there were fears in late summer that a great fleet of two hundred and twenty ships had been directly set out to revenge the losses and recover possession of Drake's great prize, a threat requiring immediate defense measures. As Mendoza heard it, a man of Raleigh's came galloping in at midnight with the news that a flotilla had been seen off Cornwall. The queen summoned the council to her bedchamber and the crisis was dealt with on the spot. Howard was dispatched in the late hours to London to embargo ships for an emergency defense fleet, and word was sent to the Medway for the queen's ships to slip out to the Channel in great secrecy. Lords lieutenants in the southern and western counties put their men in readiness for service and Leicester in the Low Countries received orders to come with force if needed. So the next few weeks were spent in a flurry; troops were viewed, arms distributed, and defenses repaired. Howard, although responsible for the preparations in Surrey and Sussex, could not leave court. His orders went to Sir William More and his colleagues, who would act for him in Surrey, and he met with his co-lieutenant, Lord Buckhurst, at Kew to co-ordinate the defense of Sussex. Previously the two had not been on good terms. Buckhurst had been the queen's representative in the Netherlands before Leicester's return; he and Leicester had quarreled violently and Buckhurst had refused to be accountable to him. Howard, as a partisan of Leicester, had been among Buckhurst's critics and had drawn a wounded cry from him a few weeks before: "he being a noble man of so great honour, my kinsman and my friend."[5] But now the quarrel was patched up, and Buckhurst proceeded to Sussex to do what he could about defenses.

5. *Cal. S. P. For., Eliz., 1587*, pp. 166–67.

This kind of drama, the sudden call for emergency preparations, had been enacted several times before and would be again before the crisis really came. Given the state of mind in England and the incomplete knowledge of Spanish plans and progress, such false alarms were inevitable, but they did give training in mobilization that would not have been taken otherwise, and they undoubtedly helped stimulate the remarkable sense of unity and purpose that Englishmen for the moment achieved.

Other preparations had been in hand earlier; the impression so frequently sustained in shorter accounts of the crisis that England waited until December to begin arming is a fantasy. Since 1579, and strikingly since 1585, Hawkins, with the full support of the crown and perhaps the grudging support of the officers of the navy, had been increasing the size and effectiveness of the fleets. By early 1587 the pace had quickened. In February of that year Parliament granted a subsidy to be used for raising armies against Spain, with the expectation that they would see service at home as well as in the Netherlands. By summer commissioners were collecting the money from citizens who, despite their patriotism, grumbled that their burdens were too heavy. Commissions, as usual, were headed by privy councilors and holders of high office, Howard among them, but the assessment and collection were made by justices, sheriffs, and deputy lieutenants. The commissioners could, if they chose, pay themselves for their trouble by setting their own assessments lighter than those of their neighbors; complaints against them were so frequent that in August the council dispatched letters all over the country, chiding them sharply for "favouring their friendes, tenants, allyes, and retayners" and for showing partiality to themselves. As money came in, so it was spent; on August 23 the council sent a letter to royal officers in Suffolk (probably similar letters went to other areas as well for other provisions) requiring them to deliver quantities of cheese and butter, purchased at their own "reasonable" prices, to James Quarles, the victualer of the navy, since the queen had found it necessary "upon great and urgent considyeracions" to keep ready "for all suddayne serv-

yces" victuals for two thousand men at sea.[6] This was among
the first of a long chronicle of special orders with which the
council occupied itself in August and September of 1587.
Local levies had to be made ready, special measures needed to
be taken for the defense of the southern counties, where the
invaders would in all probability strike, and forts and castles
had to be strengthened. To attend to such matters the council
met almost every second day throughout the late summer and
early fall, and as a result of its attentions preparations advanced steadily, in spite of Elizabeth's apparent reluctance to
spend money until all hopes of peace had been exhausted.
Howard attended the sessions faithfully; in addition to helping plan the general defense, he had special duties in the
counties under his lieutenancy and anxiously watched over the
growing needs of the navy. As early as September, for example, Howard was arguing with the Cinque Ports and the towns
of Suffolk the terms on which they would rig ships to meet the
queen's need. He rejected the offers from Suffolk with "sharp
and bitter answers," implying that too high a price had been
set upon patriotism, but the Cinque Ports took more reasonable terms.[7]

By October, time was pressing hard. In spite of the best
available intelligence, it could not be determined just when
the Armada would come, and the council pleaded urgently for
a constant state of readiness. A minute drafted by Burghley on
October 3 indicates what measures were being considered and
the importance the lord admiral played in them. Either Howard or Drake, Burghley believed, would have to instruct a
man immediately how to spy on Spanish preparations so that
the state of affairs could be ascertained with all speed. It was
time to make the whole navy ready to fight, and to put an
embargo on all shipping, so that the queen could command
the duty of every serviceable merchant ship; lords lieutenants
needed to review their forces so that they could be summoned
to serve on short notice. These were the most pressing needs,

6. Dasent, *Acts of the Privy Council*, 15:203–4.
7. *Cal. S. P. Dom., Eliz., 1581–1590*, p. 426.

and Howard had to see that all were settled. Two days later, under his signature, letters went to the vice-admirals, requiring them to locate all vessels able to go to sea and to charge the owners in the queen's name not to leave port until they heard further from the council or himself. The vice-admirals then should return to him a list of all the ships stayed, their tonnage, the size of crews, names of owners, etc., so that the queen's strength could be calculated. The embargo would apply to foreign as well as to English ships, but not to the small "crayers" used to carry grain along the coast; these should be required merely to make bond not to leave England.

The queen's ships were being fitted for war at Queenborough on the lower Thames and at Chatham in the Medway. The entire administration of the navy, from the lord admiral and the Navy Board to the clerks of cheque and the master shipwrights and gunners, had to be close at hand; Howard seems to have spent nearly all of October at one place or the other—he attended only two council meetings during the month—and Hawkins was at Chatham continuously through the fall. Little record remains as to what they did, but it is not hard to guess. The ships had to be repaired, caulked, rigged, and made seaworthy, stored with victuals, clothing, water, powder and balls, and match; ordnance had to be lifted into place and crews gathered together. From his headquarters on his own galleon, the *White Bear,* at Queenborough, Howard also had to stay in communication with the squadron of royal ships on guard duty in the Channel throughout the fall and with Drake's squadron, already at Plymouth, watching for signs that the test was at hand. He went back to court at the end of the month, entrusting the remaining details of mobilization to Hawkins and his colleagues. Although a Spanish correspondent thought that the fleet was in "very poor order" with much to be done in mid-November, by the 23d it was "in all ways" ready, and Howard testified many times in the next months to the thoroughness of the work that had been done.

In council broader policy was being debated. The adventuresome urged that Drake or Howard take the fleet to Spain and, if possible, prevent the Armada from sailing; more cautious members feared that it would be too risky to drain off the country's defense for a voyage that might miss the Armada altogether; Elizabeth was anxious to remain in a defensive posture until all peace overtures had been fully explored. Tensions, compounded by conflicting rumors, were high, and the country lived in a state of anxious uncertainty. There were rumors abroad that Drake would sail within a few days, that Drake would not sail, that Howard had already gone with forty or fifty ships. Inaccurate intelligence plagued both the Spanish and the English, and the council cried out against the queen's tendency to prepare for the most favorable possibilities instead of the least favorable. It has been pointed out many times that Elizabeth took an enormous risk by delaying her preparations so long, that if the Armada had come in September, as Philip had long planned, England would have been totally unprepared. It was a gamble, but Elizabeth counted on delays; no one could remember fleets that had sailed as soon as their commanders would have liked. When the Armada had not come by October, Elizabeth could be fairly certain that the dangers of weather would delay it until early spring. Her calculations would have been wrong had not the Spanish commander died just before he was to have sailed in January, but her luck held through the whole episode, and she made her anxious councilors look like frightened old men.

When Leicester returned fresh from his disgrace in the Netherlands, the aggressive group in council gained strength. The queen's cautiousness was for the moment overriden, and in early December orders were drawn up for the lord admiral to take the fleet to sea. His commission, signed on December 21, pointed toward a counter-Armada which would defeat the enemy in his own waters: Howard was empowered, ". . . according as there shall be occasion, and wherever and whenever he shall deem it fitting, to invade, enter, spoil and make himself master of the kingdoms, dominions, lands, islands, and all other places whatever belonging to the said Spaniards." He was granted full authority over the fleet and the army at sea, and thus would be able, "if need be, to go and to sail" to

Ireland "or to any other place, according to his own will and pleasure."[8] In theory the scope of his power was almost unlimited, but practical considerations such as the extent and nature of his supplies restricted him. The matter of supply, both in victuals and in matériel, was largely beyond his control; he had to fight with such supplies as he had, and he never believed them to be adequate. Through Burghley the queen kept her expenditures as low as she felt she could, outraging again and again Howard's standards of what was safe or even essential.

A separate commission, dated a day earlier, designated Burghley as the lord admiral's deputy during his absence at sea. This was simply an administrative device that allowed the ordinary functions of the admiralty to proceed without hindrance: someone had to sign passports and reprisal commissions in Howard's name. But the fact that Burghley was appointed suggests more than recognition of his central place in government. The impression of a close relationship between the two men is strengthened by a letter Howard wrote a few days later: he understood from Caesar, he said, how much Burghley's favor had meant to him; "I have no ways to recompense it but with my love and service, which your Lordship shall be most assured ever of."[9]

Prior to the Armada commission, Howard had divided his time between the fleet and the court. He spent most of October with the ships but returned to court at the end of the month and stayed there, with only brief absences, through mid-December. From December 21 on, his duty was to be simplified. He was the commander of the queen's fleets, a concern which overrode anything else. Between December 15, 1587, and April 1, 1588, he sat with the council only four times, even though it met almost daily during much of the period. His trips to court were quick and infrequent; he came up briefly every five or six days to consult with Walsingham.

8. S. P. Dom., Eliz., 206/41. See also John K. Laughton, *State Papers relating to the Defeat of the Spanish Armada,* 2 vols. (London, 1894–95), 1:19–23; hereinafter cited as *Armada Papers.*
9. Laughton, *Armada Papers,* 1:25.

He kept in close touch with Walsingham throughout the crisis, and it was to Walsingham that he unburdened his mind when the queen's policy seemed to him to be driving the country toward disaster.

When Howard got his commission, the terms of which must have gratified him enormously, he was on board the *White Bear* at Queenborough; he hoped, he said, to be ready to sail within two or three days, even though bad weather had delayed the loading of provisions. A few days before boarding, while looking anxiously to the great action ahead—the result of which could not but be in doubt—Howard drew up the only will he is known to have made. It was businesslike and perfunctory, purely a legal document designed to simplify disposition of his estate if he did not survive the crisis. Arrangements for most of his landed property had been made; the "mannor and lordshippe of Esher co Surrey with the advowson for life" was set aside for his wife, along with his house at Deptford Strand, called the "Sporting house," and Skynner's Place, West Greenwich, Kent; all his chattels, leases, personal property, jewels, and money, were to be used for the "educacon & bringinge up" of his two sons "accordinge to their degrees & callinges" and for the maintenance and marriage of his two younger daughters. Lady Howard was appointed executor and her father and Lord Burghley overseers (again arguing Howard's position as intermediate between the factions in the council). No mention was made of bequests to the queen or to his friends, other than the executors.[10]

Howard's position at the beginning of January, 1588, must have been entirely satisfying to him. The queen's ships were largely in good order; "if cause fall out," they would "do a better day of service for England than ever ships did for it yet." His men he found to be as "very sufficient and able company of sailors as ever were seen." Confident of himself, the justice of his cause, and the abilities of his men and ships,

10. *Collectanea Topographica et Genealogica*, vol. 8 (London, 1840), pp. 98–99.

Howard wanted only for orders to sail. He professed himself entirely at ease, eager for the job at hand, and missing only, like a dutiful courtier, the sight of the queen: ". . . If it were not for her Majesty's presence I had rather live in the company of these noble ships than in any place. And yet Would I be glad that there were something to do."[11]

Perhaps to find something to do for himself and his seagoing lords, who, he said, lived "bountifully," so that he wished he could bid them save, "to spend when need shall be," he took two of the queen's ships and some pinnaces with his principal officers around the Thames estuary from Dover to Harwich to see which ports would afford best protection to the ships in his care. The journey was taken on his own authority, and he wrote somewhat anxiously to Walsingham about it. It might be frowned upon at court, though he knew "no cause why it should be but well taken," since it had cost the queen not a halfpenny. Rather than see her spend a penny of her own, he said, he would rather spend a hundred pounds himself. Throughout the year he continued to draw upon his own resources to aid the queen in her burden. If he provoked criticism, he hoped that Walsingham, his "special good friend," would tell him frankly, "for I do assure you I will take it kindly and friendly at your hands, and think myself much beholden unto you for it."[12] It was only the queen who might have been annoyed at his initiative, and his care of her continuing good opinion, bordering sometimes on timidity, was characteristic of Howard as a commander.

Early in January, hearing a story that the king of Spain was disbanding his fleet and dismissing men, Elizabeth ordered drastic reduction in her own personnel so that her debts would not mount so rapidly. About half the men aboard the waiting ships were to be paid off and released until further need arose. It was a move that historians have criticized sharply; the queen's parsimony, many said, came close to wrecking the ship of state. If the Armada had come in January, as Philip had

11. Laughton, *Armada Papers*, 1:23, 51–52.
12. *Ibid.*, pp. 47–48, 51.

hoped it would, England could not have made an effective resistance. Like others, Howard was stricken with horror at the risk—"they know that we are like bears tied to stakes," he wrote Walsingham, "and they may come as dogs to offend us, and we cannot go to hurt them." He had an abiding fear that the queen had acted on faulty information. "If it be true that the King of Spain's forces be dissolved," he wrote to Walsingham, ". . . I would not wish the Queen's Majesty to be at this charges that she is at; but if it be but a device, knowing that a little thing maketh us too careless, then I know not what may come of it. But this I am sure of; if her Majesty would have spent but a 1,000 crowns to have had some intelligence, it would have saved her twenty times as much."[13] Howard preferred to wait for further news from Spain; if it was certain that the Spanish were disbanding, "then it were good we did so here," but, still, care had to be taken of Parma. If there was any reason to suspect a landing in Scotland from the Netherlands, Howard begged that Walsingham find three or four more ships to guard the Channel, "and I dare assure you it shall beat any power he shall be able to make." The cost of maintaining the extra ships for three or four months Howard would bear himself, "for I assure you it doth grieve me to see her Majesty at more charges than is needful, and this charge will not be great."[14] He recognized some danger from undermanning, but saw more trouble than risk, and feared that the next army would not be so forward in the queen's service: ". . . before these ships can have their full number of men again it will be a month to gather them, do what we can. And I pray to God we have them when we shall need; for many are gone abroad, and specially the chiefest men; God send me to see such a company together again when need is."[15]

The reduction in strength left Howard with sixteen royal ships carrying rather more than 2,000 men, strengthened by perhaps twenty volunteers and embargoed merchantmen. Sir

13. *Ibid.*, pp. 58, 46.
14. *Ibid.*, p. 47.
15. *Ibid.*, p. 51.

Henry Palmer had another squadron in the Narrow Seas, nine ships and pinnaces that had been in service through the winter, with eight hundred men on board. Sir Francis Drake, whose squadron was not yet united, had three ships at Portsmouth and three still at Queenborough in January. Drake had gone to Portsmouth about Christmas to begin collecting his ships and, like Howard, he could make only the briefest trips to court afterward. All together, then, the queen had thirty-three of her own ships, including two on special duty, and some merchantmen, but most were immobilized by lack of manpower.

There was a real danger that the queen's defenses would be let down still more dangerously. A small group at court, the most important member being Sir James Croft, comptroller of the household, played upon the queen's distaste for a long and costly war, reminding her that she was not yet technically at war with the king of Spain and suggesting that timely negotiations might prevent the Armada from coming at all. The duca di Parma responded, probably in good faith, and talks were covertly encouraged by Philip in the hope that they might prevent English mobilization. Through the winter of 1587 Elizabeth tried to persuade or to bully the Netherlands States-General into agreeing to a ceasefire, but it would consider no peace without guarantees of religious freedom, the only point that Spain did not consider to be negotiable. The council urged the queen not to be deceived, that as soon as she relaxed, Spain would strike. Its firmness cost it nothing, of course; the final responsibility for committing her citizens to battle was the queen's. Driven, then, by the desire to avoid war if at all possible, even at the cost of alienating the Dutch, Elizabeth announced that she would negotiate. Her determination for peace dismayed Howard, who was convinced, as were most of the councilors, that it was a trap. "Sir," he wrote to Walsingham in one of his most famous letters, "there was never, since England was England, such a stratagem and mask made to deceive England withal as this is of the treaty of peace." The next day he wrote to Walsingham in disgust that if there would be a "surcease of arms," then "it shall be but folly and to no purpose for me to lie here." Winter, Hawkins, and Borough could stay in command of the ships, and he and the other noblemen would come up to court. For him to remain at arms while the queen concluded peace would make him "a jest to many, and they have reason."[16]

The peace commissioners met after many delays, but no treaty was forthcoming. Negotiations dragged on rather hopelessly until the Armada was actually en route, thus making it more and more obvious that Spain had hoped not for peace but for a tactical advantage. The fact that Spain continued to arm, Parma wrote to Philip, was "notorious and the signs of it so obvious, that attempts at concealment are futile."[17] It was necessary, then, for the queen to recall the men she had already dismissed and to place the fleet once more in readiness for combat on short notice. By February 21, 1588, the work was well along, and Howard wrote that he would shortly be ready to sail, although the four largest royal ships, "which we shall greatly need if the Spanish forces come out," would require more time. The ships were his pride, and he gave Hawkins' management of them his full endorsement: "I have been aboard of every ship that goeth out with me, and in every place where any may creep, and I do thank God that they be in the estate they be in; and there is never a one of them that knows what a leak means. . . . There is none that goeth out now but I durst go to the Rio de la Plata in her."[18]

Within the next few days Howard and his squadron finally slipped down from the mouth of the Thames to Dover, the first step on his way around the coast to Plymouth. He was anxious to go somewhat farther afield and begged his friends at court, mainly Walsingham, to urge a more aggressive policy. For months Howard had ached for action, in spite of the fact that the weather was so unfavorable that he dared not venture out and even the ships in harbor had their sails

16. *Ibid.,* pp. 49–51.
17. James A. Froude, *History of England from the fall of Wolsey to the defeat of the Spanish Armada,* rev. ed., 12 vols. (New York, 1881), 12:407.
18. Laughton, *Armada Papers,* 1:79–80.

stretched, blocks and pullies torn, and boats lost. He reminded Walsingham that, by his instructions and "as a matter determined in Council," his squadron had two purposes, to prevent an invasion of England by Parma and to guard against any attempt upon Scotland. Of the latter the lord admiral had a strong suspicion. James VI had agreed with Lord Hunsdon not to give any assistance to Spain, but Howard was still suspicious: "For my own part, I have made of the French King, the Scottish King, and the King of Spain, a Trinity that I mean never to trust to be saved by."[19] Nevertheless, he felt somewhat later that if a pension would secure the Scottish king, Elizabeth would be "no good housewife for herself" if she refused it, for it might save her a hundred thousand pounds and a great deal of blood, "For I hold it certain if the neck of that be broken in Scotland, it will break all their intent in Spain. But it must be done in time, that it may be known in Spain before they be ready to come out."[20] Throughout the spring Howard was sure that "Scotland is the mark which they shoot at to offend us" and that to prevent a landing in Scotland it would be only common sense to "spend her Majesty's purse, rather than to hazard her honour." His own resolution was emphatic: "for my own part, [I] had rather be drawn in pieces with wild horses than that they should pass through for Scotland and I lie here."[21] Until the weather cleared he was helpless, but he chafed at idleness and at the cautious, hesitating policy the queen seemed to be following:

> If we stand at this point in a mammering and at a stay, we consume, and our Commonwealth doth utterly decay. I shall not need to speak of our estate, for that your Honour [Walsingham] knoweth it far better than I do: neither need I to rehearse how dead and uncertain our traffics be; most men in poverty and discontented and especially the poorer sort; our navigation not set on work; but the French and Scots eat us up, and grow in wealth and freights, and not assured to us in friendship. Our

19. *Ibid.*, p. 48–49.
20. *Ibid.*, pp. 69–70.
21. *Ibid.*, p. 57.

treasure doth consume infinitely with these uncertain wars, and nothing assured to us but new and continual charge. We have to choose either a dishonourable and uncertain peace, or to put on virtuous and valiant minds, to make a way through with such a settled war as may bring forth and command a quiet peace.[22]

This complaint to Walsingham is as good a statement as Howard made of his political outlook in the early years of the war, and it is a fair manifesto of the "war party." A "settled war" meant, first of all, abandonment of the negotiations at Bourbourg, it meant decisive steps to secure Scotland, and it meant sending part of the fleet under Howard or Drake to Spain to hinder further preparations. Sending Drake seemed more practical than going himself, but someone, Howard felt, had to go. On March 9 he protested to Walsingham that "the stay that is made of Sir Francis Drake going out I am afraid will breed grave peril." Despite these fears, Drake was not allowed to go; what would have happened if he had can only be guessed. But the men of the fleet, and Howard among them, believed that he might well have been able to prevent the clash in July.

Early in March, Howard, who had changed his flagship from the *White Bear* to the new *Ark Royal*—"the odd ship in the world for all conditions," so pleasing to Howard that he swore, "I think there can no great ship make me change and go out of her"—was finally able to sail. He took his fleet across to Flushing, the better to prevent any attack on Scotland and the better to bring pressure upon the independent-minded Dutch statesmen. When Leicester had returned to England the previous December, he had not formally resigned the titles given him by the States-General; the States nevertheless elected Prince Maurice, son of William the Silent, as stadtholder and commander of their armies. Maurice was to the English a rather difficult ally; when one of his generals, Sonoy, declared that he was still bound by his oath to Leicester, Maurice besieged him in his fortress at Medemblik. Sonoy was considered to be the better friend to England, and it was

22. *Ibid.*, p. 59.

the lord admiral's hope that he could at least relieve the pressures upon him, if not to effect a reconciliation. Howard was welcomed at Flushing both by the English governor, Sir William Russell, and by the Dutch towns, which made a great point of declaring that they gave all their loyalty to the queen and that they would not be commanded by any but Howard. "I gave them thanks on her Majesty's behalf," he reported, "and yet I spared not to let them know how in some things they had forgotten their duties," remembering, no doubt, their treatment of Leicester. After ceremonials and dinners were concluded "very honourably," Howard wrote to Maurice about Sonoy, but Maurice begged off, saying that the siege was the responsibility of the States; the lord admiral then prepared two ships to try to break the siege at Medemblik, but after consulting with Russell "thought it best to forbear four or five days." When the wind shifted, he returned to Margate, well satisfied with the affection and loyalty of the Dutch. He heard on his return that the siege was being raised, "which I am persuaded upon the hearing of my coming they did,"[23] but he was misinformed; a week or so later the queen sent word to Sonoy to surrender.

23. *Ibid.*, pp. 96–106.

VII: *Hour of Triumph*

So the spring passed, in tense waiting and unwanted inactivity. Impatient to be at sea, uneasy about the state of the queen's defenses, Howard wrote to court again and again to urge stronger policies and greater preparedness. And he began to grow restive about shortages and inefficiencies of supply, a restiveness that increased as the weeks passed. Several times earlier he had hinted that an army so eager to do the queen a great service might deserve unusual privileges, such as advance pay for clothing, six weeks' pay at the time of the partial demobilization, and extra rations. Throughout the action he was to display a marked concern for the welfare of the men he commanded and a keen sensitivity to the unpleasantness of their duties and the meagerness of their rewards. And, like Hawkins, he recognized that healthy men are better able to fight than sick ones.

His appeals, however, were rarely successful, not because Elizabeth and Burghley were indifferent to suffering, but because the traditional supply system could not cope with the size and demands of the service. Never had the country been required to keep up such a force for so long, and no one knew how to do it. As the weeks passed, victuals became more and more of an issue. It had been customary throughout the century to victual ships in the Channel for only a month at a time. The system had its advantages: ships were not burdened with unnecessary stores of food and could transport more powder and shot; frequent revictualing meant fresher food and less spoilage. But Howard worried—and his fears proved to be well grounded—that when the Armada appeared it would find the English fleet short on rations, and then there would be no time to get new food aboard. On April 8 he

pointed out the difficulty to Burghley. As of April 20 the fleet
would be victualed until May 18; the news from Spain indicated that the Armada would arrive about May 15. "Then we
have three days' victual. If it be fit to be so, it passeth my
reason."[1] Certainly from the viewpoint of the service at hand,
Howard was right, and his complaints had some effect; victualers did manage to get some ships supplied for as long as
three months. Still, inefficiencies remained, supplies did not
come on the dates promised, and some of the victuals turned
out to be unusable. So the problem of food for his men—one
of the most difficult in maintaining a navy until recent times
—plagued Howard as long as he was at sea.

In estimating that the Armada would be off the coast by
mid-May, Howard's intelligence sources were as accurate as
possible for the time. But if English armament was slower
than those responsible would have liked, Spanish preparations
were even more so. The death of the appointed commander
and the substitution of a new one, discovery of leaky water
casks and bad food, and the necessity to suffer through the
same fierce weather as buffeted the English coast caused endless delays. It must have been a discouraging spring for the
keener observers in the Spanish and Portuguese ports; most,
however, were swept along by the crusade fever that led some
of the Armada personnel to think that the English would
probably give up without a fight when they saw how mighty
was the arm of the king of Spain. The Armada finally sailed
from Lisbon on May 30 (English Style), more than 150 sail
carrying more than 27,000 men, only to be turned back a few
days out by heavy storms. A week before, Howard had left the
Channel squadron off the coast of the Netherlands to take his
ships to meet Drake's at Plymouth. By the 28th he was settled
in Plymouth harbor with "the gallantest company of captains,
soldiers, and mariners that I think ever was seen in England."[2]
There again he waited, eager to "make sport with them,"
confident of the outcome, but convinced still that the crown's

1. Laughton, *Armada Papers*, 1:137.
2. *Ibid.*, p. 190.

policy of inaction was wrong. As late as mid-June he wrote Walsingham that it was the belief of Drake, Hawkins, Frobisher, and others, a belief in which he concurred, ". . . that the surest way to meet with the Spanish fleet is upon their own [coast], or in any harbour of their own, and there to defeat them. . . . I [am] verily persuaded they mean [nothing] else but to linger it out upon their own coast, until they understand we have spent our victuals here; and therefore we must be busy [with] them before we suffer ourselves to be brought to that extremity."[3] He also expressed the wish that Dom Antônio were with the fleet so that a landing might be made in Portugal to divert Philip from his purposes.[4] Howard, then, was still urging preventive aggression, even though it had been estimated that the Armada was on its way or might even have made a landing in Ireland or Scotland. In truth, if a fleet could have raided Portugal even at that late date, the Armada certainly would not have sailed.

If, as he claimed, Dom Antônio could raise a popular rebellion in Portugal, then all the chaos produced by a Catholic uprising in England, an integral part of the Spanish plan of conquest, would be turned upon Philip himself. Antônio's claims of popularity, though, were scarcely better founded than Cardinal Allen's daydream that English Catholics would rise up at his signal and slay their queen. Elizabeth could not have been sure of that, but she could be sure that if Howard and his ships went south, they might miss the Armada altogether. She dreaded the human and financial cost of putting an army ashore in a hostile country, and she wanted to leave a diplomatic "out" for herself as long as there was any possibility that the Bourbourg negotiations might succeed. At most she would allow her fleet to ply between England and Spain to learn where the enemy lay. Howard argued that if a landing in Spain or Portugal were too dangerous, it would still be better to seek the fight instead of merely waiting for it, that they could be much more sure of finding the enemy if

3. *Ibid.,* p. 198, 200.
4. *Ibid.,* pp. 200–201.

they waited off his coast rather than off their own. As for plying between England and Spain, the southwesterly wind that would bring the Armada to Scotland or Ireland would also push the English ships so far leeward that there would be no contact, or they would have to lie so far out that the Spanish would be able to slip in and land on the Isle of Wight without his knowing it. "But," he added rather bitterly, "I must and will obey; and am glad there be such there, as are able to judge what is fitter for us to do, than we here; but by my instructions which I had, I did think it otherwise. But I will put them up in a bag, and I shall most humbly pray her Majesty to think that that which we meant to do was not rashly determined, and that which shall be done shall be most carefully used by us; and we will follow and obey her Majesty's commandment. . . ."[5] It is one of the ironies of Elizabethan naval history that by denying Howard the authority promised by his instructions and turning aside the advice of those he called the "men of greatest experience that this realm hath" Elizabeth made possible their metamorphosis into heroes.

During the month that Howard still had to wait, he did a great deal of plying and made one foray toward the coast of Spain, but after two days, "finding that with that wind the enemy might pass by the fleet of England undescried," he turned back toward Plymouth.[6] There, during this last respite, he "put divers things in order, watered and refreshed his ships with victuals."

Among the things put in order was the organization of the fleet itself. Howard's instructions had given him "full power and authority to lead and command" all the queen's subjects in her fleet and army at sea "in whatsoever way they have been or may be retained, or in whatever way they have been engaged in this present service." This clear grant had been reinforced by a council resolution on May 10, 1588, which stated that the navy would be "employed as by his Lordship

5. *Ibid.*, pp. 202–4.
6. *Ibid.*, p. 6.

shall be thought meet, upon such intelligence as he shall receive . . . having care, so much as lie in him, to impeach any attempt in Ireland, in Scotland, and England."[7]

Howard's instructions notwithstanding, he was not completely free to follow his own strategic inclinations—he could not seek a battle off the Spanish coast, which his training and instinct told him should be done; and the over-all disposition of the fleets was dictated by common sense. One strong squadron had to stand guard in the Channel to prevent the duca di Parma from transporting his armies to England; another had to be ready to intercept the fleet as it came from Spain; the third squadron remained in the Channel ready to come to the aid of whichever of the other two needed it first. Howard himself took the third squadron; the second, the place of perhaps greatest danger and greatest opportunity, was accepted by Sir Francis Drake, and the first squadron was assigned to Lord Henry Seymour, like Howard himself a man of highest connections and considerable naval experience. Just who picked Drake and Seymour is not clear, but it seems probable that Drake, at least, as a figure of such international reputation, had to be persuaded by the highest levels of authority to accept a position inferior to any. Indeed, there are indications that he accepted only reluctantly. In March and April he had pressed the queen to be sent with fifty ships to the coast of Spain to do battle; Williamson makes it clear that what Drake intended was to gain command of the main fighting force, "leaving to the Lord Admiral a mere titular authority and the guard of the Narrow Seas."[8] The fact that the lord admiral endorsed a Drake voyage does not mean that he accepted Drake's interpretation of his own authority or that rejection of the idea was not an affront to Drake. Drake was supremely confident of his own abilities and usually suspicious of everyone else; he was convinced that he was surrounded by traitors and cowards and was given to making peremptory commands and unexplained changes of plan, all of which

7. *Ibid.*, p. 171.
8. Williamson, *The Age of Drake*, p. 308.

made him a difficult man to deal with, especially in any kind of a secondary role. Howard took great pains not to offend his pride. He avoided, for example, giving Drake direct instructions about handling his ships and men; after a mishap at Portsmouth in which a man was killed and another injured during the testing of some guns, he suggested to Walsingham, "If you would write a word or two unto him to spare his powder, it would do well." After Howard took his ships to Plymouth he recognized the delicacy of Drake's position—experience and reputation compelled to defer to rank. He wrote again to Walsingham in the belief that a word of praise might soothe any injured feelings: "Sir, I must not omit to let you know how lovingly and kindly Sir Francis Drake beareth himself; and also how dutifully to her Majesty's service and unto me, being in the place I am in; which I pray you he may receive thanks for, by some private letter from you."[9]

Howard was also careful to consult Drake and the other prominent captains in matters of strategy. In mid-June he selected a war council, the members of which, sworn to secrecy, would be the only persons consulted or made privy to matters of strategy. Drake was the member first named in his message to Walsingham, followed by Lord Thomas Howard, Lord Sheffield, Roger Williams—a soldier who had served with Leicester and the Dutch, chosen for his experience in land warfare—Hawkins, Frobisher, and Thomas Fenner. Drake and the other sea captains were logical choices; except for Winter, serving with Palmer, and Borough, whom Drake had court-martialed and who was now commanding supply vessels at the mouth of the Thames, Howard's council included the most experienced and best-known of England's seamen, beyond any doubt the best sources of naval advice obtainable at Plymouth. The presence of the two noblemen could not be explained in the same way. They were, Howard said, "most gallant gentlemen, and not only forwards, but very discreet in all their doings"; they were also men whose careers Howard was anxious to push: "I would to God I could say for

9. Laughton, *Armada Papers,* 1:202.

her Majesty's service, that there were four such young noblemen behind to serve her. God bless them with life, and they
will be able to do her Majesty and the realm good service."[10]
Both were very young for such company—Thomas Howard
was twenty-nine and Sheffield under twenty-five. Both were
commanding ships for the first time, as volunteers in the
queen's service, and both owed at least some of their early
advancement to the lord admiral's interest in them. Thomas
Howard was the lord admiral's cousin, second son of the
executed duke of Norfolk, who rose to great favor and great
wealth from his services at sea; Lord Edmund Sheffield was
the son of Howard's sister Douglas and a link with Leicester,
who apparently had raised him and with whom he had gone
to the Netherlands. Both were on the council because the lord
admiral wished that they be given the benefit of that experience, not because of the value of their advice.

Thomas Howard and Edmund Sheffield were not the only
relatives of the lord admiral who were given opportunities to
distinguish themselves in 1588. Howard's instructions granted
him full liberty to give commands to whomever he chose, and
he made sure, as any Elizabethan courtier would have, that his
relatives and dependents were satisfactorily placed. His eldest
son, William, was given the command of the lord admiral's
own galleon, the *White Lion:* one son-in-law, Sir Robert
Southwell, had the *Elizabeth Jonas,* one of the biggest of the
queen's ships, and the other, Richard Leveson, served with
honor as a volunteer aboard the *Ark Royal,* Howard's own
ship. Also on the *Ark* was Sir Edward Hoby, the lord admiral's brother-in-law, who acted as Howard's secretary and in
the capacity of captain of the fleet. Other key fleet officers
were related to the lord admiral: Lord Henry Seymour, who
commanded the Channel fleet during the summer, was the
stepson of another of the lord admiral's sisters, the countess of
Hertford, and Nicholas Gorges, who was in charge of the
victualing ships for Howard's squadron, was his second cousin.
Thomas Knyvet, another cousin, commanded a squadron of

10. *Ibid.,* pp. 210–11.

London ships.[11] These appointments, of course, did not make Howard a nepotist on a large scale—all but a handful of the captains and officers owed their places not to ties with the lord admiral but to long experience and demonstrated ability; the list of captains and masters closely approximated the several existing lists of those eligible to serve at sea. At the same time, the lord admiral placed in the higher levels of command men who had special reason to be loyal to him and in whose success he would like to share.

Of the role of the council appointed in mid-June it is difficult to be sure. It met on most major tactical matters, and its decisions seem to have been accepted by the lord admiral. But since there are no records of its proceedings there is no way of knowing how the decisions were reached or who dominated the proceedings. The fact that councils were held at all is indicative of Howard's moderate use of power—his instructions did not require them, as did the orders he and Essex received in 1596, even though they had by that time become customary. The council was his instrument and he could use it however he chose; he chose to summon it frequently, seek its advice freely, and follow the recommendations it made. To Howard belonged the final responsibility of preventing the invasion of England by a Spanish army; it was a responsibility whose full seriousness he accepted, and though he continually expressed confidence in his victory, he sought and followed the advice of those best able to help him achieve his object. Although his personal vanity was formidable, he was never headstrong and he had no illusions of possessing unusual insight into men or events, as did Drake and some of his colleagues at court; he was therefore able to accept in-

11. There were five Thomas Knyvets active during this period, all of them cousins—more or less distant—of the lord admiral. Laughton believes that the Knyvet who commanded London ships was Thomas of Buckenham Castle, Norfolk, who was knighted in May, 1603, but it seems more probable that it was the Thomas who later became Lord Knyvet of Escrick, who had far closer ties with London and with the Howards.

formed opinion and to be convinced by the arguments of experts.

There can be little doubt that once plans were made the lord admiral had sole authority for putting them into effect. His letters to Walsingham and Burghley tell, always in the first person, of steps he has taken, and the letters of his subordinates, even of such persons as Seymour and Drake, refer to his directions at every turn, always in properly deferential terms. After the battle began, communication between ships became hard to keep up, and each had a tendency to act rather independently of others; nevertheless, reports of preparations and battle despatches leave the unmistakable impression that Howard was the principal officer of the queen in fact as well as in name. Later every man took what credit he could, but, at the time, each knew from whom his instructions came and to whom he had to answer for their completion.

On July 19 (English Style) the long months of waiting, of preparations made and made again, of victuals spent and storms weathered and damages repaired, were finally over. Captain Thomas Flemyng brought to Drake and Howard the news that he had that morning seen a great number of ships off the Lizard. The Armada was trying to collect itself after being tossed about by a summer gale, but Howard could not know this; for all he knew it was ready to attack Plymouth, where the bulk of the English fighting fleet lay in harbor. His ships had to get into the Channel and a defensive position with all speed; so, as he wrote to Walsingham, ". . . we first warped out of harbour that night, and upon Saturday turned out very hardly, the wind being at South-West; and about three of the clock in the afternoon, descried the Spanish fleet, and did what we could to work for the wind, which [by this] morning we had recovered. . . ."[12] His words gloss over one of the acts of seamanship for which he has been most commended. He brought the English fleet safely out of Plymouth, close ahead of the advancing Spanish, and then, in spite of

12. Laughton, *Armada Papers,* 1:288.

difficult winds, maneuvered it into a position behind the Armada, where he could attack or pursue at will, with the advantage of the weather gauge. The move was made possible by the weatherly qualities of the English ships, which gave the English an initiative they kept through most of the action.

The fleet Howard saw before him he reported to consist of 120 sail. After much research Sir J. K. Laughton confirmed this estimate but pointed out that about half were transport or victualing vessels and many were pinnaces that took no part in the fighting. The effective fighting ships carried, Laughton guessed, 10,000–12,000 men. Howard's own force, including the Channel fleet, was not far from the same size but was more seaworthy, better armed, and closer to sources of supply. During the year, he had under his command at one time or another 197 vessels of all sizes and kinds; again, half or more were supply vessels and others were too small to take any real part in battle. His ships were roughly the same size as the Spanish but looked smaller because of their lower construction. They carried fewer soldiers for hand-to-hand combat but more seamen for long-range fighting. With the same strategy in mind, they had more and bigger guns but fewer hand weapons.[13]

The Spanish hoped simply to avoid a great battle until contact had been made with Parma, then overwhelm the English by weight of numbers and land Parma's armies on the English coast. Howard's policy was therefore dictated; he had to try to prevent any union with Parma or any attempt on an English port by, as he said, "coursing the enemy as that they shall have no leisure to land." And he had to do so without close fighting, at which his lower, less strongly manned ships would be at a great disadvantage.

On the following day the celebrated battle began. The lord admiral sent his own pinnace, the *Disdain,* to deliver his formal challenge to the enemy, a medieval ceremony that had long since ceased to be relevant to the conduct of war. Then he led his ships against the ship he thought to be that of the Span-

13. *Ibid.,* p. xxxix–li, 288.

ish commander, the duque de Medina Sidonia, on one extremity of the Armada's crescent formation. Much powder and shot were consumed—the English attempting to cripple Spanish ships from long range, the Spanish trying to close and grapple —but without much result. Two accidents, however, were ill omens for the Spanish: the flagship of the Andalusian squadron collided with another ship and received such damages that it later had to be left behind to be captured, and another of the great galleons burned when a store of gunpowder caught fire. The English could take no special credit for either, but such accidents helped to determine the fate of the Armada.

That evening Howard's war council appointed Drake to lead the English ships through the night as they followed the enemy fleet; Drake got lost and went off following some German merchantmen, but Howard and two other ships went on, thinking they were following Drake. In the morning they found themselves almost inside the Spanish fleet, isolated from their own ships, and had to scramble out as best they could.[14] It was late in the day before the English re-grouped, and there was little fighting. The next day was a different matter. The wind had shifted to give the Spanish, who had been moving steadily eastward up the Channel, the advantage. Howard tried to lead his ships around by the shore to recover the wind, but the Spanish challenged him, and in the words of the official account, "there grew a great fight."[15] Frobisher and a small squadron became separated from the rest and were set upon by four galleasses, so Howard brought a line of ships to the rescue, exchanging heavy broadsides with the Spanish. The battle of July 23 was enormously expensive in terms of powder and shot, and English supplies were running low, but again not much damage was done on either side. Howard's own tactics, however, forced by circumstances, had been unimpeachable.

After another indecisive engagement the next morning, and while pinnaces were coming from the Hampshire ports with

14. Mattingly, *The Armada*, pp. 290–94.
15. Laughton, *Armada Papers*, 1:10.

new munitions, Howard called a council which determined a change in strategy. He divided the fleet into four squadrons, to be led by himself, Drake, Hawkins, and Frobisher; it was his plan that six ships from each squadron would attack the Spanish during the night "to keep the enemy waking," but the weather was too calm to attempt anything that night. Howard's and Hawkins' squadrons had heavy engagements the next morning without inflicting or suffering much damage, but Frobisher in the *Triumph,* trying to slip around to the windward of the Armada, again found himself cut off and escaped only after Southwell and Sheffield helped to draw off his attackers. The fighting that day and the two days before had been heavy; the Armada had not been defeated—the two accidental losses of July 21 were still the only major casualties —but a landing on the Isle of Wight (which the Spanish, in fact, had not intended) had been prevented, and Howard had seen his officers conduct themselves valiantly. So on the morning following he summoned some of those with whom he was most pleased to the *Ark* and conferred knighthood upon them, "as well in reward of their good services . . . as also for the encouragement of the rest." Thomas Howard, whose *Golden Lion* had stood by the lord admiral in the fighting of the previous morning, Sheffield, who had borne himself well in coming to Frobisher's aid, Roger Townshend, Hawkins, Frobisher, and George Beeston, captain of the *Dreadnought,* were the new knights. It was a modest list indeed, compared to those honored for lesser services in 1596 at Cádiz and still later in Ireland at Essex's hands. If Howard's relatives had a prominent place on the list, it can scarcely be surprising. The relatives knighted were noblemen, sons of families bred to command, and they had upheld the honor of their names. They could therefore expect the reward that had become customary to members of their class.

There was little fighting during the next two days; Howard's chronicler wrote that "the Spaniards went always before the English army like sheep."[16] That is, the Armada continued

16. *Ibid.,* p. 14.

on its course through the Channel toward a rendezvous with Parma, while the English followed, replenishing their spent magazines with supplies sent from the coast in answer to Howard's frantic appeals. On the night of July 27, Medina Sidonia anchored his fleet, harassed but not badly damaged, off Calais to wait for positive word from Parma. That same evening, Howard was joined by the Channel fleet, strong and fresh but short on provisions, commanded by Lord Henry Seymour, who had been chafing with impatience at his passive (though important) role in the great action.

Seymour's duty in keeping Parma from putting to sea had been taken over by the small warships of the Dutch admiral, Justin of Nassau. And, as Mattingly points out, Spanish strategy required Parma to meet the Armada on the open sea or off the English coast; when Parma could not get out and the great Spanish ships could not enter the shallow waters around Dunkirk to get him out, the whole enterprise became impossible.[17] Howard and his officers, however, did not know it was impossible. They knew that the Spaniards had to be defeated before they met Parma, whose strength they did not know. So on July 28 Howard's war council debated the means for a decision. Sir William Winter, who had been with Seymour and was, like everyone else, anxious to make the most of his contribution to victory, claimed just afterward that it was he who suggested fire ships to the lord admiral.[18] Conditions were right—the English fleet lay to the windward, the Spanish were against the bank with the current running toward them—and the suggestion was a natural one. That night eight hastily improvised fire ships were sent out; the Spanish manned boats to tow them aside, but some drifted on into the fleet, decks blazing. It was the turning point of the campaign. The Spanish ships had orders that under such circumstances they were to slip out and come to anchor again as close by as possible, but panic spread; many cut their cables and stood out to sea with no sign of a formation and no semblance of order. The

17. Mattingly, *The Armada,* pp. 318–21.
18. Laughton, *Armada Papers,* 2:7–8.

English fleet, now at its strongest, found them in that condition the next day.

With the scattering of Spanish ships, some at sea, some anchored offshore, Howard had his best opportunity to sow destruction. He allowed Drake to lead the attack, and his own efforts turned toward one of the greatest of the galleasses, which had become rudderless in the panic of the night and was now trying to reach Calais harbor. It was too close to shore for Howard's *Ark* to follow, so he sent out his longboat under Amyas Preston to take it. Preston did so, but only after the ship went fast aground and its commander was killed. The English stripped the galleass of everything valuable, but the governor of Calais, with whom Howard had exchanged polite visits in the spring, now claimed it as his prize and turned the guns of the castle upon the lord admiral. Howard, once he was sure that the galleass would fight no more, turned to the sea, where the battle had by this time become heated. During the course of the day the Spanish managed to recover their crescent formation, but only with great difficulty and under terrific fire from the English, whose supplies of shot were far more ample. By the end of the day the Armada was very badly crippled indeed; Howard wrote Walsingham that his fleet had "distressed them much" and would "by God's good assistance . . . oppress them." Although the feathers of Spanish pride were being plucked "by little and little," "their force is wonderful great and strong," and Howard still feared a landing. He could see no end to the fight and knew that he lacked enough munitions for another day—he combined his report of the day's battle with an appeal to send "with all speed as much as you can." Actually the Armada had been plucked more thoroughly than he realized. Most of the major ships were leaking and a couple had gone down; all had suffered heavy casualties, and none had more than a few rounds of shot left. The next day the English, their own ammunition too far gone to provoke a fight, stood by hoping to see the Armada driven by winds onto the Dutch coast. The wind changed just in time and the Spanish fleet moved northward. Howard's course was clear; he had to pursue, hoping for new supplies of powder and shot but determined to prevent by any possible means an attempt upon Scotland. Another great battle, though, would not be possible without the supplies for which he had been begging. A council of war resolved on August 1 to follow the Spanish beyond the Firth of Forth, then return to revictual; it also added a formal protest, signed by all the regular council members plus the earl of Cumberland, a volunteer, and Sir Edward Hoby, that "if our wants of victual and munitions were supplied, we would pursue them to the furthest that they durst have gone."[19] Lord Seymour was ordered back to his post off Flanders, since there was still danger of some move by Parma. He protested hotly; he had given the cause "the uttermost of my good will (to the venture of my life)" and he now wanted some of the honor that might come from another battle. The lord admiral, he wrote Walsingham, even after all he had done, was too petty to give him the credit he had earned: "I find my Lord jealous and loth to have me take part of the honour of the rest that is to win. . . ."[20]

There was, however, little honor left to win. The fleets did not meet each other again. What happened to the Armada is as familiar as it is tragic. Hoping for a chance to take some English port where they might accomplish part of their mission and get new supplies, the galleons continued northward, unable to do anything but try to get home. And as they tried, great new storms finished the work the English had lacked ammunition for. Ships were wrecked and cast up on the Scottish and Irish coasts, and many of the men aboard, trying to find refuge in a hostile country, were hanged or massacred on the beaches. The others, still a great part of the fleet that had set out, slowly made their way back to Spanish ports, those on board suffering enormously from exposure, lack of food and water, spreading disease, untended wounds, and from the painful knowledge that the great enterprise had failed.

For Howard the next month was one of vexation, uncer-

19. *Ibid.,* p. 6.
20. *Ibid.,* p. 3.

tainty, and bitterness, but one not unmixed with reward. He could not know how badly the Armada had suffered in the fight of July 29 or that its ammunition was gone; he did know that precious few of the Spanish ships had been destroyed and that they had moved northward in fairly good order. They might still be able to land in Scotland, and Howard's only weapon was bluff. "Notwithstanding that our powder and shot was well near all spent," he told Walsingham, "we set on a brag countenance and gave them chase, as though we had wanted nothing." He followed past the English coast and part of Scotland, then, leaving some pinnaces to "dog" the Spaniards, made for the Forth to get munitions and fresh food, "whereof most stood in wonderful need." The greatest danger was obviously past, but he begged still that the queen "be not too hasty" in relaxing the country's defenses. For himself, Howard swore that he was anxious for more service and suggested "some exploit" against the privateers of Dunkirk.[21]

By August 8 Howard and his ships had returned to Margate, from which they had set out months before. His concerns now were to make sure that England was protected from any new attempt and to look after the welfare of the men who had fought so loyally. In both he is seen at his most statesmanlike. For the next five or six weeks, he felt, "there cannot be too great forces maintained"; it was altogether possible that the Armada, instead of going round Ireland to get home, might make its way to Norway, Denmark, or the Orkneys, find new supplies, and try again. After all, as he pointed out to Walsingham, Spain and Catholic Europe had placed their whole hope and trust in the enterprise, making a great gamble in the expectation of great rewards, and the men appointed would venture all for its success: ". . . they dare not return with this dishonour and shame to their King, and overthrow of their Pope's credit. Sir, sure bind, sure find. A kingdom is a great wager. Sir, you know security is dangerous; and God had not been our best friend, we should have found it so. . . ." He had never minimized the Armada's strength, and did not now:

21. *Ibid.,* pp. 54–55.

"Some made little account of the Spanish force by sea; but I do warrant you, all the world never saw such a force as theirs was." After all, the stronger the enemy, the greater the victory. Some of the prisoners he had taken had said that the least of the four battles against the Armada "did exceed far" the great conflict at Lepanto, and that on the 29th twenty times as much shot had been fired. Realizing the greatness of the action, Howard gave way to a rare expression of religious sentiment: "Sir, I pray to God that we may be all thankful to God for it; and that it may be done by some order, that the world may know we are thankful to him for it."[22] To make sure that the Spanish would not be given succor elsewhere, Howard thought it "not amiss" that an envoy go to Scotland to urge James to refuse them, but he feared that a landing in Danish territory was even more probable. He had also heard of naval preparations at Dieppe and Le Havre, which strengthened his conviction that the fleet had to be made ready for further action. Any serviceable ships in the Thames or in coastal towns should be sent to him so that new squadrons could be formed for keeping guard. On August 22 a new council of war—Seymour, Drake, Winter, Hawkins, Palmer, and Fenner—met at Dover and divided the ships into two groups for revictualing, stationing one at the Downs and one at Margate so that when word came where the Armada had gone, "we shall be able, with the help of soldiers from the shore, for to be ready within a day for the service." Later the same day came a rumor that the Armada was indeed returning, and Howard wrote "in greatest haste" for all the powder and shot he could get, for pitch and tar, for more ships, and for fireworks, upbraiding the court for allowing land forces to be dismissed.[23] The rumor, like so many others, proved to be false, but to Howard it was a valuable moral lesson in the dangers of a quick complacency.

Strength, he felt, ought to be maintained for the defense of England, but he saw none to spare for other ventures because

22. *Ibid.*, pp. 59–60.
23. *Ibid.*, pp. 142–43.

of the sickness among the men, the difficulties of discharging ships, problems of victuals and munitions, and above all the foulness of the ships themselves. So when the queen expressed the wish that an attempt be made against the treasure fleet in the fall, Howard discouraged her as strongly as he could and sent Drake to court "with all speed" to "inform you rightly of all." It would be utterly impossible, he believed, to get the ships ready before it was too late to go out. With that idea quashed, he picked nine of the fittest ships to stay with Sir Henry Palmer in the Narrow Seas and soon returned to court, feeling by the end of August that the probability of any further action had largely disappeared.

During this same month, the problem of the men who had fought off the Spanish fleet was one that distressed their commander deeply. Their condition was only relatively better than that of their defeated enemies; they were in "wonderful need" when they last saw the retreating Armada and they grew steadily worse in the weeks that followed. Given the conditions of naval service, suffering was to be expected. Food, even spoiled food, was never in great supply; the ships, after months at sea, were always foul, unsanitary, and stinking; treatment of wounds was primitive, and knowledge of disease prevention was non-existent. So commanders had to expect to lose more men from "natural" causes than from battle. "It is a thing that ever followeth such great services," Howard wrote to the queen,[24] but it was a spectacle that angered and shocked him nevertheless, and he felt that the lack of supplies and food was to blame. When the fleet returned from Scotland, Sir Thomas Heneage heard that "they [were] driven to such extremity for lack of meat, as it is reported (I wot not how truly) that my Lord Admiral was driven to eat beans, and some to drink their own water." The story he heard was no doubt an exaggeration, but shortages of both food and clothing were severe. When he reached Margate, Howard wrote immediately to Burghley to beg that money be sent to pay the men and that a thousand pounds' worth of clothing be sent

24. *Ibid.*, pp. 138–39.

quickly, "for else, in very short time I look to see most of the mariners go naked." They were not only cold and hungry, but increasing numbers were sick and dying. "Sickness and mortality begins wonderfully to grow amongst us; and it is a most pitiful sight to see, here at Margate, how the men, having no place to receive them into here, die in the streets. I am driven myself, of force, to come a-land, to see them bestowed in some lodging; and the best I can get is barns and such outhouses; and the relief is small that I can provide for them here. It would grieve any man's heart to see them that have served so valiantly to die so miserably."[25] An "infection," probably typhus, continued to spread throughout the fleet; it had started on Southwell's ship, the *Elizabeth Jonas,* which, Howard said, lost 200 of its 500 men by the time it had been in Plymouth a month. The ship was cleaned and fumigated and a new crew was brought in, but the plague broke out again worse than ever and infected other vessels. Men, Howard reported, sickened one day and died the next; by August 22, he said, many ships had not enough men to weigh anchor, which made the state of preparedness he was urging impossible unless fresh men were sent and the sick ones discharged. It was about the end of the month before the infection died, by which time the mortality had been great. Lack of proper food and clothing had no doubt contributed—the men, Howard said, blamed the sour beer—but the principal cause had certainly been the unsanitary conditions with which fleets during periods of long service were to be harassed for more centuries.

Another vexation was the matter of pay. At the end of the service the men very naturally felt that they ought to be paid and allowed to go home, but there were many delays and frustrations. The fault, as in the matter of victuals, lay with no one in particular; the fiscal system was intrinsically inefficient and was how being subjected to greater strain than ever before. Money for wages was approved by the council and delivered by the lord treasurer's warrant to the treasurer of the navy; by custom the money was his until it was demanded of

25. *Ibid.,* pp. 96–97.

him, and he was entirely free to put it out to loan at interest or to adventure it on the seas if he so chose. It is rather unlikely that Hawkins in 1588 did much speculating—he probably never got his hands on more than the first quarter's pay—but still, when Howard needed the money to discharge his sailors as ships came into port, it was seldom at hand, and when he got it, it was seldom enough. His "poor men," Howard said in Margate on August 9, "cry out for money, and they know not where to be paid." He had pledged his honor that they would be paid and hoped the matter would be taken care of. Two days later he pleaded with Burghley that money be sent soon for the discharge of the sick; no doubt he pressed the matter further when he went up to court the next day.[26] On August 26, after he had brought a large sum from London, payment still had not been completed; money just was not available. Hawkins reported to Burghley that by paying the men through July 29 he could figure no less than £19,000—and Howard added a postscript:

> My good Lord, this is as much as is possible for Mr. Hawkyns to do at this time. There is here in our fleet many lieutenants and corporals, which of necessity we were and are driven to have. . . . God knoweth how they should be paid, except her Majesty have some consideration on them. The matter, it is not great in respect of the service. I think 500£, with the help of my own purse, will do it; but howsoever it fall out I must see them paid, and will; for I do not look to end with this service, and therefore I must be followed hereafter. . . .[27]

It is not known how deeply the lord admiral had to reach into his purse, but the pay of the lieutenants and corporals in his squadron was not the only drain. In December, with accounts still unsettled, he wrote to Burghley about some unusual items of victual—wines, cider, sugar, oil, and fish—ordered by Drake and himself during their stay in Plymouth, for which he hoped the treasurer would pay. Beer and wine he had ordered to be distributed among the fleet, and for this, he said, he would pay himself, "so that her Majesty may not be charged

26. *Ibid.,* pp. 92–93, 96.
27. *Ibid.,* pp. 164–65.

withal"; the bill for the rest came to £623 10s. 11d., not unreasonable, he thought, in that the goods were used for the sick and wounded and came in handy when regular food supplies were low. Howard considered that the service had been an expensive one for him. He had equipped a great ship and at least two pinnaces, supplied his own provisions, and covered extra expenses for the fleet. Then came the demands of discharging the men. Short of ready cash, he had used some of the gold aboard the Spanish ship taken in the Channel to help pay some of his men, then was outraged to find himself called to account.

> Sir, [he wrote Walsingham] I send you here enclosed a note of the money that Sir Francis Drake had aboard Don Pedro. I did take now, at my coming down, 3,000 pistolets, as I told you I would; for, by Jesus, I had not 3£ besides in the world, and had not anything could get money in London; and I do assure you my plate was gone before. But I will repay it within 10 days after my coming home. I pray you let her Majesty know so. And by the Lord God of Heaven, I had not one crown more; and had it not been mere necessity, I would not have touched one; but if I had not some to have bestowed upon some poor and miserable men, I should have wished myself out of the world. Sir, let me not live longer than I shall be most willing to all service, and to take any pains I can for her Majesty's service. . . .[28]

On August 27 he thought himself an abused man, under a cloud for a trifling matter of money, his advice unheeded and his pleas unanswered. However, he was soon enjoying some of the rewards of victory, and he enjoyed them for the rest of his life. After the great battle of the 29th the council had written him "to understande how gratiouslie her Majestie did conceave of the great paines and dyscretion his Lordship had used." He went up to court on the 11th or 12th of September and received the personal thanks of the queen and council for his preservation of the country's honor; Elizabeth never distributed praise and rewards lavishly, so Howard could savor her words—which are not preserved—the more. When he

28. *Ibid.*, p. 168.

returned to his ships, he wrote her his effusive thanks: "The great goodness of your Majesty towards me that hath so little deserved, doth make me in case that I know not how to write your Majesty how much I am bound to you for your infinite goodnesses, nor cannot be answered by any ways but with the spend of my blood and life in your Majesty's service, which I will be as ready and as willing to do as ever creature that lived was for their prince."[29] One can wonder at the sincerity of his modest disavowal of credit, but the pleasure and approval the queen found in his acts were the rewards that made courtiers compete for military duties. The gratitude of the queen and the nation was, for Howard, a fund of credit that was almost inexhaustible; it gave him a far greater influence than he had ever experienced before, and from it he forged an unassailable place. The queen's gratitude took more tangible forms. It may be that the pension of £200 that he was receiving in 1603 was part of his reward; it seems probable that the license to export cloth received the next year was.

The acclaim in which the lord admiral basked after September was not altogether universal; some voices had been raised all along against the way he conducted the fight. One of these was that of the young and elegant earl of Essex, then enjoying the first warm, rich glow of the queen's favor. The countess of Lincoln, daughter-in-law of the late lord admiral, entertained Essex and Sir Thomas Gorges at her house at Horseley on July 28. They were returning to the court from Dover, where the Spanish fleet had been seen lying against Calais and, as they thought, sending out boats to land and refresh their men and get new food supplies. They told the countess that ". . . there is much grief conceyued in the court that my Ld. Admirall hath suffered them to passe on so farre without fight, and that he prevented not the opportunity they haue now gotten of refreshing their men."[30] The letters from court, those that survive, do not reflect this criticism, which was, after all, based on ignorance of the facts. It may be that

29. Dasent, *Acts of the Privy Council*, 16:207–8; Laughton, *Armada Papers*, 2:138.
30. *Cal. Loseley MSS*, p. 645.

Essex had picked up the gossip of uninformed people; the council at least knew by then that battles had been taking place for a week. In the council, though, there were other misgivings about Howard's wisdom. Richard Drake, the queen's equerry, was dispatched from court on the last day of July with a "memorial . . . of such things as her Majesty doth desire to be informed of." Why had the Spanish ships not been boarded? It was true that some of these ships were perhaps too big for the attempt, "yet some of the Queen's ships are thought very able to have boarded divers of the meaner ships of the Spanish navy." Grappling and boarding had been the traditional way of fighting on the sea; that was why hundreds of soldiers were customarily crowded upon the decks. But the question displayed a lack of knowledge both of changing conditions of warfare and of the English position; Hawkins had built the English ships so as to avoid hand-to-hand combat. English guns were too imperfect and gunners too untrained to sink many ships, but they could cripple them, cause great slaughter on the decks, and make boarding unnecessary. The wisdom of fighting at long range was accepted by all of Howard's officers, and his position was defended later by Raleigh and all the naval historians, after long-range fighting on Howard's example began to prevail. "Our admiral knew his advantage and held it," said Raleigh in his defense, "which had he not done, he had not been worthy to have held his head."[31] Howard has also been criticized for his conduct on the great day of July 29; instead of immediately joining the fray, he slipped off to try to catch the prize in Calais harbor. Froude intimated that it was an unworthy act which showed him as a self-seeking, nit-picking kind of commander who could not think beyond the prize money he might get and who may have been avoiding the real battle.[32] To capture the galleass may have been unworthy of his efforts, but it is hard to begrudge him the few hours he spent in the attempt. It would have made a splendid prize, and its value would go not to him

31. Sir Walter Raleigh, *Historie of the World,* new ed., 2 vols. (London, 1736), 2:565.
32. Froude, *History of England,* 12:478–79.

but to the queen. Also, it was a powerful vessel, and seeing it made incapable of fighting was worth some trouble. As for his avoiding battle, his conduct in the earlier battles and later the same day makes the implication absurd.

Howard perhaps was not a brilliant tactician, but he had a reasonable plan and he stuck to it. He was a moderate man who led his ships ably; he lost not a single ship in the whole engagement, which argues not only his caution but also his discretion and skill. It is true that history was on his side—if the Armada had been better supplied with big guns and with shot, if it had been able to reach Parma, if Parma had been ready, if the storms had not completed the destruction Howard started, then his fame might have been of another kind. Accidents of fate contributed very heavily to his victory, but he gave the service the whole of his loyalty, his capacity, and his force, and it is impossible to say that any Englishman could, with the limitations of short supply and poor intelligence reports, have done any better.

Howard's own satisfaction with his accomplishments led not only to his commissioning an Italian writer, Petruccio Ubaldini, to write the narrative of the great struggle, which, suitably embroidered, has become one of the important sources of Armada legends, but also to his setting a Flemish artist, Cornelius Vroom, to work on a set of great tapestries commemorating the event. Using as his guide a series of engravings prepared by Augustine Ryther, Vroom produced a set of panels which for years was the chief ornament of Howard's London house, just as the event was the chief ornament of his life. He was expected to give them to Elizabeth in her last years but did not—only to have to sell them to James I to help meet his debts. With a fine sense of history, James hung them in the House of Lords, where they remained for two hundred years.

VIII: *The English Armada*

Philip II did not give up hope of conquering England when his battered ships came trailing home. Knowledge of that fact underlay the anxiety and dread that Englishmen felt throughout the next decade. Reports of naval preparations and expeditionary schedules so flooded the country that the queen had to maintain a defensive posture, keeping forts in readiness, trained bands alerted, and the fleet close at hand. Periodically, when the coming of a new Armada seemed imminent, more elaborate preparations were taken in hand. At those times Elizabeth naturally relied heavily on those who had served in the past, among whom Howard was conspicuous. On each occasion, by the time armament was well along, word would come that it was all a mistake and preparations would be relaxed. But still, Howard was one of the men chiefly looked to for the country's safety, a man whose claim to precedence and command could not be challenged even by an Essex.

The first of the alarms came in March, 1590; a great fleet, it was said, was arming to overwhelm England in the spring. Immediately, the defense measures of the 1587–88 crisis began to be duplicated; merchant ships were embargoed, the royal fleets fitted out, commanders appointed for a sea and a land force. It was said abroad that Howard, with Essex as his lieutenant, would command the navy, while squadrons would go to Drake, Hawkins, Frobisher, and Thomas Howard. A month later the danger passed and plans changed. For a time the council thought about using the fleet to send the lord admiral and Lord Willoughby with a large army to France, but that possibility was soon dropped. The queen's fiscal burdens—she was supporting ten or twelve thousand men already in the Netherlands, France, and Ireland, besides subsidies for German and Swiss soldiers—would not allow any large-scale endeavors, nor was she ever ready to give support on a grand scale to Henry IV.

There were other moments of panic in 1593 and 1594, but they passed before much could be done. Even when it was not felt to be necessary to call for a great national effort again, Channel fleets had to be kept ready and fortifications in good order; the lord admiral visited port facilities and fortifications at Dover and other Kent ports in November, 1593, and wrote to Burghley from Dover for help in strengthening that port.

The years 1589–95 were not only years of continuous precautions and constant anxiety over Spanish invasion, they were also among the busiest years of the naval war. Even after the limited accomplishments of Drake and Norris in 1589, other adventurers sought new commissions and ships in the hope that they would perform great services. The earl of Cumberland's voyages in 1589, 1591, 1593, and 1594, the voyage of Hawkins and Frobisher in 1590, Lord Thomas Howard's expedition in 1591, the voyage Raleigh organized in 1592, Frobisher's 1594 voyage, and the expedition of Drake and Hawkins to the West Indies in 1595–96 all were supported to some extent by the queen, and all had similar goals—to capture the treasure ships or the cities where the treasure was being loaded or unloaded and by so doing disorganize the fiscal system of the Spanish empire. Most of the voyages accomplished little; they were a considerable nuisance to Spain but returned few profits to England. The single exception was the expedition of 1592, in which Raleigh was the principal adventurer; under Frobisher, his ships, with some of Cumberland's, some of the queen's, and some of the city of London's, captured the East Indian carrack *Madre de Dios,* whose lading of jewels, spices, silks, and luxury goods of all kinds became a maritime legend.

The lord admiral was not ordinarily deeply concerned with setting these and the many smaller private ventures on the seas. There were routine administrative matters concerning the loan of royal ships, but these were handled mainly by the treasurer of the navy and the other officers. Howard was not a notable investor in other men's enterprises, so even as a private citizen he had little stake in their outcomes. Only in the voyages of Thomas Howard and Raleigh did he involve himself heavily. The reasons in both cases were unquestionably personal. Lord Thomas was his cousin and his protégé at sea; Raleigh was a distant kinsman and during these years his good friend. It was to Howard, with Cecil, that Raleigh turned for help in overcoming the disgrace of his secret marriage, and he pledged in 1594 that he would serve with Howard, if need be, as a private sailor. Probably on pleadings from these two principals Howard invested in their voyages. On Raleigh's two expeditions he sent his pinnace, the ninety-ton *Lion's Whelp;* for his cousin's great enterprise, he victualed, outfitted, and sent three small vessels, the eighty-ton *Charles,* and the *Delight* and *Disdain,* seventy tons each. But he got little in return; the Azores expedition was not a financial success, and Raleigh's Guiana voyage failed to find the gold mines of the Orinoco.

Saying that he did not customarily invest in other men's ventures, however, should not suggest that the lord admiral was not himself a privateer on a rather large scale. And there can be little doubt but that his expeditions were as successful, by and large, as most—since he could be backed by the manpower and resources of the crown and since anything caught would almost certainly be declared good prize in his own courts. Nearly all the major naval personnel from Howard down, as Andrews has shown,[1] operated ships of their own, and there are many indications that widespread use was made of crown timber and labor in building them, that royal supplies of cordage, sails, pitch, victuals, etc., were raided in outfitting them, and that the queen had to pay wages to their crews while they were searching for prizes. Not so much rigging of the navy lists and other forms of fraud occurred during Hawkins' tenure as treasurer of the navy as afterward, but there was nevertheless a great deal of shady practice. And no one was in a better position to get away with it than the lord

1. Andrews, *Elizabethan Privateering,* pp. 81–99.

admiral himself. Howard was recognized by his generation as a moral and honest man, but he was not a reforming zealot and could always live comfortably with existing practices. When he and Robert Cecil sent his new *Truelove* to the Barbary coast in 1597, they not only placed it on the lists of ships in royal service but doubled its nominal muster so that it could be victualed—at royal expense—for six months, although the fleet was out for only three. Whether this incident represented an occasional or a systematic peculation cannot be seen from available records; the presumption is strong, however, that Howard never made any sharp distinctions between the queen's navy and his own. The ventures with Cecil could be especially profitable, since Cecil could assign secret-service funds to help outfit the ships, with the justification that they would be used to gather information about Spanish preparedness.[2]

Over a fifteen-year period when privateering was most profitable, Howard is known to have used his own ships (seven of them in all) in at least nine voyages, in addition to equipping ships for Drake's expedition of 1587, the Raleigh voyage to Guiana, Thomas Howard's Azores expedition, and his own voyage to Cádiz in 1596: his *Disdain* captured sugar, brazilwood, and salt, worth more than £1,000, in 1589 and made a less profitable venture the following year; the *Lion's Whelp* with a Southampton ship captured a load of iron in 1590, squabbled with a squadron of London ships over a West Indies prize in 1597, and captured another prize of unknown value in 1598; the *Truelove* captured a cargo worth £1,800 in 1598; and a hundred-ton pinnace took a Hamburg flyboat in the Mediterranean in 1602. Howard and Robert Cecil commissioned a London ship in 1601 which brought back a gratifying profit in sugar and joined in another voyage in 1602 that resulted in a disputed judgment in the admiralty court. Some of the voyages lost everything that was put into

2. See Lawrence Stone, "The Fruits of Office: The Case of Robert Cecil, first Earl of Salisbury, 1596–1612," *Essays in the Economic and Social History of Tudor and Stuart England in honour of R. H. Tawney,* ed. F. J. Fisher (Cambridge, 1961), pp. 91–94.

them—not even queen's supplies could make a privateer turn a profit when it found no prizes. But under the conditions in which he could operate, Howard managed to get the most from what his captains did find, and it is scarcely surprising that he preferred to use his capital in his own ventures.

His attitude toward most of the 1589–96 voyages is seldom reflected in surviving papers. His honor and his name were most committed to Lord Thomas Howard, so when Thomas returned after the loss of the *Revenge,* the lord admiral felt obliged to defend him. Raleigh was among those who attacked Lord Thomas for allowing the death of Sir Richard Grenville, his cousin; he implied that for what he accomplished Lord Thomas might have been serving Spain rather than the queen of England. The lord admiral made an angry rejoinder, and for a time the court gossips believed that if they met they would fight. The quarrel was quickly composed, however, and it was one of very few serious differences between them before Raleigh's fall.[3]

First plans for Lord Thomas' expedition had called for a

3. The assertion of Donald Barr Chidsey that "the whole Howard family despised Raleigh" and that he and the lord admiral "had never been friends" (*Sir Walter Raleigh That Damned Upstart* [New York, 1931], p. 117), an opinion echoed in other biographies, does not seem to have much foundation, and there is considerable evidence to the contrary. When Raleigh returned from the Guiana voyage in 1595, a voyage that the lord admiral helped to make possible, he wrote a narrative of his discoveries; the dedication, to Howard and Cecil, testified that "your loves sought me out in the darkest shadow of adversitie, and the same affection which accompanied my better fortune, sored not away from me in my many miseries; al which though I can not requite, yet I shall ever acknowledge: & the great debt which I have no power to pay, I can do no more for a time but confesse to be due" (quoted in Richard Hakluyt, *The principal navigations, voyages, traffiques & discoveries of the English nation,* Everyman's ed., 8 vols. [London, 1903–7], 7: 272). Raleigh always signed himself "loving kinsman" or "poor kinsman" in letters to Howard, emphasizing blood ties that were extremely remote and that would have been ignored had the two men not been on good terms. And Howard seems to have favored Raleigh when he could, as in the assault on Cádiz.

great fleet to be commanded by the lord admiral himself, in which Thomas, the earl of Cumberland, Raleigh, and others would have squadrons, and on several other occasions during these years Howard almost went to sea. There were the invasion preparations of early 1590, the murmurings in 1593, and the Brest expedition of 1595, which was being considered his as early as January and as late as June.[4]

The failure of these plans left him almost continually at court, occupied with the affairs of the council and with a variety of more-or-less petty duties. The new offices of steward of Hampton Court and of Windsor Castle added new responsibilities, honorific and real. In January, 1592, he became for the first of several times a commissioner to exercise the duties of the Earl Marshal—on this occasion with Burghley and Hunsdon—and in 1593 he was a commissioner for the Order of the Garter. Also with Burghley and Hunsdon, he arbitrated a dispute between Sir Edward Hoby and Brasenose College, Oxford, over a piece of property. With Burghley and Buckhurst he spent many hours deciding on the ownership of goods in the captured Venetian carrack *Uggera Salvagnia.* In 1593 the plague was worse than usual around London, and Howard had the responsibility of restricting movements in and out of infected areas, to protect the court. There were appointments and patent disputes to be settled, imposters and forgers who solicited money on his warrant to be caught and dealt with, and the difficult case of Garrett Swift, son of a former sergeant of the admiralty, who had been arrested for piracy and who accused Howard of a variety of bizarre crimes—from seizing his and his family's livelihood to trying "by extraordinary means" to make his wife a whore[5]—to be settled.

These and more congenial tasks could fill the time of a courtier and made many of them beg the queen for a more active employment. In 1596 Howard got the active employment all courtiers hoped for: command of a major expedition against Spain. And he exploited the opportunity to the fullest.

4. *Cal. S. P. Dom., Eliz., 1591–1594,* pp. 407–8; Milton Waldman, *Sir Walter Raleigh* (New York, 1928), p. 93.
5. *Cal. Hatfield MSS,* 6:44–46.

Out of the 1596 voyage, like the Armada fight, he built an indestructable place for himself in the queen's favor and in his country's esteem.

Plans for the expedition to Cádiz in the summer of 1596 bear a close resemblance to the suggestions made by Hawkins at Deptford in December, 1587, and by Howard and Drake as they lay at Plymouth in 1588. What they had urged was essentially a defense by aggression; a fleet would be sent to the coast of Spain to interrupt and delay preparations and, if possible, prevent the Armada from sailing by destroying the ships and attacking the cities of the king of Spain. Antonio Perez, the renegade official of Philip II for years now in Elizabeth's service, had urged that the attack fall on Cádiz, a city at once rich, vulnerable, and strategic, and his arguments convinced the lord admiral;[6] it was Howard who promoted the scheme before the council. The Cádiz voyage, then, was peculiarly his achievement, even though it may have been suggested first by others. Hawkins and Drake, who had pressed for such an expedition in the past, were at sea and would never return; the only other possible rival for the honor would have been Essex, the co-commander, who specifically disavowed responsibility in a letter to the council at the time he left England:

> . . . as I was not the contryver, or offerer of the Project: so againe, if I had refused to have ioyned with him that did invite me to it, I should have benn thought both incompatible and backward in her Maties service. I saye not this, for that I thinck the action such, as it were disadvantage to be thought the Projector of it: but I saye, and saye trulie, that my Lord Admirall devised it, presented it to her Matie, and had aswell her Maties approbation, and the assent of such yor Llpps as were acquaynted wth it; as my promise also to ioyne wth him.[7]

The picture of Howard revealed in this passage is a rare one. On perhaps no other occasion in his public life is he seen clearly as the active force behind royal policy, working out a

6. Oppenheim, *Sir William Monson*, 1:363.
7. S. P. Dom., Eliz., 259/12.

plan, convincing his colleagues of its merit, and arguing it successfully before the queen. Essex's letter does not indicate the extent to which Howard was responsible for the plan that was followed at Cádiz; presumably he created the general concept upon which preparations were begun. The plan certainly must have been elaborated at council meetings in the fall of 1595, and many months passed before details were worked out. But the idea of some great enterprise against Spain the following year had been accepted by the queen as early as August, 1595; her instructions to Thomas Bodley, who was sent to the Netherlands as ambassador at that time, indicate that she expected to need a squadron of Dutch ships.[8]

We do not know the arguments Howard used to convince Elizabeth and her ministers. He could point to the continuing rumors of preparations in Spanish ports for a new Armada and to the weakness of defenses as the activities of Drake and Hawkins drew English strength to the West Indies. He might argue the damage done to Spain by the capture of cities and the destruction of fleets, and he could promise, as others had, to bring home great wealth in prisoners ransomed and goods seized. These arguments were sound, but Howard's motives included private as well as public considerations. He was nearly sixty, about as old as one could be expected to withstand the rigors of naval warfare; he might not have another chance to serve his queen on the field of honor. "My time will be past after this," he wrote to Cecil, "and therefore will do the best I can in this."[9] Whatever arguments he used, apparently he was able to secure full support from the most important members of the council. Essex was won over by the promise of joint command—another chance to immortalize himself through feats of arms. Burghley and Robert Cecil approved, though they shared little in the earliest preparations. The only complicating factor, and it proved to be a serious one, was the situation of the French king. Henry IV was gradually winning the support of the Catholics but was

8. Oppenheim, *Sir William Monson*, 1:362.
9. *Cal. Hatfield MSS*, 6:86.

losing ground in Picardy against a Spanish army from the Netherlands. If the Spaniards captured Calais or Dieppe or other Channel ports, all the dangers of the early nineties would return, and Elizabeth might have to cancel any projected invasion of Spain to send quick succor to France. Howard and Essex both must have watched the negotiations for English support between Henry and Sir Henry Unton with great concern, though there is no evidence that Howard supplied, as Essex did, information from the English plans to the French king while they were still being kept secret at home.

The value of the voyage would, of course, be lost if the plans leaked out, so the council took care to maintain close secrecy. Considering the great number of people who became involved, the secret was kept very well, and few records of the early preparations survive. Not until December, when the lord admiral sent letters to seaport mayors assigning them quotas of merchant ships for the next spring did the country know that a great fleet would be assembled. Until it sailed in June only a handful of officers knew the fleet's actual destination and purpose.

A memorial in Robert Cecil's hand, written early in January, 1596,[10] shows plans far along at that time. As the plans stood then, the ships would carry 4,490 mariners and 5,000 foot soldiers victualed for five months. At Howard's suggestion the wages, amounting to £21,400, would not be paid until the end of the voyage so that they might be covered by the plunder taken. Iron ordnance would be used instead of brass, also to save money. The lord admiral and Essex would command; Sir Edward Norris and Sir Francis Vere would be called from the Netherlands with nine or ten companies of experienced soldiers. Thirty Dutch ships would be used for carrying troops; the city of London had offered twelve ships and two pinnaces, which "much pleased" the queen; lesser seaports were coming forward more reluctantly with their contributions. Vere, one of the most eminent of Elizabethan soldiers, came in February from his command in Holland for

10. *Cal. S. P. Dom., Eliz., 1595–1597* (London, 1869), p. 347.

a conference at the lord admiral's house with Howard and Essex. They drew up schedules of the men and equipment necessary for such a voyage and, at the instance of the lord admiral, adopted a tight timetable for preparations which would have them away from England by the first of April. Vere later voiced some dissatisfaction with Howard's unwillingness to carry enough equipment to build shore fortifications and urged on Essex the need for a stronger army—a prelude to later quarrels over whether precedence should be given to the land or the sea army. But he promised that there would be no difficulty in getting the troops from the Low Countries ready by the appointed deadline. As yet, even he did not know precisely where he would be going; from the discussions that had taken place he assumed it to be either La Coruña or Cádiz, and he decided that Cádiz offered the more favorable target.

The commissions had not yet been signed, but an informal division of authority was clear from the first: the lord admiral would be responsible for the naval force, Essex for the army. Preparations were handled in the same way. Under Essex's name went letters to the lords lieutenants for the levy of troops; with him Vere negotiated the withdrawal of forces from the Low Countries, over the indignant but futile protests of the States-General. Essex's popularity and reputation attracted young gentlemen from all over the country, but the ranks of the foot soldiers had to be filled by emptying the jails of able-bodied prisoners and scouring the taverns and dives for "masterless men"; the mortality in foreign wars was well enough known to send those who did not thirst for glory and plunder scurrying for protective cover.

Howard had even more difficulty in finding fit mariners and in collecting and equipping the fleet. Victuals and supplies were ordinarily handled by the treasurer of the Navy and the designated contractors, Marmaduke Darrell and James Quarles, but the treasurer, Hawkins, had died at Havana. That fact was not yet known in England, so no successor had been appointed. As a result, many of the treasurer's duties had to be attended to by the lord admiral himself. His presence was required at the naval yards; every day, he wrote Cecil on March 7, "bringeth on that which cannot bide delay." The day before, he had worked at "Mr. Quareler's" until three in the afternoon with Thomas Howard and Raleigh; then he and Raleigh "were up and down on the river" inspecting ships. "There is nothing," he said with obvious pride, "that can pass but by my hand." His time was so taken up by details that he saw no chance of coming to court, and to the crowd of workmen and contractors who begged to speak with him when he was not busy, he had begun to say, "When is that?" Nevertheless, he hoped to have everything ready within a few days of the appointed time. "I promised at the first the first [sic] beginning of April, and let but the first go to the 15th at the uttermost, and I hope to be master of my word." No other queen's general or private outfitter within living memory "hath kept promise in their going out, by two months whatsoever and more."[11] Howard would not be able to do so either, but the fault lay not in his lack of care.

He was, in fact, very pleased with his achievements as an administrator. He had promised that two new ships would be ready by March 20, and they were ready two weeks early, a feat which Hawkins himself would have had difficulty matching. "Every body said it was impossible, but I assure you my often eye and my purse was the furtherer of it." Delay would mean greater expense, and people would say that Drake or Hawkins could have done better. Howard was anxious to prove that he could handle anything they could: "It is not with me as it hath been with other admirals," he wrote to Cecil, "all things ready to their hands, so as they had nothing to do but to make their living and to provide bacon meats and so go aboard."[12]

According to Cecil's memorandum, Elizabeth promised to pay wages and victuals, estimated at £56,366, and the expenses of fitting out her ships, some £20,000 more, but much of the remaining cost was borne by Howard and Essex them-

11. *Cal. Hatfield MSS*, 6:85–86.
12. *Ibid.*

selves. Both found their resources heavily taxed by the voyage. "A heavy charge now daily lieth on me," Howard told Cecil. "We have 260 men that feedeth and hath wages of us, for now the victuals be taking in every ship, which is not the Queen's charge." The next day Essex wrote to Cecil begging him to expedite those matters which passed through his hands, "for so you shall both advance Her Majesty's service greatly and pleasure us two, who, by want of despatch, may be ruined in our estates."[13] Essex was always notoriously lavish in his expenditures and during most of his career was heavily in debt; Howard was much better able to finance a great expedition than he had ever been before, thanks to the activity of the privateers; but neither spared his purse in the effort to get the fleet on the seas.

Robert Cecil wrote the queen's commission to her generals to "invade the realms and dominions" of her enemy the king of Spain and presented it to her on March 15. She examined it, then sent it to Burghley with word that he should alter it so as to restrain "the general" from offending neutral nations: Burghley added a few "special words," as he put it, which "will manifestly direct them whom justly to invade and offend"[14] and whom to leave alone. Thus amended, the commission, which had not yet been seen by the generals themselves, was taken back to the queen and signed.

Elizabeth, however, could rarely commit herself to any great decision without suffering painfully from second thoughts, and the next morning during her sermon she sent word that the commission should be prevented from passing under the Great Seal; later in the day she summoned Cecil and told him that she was distressed by the discretionary powers given the commanders. She had, however, told Essex that it was signed, and Cecil sent word to Howard, who wrote late the same day thanking him for the "good news." The amendment made was a minor one, binding the generals to

13. *Ibid.*, p. 88.
14. Read, *Lord Burghley and Elizabeth*, pp. 515–16.

act on the advice of their council in making a landing, and the next day the commission was sealed and delivered.

At about the same time[15] Burghley wrote a memorial "To the Queen's Majesty's only most fair hands, from a simple weak head," expressing some misgivings about the powers that had been given to the generals. They ought to be required to tell the queen, he said, ". . . what course they intend to take, if wind shall favour them, and to what coast and port of Spain or Portugal they intend enterprising, and where to land any forces, and what numbers; how far west or south they intend to pass or send ships, and for what purposes. Though they may have cause to change their present determination, yet Her Majesty may be better satisfied if she thinks their determinations likely to bring good effects."[16] Burghley thought that either the generals were keeping too many secrets from the queen and, presumably, from himself, or decisions had not yet been reached, and he felt it was time that these matters were settled. Later on, Essex did make secret plans that went beyond his instructions; perhaps Burghley heard some rumor of such plans and wanted them clarified. The fleet's destination was still secret, so the generals apparently answered Burghley in person. But at the same time Burghley asked other questions, which produced from Howard and Essex on March 23 a detailed statement of the organization of their expedition. The fleet would include seventeen of the queen's ships, three pinnaces, ten double flyboats for victualers, twelve ships from the city of London, a Dutch squadron of twenty-four vessels, and as many more ships furnished by the port towns and by private adventurers, divided into four squadrons commanded by Essex, the lord admiral, Lord Thomas Howard, and Sir Walter Raleigh. Sir George Carew, lieutenant of ordnance, would have charge of ordnance. Sir Robert Southwell would be treasurer, Sir Francis

15. Read (*ibid.*, p. 516) indicates that the memorandum was written on March 16; *Cal. S. P. Dom., Eliz., 1595–1597,* gives the date as March 20.

16. *Cal. S. P. Dom., Eliz., 1595–1597,* p. 189.

Vere marshal, and Sir John Wingfield, Sir Thomas Gerard, Sir Conyers Clifford, and Sir Christopher Blount would be colonels. Vere and the four colonels would be council members for the land forces and Thomas Howard, Raleigh, Carew, and Southwell would serve in that capacity for the navy. Sir Edward Norris, the commander of English troops at Oostende, had been named at first to go, but his name does not appear in these papers, nor does that of the earl of Cumberland, who wanted to command the squadron given to Thomas Howard. Cumberland came to the lord admiral "much grieved," but, Howard wrote to Cecil, "I dealt so with him as he knoweth how it must be. He seemed that now he would not seek for anything to supplant my Lord Thomas."[17] Cumberland instead went to sea with his own ships.

Howard reported that so far they had spent £7,180 in the queen's name, for prest, coat and conduct money, sea stores, grounding the ships, and for canvas, and £18,000 more, for wages and the like, had been committed but need not be paid until the fleet's return; this did not include the wages of the land forces, 1,000 of whom Essex promised to pay himself, 1,500 of whom he would furnish with armor. Howard, so far as is known, made no such promises; his more cautious nature forbade such generosity with prizes yet untaken, just as it discouraged speculation in the naval fortunes of other men. The queen would appoint "some sufficient person," who turned out to be Anthony Ashley, to "keep perfect books of all her charges" and of the value of prizes taken and their disposition.

A few days later came news which almost disrupted the entire plan and which completely shattered the lord admiral's cherished hope of leaving by mid-April. Archduke Albert, the new viceroy of the Netherlands, suddenly descended upon Calais, within sight of English shores, and put the unprepared town under siege. Relief had to be sent, and the ships and men readied for Cádiz were the nearest at hand. There was no knowing how long the siege might last, and while it lasted

17. *Cal. Hatfield MSS,* 6:102.

neither ships nor men nor money could be spared for a great effort in Spain. Howard must have learned of the siege with great shock and disappointment, since he believed his prospects were bound entirely in the Spanish venture. Still, it was possible that some service might be performed at Calais and something gained for his effort and expense. Burghley was of the same mind. "My Lord of Essex and Lord Admiral cannot with more honour employ themselves" and their forces than in the town's defense, "their whole pay to be answered by her Majesty," he wrote privately to his son.[18]

Essex agreed that England's honor was tied to Calais, and he made certain that he would be the instrument of its relief. When news came of the siege he hurried down to Dover, then began flooding Howard, Cecil, and others with letters to rush preparations for immediate aid. On April 3 he wrote Howard that the port was still open and could receive ships. "Your Lordship may offer to the Queen to put them in, for it is easy. Pray urge her to resolve." That same day he sent one of his men to slip inside the city to get accurate news and in another letter to Howard expressed his resolve to die fighting, if need be, to save the town. "Assure yourself if we offer to carry succours and come there," he said, assuming that the commission already granted would be altered to send forces to France, "we must do somewhat to purpose, or bury ourselves before it, for you would not come to see an enemy take a town before you, when the world looks you should relieve it."[19]

Always anxious to achieve military greatness and restless for physical activity, Essex could not fail to be deeply impressed by the needs of the town on the horizon and could not but chafe at the delays in getting the necessary means to him. Elizabeth, however, moved less readily. She began to negotiate terms with Henry IV, gave orders on April 7 to raise troops, then rescinded them. On April 10 the levies were summoned again, just as Essex came up from Dover, frantic with worry. He had worked day and night to get ships loaded with victuals

18. Read, *Lord Burghley and Elizabeth*, pp. 516–17.
19. *Cal. S. P. Dom., Eliz., 1595–1597*, p. 197.

and ready for the troops he would lead, all the while bombarding Burghley and the council with appeals and plans for gaining entry to Calais. He got permission to take 6,000 troops across the Channel and returned to Dover the same day to complete his preparations. The lord admiral, meanwhile, had stayed with the fleet in the Medway, sending ships around to Dover as they were readied. When word came to him of the queen's final resolution, he hastily ended his preparations and went to Dover to join his colleague in command.

Howard came to Dover on April 13, just as the formal commission was received. To his utter dismay he discovered that he was left out of it. Elizabeth instructed Essex to transport the men levied from London, Middlesex, Essex, and the southwestern counties "with all expedition" to join the army of Henry IV in succoring the citadel of Calais. He was to act "with the advice of our said Admiral, when he shall be with you." Howard was simply to assist and advise Essex, not, apparently, as an equal but as a subordinate.

Perhaps the queen had finally become impressed with the need for haste, did not believe that Howard would arrive at Dover in time to go, and did not want the expedition to await his arrival. She had Cecil write an explanatory letter which, unfortunately, does not survive. But Howard felt mortally offended at the sudden and unexpected loss of status, and he saw in it the complete ruin of all his hopes. The voyage to Spain was postponed, perhaps to be canceled, and he was being excluded—deliberately, he thought—from the only service at hand. He had "little looked" ever to receive such a letter, he wrote to Cecil in a storm, and he thought he had deserved more than the disgrace visited upon him. "I wish I had drowned by the way before I arrived at this place." Now he begged to be discharged of all his offices and commissions, "for I vow it by the Lord that made me I will never serve but as a private man whilst I live, and if her Majesty lay me in the Tower it shall be welcome unto me." His anger was almost treasonable. In all the history of England, he said, no man had ever known such a landing to be entrusted to anybody but the lord admiral, "yea, and by admirals of my name." He accepted his fate but refused to continue in his present place, asking that someone be appointed to replace him, "for I hold myself accursed to be here, and it cannot but torment me to find her conceit of me." To have joined him in commission with the earl of Essex in the first place was, he said, "an idle thing, for I am used but as the drudge. But since I see it is the account of me, I will take care of myself and estate in time." Since his disgrace "cannot now be salved" except by "importunate suit," to which he absolutely refused to stoop, he prayed that he would not be "pressed" for "the other journey" after Calais was relieved, "for I vow it to God I will not stir in it." Now he planned to return with his own two ships "and not lie in Dover to my shame." "And thus," he concluded, "I leave for ever farther to deal in martial causes." It was indeed, as the clerk who received it noted on the endorsement, "a passionate letter,"[20] an outburst of jealous rage and trampled pride that scarcely sounds as if it came from a man of sixty.

Essex was generous in his sympathies. He had never, he wrote to Cecil, seen a man so afflicted. "By Christ, I am so sensible of it as I have written to the Queen in passion." He hoped that Cecil, "as you love either of us, or the service," could get the order changed. He had seen Howard's letter to Cecil and begged him not to show it to the queen, "for it is too passionate, and it may break all our actions, if she take him at his word."[21] The caution was probably unnecessary; Cecil was not so indiscreet as to betray a friend's ill-considered anger. But apparently the queen learned of Howard's anger anyway; in a "sharp postscript" she reproved him for his disloyalty and told him to look about his duties.

Before nightfall Essex was able to persuade Howard that the slight had been unintentional, and both signed a letter to Burghley at nine o'clock, asking him to expedite the departure of a hoy loaded with pioneering equipment from the Tower wharf. It is unlikely, however, that an amended commission completely cleared the air. In his anger Howard released

20. *Cal. Hatfield MSS,* 6:144.
21. *Cal. S. P. Dom., Eliz., 1595–1597,* p. 204.

resentment at being the "drudge" of his young and shining companion, and the resentment apparently lingered despite Essex's quick defense. This was the first expression of open hostility between the two men, and it is easy to imagine that an undercurrent of suspicion and jealousy continued.

In the next weeks there were stories afloat that reflected something of the cloud over the lord admiral—the only time he was ever in Elizabeth's bad graces. At the end of April a boy named Smith who had been among the levies at Dover was hauled before the Star Chamber and severely sentenced—to lose one ear at Westminister, the other at Windsor, to be whipped, imprisoned "during pleasure," and fined £20—for retailing a slander against the lord admiral. According to Smith's story, the earl of Essex had searched the lord admiral's ship and opened some barrels that were supposed to contain gunpowder but in which he found only ashes, dust, and sand. Essex had called Howard a traitor, and he and Cumberland had taken the lord admiral to face the queen, who seized him by the beard, exclaiming, "Ah, thou traitor!" In May, perhaps hearing an enlargement of the same theme, one of Burghley's correspondents in Germany said he had news that the lord admiral had been committed to prison. The stories were preposterous, but they show how hints of what was going on in the highest levels of society trickled down to the ignorant, who filled them out with details that suited their own inclinations: Essex was the popular hero and could not yet sin, but Howard was a rich and avaricious old man. The scenes Smith described may indicate what the populace was willing to believe of each, given the information at its disposal. In both of the great actions of his life, then, Howard was coupled with a far more popular and attractive figure, who could easily overshadow his more stolid accomplishments.

In spite of the anguish it caused Howard, the commission came too late to help Calais. Only a day after the queen had given permission to sail, the citadel surrendered. When the news came, Howard was aboard his ship and Essex was having supper on the *Rainbow;* they had spent all day embarking their army. Now there was nothing to do but release the men so lately levied, return to court, and take up the enterprise that had been left off. Essex was mortified. He had personally promised Henry IV that he would bring help, but had been compelled to stand by in idleness as the Spainards marched into the city. "I wish myself in another world," he had written the previous midnight, "where I might not hear the complaints that through all Christendom will run upon us for losing such a place, and in such a manner as this is like to be."[22]

Now the other world where his honor might be redeemed was the harbor and streets of Cádiz, and toward it he turned. Howard, no doubt, was more easily consoled than Essex because of the thought that his own expedition would not be diverted, no matter how keenly he felt the blow to English prestige. Anyway, he had little time to grieve. As Essex left to take the news to the queen, word came that Spanish ships were in view. Every man went to his ship "with all diligence aboard so fast as I have not seen the like and ships so soon under sail." But it was another false alarm, and preparations for Cádiz were resumed immediately. From Dover Roads on April 17 the generals wrote to Burghley to send £4,000 imprest money to Portsmouth to pay the soldiers who had come long distances without so much as a change of clothing. It was important now to get away as soon as possible because, until the fleet was at sea, both the land and the sea army had to be paid by the generals, who "are already at a greater charge than any two subjects have been at in the like service this long time."[23]

So the lord admiral took a few days to finish watering, then set out with most of the fleet and the army for Plymouth, urging Cecil to hurry Raleigh, Thomas Howard, and Southwell with the remaining ships and supplies. He left Burghley a commission to act as lord admiral in his absence and an affectionate letter of farewell, vowing himself "so much bownd unto your lo[rdshi]p as I must confese, to no man that

22. *Ibid.*, p. 205.
23. *Ibid.*

ever lived more, only my father excepted." He thanked Burghley for his "kynd and most honorable favors" and hoped for so much favor in the future that he would not be condemned for whatever befell by accident, adding, significantly, "for I have no menynge to conne any rashe or unadvysed course." He promised never to rush into any action on his own unsupported judgment but "to yeald to those that shall show best reson." In the past "I have ever desired to follow, as neer as I could, the many good excamples you have showed; but it was not in me to comy nere it, but that little I have, I did, and must ever confese, I gathered it from you." He was therefore bound to love "you and yours" and if he thought his son would not do so after him, that son would never taste his favor.[24] Although extravagant vows of duty and debt were the fashion, Howard's choice of words indicates a feeling of special relationship. The farewell has particular poignancy because of the realization that Burghley was declining so rapidly that he might not live to see the fleet return. Aside from a businesslike note to Cecil, there were no other farewells, but there would be time in Plymouth for that. He was now contritely at the queen's command, asking Cecil to remember his "humblest duty" to "her sacred Majesty." "By her commandment I did master myself with patience and with duty obeyd, but shall ever think myself more else worth than I have done." Now he hoped God would allow him to do "that service which my unspotted heart hath ever desired, and after this service with her gracious favour to live quietly."[25]

Once in Plymouth, about April 28 or 29, he began a long and restless wait for the other officers and for permission to sail. Essex had left the court on April 25 and arrived at Plymouth after three days of hard riding ready "to rest my brains and my bones." He brought with him a "Declaration of the Causes moving the Queen's Majesty to prepare and send a navy to the seas for defence of her realm against the King of Spain's forces" which Burghley had written just before Essex

24. Lansdowne MSS, 116/22, art. 13.
25. Devereux, *Lives and Letters of the Devereux*, 1:339; *Cal. Hatfield MSS*, 6:146.

left for Plymouth and which the generals published. It was a piece of propaganda protesting that Spain had sent a great fleet against England in 1588 even while peace was being negotiated and that now she was preparing another; the king had "those many years openly professed great enmity . . . without any just cause," so now the queen was obliged to retaliate. The generals promised not to offend any person other than subjects of the king of Spain and those who aided him; they would "use as friends" all those who would assist them. But any who refused their protection would be considered "manifest aiders" of Spain; if such persons suffered damages, they would have no cause for complaint. The declaration was to be published in French, Italian, Dutch, and Spanish, and would be distributed in "as many ports of Spain and Portugal as conveniently might be."[26]

Just before Essex and Howard met at Plymouth, news came from Sir Nicholas Baskerville, the surviving officer of the West Indian expedition, that Drake and Hawkins were dead and that their fleet had suffered one disaster after another. To Essex this meant "it was time to draw swords" with Philip II, but the queen could not be so bold. Her two most prominent naval officers had been lost, Drake whose name was the terror of the Spanish seas, and Hawkins, no less intrepid and a trusted administrator as well. Only a few ships had come straggling in; Elizabeth did not yet know how many had been lost. Those that returned would spend months in dock being grounded and refitted before they could sail again. The early estimates of shipping for Cádiz had figured that Hawkins and Drake and their fleet would be available for the defense of the country while the rest of the ships were gone. Now it seemed that England would be left naked and undefended while the greatest personages in the country took most of the country's armed strength on a risky piratical cruise. The queen and the principal adventurers had already spent so much money on the expedition that she could not back out, but she could reduce its scale and send commanders less important to her

26. *Cal. S. P. Dom., Eliz., 1595–1597*, pp. 207–8.

and the realm. Essex and Howard could stay at home to defend her, and some worthy knight and seaman could go in their places. For a month the queen agonized over that thought while her generals waited, horrified by their mounting costs. Essex protested that there was "a little world" eating daily at his table and that he had spent more in the voyage "than my state is worth." In mid-May, Elizabeth reached a resolution: she could not afford to see the expedition go out as it was presently constituted, so letters went from court that it was her wish to change the nature of the voyage and provide new commanders. There was an inevitable protest. From Howard himself, nothing is heard; perhaps, remembering how he lost his temper at Dover, he let Essex and his subordinates write for him. Essex wrote an angry but lucid letter to the Privy Council reminding the lords of the great expenditures made not just by the crown but by private citizens and towns as well, the loss of prestige to the country that would follow, the dangers from a new Armada or an invasion of Ireland, and the distress given to the French and Dutch.

The chief naval officers, headed by Lord Thomas Howard and Sir George Carew, perhaps speaking for the lord admiral as well as themselves, wrote a similar letter to Sir Robert Cecil. If the generals are recalled, they said, "the reputation of the voyage . . . will be much blemished," since armies "under great commanders do terrify and discourage an enemy." Many of the gentlemen who joined the service had come "out of particular love unto the Lords Generals" and would not serve under any other, and those baser men who were imprest would run away. Nor, they believed, would the Dutch contingent be willing to serve under generals of lesser reputation. And if the king of Spain had learned who was leading the forces against him, his preparations would undoubtedly have been the greater, so reducing the strength of the English fleet would mean imperiling the whole cause. For all these reasons, they concluded, if Essex and Howard were recalled, no other man would be found willing to take the charge.[27] The queen

27. *Cal. Hatfield MSS*, 6:188–89.

did not appreciate such insubordination, but she did not recall her commanders; after much urging she finally sent a letter by Fulke Greville giving them permission to go at their earliest convenience. Within a day or two Sir Walter Raleigh arrived with the rear guard of the fleet, and little more time was lost in loading and getting to sea.

By the time Greville finally came, the long wait and the cancerous expense of feeding and housing a great army had worn thin the patience of the commanders. To the world, Howard and Essex maintained a united front, but there were secret jealousies. After the final loading had begun, an officer as close to the generals as Sir George Carew, lieutenant of ordnance, had written to Cecil that although "we are grown extreme dull" by the drain to their hearts and purses, "Our generals do yet hold their good corresponditie."[28] But not five days earlier there had been a petty disagreement over signing a letter; Essex signed a joint report so high on the page that Howard could not sign except below, so, insisting that the joint commission gave him equal precedent in spite of his lower rank, the "unruly admiral" cut out Essex's signature. Essex was now beginning to irritate him with the smallest act, an irritation spurred, no doubt, by the knowledge that this brilliant figure not half his age had the far greater reputation as a general and would monopolize the glory in Spain.

Nor were the other commanders entirely comfortable. Early in May, Essex had written that he was, with the advice of the lord admiral and the council, "setting down every man's place and degree for avoiding of quarrels." A notable quarrel developed between Raleigh and Sir Francis Vere, who was being much consulted and patronized by Essex. Both claimed precedence; after several "open jars," the council decided that Essex's friend Vere, a soldier, would take precedence on land but would yield at sea to Howard's friend Raleigh, a mariner. Such rivalry was in a sense stimulating, because when the attack came, each wanted to be in the forefront of the fighting to steal the glory from his peers. But it could not be conducive

28. *Ibid.*, pp. 199–200.

to a smoothly executed campaign in which each person subordinated his own interests to the success of the whole. For the moment, however, all seemed in harmony when the time came to embark. The fleet cast out to sea on June 3, on a signal from the lord admiral aboard the *Ark Royal.*

The departure was undoubtedly an impressive sight. The ships carried two earls, Essex and Sussex (who was a volunteer), and two barons, the Howards, some of the most famous of England's knights, and a great body of gentlemen, all magnificently garbed for war and accompanied by as many liveried retainers as they could turn out. There were more than ten thousand men aboard, well, indifferently, and poorly equipped—a large army for the time and one capable of nearly any action on land or sea. The fleet itself was the greatest ever sent from England on a mission of aggression— perhaps 120 sail in all, with probably as great a tonnage as the Spanish Armada itself. It included from fifteen to seventeen of the queen's ships, two of Howard's, seventy-five or so furnished by London and the port towns, and nearly thirty sent from the Netherlands. The expedition represented an enormous effort, and there is a little wonder that Elizabeth felt pangs at seeing it go, even apart from her personal regard for some of those aboard.

IX: *The Capture of Cádiz*

After the many delays in departure, the voyage itself passed without serious incident. Reaching the Spanish coast took about two weeks, with some time lost because of bad weather. The lord admiral's scouting vessels captured an Irish bark, from which he received an important intelligence report: a great naval concentration lay inside Cádiz Roads, including two argosies loaded with grain and perhaps as many as thirty other ships of war. The Irish count was not altogether accurate, but the news was decisive. It was resolved that Cádiz would be the goal.

On June 18, the council of officers met in Howard's quarters on the *Ark* to decide on a plan of attack. They agreed, on whose suggestion it is no longer known, that the first effort should be against the town. Essex would lead in such ships as carried companies of soldiers, and the others, except for the few under Sir Alexander Clifford sent to immobilize the galleys at nearby Puerto de Santa Maria would stand guard in the harbor until the town was taken. Or, if conditions proved sufficiently favorable, the ships might be attacked at the same time as the town. Raleigh was assigned five ships and instructed to intercept the argosies. Overnight, however, members of the council began to entertain misgivings, and the next day substantial changes were ordered: Essex would land his troops at Santa Catalina, then Howard would put his men ashore south of Cádiz Island; it was to be a double attack. Raleigh and the Dutch squadron would ride at the entrance to the harbor to make sure that none escaped. The change in plans may have been required by Howard's reluctance to take such a passive role, but the new plan could not have been more satisfactory to Raleigh. There was throughout the expedition a rather undignified scramble for places of honor, an anxiousness to be in the forefront whenever there was a chance to win distinction, from which none of the principal officers was exempt.

On June 20, a Sunday, the fleet came to anchor in the bay of San Sebastián, just off Cádiz. The city was not defenseless; a strong fort guarded the entrance to the harbor, and inside lay four of the king's great ships of war and many armed merchantmen. But the defense was disorganized; the Spanish had known about England's fleet, but had guessed it would aim for Lisbon. The council renewed its decision to make a landing to the south and capture the town before entering the bay to attack the fleet. The reasons offered suggest that it was Howard's plan that was adopted: if the town were surprised before it had time to prepare its defenses, then the fleet could enter the harbor without being subjected to devastating cannonade from the fortress and could destroy shipping there at the cost of minimal damages to itself. But when the ships' boats were lowered, it was discovered that the sea was too heavy for such an attempt; one boat capsized, resulting in several casualties, and the rest had to be taken back. According to Sir Walter Raleigh's own version of the events, he returned from an errand while the soldiers were still being disembarked, saw immediately that an attempt at landing would be impossible, and boarded Essex's vessel and told him so, "in the presence of all the colonels." Essex "excused himself, and laid it to the Lord Admiral; who, he said, would not consent to enter with the fleet, till the town were first possessed." The commanders all recognized the danger, but would not cross the admiral. However, by his testimony, Raleigh hurried to the *Ark Royal*, convinced Howard of the folly of the present course, and obtained his consent to attack the fleet first. He then returned with the good news to Essex, who shouted and threw his hat into the sea to vent his enthusiasm.[1] Sir William Monson, however, also claimed the honor for the change of plan,

1. Edward Edwards, *The Life of Sir Walter Ralegh . . . Together with his Letters,* 2 vols. (New York, 1868), 1:210–11.

although he did not suggest how it was adopted. He made no mention of Raleigh's comings and goings, but said that the day "was spent in vain, in returning messengers from one General to another." Finally, he said, "they were forced to resolve upon a course which Sir William Monson . . . advised him [Essex] to the same morning he discovered the town," which was to surprise the ships and capture the harbor "before they attempted landing." With that decision, the great question became "who should have the honour of first going in?"[2] The conflict between the two versions is one that appears again and again in accounts of the exploit. The honor that was won made each commander anxious to stress his own role, and half a dozen narratives were later written, contradicting one another at almost every point. Monson's account, though undoubtedly much exaggerated with respect to his own importance, is supported by a letter from Howard to Essex which seems to have been written that day and which indicates that Howard was not at all so stubbornly set on protecting the ships at the risk of exposing the men to drowning and death. It was written after Howard received an angry note from his co-general. The implication is strong that Essex wanted to take the troops in as planned, but that Howard had decided the waves were too high and discouraged it. Then Essex wanted to lead the ships in to attack, but Howard would not give his consent to that either. Essex, always quick to imagine insults, looked upon this attitude as a personal attack. "My lord, if I could think that you had this day received any 'gote' [sic] of scorn I should be sorry," the admiral wrote, "but I protest before God I can not think of any; for who can attempt anything when God shall cross him with the weather?" He went on then to justify his refusal to allow Essex the point of honor in the naval assault:

> But, my lord, to adventure you and the principal ships of this army, to the utter overthrow of the whole journey, I cannot like it. My duty tieth me to my instructions, and I do pray your lordship to remember your promise to her Majesty. But

2. Oppenheim, *Sir William Monson,* 1:347–48.

to have the ships destroyed without hazarding your person and the principal ships of her Majesty I can like it, and for us to give countenance unto it, and if it please you that Sir W. Ralegh may have the charge with his own ship. . . . And this far I do agree and like of; against your lordship's adventuring I do protest and so did Sir Conyers Clifford and Mr. Ashly, and so I think will all of judgment; and therefore, my honoured lord, bear with me not to lose her Majesty's favour and undo myself. I perceived by Mr. Ashly that if we had gone forward this day in setting on them it had been laid on me as the first author of it. . . . Good my lord, think there is more to do than this, and let not a mischance overthrow all, and when the spoiling of such is most likely to be requited with the loss of better. This far I dare adventure as I have set down; farther I cannot.[3]

According to Monson, Howard had been "straightly charged by her Majesty that the earl should not expose himself to danger, but out of necessity," and to care for the safety of the royal ships.[4] A role of moderation and caution had been forced upon him, which he scrupulously carried out.

Others also claimed the right to be the first to enter the harbor; that night the council gave the honor to Raleigh, after supporting Howard against Essex, but Thomas Howard as vice-admiral contested him, and successfully pleaded the privileges of his rank. That night, however, Raleigh moved his ship in so close that none could pass him. The next morning it was he who sailed first; he began to batter the galleons *St. Philip* and *St. Andrew*, which had been among the fleet that captured Sir Richard Grenville. Thomas Howard was soon after him, but Raleigh's example destroyed all thought of preserving order as each commander tried to force his way into the vanguard. Both generals had been assigned places in the body of the fleet, but Essex had never been able to hold back while others were doing battle for honor and fame, and he pushed to the front. Monson later claimed that it was he who "put him [Essex] in mind of his honour, for that many

3. *Cal. Hatfield MSS,* 6:239.
4. Oppenheim, *Sir William Monson,* 1:347.

eyes behold him." Howard found the entrance to the harbor so crowded with ships that he could not get through, so he and his son William took to a longboat in order to go where the fighting was thickest.

As the English ships entered, they found that the Spanish had taken what precautions they could. Four great warships lay across the mouth of the harbor, supported by galleys, two Lisbon galleons, three war frigates, two argosies "very strong in artillery," and perhaps forty or so armed merchantmen. After a fierce contest that lasted five or six hours, the English made ready to board; the two galleons were captured and taken home, but two of the warships were finally fired by their commanders, with the crews still aboard. As Raleigh observed the scene, many jumped into the water in flames; others hung by ropes to the ships' sides, "under water even to the lips . . . and grievously wounded." When the powder and shot on the *St. Philip* began to explode there was so great a fire that "if any man had a desire to see Hell itself, it was there most livelily figured." The Dutch squadrons had taken little part in the assault, but now they "used merciless slaughter" against the survivors until Raleigh and Howard had to row up and down beating them off, doing what they could to prevent complete destruction of the ships as well. English casualties had been few, but Raleigh himself was wounded and could not take part in the assault on the town, a fact which he bitterly resented.[5] Some twenty of the galleys were captured by Captain Robert Crosse, but others moved up the bay and later were able to make their way to the open sea. The greater part of the merchant fleet, much of it loaded with goods for Mexico, moved farther into the harbor.

Preparations now were made for an immediate assault on the town. Leading the troops ashore was an honor that Essex could not be denied; he and Sir Francis Vere landed 2,000 soldiers on a beach near the city, while others went to capture and destroy the only bridge that connected Cádiz with the mainland. The town, suffering from shortages of supplies and

5. Edwards, *The Life of Sir Walter Ralegh,* 1:216.

from the lack of a recognized military authority, had hastily put together a few companies of cavalry and foot soldiers; these came out to challenge Essex, but after some skirmishing they retreated again in such haste that many left their horses behind and scrambled over the walls. With Essex in the lead, the English were close behind. Essex himself was first on the wall, ordering his men to jump down into the streets, until Vere forced open the gates. They encountered strong resistance in the market place, where Sir John Wingfield, a regimental colonel and camp master, was killed, the only notable English casualty. But the arrival of Lord Admiral Howard with his sea regiment of 1,200 men soon put an end to a battle whose outcome had never been in serious doubt. Other resistance soon ended, and the city was captured. Some of the wealthier sort took what they could and fled to the citadel, where they hoped to negotiate terms better than abject surrender, but the rest of the population gave up. That night both Essex and Howard lodged—one at the fort and the other at the priory—in "her Majesty's city of Cales, not in fancy, but won and yet held by her soldiers' swords."[6]

Until that time, despite adolescent competition for honors and jealousies over place and precedent, the exploit had probably been managed as well as any Elizabethan military venture. The city had been taken with spectacular ease; loss of life had been minimal, the prestige gained considerable, and the prospect of plunder enormous. There had been some friction between the commanders, but the recognition of common purposes had allowed them to co-operate effectively if not harmoniously. Hopes of winning glory for self, queen, and country had made not only the generals but the whole rank of officers zealous in forwarding the attack. However, planning had been aimed simply at the capture of town and harbor; no one had considered seriously how the victory should be consolidated, how the greatest material and political gain could be realized once the fighting stopped. Even after arrival, the generals seem to have made no effort to plan, in spite of

6. *Cal. Hatfield MSS,* 6:229.

the queen's known wish and their own promises to make the expedition pay for itself and bring home great treasures. The result was that the authority of the generals suffered some collapse in a melee of plundering, and Elizabeth lost much of the wealth with which captains and private soldiers filled their own pockets. The soldiers themselves cannot be blamed; enrichment in stolen goods was a principal motive for coming, and both officers and men could justify wholesale spoilage by citing hardships, expense of service or inadequate pay, cherished military precedent, and rights of conquest. But by not controlling their men more stringently, by never meeting to form a deliberate course of procedure, and by not acting with greater initiative, the commanders lost or wasted more than they saved.

Most important was the loss of the merchant fleet. Some fifty or so ships had retreated deeper into the harbor when the warships fell; the whole English fleet blocked the way out, so they were left to their own devices while the town was being stormed. Failure to capture the merchant ships is usually laid to the lord admiral: it is suggested that he wanted no part of the pedestrian duty of taking over a fleet already defeated, so he neglected his proper duties in order to share in winning the town. Monson, however, who was a captain in Essex's own regiment, enlarges somewhat on the story. According to his version, he had—predictably—urged the earl to master the ships first, for ships brought back to England "would be always in the eyes of men, and put them in remembrance of the exploit in gaining them," while the town might be easily won but would not be long enjoyed, "and so quickly forgotten." But Essex was eager to land and fight; he took his troops ashore without consulting his co-commander, merely leaving a message suggesting that Howard should see to the ships. In spite of his admiration for Essex, Monson concluded that this was a serious fault: ". . . the earl's sudden landing . . . which should have been resolved upon mature deliberation, was a great oversight in him, and questionless the Lord Admiral found his honour a little eclipsed, which perhaps hastened his landing for his reputation sake when as he thought it more reason to have possessed their fleet."[7] Monson's story cannot be corroborated, but it is in keeping, at least, with Essex's behavior on other occasions. And Howard's quick response is what one might expect of him if he found himself suddenly left behind with instructions to do work that could well be looked after by an inferior. It has also been suggested that he felt once again the responsibility to look after the earl's safety, but it is a bit difficult to see how his presence in the battle might have protected Essex. It is sometimes said, too, that Raleigh may have been partly at fault—because of his wound he could not go ashore, but he declined an offer from some of the captains to attack the ships, in the belief that they would be safe until the next day, and allowed his officers to join the fighting on shore.

At any rate, the following day the port officers offered to pay two million ducats for the ships and their cargoes, an offer which Howard disdained, saying that he had not come to Spain for chaffering. He ordered a squadron of the lighter vessels to capture or sink the merchantmen, but before his ships were ready a fire swept through the Spanish fleet and destroyed most of the ships and whatever cargo had not been secretly unloaded. The English managed to salvage a few pieces of ordnance, but little else. The fire had been ordered, it turned out, by the duque de Medina Sidonia, Howard's old opponent, now governor of the province, who preferred to see the goods spoiled altogether rather than allow them to fall into English hands. Cargoes of oil, wine, silks, and other goods bound for the Americas were destroyed; estimates of value ranged as high as 24,000,000 ducats. The blow to Spanish finances, of course, was tremendous, but to Spain the goods were lost anyway, and the fires removed a great source of profit for the invaders.

Meanwhile, those who had taken refuge in the citadel arranged for a conditional surrender. They agreed with the generals to pay 120,000 ducats for a promise of personal safety. The English kept fifty leading citizens as hostages, sent a group to Seville to collect the ransom money with instruc-

7. Oppenheim, *Sir William Monson*, 1:351–52.

tions to return within twelve days, and allowed the others to leave peacefully. In a gesture of punctilious gallantry, the Spanish ladies were allowed to carry with them whatever personal belongings they could, an act which gained both commanders some local reputation.[8]

After the city was evacuated and measures had been taken for the safety of religious building, it was surrendered to the soldiers for still more plundering. Officers and those who had earned special merit were assigned wealthy houses, whose contents would be their shares of the prize; some areas were set aside for indiscriminate looting by the common soldiers. Pillaging occupied practically everyone but the two generals during the next days, but it was conducted in so unsystematic a fashion that some wealth was overlooked and more destroyed. Rumor had it that £11,000 had been left in the fortress. In the confusion of the capture, the customs house, which should have been a great source of wealth, had been forgotten, and when soldiers finally were sent, they found it had already been ransacked by the natives, and nearly everything of value was gone. The ships captured, of course, were to be reserved for the queen, as were other classes of goods—including ordnance, powder and shot, coin and bullion, spices, and jewels—but the soldiers were so uncontrolled and the generals, especially Essex, were so openhanded in their rewards that again much was lost which might have helped pay the expenses. Stories later circulated of great diamonds spirited away, of coffers containing hundreds of pounds disappearing, of treasures of all sorts hidden on the ships or sent home by private vessels, of chests of spices thrown away, and of silks trampled under foot.

The business of spoilage was so attractive that ships were left virtually unattended and posts unguarded from the time the city fell, which produced waste of life as well as of treasure. A detachment had gone to guard the mainland bridge, but the prospect of riches lured the officers away. The remaining soldiers got drunk on native wine; then they were

8. Devereux, *Lives and Letters of the Devereux*, 1:369; *Cal. S. P. Dom., Eliz., 1595–1597*, pp. 271–73.

set upon and killed. The bridge was broken down, and the galleys which had sought safety behind it went out again and escaped. Later these galleys hung around the edges of the English fleet and made themselves a considerable nuisance, although they were not powerful enough to inflict serious damage.

On Sunday, just a week after the fleet had first come into view, a pause in the pillaging was ordered to grant knighthood to the most conspicuous members of the company. The list was a long one; Essex was always profligate with honors, and now Howard followed his example; he created more knights at Cádiz than during the rest of his long career in the service of the crown. Always jealous of being overshadowed, he was determined to exercise every privilege that his colleague did, so instead of restraining Essex, he seconded him. That day sixty new knighthoods were conferred, thirty-three by Essex and twenty-seven by Howard. By the end of the voyage there were sixty-six knights of Cádiz—"all who deserved it or affected it or did not neglect and refuse it, as some did." Each of the commanders knighted several of his own followers but also knighted as a courtesy a few of those especially close to his colleague: it was Howard who knighted George Devereux, Essex's brother, and Gelley Merrick, his confidant and secretary; and Essex knighted Howard's son William and his son-in-law Richard Leveson. No doubt each of the new knights felt that he deserved the honor, but the rest of the country did not, and the "knights of Cales," who in doggerel verse could be bought out, along with Scottish lairds, by a yeoman of Kent, were the objects of some derision at court.

The two generals, in spite of their great expenses in setting the expedition to sea, scorned to take part in the pillage of Cádiz, a fact upon which most observers commented. They felt, perhaps, that they would receive from the queen rewards that were sweeter and more legitimate than those they could seize in a captured city. While they waited for the arrival of the ransom money, Howard undertook a polite correspondence with Medina Sidonia to suggest an exchange of prisoners.

There were thirty-one Englishmen, he discovered, in the duke's galleys; to recover them he would free as many of his own prisoners of equal or higher rank. But if the duke refused, after the gentle treatment given the people of Cádiz, he warned that "a different style of war must be followed in future." Within a few days came a galley bearing the prisoners, some of whom had been captives for many years.[9]

Since the Spaniards sent to raise the ransom money did not return within the twelve-day limit, delay in leaving became more and more dangerous. The longer they waited, the more likely became an attack from a strong land army or an ambush by a Spanish fleet. Essex was not one to shrink from such a prospect; he even wanted to lead an army into the interior to seek out the forces that Medina Sidonia was reported to be gathering. When that suggestion was rejected by the council, he proposed another: the town ought to be fortified, garrisoned, supplied, and held for the queen as a thorn in the side of the Spanish empire and a constant affront to the prestige of the Spanish arms. This, perhaps, had been his real intention from the beginning; he had pointed out the advantages of such a proceeding in the letter he sent to the Privy Council as he left England. There were ample stores of food in the town; more might be taken from the ships, and arms and powder could be supplied until reinforcements were sent from England. At first his enthusiasm and the momentum of victory carried the council. In a meeting on June 29 the generals decided that they should take only the weakest vessels home, that Thomas Howard and Raleigh would take a detachment to the Azores to watch for the West Indies flotilla, and that the rest of the ships and men would stay at Cádiz. Sir Anthony Ashley was ordered to England to inform the queen.[10]

The next day Essex let it be known that his real plan was to

9. Sir William Slyngisbie, "Relation of the Voyage to Cadiz," in *Naval Miscellany,* ed. John K. Laughton (London, 1902), 1:81–82; *Cal. Hatfield MSS,* 6:241–42.

10. Devereux, *Lives and Letters of the Devereux,* 1:353–55; Oppenheim, *Sir William Monson,* 1:352.

command Cádiz himself; he did not fancy returning home while great things could still be done. This was unthinkable: if the rest of the expedition, and Howard in particular, came home without the favorite, Elizabeth's displeasure would make the strongest tremble. And by that time sober second thoughts had cast doubts on the value of the exploit. It was true that maintaining an English garrison in a Spanish city would be a constant hindrance to Spanish effectiveness elsewhere. True, if a fleet could be maintained at Cádiz, it would make possible a blockade of the coastline and perhaps the never-accomplished capture of the West Indian flotilla. But the chances of success, especially under Essex, were remote. The garrison would be subjected to the most determined attack the Spanish empire could muster; it could expect every effort to revenge the dishonor of the capture. Keeping the garrison alive would require continual reinforcements and supplies, an outflow which would be hard to maintain. It would mean a radical departure from the queen's policy, taken without her knowledge or approval. And Essex as a commander could not be expected to hold the hostile city against a prolonged sieze; his impulsive nature and reckless chivalry were not suited to a warfare of privation and waiting in which opportunities to lead charges and scale walls would be few. So the other members of the council, led by the lord admiral, began to raise objections. They discovered that there were not sufficient supplies on the ships to last until more could be sent from England, so the council, over Essex's objections, resolved to "quit the town with as much expedition as they may."[11]

For this decision, Howard laid himself open to later criticism. Essex's biographer deplored the fact that Essex's "colleague in the chief command was so aged that the exertion attending the capture of Cádiz had exhausted his energies."[12] Essex himself could later blame the lord admiral for his caution and could attempt to claim the entire credit for what was accomplished; when Howard was honored for his role,

11. *Cal. Hatfield MSS*, 6:229.
12. Devereux, *Lives and Letters of the Devereux*, 1:371.

Essex chose to be mortally affronted. Howard's position was dictated by neither fatigue nor conservation, but by prudence. He was exercising, as he had from the beginning, his role of curbing Essex's ebullience, of moderating Essex's enthusiasm with his own common sense, and of preventing Essex from exposing himself to extreme danger. "My duty tieth me to my instructions," he had said, and it still did.

On Howard's insistence, the council prepared to give up the city. As the soldiers were re-embarked, detachments set fire to everything that would burn, and the fleet moved out of the harbor on July 4. That night it was agreed to attack again at Faro, a large town on the southern coast of Portugal. Howard, according to Monson, was "utterly against" making a landing there, for what cause it is not clear.[13] But once the fleet arrived on July 14, he demanded the right to lead the army ashore, as his colleague had led the attack at Cádiz. After some debate, however, "being distempered with the heat of the day and very faint, not able to endure a long march, by persuasion of the Earl and others, much against his will, [he] was persuaded to return to his ship." So it was Essex who again gathered to himself the few honors that were available. The town was abandoned as the English approached, and little of material value could be found. After two days, finding neither spoil nor an army to fight, Essex burned the city, and the general and his troops marched back "three great Spanish leagues" in weather "extreme hot" across "deep sand which was painful unto us." Characteristically, Essex refused the comforts of a horse to endure the same hardships as his men.[14]

A few prisoners taken at Faro said that the next town of any importance was Lagos, near Cape Saint Vincent. They commended its strength and reported that all the gentlemen of the countryside had gone there to await an attack. The news was "exceedingly acceptable" to Essex, who at once proposed that they attack; again it was the lord admiral who had to point out that if the town had been given plenty of

13. Oppenheim, *Sir William Monson*, 1:354.
14. *Cal. Hatfield MSS*, 6:268.

time to prepare its defenses, more would probably be lost than gained in making a landing. He maintained, too, that the place was nothing more than a big fishing town which had no wealth, and that the citizens were not Spanish but Portuguese, "who in their hearts were our friends." After the winning of Cádiz, he said, there could be no honor in attacking such a place, and if it were to be won, it would be at the loss of their best soldiers, "who would rather desire to die than to receive the indignity of a repulse." Essex, "much against his will, was forced to yield to these reasons," and the idea was given up.[15]

Every expedition sent out from England hoped to capture or destroy the great shipments of gold and silver from the mines of the New World, so after leaving Faro, Essex and Howard by common consent bore westward for the Azores, where they planned to lie in wait. A change of wind, however, carried them much farther north. At a new council meeting, Essex and Thomas Howard "offered, and that with great earnestness," to take twelve ships, victual them from the others, and stay behind to wait for the treasure ships. But they did not prevail; the rest of the council was ready to go home, and they knew it would be foolish to leave Essex behind in a risky enterprise. This time it was Raleigh who led the opposition, arguing the scarcity of victuals and the growing disease among the men, always a great handicap to an extended voyage. Monson felt that the real reason was the success of the pillaging at Cádiz; "the riches of Cadiz kept them that had got much from attempting more, whereas if they had been poor, want, and not honour, would have enforced them to greater enterprises."[16]

In general, later students have agreed with him; it was mainly the desire to enjoy their stolen wealth which prevented further adventuring. Such cupidity, however, did not account for Howard's conservatism; he had gained little, if anything, in material reward. His position now was probably what it had been at Faro: any further exploits would risk what they

15. Oppenheim, *Sir William Monson*, 1:354–55.
16. *Ibid.*, pp. 355–56.

had already won. And it is true that there was a kind of law of diminishing returns in operation; the longer a fleet stayed out and the more actions it attempted, the greater would be its weakness from disease and exposure and the smaller its chances of continued success. The longer they stayed in Spanish waters, the greater would be the odds that Philip II would be able to assemble a fleet of his own, as he had against Thomas Howard and Richard Grenville in 1591. Howard's prudence, however, lost its persuasiveness when the treasure fleet arrived only a few days after the English had gone. Still, there is some doubt as to what Essex could have accomplished with twelve ships manned by disgruntled sailors who wanted to go home.

In the preceding weeks many and conflicting reports had reached London as to what had happened at Cádiz. The first rumors were exuberant: Cádiz had fallen, the Spanish fleet had been destroyed, and wealth of many millions had been taken; an Italian account said that six hundred pieces of artillery and ships and goods worth two-and-a-half millions were captured. But later stories began to equivocate. Burghley got a report that 1,300 Englishmen had been slain, which he concealed from the queen, but which he confessed "much perplexed" him.[17] By mid-July, more accurate information was being received; George Carey of Cockington sent to Robert Cecil a fairly accurate account he had received from an English captive who had escaped from Sanlúcar, a few miles from Cádiz, at the time of the attack. As the later reports came, they gave more and more emphasis to the pillaging and to the loss of the merchant fleet. Elizabeth became more and more restless, more and more fearful that the profits had been squandered, and her first feelings of triumph and gratitude began to give way to irritation. At the beginning of August, Lord Burghley commenced preparations for recovering as much of the treasure as possible. A commission of gentlemen—including Sir Ferdinando Gorges, William Killigrew of the privy chamber, and Richard Carmarthen and Thomas Mills, cus-

17. Read, *Lord Burghley and Elizabeth*, p. 521.

toms officers—was sent to Plymouth, where the fleet was expected to anchor. They were reminded that "it was always intended" that the queen should be recompensed out of the prizes, so it would now be necessary to recover and value them, with the help of the generals, to pay the men out of the spoils, and to see the goods locked up and inventoried. It was further pointed out that Essex had promised to pay for a thousand of the soldiers at twopence a day, but all payments would be suspended until the spoils had been surveyed.[18]

A few days later the council began to send letters to the generals. A letter of August 7 told them that the queen had heard reports of great spoilage, so they should search all the ships before the soldiers were disembarked. They were reproached for their failure to capture the treasure fleet and were warned to ready a thousand of their men as soon as they landed to go to Ireland. If they were already in England when they got the letter, which was the case—Howard landed at Plymouth the same day—they should consider sending part of their ships back to the Azores, "for wee assure yow her Majestie greatlie affecteth the compleatinge of the vyctorie by that adventure." Two days later another letter arrived. The generals, still presumed to be at sea, should decide how to discharge the troops immediately to save unnecessary wages, since they knew ". . . howe greatlie it is to her Majesty's misliking that she be now sollicited to be put to anie further expences . . . remembring the assured promises which her Highnes saieth she received with so earnest protestacions from both your Lordships, not only to see her eased of that burthen but of assured hopes of great profitt and gayne."[19]

By August 11 it was known in London that Howard had returned. Actually, Essex arrived only a day later, but Howard, as the first commander to return, had to bear the queen's wrath. The council wrote to let him know "how ill her Majesty took it to hear of so much taken and so ill a reckoning like to be made to her." The lords did not choose to

18. *Cal. S. P. Dom., Eliz., 1595–1597*, pp. 264.
19. Dasent, *Acts of the Privy Council*, 26:84–89, 102–5.

meddle between them, but wanted Howard to know what the queen expected. Good search should be made of all ships and passengers; he should recover and preserve unused victuals which might be used for the return to the Azores; he was not to ask money for wages, "since if good search be made," it would be found that each ship had "pillage enough" to bear its own charge. So he, who had treated the matter of wages so lightly in advance, should now take the pillage and pay the men, or leave the pillage and pay no wages, whichever would be better for the queen.[20]

Actually, some of what the queen and council demanded had been anticipated by the generals. On July 9, just after leaving Cádiz, they sent written instructions to Sir Anthony Ashley and Sir Gelley Merrick, who had gone ahead with news, to arrest and examine all ships that had been in the service as they arrived at western ports, and to seize all treasure and munitions. As it turned out, their choice of commissioners was not a wise one, for both Ashley and Merrick were guilty of concealing treasures of their own and were partly to blame for some of the losses of coin and gold during the plundering spree. Now their authority conflicted with that of Gorges and his associates, which helped to confuse the matter of taking inventory.

The queen's displeasure, however, was gradually mitigated by the recovery of some of the spoil, even though the lord admiral advised her that it was impossible to send men or ships out again without several weeks of rest and refitting, by which time it probably would be too late in the year. Virtually the whole fall was spent examining the returning captains, searching for hidden spoil, and accusing and answering in an atmosphere of recriminations and hostility. Knights accused each other of corruption and malversation, of taking bribes and of gambling with the crown's profits, of selling prisoners for private gain and of despoiling each other. The council and the commissioners spent weeks trying to track down goods that had disappeared and to assess what actually had been

20. *Cal. Hatfield MSS,* 6:329–31.

salvaged. The final settlement remains obscure; in some cases gentlemen were forced to disgorge; in others, if it seemed they had merited some reward and had not taken any of the goods that the queen could claim, they were allowed to keep some or all of what they had. A correspondent of the king of Scotland summarized the scene in September: "The prosperous success of this late action of Cales hath been so strangely carried by bad advice of late, some ransacking the vessels for the Queen's advantage, some accusing their companions for their own advancement, the Queen complaining of want of care in the generals to conserve the treasure, the generals excusing themselves by impossibility in so great confusion upon the sudden taking of a town."[21] Just how much was finally recovered and how much the voyage cost cannot now be judged; Burghley's note of December, 1597, listing expenses of £38,269, may or may not be complete and may or may not have been canceled by the recovery of pillage.

In other than financial terms, however, the gain was considerable, in spite of its limitations. Elizabeth slowly recovered from her inclination "rather to find fault with that which was left undone than to praise that which was done." The official summary of the action, prepared mainly from Howard's own report and corrected by Robert Cecil, provided testimonial to the accomplishments: ". . . The Spanish King has received manifold loss hereby, his dreadful galleys being shamefully beaten, his invincible galleons and apostles taken and burnt, and his Indian fleet forced to destroy themselves. . . . The greatest magazine that has been seen has been fired and wasted; the quantity of ship provision was infinite. . . ."[22] In fact, the expedition to Cádiz was one of the great military exploits of the age; one of the principal cities of Spain had been captured and plundered and a great fleet was destroyed, with losses that were small indeed, even though Elizabeth finally did have to pay some of her soldiers' wages.

21. *Ibid.*, p. 372.
22. *Cal. S. P. Dom., Eliz., 1595–1597*, pp. 271–73.

X: *Earl of Nottingham*

In spite of some doubts as to the success of the Cádiz voyage and despite some rather unstatesmanlike attempts by the commanders to monopolize credit, the expedition still represented a high point in the careers of both Essex and Howard. For Essex it had been the justification in deed of his martial pose, which had so often failed to take substance in the past and which in fact never materialized again. He had proved himself at Cádiz to be the soldier he had been acting like at court—the first defender of the English cause in foreign lands, the military hero of a glory-minded people. For Howard, it was a satisfying sequel to the victory over the Armada; he could now spend his declining years in the immensely comfortable knowledge that he had led his nation during the two proudest moments of the reign. And the irritation the queen felt was temporary; she had a warm regard for the rival generals, both of whom continued as high in her favor as ever in the past.

But the Cádiz voyage had another and rather ugly consequence. The hostility that flared up several times between Essex and Howard gradually hardened into an obvious and lasting enmity. Howard was placed in the somewhat undignified position of being an open rival of a man young enough to be his son and attractive enough to excite the admiration of the entire country. There still were, of course, protestations of love and service between them and perhaps sincere reconciliations, but the old scars opened when subjected to new tensions.

As a rival of Essex, the lord admiral was one of a goodly company: Raleigh, Sir Robert Cecil, Lord Cobham, and sometimes others were viewed by Essex himself and by the court as his competitors and therefore his enemies. So Howard's opposition to Essex made him their natural ally. In earlier years he had maintained some independence at court, being a friend of Leicester but also a friend of Burghley and Hunsdon. Before 1595 it is not possible to place him unconditionally in any "faction" in court or council, but after the Cádiz voyage he became irrevocably a factionalist, and at critical moments a zealous one.

Actually, Howard had ties with Essex's enemies beyond his own quarrel. His relations with Raleigh had usually been friendly, although never close and sometimes rather hard to define. Raleigh had executed naval commissions that held the lord admiral's respect, and they had co-operated without friction several times in the past. In 1600, Lord Cobham, with whom Howard had never been closely associated in the past, married the widowed Lady Kildare and became Howard's son-in-law. But far more significant was the lord admiral's increasingly close association with Robert Cecil. They had been in almost daily association at court for years, from the time that Cecil began to receive responsibilities, and apparently during these years association turned to friendship. From the time Cecil first appeared as a major figure at court, during his father's last few years, Howard considered himself a devoted friend. When Cecil's wife died in January, 1597, Howard wrote that "the loss of the dearest sister I have . . . could not have grieved me more." He swore that he had not visited Cecil, "whom I do protest before the Lord, I do love as well as myself," because he had not been able to master his own sorrow. As long as God would spare his life in this troubled world, he said, there would not be "any tread on the earth that shall love you better than my poor self: and I vow it to God I think none doth or can so much as I do."[1]

At the same time, Howard and Cecil had also begun to appear as partners in commercial ventures, and they acted jointly on matters of state with increasing regularity. Both were unflagging in their attendance at court and at the council

1. *Cal. Hatfield MSS,* 7:39.

table; matters which might appropriately be considered by the council were often sent to the two of them, and they frequently signed the letters going from the council or from the queen to Ireland or to the shires. In itself, this means little; any two members of the council might do the same. But the frequency and scope of letters addressed to them or sent from them suggest that by 1597 they were beginning to handle between them much of the routine of administration, especially during those times when Essex was away from court. In many cases, reports from informants in Catholic Europe, like Edmund Palmer at Saint-Jean-de-Luz, or officers in the Low Countries, including Sir Francis Vere, were directed to them both and received joint replies. They acted together to send out reconnaisance ships into Spanish waters or to have repairs made to the harbor at Chatham; they wrote together to the Irish council to convey the queen's displeasure over the loss of the fortress at Blackwater or to offer protection to a loyal Irishman. Volumes 7 and 8 of the calendared Hatfield manuscripts contain reference after reference to co-operation in activities covering nearly the whole range of Elizabethan government.

The several surviving letters between them, mostly from the lord admiral to Cecil, indicate the easy informality of their friendship. The lord admiral rode out with Sheffield and Hunsdon to try out Cecil's hawks, then saw the queen at Hampton and wrote enthusiastically about her praise for Cecil. He described in detail how he treated his children's measles, and he gave Cecil periodic reports on his own and his wife's health. Cecil wrote to him for flowering trees the lord admiral had brought from Holland and for a water spaniel to present to the king of France. Their relationship was apparently such that they could interfere in each other's affairs without fear of offending. When Cecil went to France early in 1598, he witnessed a severe storm on the south coast that damaged naval installations and coastal defenses; he gave directions for making repairs, then wrote to the council and the admiral requesting confirmation of his instructions. When the lord admiral received a packet of letters from Plymouth in

September, 1599, he told Cecil that he "opened Mr. Stallinge's [the customs officer at Plymouth] because it was to you," and he sent the letter itself accompanied by his own advice as to what action was called for.[2] If he felt safe in opening letters directed to another officer of state, no doubt he was quite sure of that officer's friendship.

Their relationship, however, was a curious one. The lord admiral was a person rich in years, in experience, in dignities; in normal circumstances he might be expected to patronize the rising young administrator, son of an old colleague. But Robert Cecil was no ordinary administrator; he was a man of keen perception, shrewd ambition, and sure political instinct, of capacities that were apparently much greater than Howard's. He seems to have slipped very easily into the position his father had held with the lord admiral at the times when they had worked together most closely. If the relationship can be called a political partnership, then it was Robert Cecil who was the senior partner, just as Lord Burghley had been the senior partner. The lord admiral lacked the kind of ambition that requires domination over other men, just as he lacked the kind of ability that would enable him to dominate, apart from the exercise of command at sea. His ambition was for place and honor, and he was quite willing to accept political tutelage from a more vigorous personality in order to achieve them. For Cecil, of course, he was a formidable ally: Howard's name, his nearness to the queen, his entrenched position, and his martial reputation made him as valuable a friend as could be found.

Early in 1597, however, the observer at court would have judged that Howard and Cecil were being drawn together by their mutual hostility toward Essex, even though they were not at the moment voicing that hostility openly. Essex appeared in public on a friendly basis with Cecil, Raleigh, and Howard alike, although he felt obliged to contest Cecil's candidacy for the chancellery of the duchy of Lancaster and Cobham's bid for the lord wardenship of the Cinque Ports,

2. *Ibid.*, 9:347.

and to offer himself for a variety of appointments. But the accord did not last through the next year.

The triumphal return from Cádiz had been followed by disquieting rumors of new invasions which continued through the winter and early spring, keeping the country in a state of unrest. To forestall a raid, the council began to consider another offensive. Several royal warships were made ready for sea; word was sent to the Netherlands for 5,000 seasoned troops, and an expedition similar in scale to the Cádiz voyage was the result. By the end of May, Essex knew that he would lead it. Walter Devereux suggested that Essex may have been "drawn in" by the "other faction" to offer himself as the commander by the earlier proposal that he put in writing his opinion on Spanish affairs, and that his appointment was the final fruit of that effort.[3] Such a conclusion has a logical plausibility, but Essex was, in fact, the only obvious commander of a large-scale expedition, and he would have felt a personal humiliation if it had sailed under any other general. Howard was the only man of comparable reputation, and he disqualified himself. He suffered from bad health in the later weeks of the Cádiz voyage, and some of his complaints had persisted. For him now to lead a hazardous foreign invasion might mean risking his army's safety as well as his own.

The months during which the voyage was planned and undertaken were a time of apparent good feeling between Howard and Essex, though it is impossible to say how deeply the current ran. But the voyage turned out badly and Essex came home embittered. The only accomplishments were the capture of a few minor prizes and an attack by Sir Walter Raleigh on the island of Fayal, with which Essex had nothing to do. Since the latter had been carried out without Essex's knowledge, it offended him deeply, and he made Raleigh apologize before his council.

While Essex was failing in his effort to harass and impeach the Spanish but succeeding in reopening his feud with Raleigh, Burghley and his son and their friends were having

3. Devereux, *Lives and Letters of the Devereux*, 1:411–12.

better luck at home. The course of domestic affairs had been relatively smooth, which meant that there was opportunity to press on the queen Robert Cecil's obvious claims to preferment. Howard, too, was able to press a claim of his own. Just after the defeat of the Armada, the queen had intended to create several new titles of nobility, one of them for Howard. The titles had not been granted, perhaps because of Burghley's reluctance to accept. Howard, however, had none of Burghley's reservations about becoming an earl. He was not, like Burghley, from the middle classes. His forebears had been dukes as well as earls; he had some of the queen's own blood, and his services to his country, he sincerely believed, were as deserving of reward as any man's. His service in 1596 strengthened an already potent claim on his sovereign's gratitude. There is no documentary evidence—nor is it likely that much ever existed—that Howard sued to the queen for an earldom, but such honors rarely came unbidden. At any rate, on October 23, 1597, as she came from the chapel, Elizabeth handed him his patent as earl of Nottingham.

The lord admiral's elevation was timed to coincide with the opening of a new session of Parliament the following day, for which he would act once more as lord steward. His ceremony added to the pageantry of that occasion; clad in the formal robes of the earl of Pembroke, he was presented to the queen by the earls of Shrewsbury and Worcester and was attended by the earl of Cumberland, carrying his sword, and the earl of Sussex, bearing his cup and his new coronet. Elizabeth spoke graciously in acknowledging his services, and Secretary Cecil read his patent aloud. The formal patent, prepared by the Heralds' College, was designed to magnify his prestige, dwelling especially on the defeat of the Armada and on the action of the past year, when he, "jointly with our most dear cousin Robert earl of Essex . . . valiantly and honourably" took the island and city of Cádiz and destroyed a Spanish fleet. The next day, in an aura of new glamour, he presided over the formal opening ceremonies of Parliament and took his seat in the House of Lords as earl of Nottingham, lord of Effingham, lord admiral, and lord high steward pro tempore. His great offices allowed him to take precedence over every other earl except Oxford, hereditary lord chamberlain. For a man who enjoyed ceremonial and public honor, it was a moment to be savored. But the taste of honor was undoubtedly somewhat soured by new stories which reached London on the same day, that there was a Spanish fleet headed for England after all, stories which put the city in a high state of alarm for weeks. The rumors were substantially true; there was a large fleet at sea, which was turned back by storms only after it reached the Channel.

The earl of Nottingham's enjoyment of new honor and precedence was further spoiled by the return of Essex, who managed to turn the new peerage into a major political issue. Essex landed at Plymouth on October 24—his fleet having been battered by the same storms that broke up this new Spanish armada—frustrated in his hope of new military triumphs. But he went to court apparently expecting some thanks for his efforts and some sign of rejoicing at his safe return. There was some sense of relief in London, and panic over invasion rumors began to subside. But from Elizabeth he got not praise but blame: he had spent great sums of public money and accomplished little or nothing; he had disobeyed her orders in not attacking El Ferrol and in returning when he did. And Essex discovered that his censure of Raleigh had been misinterpreted; his enemies had influenced the queen to think that it had been unjustly prompted by Essex's own vanity. He was deeply wounded, even after Sir Francis Vere defended him, and went into seclusion. He could not blame the queen herself, not openly anyway, but he could vent his pique against those false friends who had showered him with good wishes when he left and then used his absence to advance themselves and destroy his own credit. His "Official Relation" of the voyage, published soon afterward, ended with a cut at "others, that have set warme at home and descant upon us": "wee know they lacked strength to performe more, and beleeve they lacke courage to adventure so much."[4]

Those who had sat comfortably by their firesides now were

4. Laura Hanes Cadwallader, *The Career of the Earl of Essex from the Islands Voyage in 1597 to his Execution in 1601* (Philadelphia, 1923), p. 22.

enjoying preferment gained without his knowledge or approval and at the cost of his reputation and prestige. Rankling recognition of that fact turned his disappointment into sullen rage. Cecil's appointment as chancellor of the duchy of Lancaster on October 10 removed from Essex's reach yet another office he had sworn to possess for his friends; there was a chance that his following at court, faced with apparent loss of influence as well as failure in the Azores, would dwindle. This was bad enough, but he chose to interpret the lord admiral's elevation as a deliberate insult. Essex now had to yield to Nottingham in the House of Lords; he bitterly imagined that the terms of the patent slighted his own role at Cádiz. He refused to appear at council or to take his seat in Parliament while such injustice prevailed. He demanded a special commission to investigate the circumstances of the capture of Cádiz, and he offered to appeal his claim for the honor of that victory to the judgment of God in single combat with Nottingham or any of his name that would defend him.

The outburst was a close approximation of a child's tantrum. He and Nottingham had been joint commanders at Cádiz, and the patent gave them joint credit, but Essex wanted public and formal acknowledgement that the principal glory belonged to him—in a document designed to flatter and honor his colleague. To quarrel with the terms of such a document, granted directly and exclusively from royal prerogative and amounting, after all, to empty ceremonial, showed poor judgment and disrespect for his sovereign. But Essex also demanded that the patent now be altered to give him his rights, a direct affront to the majesty of the queen as well as to the prestige of the new earl. Nottingham, of course, refused altogether to hear of altering the patent or of opening an investigation or of allowing a trial by combat; he, too, was sensitive on points of honor and could not admit any shadow of truth in the charges. So Essex withdrew to his house and reported that he could not attend court, council, or Parliament, because of a "violent throbbing in the temples, when exposed either to cold or to long speeches." His illness may not have been completely a pose; it often took some time to recover from the effects of a prolonged sea diet. But his excuse was not couched in terms that would permit a favorable interpretation.

The feud lasted through the fall and preoccupied the whole court. The French ambassador complained that it was impossible to get anything done because the queen refused to settle matters in Essex's absence, and Essex refused to sit at council. But after the first weeks, Nottingham's attitude became more conciliatory. In November he wrote to Essex pledging his friendship and swearing to the purity of his motives:

> If I have not dealt in all things concerning you, as I would have been dealt withal, had I been in your place, let me never enjoy the kingdom of Heaven; if there hath been any such sycophant that hath abused me, if I do not, before you, make him give himself the lie, let me bear the shame. I am not base; I know what belongth to honor; and to such an one as you are, if my love were not to you, and that I desired the continuance thereof, your Lordship's earldom should not make me write this.[5]

His appeal to Essex's generous nature did him credit, but it may have been made with an eye to his own interest. When it was written, he still had all he had been given, and if Essex had returned to court after making such an issue, it would have been at a heavy cost in injured pride. Now Essex's friends were beginning to argue that he had reason to feel aggrieved and that a compromise might restore normalcy. Parliament was in the middle of its session; it was necessary to get great sums of money for public business, which might require the support of all factions. This was a line of reasoning which might have appealed to Elizabeth herself. She was fond of Essex, in spite of his petulance, and she did want him consulted in military matters. She was repeatedly able to forgive conduct in him that would have ended the public career of a lesser man. At one point she seems to have considered giving in to Essex and sent two of her court gentlemen to him to talk about altering the patent. But the attempt failed; nothing

5. Quoted in Devereux, *Lives and Letters of the Devereux,* 1:469–70.

Nottingham would permit satisfied Essex. In December, at the queen's direct suggestion, Raleigh tried to persuade Nottingham to give in enough to permit a reconciliation, but nothing was gained. Finally, another compromise was suggested, probably by Raleigh or by Robert Cecil. Essex had pleaded for offices himself early that year; let him now be given one that would restore his formal precedence, but require him to stop the foolish talk about changing Nottingham's patent. Just before Christmas—the day after Parliament adjourned for the holiday—Elizabeth let it be known that she would appoint Essex as Earl Marshal, which would give him precedence over Nottingham under the terms of a statute dating from Henry VIII.

Essex was finally placated. It is barely possible that this was what he had been after all along. But now Nottingham felt injured; it seemed to him that the queen had given in to the insolent demands of the favorite and had taken the heart out of his own prize. His duties as lord steward now finished, he retired to Chelsea, where it was reported he intended to take his own turn at being sick.[6] His petulance, assuming that his illness was not genuine, was not as prolonged as Essex's, since he was back in his place when Parliament reopened on January 11. By February he and Essex were acting together again in the ordinary affairs of the council, the feud apparently ended. But both harbored feelings of resentment and injury. Nottingham actually came out of it rather better than Essex. He had lost a little of his newly won dignity, but, by not allowing his wounded pride to interfere with the execution of his duty, he had kept intact what was far more important, the respect and esteem of his sovereign. Although the queen did what she could to conciliate her impetuous friend, from that time on, relations between them tended to be increasingly strained. Essex was too shallow and too egocentric to realize

6. Arthur Collins, ed., *Letters and memorials of state . . . Written and collected by Sir Henry Sydney . . . the famous Sir Philip Sydney, and his brother Sir Robert Sydney . . .* , 2 vols. (London, 1746), 2:77; hereinafter cited as *Sydney Papers*.

that his credit with Elizabeth was not inexhaustable, and his arrogance became increasingly troublesome.

According to an old story, the first Howard of Effingham had been denied an earldom because he lacked the property to maintain it. When his son was elevated, he had scarcely more, but at the time he did not need a landed income—the wealth of the admiralty would support almost any dignity. And he was living as richly as any earl in the country. During the summer of 1588, while he was at sea, his household moved into the mansion of Chelsea, one of the most notable country houses near London; built by Henry VIII, it had been the main residence of his widow as long as she lived. Until 1591 it had been leased from John Stanhope, but when his lease expired, Elizabeth gave the house and its lands to Lady Howard. It was a most valuable property, still regarded as a country seat, but within a short ride of Whitehall and the court. In the next years the council met there often and the queen was entertained at least four times. It was not the least aspect of Chelsea's desirability that it was so near the queen's own residences that she never inflicted on its owner the expensive honor of entertaining the whole court for an extended time.

Chelsea was an eminently suitable base of operations for a courtly grandee, but Nottingham kept accumulating houses in and near London far beyond the requirements of practicality and comfort. Reigate and Blechingley were not inconvenient to the court, and he may still have been maintaining Esher, since he had designated it and another nearby house, Skynner's Place, Greenwich, as part of his wife's jointure. In 1591 he leased another establishment, Haling House, near Croyden. It had been taken from its Catholic owners, the Gages, at the time of the Babington plot, so Howard's lease was from the crown; when the lease expired in 1611, James I gave it to his lord admiral outright. It was a large house described later as being "in the midst of a pleasant park"; Nottingham enjoyed it enormously and spent as much time as he could there, but even after he turned Blechingley over to his son he scarcely needed another house in northern Surrey.

Part of the base in landed property the new earl lacked in 1597 was supplied in 1600 by a magnificent gift from the crown—which included yet another great house not far from court. His servants Nicholas Zouche and John Ware received in trust for him—and formally conveyed to him the next year —Merton Priory in Surrey with its attached lands, the manors of Lymington, Hampshire, and Leckhamstead, Berkshire, and the castle, manor, and lands of Donnington, Berkshire. Leckhamstead, Lymington, and Merton were all sold within a few years after the value of admiralty incomes had dropped. Donnington stayed in family hands a little longer and may have produced some income, but it also involved Nottingham in one of the most celebrated property suits of his age, so that he got very little comfort from its possession. He had claimed residence rights as constable of Windsor Castle and its forest, on the edge of which Donnington stood, but his claim was disputed by Lady Elizabeth Russell, one of the learned daughters of Sir Anthony Cooke and a formidable and determined antagonist, who had been appointed custodian in 1589. Her custodial rights ended when the castle was alienated from the crown; she then claimed rights of lease, upon which she had spent five hundred pounds in gifts. The battle lasted fifteen years and nearly became a blood feud: hostages were taken and forcibly released, fields were harvested under guard, castle doors were stormed by armed parties, and the Privy Council was appealed to for protection against the "horrible riots" of the enemy. It has been said that the opening scene of *The Merry Wives of Windsor,* in which Shallow threatens to take Falstaff before the council for beating his men, killing his deer, and breaking open his lodge, is a reference to one phase of the quarrel.[7] Lady Russell, a widow who was by no means defenseless, bombarded her nephews, Francis Bacon and Robert Cecil, with appeals and finally got a hearing before the council. Not at all overawed by that body, she insisted—even though the members were supposed to attend the king after

7. There is a detailed summary of the proceedings over Donnington in Violet A. Wilson, *Society Women of Shakespeare's Time* (London, 1924), pp. 12–15, 223–37.

dinner—on delivering herself of a long vituperative and irrelevant speech which may have helped the council to decide
against her. Nottingham's possession was finally secured by
council act in November, 1606; within two years Donnington
had been granted to his son, who leased it and then sold it to
Lionel Cranfield, to whom he was heavily in debt.

The lord admiral never stayed at Donnington for more
than a few days, with Lady Russell holding it most of the time
on one basis or another until 1603, but its income may have
helped to support for a time another great house in London
which became a favorite residence. In 1602 Nottingham was
given a lease for Arundel House, one of the best known of
London mansions, and it became his by a grant early the next
year. It had begun as the London house of the bishop of Bath
and Wells, was "new builded" by Lord Admiral Thomas
Seymour, and on his attainder was given to the earl of Arundel. When Arundel's grandson, Philip Howard, heir of the
executed duke of Norfolk, died in 1595, it returned to the
crown. It was on the Strand between Somerset House and
Essex House and possessed remarkably fine gardens extending
down to the river. Eighteenth-century writers scorned its "dull,
heavy" architecture, but the duc de Sully, who stayed there in
1607, called it "one of the finest and most commodious of any
in London." It was at Arundel House that the lord admiral
hung his Armada tapestries, and it was there that he lived
most of the time until 1607, when James I made him sell it
back to Philip Howard's son.[8]

Reigate, Blechingley, Esher, Skynner's Place, Admiral
House, Chelsea, Haling, Arundel House—all were establish-
ments within a day's ride of court. Not all of them were
maintained at the same time; Esher and Blechingley, and
maybe Admiral House on King Street, were disposed of before Nottingham moved into Arundel House. A little later he
leased another house, at Carsholton, Surrey, where in James's

8. David Hughson [Edward Pugh], *London, being an accurate
History and Description of the British Metropolis . . .* , 4 vols.
(London, 1807), 4:170; see also *Cal. Hatfield MSS*, 18:337,
478–79.

time he took the Prince of Wales to fish, and he leased a house at Deptford which would be convenient to the navy yards. His "vast" expenses in keeping up seven houses were sufficient explanation to Fuller that "he died not very wealthy."[9] Nottingham was not a great builder like Burghley, who left three mansions as "a monument of her Majesty's bountifulness to a faithful servant,"[10] but he was a "maintainer" of houses second to none in England. For twenty years after the Armada fight, and especially the years immediately after his elevation to earl, he was living with all due magnificence, surrounded by an aura of dignity, honor, and expensive glitter, all of which he thoroughly relished but which proved to be somewhat illusory.

9. Fuller, *The Worthies of England,* 2:361.
10. Read, *Lord Burghley and Elizabeth,* p. 217.

XI: *Lord General*

About six months after Nottingham's elevation, the ugly quarrel that took place over the choice of a new lord deputy for Ireland reflected Essex's changing status at court. In the heat of discussion Essex forgot himself and turned his back upon the queen with a scornful look, a flagrant disregard of court etiquette. She interpreted it, probably correctly, as a gesture of contempt, gave him an angry box on the ear, and told him to go and be hanged. Automatically, he put his hand on his sword and might have drawn it if Nottingham had not stepped between them. As he left, the unrepentant favorite swore that he would not have received such an indignity at the hands of Henry VIII himself, and again he withdrew from court to nurse his pride. This was a more serious estrangement; by now his constant attempts to monopolize favor and even to dominate the queen herself had stirred deep resentment in Elizabeth, despite her personal regard for him. Nottingham's gesture had been one of mediation, the instinctive response of the bystander, but it served once again to further his standing with Elizabeth at Essex's expense.

There was, however, no break between the two earls at this time, and during the summer, assisted by Buckhurst, they were able to deal together with the complaints of the Dutch that the English, in violation of treaty rights, were seizing Zealand ships loaded with corn for Spain. The English were immune to any threat or pressure and threatened to cut off further supplies, so the deputies from the States-General had to content themselves with a written expression of the queen's good will and her intention to follow the war to a successful conclusion.

In the past Lord Treasurer Burghley had taken the leading

part in almost all important negotiations with the Netherlands or any other foreign country, and he had exercised a moderating influence on court politics which had helped to soften the lines of factional conflict. But in August, 1598, he died, to the sorrow and loss of the queen and a great part of the court. To Nottingham, who was one of the principal official mourners at his funeral, the loss was a personal one. He had written Burghley that he cherished him like a second father; their friendship had never been seriously interrupted. Burghley's death made Nottingham the oldest and most experienced of the queen's councilors; he and Whitgift were the only men left at court who had been the queen's servants, in even an occasional and minor way, at the time the reign began. This fact created a closer bond between the admiral and his mistress in her last years, but it did not mean that Nottingham supplied Burghley's place. Burghley had been an unusual kind of political figure: deeply enmeshed in politics, yet in a sense above them; not blind to his own interests, but faithful always to a high concept of loyalty. Near the end of his life he had gained a certain aloofness from factionalism, in spite of his zeal for his son's advancement, and his presence had a steadying influence on younger and less dedicated men. Nottingham, although a devoted servant of Elizabeth, did not have that kind of maturity in 1598 and never achieved it.

Without Burghley's influence, and with the queen gradually losing the sharp edges of her perception and control, party squabbling around her intensified. By the fall of 1598 Essex was once more received into favor—to most observers as securely as ever—and again attempted to dictate to the court. In October John Chamberlain predicted that sooner or later he would be appointed master of the Court of Wards, the patronage plum which had helped to enrich Burghley and which Burghley's son coveted for himself. But the greatest issue at court was not filling Burghley's vacant posts; it was the Irish war and the selection of a commander to prosecute it.

In the summer of 1598 Hugh O'Neill, earl of Tyrone, was stirring the Irish to fresh hostilities. His victories made him the hero of the discontented Irish, and his rebellion spread from Ulster the length of Ireland. As Essex and his queen quarreled over the appointment of the lord deputy, the Irish were burning villages and attacking English castles, and Tyrone was swearing his loyalty to the king of Spain. During the fall the English garrisons were strengthened, but the provisional government proved unable to keep the rebellion from spreading. The appointment of a vigorous commander with full powers and generous support was essential if the loss of all Ireland outside the Pale was to be prevented.

The queen and most of the council now leaned toward Lord Mountjoy, a proven soldier, though still a young man, and the man who finally did bring Ireland to heel after Essex's death. But Essex objected that Mountjoy was too young, too inexperienced, a man of too little an estate and reputation and too much book-learning. The objections that he raised to other names and the qualifications that he demanded of the lord deputy seemed to indicate that he considered himself the only man able to do the job. Inevitably he became a candidate, though a rather reluctant one. As early as October 20 Chamberlain sent Dudley Carleton word of rumors that Essex would take the Irish government upon himself with a commission under the Great Seal which would allow him to return after a year if he liked.[1] Not long afterward, Francis Bacon advised his patron to be cautious; committing himself to a long campaign in Ireland and a long absence from court would risk his reputation and his influence. But Bacon apparently believed that Essex as lord deputy might not have to go to Ireland at all, that the prestige of his name and the reputation of his prowess might induce the rebels to submit.[2] Others of Essex's friends, of course, were clamorous to win their fortunes under him and gave less heed to the risks.

It is often suggested, too, that Essex's rivals at court encouraged him to offer himself, in the belief that his rashness would destroy him. It was, indeed, too choice an opportunity for

1. *Cal. S. P. Dom., Eliz., 1598–1601*, p. 110.
2. James Spedding, *The Letters and the Life of Francis Bacon*, vol. 2 (vol. 9 of *The Works of Francis Bacon*, 15 vols. [London, 1868–90]), pp. 94–129.

Cecil and Nottingham and their friends to miss. If Essex were safely removed to Ireland for months or years, he would be unable to interfere with what they believed to be sane government in England. If he won a great victory, he would come home with new powers and represent new dangers. But one of their own greatest headaches would be solved, and they would have been given many months in which to secure themselves. At any rate, the chances for such success were remote. No one yet had led the ill-equipped, disease-racked armies in Ireland to any substantial victory, and Essex was too tempestuous, too impatient, and too romantic to endure the kind of fighting he would find. So it is altogether likely that Nottingham and Cecil did all they could to draw out Essex's objections to the other names that were suggested, until he had isolated himself as the only acceptable nominee. Very early in November Cecil wrote confidentially to a friend that he believed Essex would be nominated and given complete powers to bring an end to the war, a prospect he apparently faced with complete composure.[3]

The appointment was not formally announced to the Irish government until January 14, 1599, but as early as November 24 Nottingham wrote to Essex that he had sent for Sir Henry Palmer to fit the ships for Ireland to Essex's contentment, recommending that Essex use either the *Dreadnought* or the *Antelope* for his flagship.[4]

Essex did not accept his new task with blind optimism. His famous letter of January 4 indicated that he expected the worst:

> . . . I am not ignorant what are the disadvantages of absence; the opportunities of practising enemies when they are neither encountered nor overlooked: the construction of princes under whom *Magna fama* is more dangerous than *mala*, and *successus minus quam nullus:* the difficulties of a war where the rebel that hath been hitherto ever victorious is the least enemy that I shall have against me; for without an enemy, the disease of that country consumes our armies, and if they live,

3. Cadwallader, *Career of the Earl of Essex*, pp. 29–30.
4. *Cal. Hatfield MSS*, 8:452.

yet famine and nakedness make them lose both heart and strength. And if victuals be sent over, yet there will be no means to carry it. . . . All these things which I am like to see, I do foresee.[5]

Yet he was committed to go and committed to win, if he hoped to keep any shred of reputation or influence. The cruel dilemma and evil prospects he faced took a heavy toll on his disposition. Again he gave vent to his irritability in a petty quarrel. Just after Twelfth-night, he exchanged hot words with the lord admiral over the appointment of Sir William Woodhouse, who was rumored to be a suitor for Nottingham's granddaughter, to command a company in the Low Countries. The matter was insignificant, but the quarrel was prolonged and again divided the court. A month later Chamberlain wrote that the jars between them grew worse by being daily renewed; in March the issue still was not settled.[6]

It was a bad time for a feud; an army had to be raised and supplied, ships and provisions provided, and officers selected. The lack of co-operation between two of the principal councilors necessarily handicapped and delayed preparations. The victualers had first been ordered to have their stores ready by February, but that deadline was quickly postponed for a month and had to be postponed again. On March 1 Cecil grumbled to Thomas Windebank, clerk of the signet, of the delays the squabble had caused, which no doubt forced him to take over the main burden of preparations himself.

Essex finally got away from court at the end of March and arrived in Dublin in mid-April. He commanded the biggest army sent to Ireland so far—nominally 16,000 foot and 1,300 horse. But almost immediately he began to quarrel with the English council over the inadequacy of his support and to chafe at the overwhelming difficulties of the service.

During the next few months Essex managed to arouse the suspicion and apprehension of the queen and to destroy most

5. *Ibid.*, 9:10.
6. Norman E. McClure, ed., *The Letters of John Chamberlain* (Philadelphia, 1939), 1:62, 67, 69, 72.

of his strength in the council while he tried to solve the problems of Ireland. He was a brave and experienced, though not very level-headed, soldier, and under normal conditions of warfare and against a conventional enemy he might with good luck have been able to accomplish part of what was expected of him. But in Ireland he was faced by conditions he had not expected and which the ministers in London never appreciated. Those conditions forced him to abandon the plan of attack that had been worked out at court, and he was never able to return to it. His failure to follow instructions caused alarm, then suspicion, and finally anger and hostility, which ruined him.

The queen's tone in letters to Ireland became more and more peremptory; finally she ordered Essex to stop delaying and march directly to Ulster to seek the enemy. Her harsh attitude is only partly explained by her lack of knowledge of the conditions of Irish warfare; she was confronting at the same time what seemed to be a grievous crisis at home. Invasion from Spain seemed imminent, and she felt that she might have to recall Essex or his troops for other duty; she wanted Tyrone effectively dealt with, if at all possible, before that happened. The invasion panic of the summer of 1599 was a brief one, but it was severe, and on July 30, when it started, there was no way of knowing that the danger was a mirage. Word had suddenly been received that a great fleet of a hundred ships under the *adelantado* of Castile was leaving Spain, and that the *adelantado* had vowed to capture and sack the city of London. There was no conclusive evidence that it was an invasion fleet, but intelligence reports were not always trustworthy, and there were always rumors afloat of the most alarming nature; a few weeks earlier a fleet of fishing vessels had caused a momentary panic. England had been taken by surprise when the *adelantado*'s fleet was discovered in the Channel in 1597, and the government could take no chances now. It was necessary to prepare for the worst, and the preparations taken meant new advancement in prestige and power for Lord Admiral Nottingham.

The council made some attempt at first to maintain secrecy

so as to prevent the spread of panic; when Nottingham received a report from Captain George Fenner on July 27, he sent it on to Cecil with a caution to "note it well, and to keep it unto yourself until I have spoken with you."[7] Raising a defensive army and preparing a defensive fleet, however, had to be public steps, and by August 1 London was "in a hurle as though the ennemie were at our doores."[8] The plans laid by the council in many respects repeated what had been done at the time of crisis in 1588. A fleet would be put to sea at the earliest possible moment; it would include whatever royal ships were available and what ships could be readied by the city of London and other seaports and sent from the Netherlands on short notice; it would be manned by sailors immediately pressed for duty throughout the southern ports. As in 1588, the fleet would be the first line of defense, but an army had to be raised also, in case the fleet failed to prevent a landing. The lords lieutenants of the southern counties got orders to put their local levies under arms with all speed, to see to the coastal defenses, and to place shipping under immediate embargo. To defend London and the court, a great army would be summoned from the trained bands of the city and the southern counties, and an encampment like that at Tilbury would be re-created.

If Essex had been in England at the time, he could have pressed an irresistible claim to command the army. His was still the greatest military reputation in the country. But he was not available, and in his absence Elizabeth again turned to the old friend who had presided over England's triumph in 1588 and who had shared Essex's glory in 1596. She appointed Nottingham as "Liuetenante and Captayne generall" over all the forces to be raised south of Trent for the defense of the country against foreign invasion. She authorized him to receive "apte and able Subiectes for the warres . . . well and suffetientlie armed & furnished," to direct them to whatever rendezvous seemed convenient, to assemble them into "an

7. *Cal. Hatfield MSS*, 9:249.
8. McClure, *Letters of John Chamberlain*, 1:78.

Armye or armys to staye and resist the invasion of our realme by any forraine forces," and to "order governe and Comaunde" all her subjects brought together for that purpose from any part of the realm. He was given complete authority to organize the army, to meet and defeat any invaders and rebels by whatever means he saw fit, to declare and execute martial law over the entire south of England, to "make Constitute and ordaine, Statutes, ordinances and proclamac'ons" necessary to the good government of her armies, and to punish contempt, disobedience, and disorder at his own discretion.[9]

Nottingham's commission was not formally issued until August 10, but he was acting as supreme commander of England's defensive effort from the first of the month. The patent named Lord Mountjoy to be his deputy; it allowed Nottingham to name his own marshal, and he immediately summoned Sir Francis Vere from the Netherlands. The earls of Northumberland and Sussex took command of the horse and the infantry, and Lord Hunsdon led the bodyguard. As lord admiral, Nottingham remained nominally responsible for the fleet as well, so his position was one of enormous power. However, he could not effectively command both ships and soldiers, so a separate commission was given to his friend and relative Thomas Howard to "execute upon the enemy whatsoever shall seem necessary for the defence of our kingdom, either by impeachment of his forces from landing, or using any other means to the overthrow of any fleet of the King of Spain's."[10]

The first days of August were spent in frenzied activity. Nottingham could not know precisely when the Spaniards would leave port, if they had not already gone, or on what day they would descend upon the coast. An army had to be put together from those trained bands nearest at hand, so the council on August 2 ordered 6,000 men to be levied immediately in Kent and 4,000 more in Sussex; they were to be

9. Patent Rolls, 41 Eliz., pt. 24, fol. 246, Public Record Office, London; another copy can be found in the Harleian MSS, 168/138–40.

10. *Cal. Hatfield MSS*, 9:316–17.

furnished with arms and armor and assembled at Sitting-bourne by the 10th. Another 2,000 were called from Surrey. Smaller components were summoned from Hertfordshire and other nearby counties and were to meet at Tottenham on the 12th. Letters were sent to the noblemen and bishops seeking their commitments of horse soldiers "as yf the ennemie were expected within fifteen dayes." Councilors and courtiers set an example for the rest of the country by pledging to raise whole companies of cavalry: the earl of Pembroke promised 200 horse; and Nottingham, Shrewsbury, Worcester, Northumber-land, Cecil, and Whitgift a hundred each; others "according to theyre abilitie."[11]

The city of London, the apparent target, was called upon for a tremendous effort. Chamberlain heard at first that the city had been asked to provide sixteen of "theyre best ships to defend the river" and no less than 10,000 men, of whom 6,000 would be set to training immediately, and that the whole population had been advised to ready its arms. He was probably exaggerating; later letters between Stephen Soame, the lord mayor of London, and the Privy Council mentioned twelve ships and 6,000 men, half under arms and half as reserve. To keep the Spanish from slipping past the English fleet and sailing up the Thames, Nottingham instructed the city to take the desperate step of blocking the channel with sunken ships. Soame, however, protested the "many and great inconveniences" involved and suggested instead that they ready all the ships in harbor for defense and line the banks with ordnance, or else build a floating barrier of hoys and barges, the latter of which the council allowed.[12]

England's defenses took shape with surprising speed; by August 9, nine of the London ships were already on their way to Gravesend, the 3,000 London soldiers were in arms, and foot soldiers were arriving at Sittingbourne, Gravesend, and Tottenham. On August 6, the earl of Bath, lord lieutenant of Devonshire, wrote from Plymouth that he had taken order for

11. McClure, *Letters of John Chamberlain*, 1:78, 80–81.
12. *Cal. Hatfield MSS*, 9:280–82.

the defense of the southwest: he had 2,000 men at Plymouth and 3,000 more at Dartmouth, Totnes, and Torbay; all shipping had been stayed; and surplus mariners had been dispatched to Chatham. On the 11th, Sir John Stanhope and William Meredith were commissioned as treasurers at war, and Stanhope was given a warrant on the Exchequer for £10,000, which Nottingham was already demanding in order to pay coat and conduct charges as the soldiers poured in.

As these preparations proceeded, the country continued to be swept by panic, confusion, and conflicting rumors. There was no way to disseminate the news upon which the council acted, and no wish to do so; the lower orders, then, had to guess from the preparations what was going on. One of Cecil's correspondents heard stories that the Spanish were sending 150 ships and 70 galleys; that they had 30,000 soldiers with them and would get 20,000 more from the Netherlands; that the king of Denmark was sending a fleet to assist the Spanish and the king of Scotland had 40,000 men in arms, ready to invade; that the enemy had landed at Southampton and the queen had left London by night; that the Spanish army had invaded but was broken and defeated, "with 100 other strange and fearful rumors, as much amazing the people as [if] invasion were made."[13] Henry Wake in Northampton heard it "secretly spread and whispered" that the queen was dead or dangerously ill.[14] A rumor that a landing had been made on the Isle of Wight "bred such a feare and consternation" in London, Chamberlain wrote, ". . . as I wold litle have looked for, with such a crie of women, chaining of streets and shutting of the gates as though the enemie had ben at Blackewall. I am sorry and ashamed that this weakenes and nakednes of ours on all sides shold shew yt self so apparantly as to be carried far and neere to our disgrace both with frends and foes."[15] "The vulgar sort," he told Carleton in his next letter, "cannot be perswaded but that there was some great misterie" involved in the sudden creation of an army. "Because they

13. *Ibid.*, pp. 282–83.
14. *Ibid.*, pp. 302–3.
15. McClure, *Letters of John Chamberlain*, 1:80–81.

cannot finde the reason of yt, make many wilde conjectures, and cast beyond the moone." Many believed that the queen was dying; some were so ungenerous to Nottingham as to suggest that the whole mobilization "was to shew to some that are absent, that others can be followed as well as they, and that yf occasion be, militarie services can be as well and redily ordered and directed as yf they were present."[16] The idea that a panic might have been created to show Essex that he was not needed must indeed have been the product of "vaine and frivolous ymaginations," as Chamberlain said, but such stories do suggest how much a popular hero Essex remained, despite his lack of success in Ireland, which became more and more obvious as weeks passed.

The panic that Chamberlain described may have suggested the show of bravado which took place after the horse soldiers had been mustered. With a great display of "feathers, skarfes and such other light ware," the earl of Nottingham "with all the great officers of the field came in great bravery to Powles Crosse . . . and dined with the Lord Mayor."[17] At that time it was widely believed that the Spaniards were at Brest, and it may have been felt that such a ceremonial show of martial finery might help restore public calm and give confidence to nervous Londoners.

The air of uncertainty and the sudden appearance of armies of hungry men around the city caused rapid inflation through the month of August. Late in the crisis Nottingham was obliged to issue ordinances fixing maximum prices on beer, wheat, butter, cheese, eggs, and other commodities, and victualers were prohibited from hoarding, under penalty of imprisonment and fine. Panic was never great enough to destroy the profiteering instinct, and controls remained in effect until after the troops had been dismissed.

But at the height of the panic, some expressions of doubt began to appear. From the Netherlands, Sir Francis Vere, summoned to be marshal for the army, wrote that intelligence

16. *Ibid.,* pp. 82–83.
17. *Ibid.*

reports received by the States-General indicated no preparations in Spain which would threaten England, and that the Dutch were thus reluctant to spare ships or men. From Flushing Sir Robert Sidney wrote that the story of forty ships sailing from Spain was false— he had heard that such a fleet had been proposed and debated but never decided upon and never prepared.

By the time these letters reached England, the country was beginning to calm. The army was being assembled in good order, although, as usual, the numbers called for did not materialize, and the fleet gathering at Chatham and Gravesend was preparing to sail. Nottingham himself was still apprehensive and was deeply embroiled in details. He dashed off note after note to Cecil and the council, reporting his own comings and goings and asking for advice and instructions. He found that the trained bands had neglected their drilling and that their numbers had been filled out with dead pays, which made him long for the arrival of Vere and his Dutch veterans. "I protest I think 2,000 of them worth my 8,000 of those called trained men," he grumbled. "There was never prince so deceived as her Majesty has been with this word of trained men. . . . Not one thousand . . . can so much as march in good and just order." Only half of the men levied from Sussex ever showed up, he complained: "those deceits are good to lose a realm." During these tense days Nottingham felt very keenly the weight of his responsibility: "God bless me with this heavy burden, and I pray God that one fair day breed not opinion that it will be never foul weather again. A house is sooner broken down than builded."[18]

It cannot have been long after this letter was written that the air of imminent disaster began to clear. The Spanish were supposed to have left La Coruña about the first of the month, so after two weeks, when nothing had been seen or heard of the fleet, hopes began to rise that it had been delayed or turned aside. And, despite the dismaying rawness of the troops, the country was now much better able to defend itself.

18. *Cal. Hatfield MSS,* 9:338.

On paper, Nottingham's army swelled to a formidable 30,000, though this number never actually existed in the flesh. Many of the noblemen never brought their companies of horse, and only 2,000 cavalrymen were actually mustered; the foot certainly never passed 20,000, but may not have been far from that number. So, in spite of the deceits that threatened the kingdom, the lord admiral had a massive force at his command. If well disciplined, his army could make invasion very difficult. The additional trained bands levied in the western counties for local shore defense meant, according to the estimate of the Venetian ambassador in France, that 50,000 men had been placed under arms in less than three weeks. And the trained soldiers from the Netherlands were expected daily. About August 20, the fleet, under Thomas Howard and Raleigh, was able to get under way, "prettilie stronge and in goode plight, for so short warning." It included twenty-three of the queen's ships, the twelve furnished by London, and six commandeered vessels, plus a squadron of armed hoys. Again, a re-enforcing squadron from the Dutch was looked for, which would create an impressive emergency navy.

The main function of the hastily summoned army had been to resist an invader if he came before the fleet got out; it was not meant to be more than a makeshift for a few weeks. If the danger materialized, it could be summoned again, or replaced by a more regularly constituted force, but keeping thousands of men waiting restlessly in camp at harvest season was a needless expense to the country as well as the crown. So on August 20 Nottingham began dismissing "our loving subjects assembled together by virtue of our former commandment."[19] As usual, the queen was not able to reward them as they deserved, but they all got something; some were paid for four days' service, some for five, and some for a whole week. Some levies had never been mustered; Nottingham wrote Cecil on August 22 that he planned to dismiss the trained bands of Norfolk and Suffolk without reviewing them, "and save her Majesty a day or two's pay." Nor had the reserves from

19. *Ibid.*, p. 315.

London been mustered; the day appointed was St. Bartholomew's Eve, which would bring great throngs to the city, and the artificers would stand to lose a profitable holiday, so the lord general resolved to send them home "with as much speed as is possible."[20] Dismissing the army was almost as tedious as calling it together, but a few days later Nottingham could report that all the levied horsemen were gone and that the volunteers would go the next day. By now the lord admiral himself was beginning to feel some confidence that the crisis would not come. He suggested to Cecil that word be sent to Sir Francis Vere to hold his troops in readiness on the Dutch side of the Channel rather than incur the expense of bringing them over before it was certain they would be needed.

The next day, though, there was a momentary renewal of the panic; someone said an armada had been sighted off the French coast; with favorable winds it could be landing at any time. So the Privy Council sent hasty word to London that everything be stopped: "there is now high time for every good subject to show his duty and affection to their Sovereign and country." The trained bands came out again, and available vessels were positioned in the river. Any horses that had been dismissed and were still about the city were stayed.[21] The sense of urgency was as great on August 25 as at any time, but it passed quickly. This new story had grown, it turned out, from the appearance of six galleys in La Hogue; a few days later George Fenner and Ferdinando Gorges were sent from Plymouth with what ships they could get together to capture them.

Before the end of the week Nottingham wrote Thomas Howard that the main flotilla commanded by the *adelantado*, seventy sail in all, instead of descending upon England, had gone to the Azores to intercept a Dutch treasure-hunting expedition, and that its supporting galleys had been left in port, suffering severely from hunger and disease. England had been the planned destination, but the orders had been counter-

20. *Ibid.*, p. 317.
21. *Ibid.*, p. 322.

manded from court because of the danger to the treasure fleet in the islands and because of the "rashness" of the *adelantado*. The lord admiral expected the Spaniards to stay where they were through the winter, which meant they would lose half their men by spring from disease and storms. So, unless he heard something to the contrary within a week, Howard would bring his own fleet home with all care and safety. By August 28, the month-long crisis was over, and all that remained was to complete the business of discharging and paying the troops and seeing the ships safely home.

This was the last great invasion scare during the Spanish war; four times Spain had attempted to overwhelm England with a seagoing army, and four times the attacks had failed. On two of those occasions England had been caught completely off guard, but this last time at least, in spite of panic, an impressive defending force had been put together within a few days. The fact that the country had mobilized perhaps 50,000 men and a navy of forty or so vessels in less than three weeks is a testimonial to the efficiency of Elizabeth's government, to the responsiveness of her people, and perhaps not least of all to the effectiveness of her appointed commanders.

The futility of hastily summoning an army with a great show of bravery to defy an enemy that was not there made it seem a bit ridiculous, like old men playing with war toys. But it was a serious matter, and Nottingham performed a highly creditable service. However, the scrambling haste of the mobilization does suggest that the country was in the habit of gambling with its safety. If the government received adequate warning, it would be ready to withstand attack. But the possibility that a Spanish fleet might suddenly appear off the Lizard or outside Plymouth harbor was real enough to frighten more than one Elizabethan statesman. Nottingham's truism that "one fair day [should] breed not opinion that it will never be foul weather again" expressed the need for some more permanent kind of defense arrangement and an unwillingness to accept the seas as an adequate frontier barrier. He wanted to create at least the nucleus of a standing army, but of course it was not his responsibility to find the money to support it or to convince the country of the necessity of keeping it.

England had responded quickly in the August crisis, but there was missing the great sense of common purpose and single determination which had animated Englishmen in 1588. Perhaps the country was beginning to tire of the war and of the cry of wolf—three times before the same stories had been told, and the enemy had not set foot on English soil. Perhaps there may even have been some lack of confidence in the commanders; Nottingham certainly was not as popular a general as Essex would have been, despite his dinner at Paul's Cross. London was not eager to make such a great effort for its defense, and the fathers did not consider the situation as grave as did the ministers. There was some bickering about payment for the city's share in the mobilization, and when the last flurry of rumors came on August 25, the council reminded the lord mayor and his colleagues very sharply that it wanted none of the "disputation and backwardness as heretofore hath been used, as you will answer it at your peril."[22] In the counties, too, there was some reluctance; the earl of Bath wrote that there was some dissatisfaction over the great number of people, especially those of "poor estate," assembled in the busy harvest season. But such restlessness may not have been widespread, and certainly it was no handicap to the efficiency of the mobilization. When the queen called, her subjects would still answer, though perhaps not with the former gladness of heart.

22. *Ibid.*

XII: *Essex and Elizabeth*

During the August crisis the hero of the London masses was still struggling with his own crisis in Ireland. He solved it with characteristic boldness, by substituting his own policy for the crown's, negotiating rather than fighting, and then returning to England in direct violation of Elizabeth's explicit orders. Essex must have believed that his old charms would still be enough to win the queen's forgiveness for his coming; having accomplished that, he might be able to combat the influence of his rivals and return to Ireland with new support or perhaps avoid returning at all. But his favor was too far gone to be revived by an illegal visit; complete abandonment of his duties seemed the final act of disobedience and defiance. On September 29 when he first burst in on Elizabeth "newly up" from bed, still in his muddy boots and traveling clothes, she received him kindly—as Miss Handover points out, she had no way of knowing whether or not he had an army outside.[1] But her attitude soon changed; the same afternoon she criticized him sharply and before the end of the day confined him to his chamber.

During the next few weeks it seemed possible that the factionalism of which Essex was the center might fade. On October 21 his rivals declared themselves satisfied with his submission and urged the queen to release him. But her disfavor was not lifted, and for the rest of his life Essex held uncertain status, little influence, and few prospects. His cause for the next year and a half was inevitably the cause that preoccupied court and country. In it the place of the lord

1. P. M. Handover, *The Second Cecil: The Rise to Power 1563–1604 of Sir Robert Cecil, later first Earl of Salisbury* (London, 1959), p. 196.

admiral is a bit hard to define with precision. He was the senior member of the Privy Council, and the council's function was to defend and carry out the queen's purposes concerning Essex. There is no suggestion that he felt any discomfort in this position, and he seems to have been as actively concerned as anybody in seeing that Essex did not regain favor. In November he remarked in public that with such an army as he had, Essex should have been able to drive Henry IV out of France, at which the French ambassador is said to have lodged a complaint.[2] Later, an anonymous correspondent indicated that Nottingham and Cecil might have planted informants in Essex's house, to see if anything untoward was said at the christening of his son. But this vindictiveness gradually waned; there was, after all, no reason for them to oppose Essex once the queen became his enemy. When the council met the public in the Star Chamber to defend the queen's proceedings against him, Nottingham was one of those who spoke, not so much attacking Essex as defending the queen's treatment of him, in order to stop the "railing speeches and slanderous libels" circulated in London, the spreaders of which Buckhurst said "deserve death more than those who commit open rebellion, and are easily suppressed."[3] The lord admiral dwelt upon Essex's inconsistency with himself as well as his disobedience of instructions:

> . . . he shewed how the Queene had assembled her wisest counsellors best insighted into the affaires of Ireland, to a consultation about this Irish rebellion, and that all or most of them, adiudged it fittest, first to reduce Vlster to obedience. That Essex also was of the same mind; who oftentimes had reiterated it in these words, that not the boughes of rebellion, but the root must be taken off. But that he was very sorry that he had done otherwise: withall affirming that fiue of the Queenes ships, with others, ready to be vsed in warre, had been sent ouer to Vlster, and there lay six whole moneths without any vse.[4]

2. Collins, *Sydney Papers*, 2:139.
3. *Cal. S. P. Dom., Eliz., 1598–1601*, pp. 347–54.
4. William Camden, *Annales: The True and Royall History of the famous Empresse Elizabeth* . . . (London, 1629), bk. 4, p. 249.

Nottingham's indictment cannot have been among the most telling; as a man of military experience he should have known that conditions in Ireland might not have been anticipated by even the "best insighted" councilors in England. Nor was the public justification of the queen's anger effective in producing any change. Essex remained as popular as before, and his confinement continued to be as close.

Despite the incessant appeals of his friends, it was not until mid-summer that any change was made in Essex's status, and even then the change was not in the direction he had hoped for. In June the queen summoned a commission of peers and judges to meet at York House to try Essex's crimes, on which commission Nottingham appeared. The burden of the prosecution was carried by Yelverton, Coke, and Bacon, but after Essex answered their charges Nottingham put to him one of the critical questions: what had persuaded him to abandon his duty in Ireland and force himself on the queen? Essex's reply was that he had come seeking her pardon, as Leicester had sought it under similar circumstances. When all was done, after a day-long session, the commissioners were polled as to his guilt and his sentence. Most of them were conciliatory; Essex had offended grievously against the majesty of the queen, but they did not seek his life or his total ruin. Nottingham was unwilling to see him sent to the Tower, although he might be fined, and others took similar attitudes. The final sentence was mild: Essex was to have his major offices sequestered and he was to be returned to confinement in his own house until the queen's further pleasure was known. He was held guilty of disobedience and contempt but not of disloyalty, which left open the possibility of forgiveness.

By mid-November, however, Essex apparently had given up any hope of recovery by normal means, especially after the lapse of his monopoly to license the sale of sweet wines sealed his financial destruction. He became hostile, resentful, and contemptuous so suddenly, Sir John Harington believed, as to prove him "devoide of goode reason or righte mynde."[5] He threw his house open to radical Puritans and discontented

5. Cadwallader, *Career of the Earl of Essex,* p. 73.

soldiers and it became a center for disaffected talk. Out of the talk a vague plot began to take form, directed against those who were monopolizing favor and preferment. It was thought that if only Essex could gain the queen's presence by some stratagem, all would be well; the enemies could be driven out and grievances reformed. Probably precise aims were never defined nor detailed plans made; Essex was a person who had little need for elaborate plans and felt himself under little constraint to follow them when they were put forth. Later he swore that all he had intended was to use whatever means were necessary to make his way to the queen, then to throw himself at her feet and beg for forgiveness and for the release of those who had mismanaged the state.[6] Almost as important, he hoped to force Elizabeth to recognize James of Scotland as her successor, which would insure his own position in the next reign as well as during her remaining years.

Essex's growing disaffection and the disorderly gatherings at his house and Southampton's were no secret. Nottingham and Cecil, among others, had no doubts that they were objects of whatever plotting was going on. Some of Essex's followers had said more than once that Nottingham and Cecil "and none else" were to blame for his troubles, and that if he were to go suddenly to court and kill them, "it would be a fillip matter" and "nothing would be made of it."[7]

It was a message from the Privy Council that finally touched off the explosion. On February 7, 1601, Essex was asked to appear before the council, presumably to be warned of the dangers of his conduct. The message seems to have caught Essex and his friends by surprise; only the day before, his clerk had written to the lord admiral asking for payment of £230 19s. as his maintenance for the week just past and for the weekend coming. Fearing that the plot had been found out, Essex refused to go, pleading illness. He called his closest

6. J. S. Brewer and W. Bullen, eds., *Calendar of the Carew Manuscripts preserved in the archiepiscopal library at Lambeth*, 6 vols. (London, 1867–73), 4:35–39; hereinafter cited as *Cal. Carew MSS*.

7. *Cal. Hatfield MSS*, 11:123–27.

friends together, and they decided that they must strike or perish. They had no weapons with which to capture the court, so they adopted an alternate plan—they would make an appeal to the city of London the next day, just before the end of the sermon at Paul's Cross. If the response was good, they would attempt the court; if not, they would take refuge in the countryside. That night word was sent out to Essex's friends to come at once to defend him against the plottings of Raleigh and Cobham. The next morning the crowd that gathered at his house heard that Essex would go to the queen to tell her that there were designs on his life and that, with the support of the city, he would revenge himself.

That same morning the Privy Council was in anxious session at Whitehall. Essex's exact intentions could not be known, but the tenor of his behavior was clear. Orders were sent to the constables to levy two or three hundred men to guard the court gates and to the lord mayor to raise a thousand men to defend the city. Watch was to be kept at the city gates, the Office of the Rolls, and the Tower, and the readers and benchers of the Inns of Court were to stand by with their arms. But in the hope of preventing bloodshed, four councilors who had been Essex's friends went to his house to bid the crowd disperse and to promise that if Essex had grievances against any they would be heard. Essex, however, insisted that his life was threatened and that he must defend it. His followers raised a tumult, and the councilors were taken to the house as hostages. This act of defiance made it necessary to carry though the rest of the plan, so Essex and a crowd of soldiers poured out into the streets, crying plot, murder, and treason, begging the citizens to arm. Londoners came to see but not to follow.

Robert Cecil's brother entered the city at about the same time to proclaim Essex a traitor. The citizens, despite their love for Essex, could not in all the confusion decide to risk themselves in a cause they little understood and from which they could expect no tangible gains, so not only did Essex fail to attract a following, but his own men began to slip quietly down the side streets.

Simultaneously, more elaborate precautions were being taken at court, and it was Nottingham who took charge of them. His health again was not good; he had just recovered from a severe illness and still complained that he was "troubled with some imperfections" in his head.[8] But his old commission as lieutenant general, granted during the 1599 invasion scare, was revived and he took command of the soldiers being assembled.[9] It was, no doubt, a rather ragged army that gathered at court, but it was a far more effective force than Essex had been able to attract. And it was largely in the hands of men who were loyal not only to the queen but to the lord admiral as well—his son Lord Effingham; his cousin Thomas Howard, the constable of the Tower; his son-in-law Lord Cobham; his friends Sir John Stanhope and Sir Fulke Greville; and his allies Lord Grey and Lord Burghley. A few —Cumberland and Lincoln, Compton and Sir Robert Sidney —had no personal tie with Nottingham, but their loyalty could be counted on.

By the time the force was drawn together, the attempt to storm the city had failed and Essex had decided to defend himself from his house. But as he returned, he found the way blocked near Paul's Cross by a chain and a company from the trained bands. A skirmish followed in which two or three were killed and a few wounded. Essex and his friends managed to make their way back to his house, but they discovered that Ferdinando Gorges, who had been left behind to guard the hostages, had released them, an act which weakened their position still more but which Gorges could later plead in mitigation of his own crimes.

By nightfall the lord admiral's army had surrounded the house. He and his son-in-law with three knights took possession of the garden on the river side; the others were stationed at the street entrance. Ordnance was sent for from the Tower so that the house could be blown up if necessary, and Sir Robert Sidney, again a man who had been Essex's friend, went

8. *Cal. Carew MSS*, 4:23.
9. Dasent, *Acts of the Privy Council*, 31:156.

to him to demand surrender. Essex tried to bargain; if he were given hostages, he would be willing to go to the queen, ask her pardon, and lay the blame on those who deserved it. His position was impossible and Nottingham refused all conditions, but while the ordnance was being brought he gave Lady Essex and other women in the house a chance to leave.

Essex apparently considered trying to force his way out, but finally gave up and promised to surrender if given the lord admiral's pledge that they would be treated according to their rank, that their cause would by justly heard, and that Essex might have the solace of his chaplain in prison. Nottingham again would agree to no conditions but promised to intercede for reasonable requests. And he kept his promise; the minutes of the Privy Council later record that he had moved the queen to allow the chaplain to visit the Tower, but since he was "well at his ease," a substitute was sent.[10] So about ten in the evening of February 7 the rebellion ended. The noblemen— Essex, Rutland, Southampton, Sandys, and Cromwell—came out, fell on their knees, and gave up their swords. They were taken to the archbishop's house that night and to the Tower the next day, and eighty or so of their servants and hangers-on were distributed to other prisons in the city. On the 9th the lord admiral sent to Rutland House and to Essex House for furnishings for their new quarters in the Tower; Rutland asked for his canopy bed with curtains and valance of ash-colored damask, but Essex in his despair was satisfied with whatever furniture was convenient.

The danger, such as it was, was over, but at court the state of emergency continued for weeks. It was uncertain whether London would submit peacefully to Essex's imprisonment and inevitable trial. The masses were not inclined to consider his demonstration a rebellion, and if the court seemed ready to execute him, they might be stirred to the violence they had not yet shown. Efforts to change the public mind met with a mixed reception; no doubt some were impressed with what they were told, or sufficiently confused to prevent their partici-

10. *Ibid.*, p. 165.

pation in any action. But there was loose talk among apprentices of a raid on the court, and a soldier, Thomas Lea, did try to force the court on Essex's behalf. His plot was immature and foolhardy and was quickly punished. It may, however, have been a spur to the council's proceedings, for the day after his arrest was one of great activity. Justices and constables of Middlesex were told to assemble their trained bands at Charing Cross, and garrisons under the lord admiral were to be stationed around the city to prevent any new public stirring. Ports from Plymouth to the Wash were closed in case the plotters broke free and tried to leave the country. A commission began to examine everyone who had been privy to the treason, and letters were sent to most of the noblemen of England to come to court within the week "to be further acquainted with the treasons" and to be present at the arraignment.[11]

The day after Lea's arrest the council met in public session in the Star Chamber to explain the enormity of Essex's crimes. Lord Keeper Egerton spoke with great emotion of the danger in which the queen had been placed. After Egerton broke off in tears, Nottingham praised the queen's great courage; he swore that she had been so little dismayed that she could scarcely be prevented from confronting the rebels to see if any dared to face her openly. It was Cecil who undertook the principal accusation, claiming that Essex had been planning for some years to make himself king of England and to become "Secretary, Admiral, and what not," that he would have brought over an Irish army and granted toleration to the Catholics.[12] For such charges there was no tangible evidence, but they might help to destroy Essex's credit.

When there was no new uprising, tension slowly relaxed. By February 17 the council was satisfied that there would be no escape from the Tower and allowed the ports to reopen. The levies, however, were not dismissed until the end of the month. Essex's arraignment in Westminster Hall was set for

11. *Ibid.*, pp. 150–52.
12. *Cal. S. P. Dom., Eliz., 1598–1601*, pp. 582–85.

February 19, which allowed almost two weeks for preparation of the case against him. The lords of the council themselves took part in examinations; Nottingham examined Essex at least once and pressed him to reveal the location of an incriminating black bag which some underlings said he had worn about his neck. Essex denied having it, so Sir John Payton was instructed to search his chamber for it "in the morninge early before he be up yf this come time enough." At the same time, others were told to search through a trunk for papers "or other thinges which concern her Majestie or the State." But if the black bag ever existed, Essex had burned it with his other papers the day of the rebellion, for the searches revealed nothing.[13]

Even without the black bag, however, the case against Essex when he appeared for arraignment was strong, leaving little doubt that he would be found guilty. He had held four councilors as prisoners and he had taken arms against the authority of the crown and the ministers of state. Even if there had been no suggestion of hostility against the queen herself, he had attempted to redress private grievances by a show of force against an established and successful government. Of more than forty nobles summoned, twenty-five sat on the court. Some, including Nottingham, Thomas Howard, Cobham, Grey, and Burghley, had been open enemies of Essex and his devoted but reckless colleagues, but personal animosities no longer counted for much. The proceedings lasted for ten hours without interruption. The lord admiral, among others, took part in examining witnesses from his seat on the court: he commented on the outcry against the councilors at Essex House, but the witnesses refused to say whether Essex had encouraged the disturbance or not; he pressed Sir Ferdinando Gorges, who had abandoned Essex at the last possible moment, to "unfold openly" everything that had passed between him and Essex, but Gorges had nothing to say. Still interested in the search for missing papers, Nottingham

13. Dasent, *Acts of the Privy Council*, 31:163; *Cal. Hatfield MSS*, 11:69.

wanted to know "for the better satisfacc'on of my Conscience" if Essex "did at anie tyme delyver owte anie articles in writinge . . . layinge open the projects of his purpose," but he discovered nothing.[14] After a melodramatic confrontation with Cecil, Essex was finally driven to admit that he was a traitor in the eye of the law, for which he was willing to die, but he insisted always that he had never entertained disloyal purposes. When all had been heard, the lords were polled one by one as to whether Essex and Southampton had committed treason. Beginning with the newest baron, Thomas Howard, they each pronounced them guilty.

Throughout the trial Essex had maintained a firm attitude of innocence of motive, but after sessions with the dean of Norwich and his own chaplain the next day, he asked for an interview with Egerton, Buckhurst, Nottingham, and Cecil to "discharge his conscience, and confess his great obstinacy." According to Cecil's account, he unburdened himself freely, admitting not only his treasonable intent but also blaming his confederates, including his sister, Penelope Rich, for inciting him to rebellion.[15]

Essex lived only a week after he was condemned as a traitor, in spite of whatever misgivings Elizabeth must have felt and whatever appeals friends made on his behalf. It is tempting to speculate that the council pressed the queen to follow a prompt hearing with a speedy execution of justice, while troops were still on hand to prevent any demonstration. It is said that in his confession Essex admitted that she was not safe as long as he lived. Later, when the lords urged her to pardon Tyrone, Elizabeth reproached them for the fact that they would forgive a rebel who had made war on her for seven years but would not permit her to spare Essex for one day's disobedience.[16] But it cannot be known how accurate her own retrospective feelings were.

14. Additional MSS, 34,218/210–18.
15. *Cal. Carew MSS*, 4:35–39.
16. Edward P. Cheyney, *History of England from the Defeat of the Armada to the Death of Elizabeth,* 2 vols. (London, 1914–26), 2:572.

The council was preoccupied for weeks after Essex's death in disposing of his partners in folly and settling administrative details. In these procedures it was Nottingham and Cecil who carried authority. Theirs were the signatures necessary for the payment of rewards or accounts; it was they to whom the letters of appeal and excuse were sent and to whom the seditious remarks were certified. It was their influence that the now-widowed Lady Essex still needed. Essex's property had been seized immediately after the uprising, and now she had a mountain of debts and small means to pay them. Apparently she made, or believed that she had made, a deal of some kind with Nottingham for his influence in getting some property belonging to the other plotters to help pay her husband's obligations. But as Julius Caesar had complained years before, she found his promises easy but his fulfillment wanting. Later she wrote to Cecil hoping that he would "break the ice" with the queen, adding, "My Lord Admiral, to myself and my friends, uses many kind words, but in the main point never opened his mouth, which moves me to despair, and rather to rely upon the remnant of my own hard fortune which is sure by law, than to build upon uncertainties depending upon my Lord's pleasure."[17] There is no other hint as to what had been said, but clearly Nottingham was the individual she believed would be able to plead her cause successfully.

Essex's death, in fact, left Nottingham and Cecil without serious rivals. Those who had said that they caused Essex's troubles could now say with real truth that they would rule the country. While he lived, Essex had been the center and primary cause of competition among the queen's advisers. But the more prudent of his followers had found new allegiances after his return from Ireland, and those who stayed with him were discredited and disgraced. Factionalism had been removed at the cost of destroying one faction. The influence and prestige of the admiral and the secretary stood higher than ever, and none could hope to compete with them successfully.

These were months in which Nottingham lived grandly

17. *Cal. Hatfield MSS*, 11:546–47.

and expansively, fully enjoying the gaze of the country and court which fell squarely on him and his colleague. He had stood for years on the fringes while, one by one, the more exciting and more dominant personalities disappeared. Others had come to carry on their functions, but they seemed to lack the strength or the dash of their predecessors; Nottingham had not really grown in stature except in relation to those around him. But now, not only was his influence critical, but his incomes were magnificent and his spending lavish. These were the years when he maintained as many houses as the Spanish war would support, and maintained them generously. He was an old man, but he displayed himself bravely at court in his white satins and his tawny velvets. The cut of his doublet and the style of his collar were noticed and copied by the young men who wanted to be seen. Philip Gawdy was one of those who accepted a novelty on the strength that "my L. Admyrall, and some others suche," had appeared in it.[18] Nottingham amused himself in the same fashion. When he hawked or hunted, he did it conspicuously—an Irish office-holder was driven to wish that he could command as much revenue to meet his responsibilities as the lord admiral "hath means to hunt the hare." He still extended the protection of his livery to one of the two companies of dramatic players licensed to appear at court, but there is no more evidence for 1601 than there had been for 1584 that he had a personal interest in what they were doing. Such patronage was part of the role of a great man; Nottingham apparently enjoyed the role more than the acts which gave it substance. As with other favorites and statesmen, his name lent dignity and authority to anything touched, and the magic of the connection was eagerly sought. He had accepted the stewardship of towns scattered across the country, Windsor and Scarborough being the most notable; he accepted dedications in books published on navigation and seamanship. But again his patronage tended to

18. I. H. Jeaves, ed., *Letters of Philip Gawdy* (London, 1906), p. 92.

be rather negligent, and he gave little more than his name in return. He did intercede for Windsor early in the new reign for a revised charter which the borough had long been seeking, but for the most part, even in areas where his sympathy was assured, his patronage brought no results. Richard Hakluyt dedicated the second edition of his *Principal Navigations* to him—with fulsome accounts of the defeat of the Armada and the capture of Cádiz—in the hope that the lord admiral would endow a permanent lectureship in the art of navigation. But Nottingham did not choose to do so, and there would have been no public instruction in the field had navigation not been included in the offering of Gresham College.[19]

Nottingham also tended to be somewhat diffident in his cultivation of the parliamentary following that most of the court figures maintained to one degree or other. It was the perennial hope of the queen and council to find Parliament diligent, tractable, and co-operative; those individuals like Nottingham, who had been raised to great heights by chance, industry, ambition, and royal grace, could be expected to marshal their followers and use their own resources to help make it so. Nottingham did, but only rather offhandedly. He was almost uniquely fitted by inheritance, marriage, and office to be valuable, and for several years there was a sizable group in Commons predisposed to loyalty at least partly because of some tie with him. When Elizabeth's last Parliament met in October, 1601, that collection was at its largest. Two of Nottingham's sons were knights of the shire, for Surrey and for Sussex, and he had dependents and relatives sitting for Reigate and Blechingley, boroughs that were for a time under his outright control, for Windsor, Appleby, King's Lynn, Malmesbury, and Cardiff—ten or eleven members in all.[20] But two of his dependents, Sir Richard Trevor and Sir Robert Mansell, had tried for county seats they did not get, and as far

19. See David W. Waters, *The Art of Navigation in England in Elizabethan and Early Stuart Times* (London, 1958), pp. 242–43.

20. For a fuller account of Nottingham's political patronage, see *Journal of Modern History,* 39 (1967):215–32.

as can be seen, the lord admiral had not tried to help them.[21] Nor did he exert any control over those who were his followers; for the most part they did not speak up even on issues that affected him directly. Largely self-created, the following existed, but Nottingham did not really try to build it into a power bloc, as Essex had with his Welsh following a few years earlier.

In spite of some carelessness in the use of power, Nottingham and Cecil had never commanded greater influence. Circumstances, however, gave their triumph a rather hollow ring. The queen was an old woman; her health and her powers were declining; she was often ailing and more often moody. Logic argued that she would not live much longer, and when she died their powers would die with her. It was, in a sense, a kind of caretaker government in their hands. But age, infirmity, or lack of contradictory advice did not mean that Elizabeth delivered herself up to them; she was not to be ruled by a secretary any more than she had allowed herself to be ruled by a soldier. If anything, she became rather harder to govern as she saw her death approaching.

Nor did the death of Essex mean that there was no more competition for the gifts of office or honor from the crown. Letters of observers during the next months reflect the passionate personal ambitions, eager cultivation of the great, and the hypocrisy of commitments which may have come to full flower while Essex lived, but which continued to flourish after he had become the victim of his own ambitions. It was, in fact, an atmosphere of suspicion in which the most accomplished practitioners felt ill at ease. Cecil, whose power had become the envy of all, including those who had been his friends, wrote Sir George Carew early in 1602 that "of all our number," except for two persons identified by ciphers, presumably

21. Full accounts of these elections are given in John E. Neale, "Three Elizabethan Elections," *English Historical Review,* 46 (1931):219ff.; A. H. Dodd, "North Wales in the Essex Revolt of 1601," *English Historical Review,* 59 (1944):359ff.; and A. Hassell Smith, "The Elizabethan Gentry of Norfolk: Office-holding and faction" (diss., University of London, 1959), pp. 322ff.

Nottingham and Buckhurst, "I have none but vipers."[22] To Nottingham he had already confessed "so ominous a spirit" that he could "yield to my genius no other reckoning than to assure it, that whatsoever can wound me will betide me."[23]

Nottingham and Cecil could not be overborne, but every courtier, if he maintained his following, had to be an advocate for his friends. Now the problem of succession to the crown made the competition especially urgent. Those with established places stood to lose them if they were not high in the favor of the successor; those who had not fulfilled their ambitions in the old reign hoped to do so in the new if they cultivated the heir assiduously enough. But the situation was complicated by the lack of a recognized, legitimate heir apparent; for reasons of policy and preference Elizabeth steadfastly refused to discuss what would happen after her death. However, though no direct heir existed, the crown was not "like to fall to the ground for want of heads that claims to wear it." Thomas Wilson listed twelve foreign princes and English noblemen with claims. All, he found, suffered from some kind of handicap—foreign allegiance, bastardy, sex, or religion—but one of them had to succeed, and those courtiers who had been the instruments of decision could reap a rich harvest of gratitude. So talk of a successor was a matter in which "the pulse beates extreamely,"[24] in spite of the queen's strict prohibition of discussion. Nottingham's pulse was no less affected than others, but it is significant that he took no overt part in any intrigue; Cecil looked after his interests.

While he was yet a figure of influence, Essex had been one of the most avid of the speculators in succession. He, like Thomas Wilson and probably most other Englishmen, believed that "the King of Scotland will carry it." Along with many others, including Sir Walter Raleigh and Sir Robert Cecil, he had sent James expressions of good will and offers of service. But always the monopolist, he had undertaken to

22. *Cal. Carew MSS*, 4:221.
23. Quoted in Handover, *The Second Cecil*, p. 274.
24. Thomas Wilson, "The State of England, Anno Dom. 1600," in *Camden Miscellany*, vol. 16 (London, 1936), p. 2.

freeze out his rivals and make James owe England's crown to him alone, particularly after his relationship with Elizabeth turned sour. When he tried to raise the city, Essex had used the story that his enemies were planning to force the Catholic infanta on the nation; he repeated the charge, now aimed specifically at Cecil, at his arraignment, until Cecil in great anger forced him to back down.

Despite Essex's retreat, there was almost inevitably some truth to the charge that Cecil had negotiated with the infanta and others, though it would have been a mortal affront to Elizabeth to admit it. Cecil and Nottingham, regardless of which candidate they found most suitable, could not afford to risk their futures on one. It was suggested at one point that Cecil, a widower, might marry Lady Arabella Stuart, an alternative representative of the Scottish line; although he swore more than once that "I know no soul on earth that I am married unto, or would be if I might,"[25] he still might profit by a flirtation if her candidacy became stronger. Another time both Nottingham and Cecil were identified with Lord Beauchamp, son of the earl of Hertford and the most prominent heir in the line of the younger daughter of Henry VII. A Catholic letter deciphered in November, 1600, noted that Beauchamp was related by marriage to Sir John Stanhope, a friend of the lord admiral and Cecil and a favorite of the queen, and that the lord admiral's friendship with Hertford was notorious, even after the death of his sister, who was Hertford's second wife.[26]

Father Leo Hicks showed that Cecil, Nottingham, and Buckhurst had at least passing interest in other candidates as well, specifically the Spanish infanta, and that especially in 1600 they were not opposed to one that could command Spanish and Catholic support. If Essex managed to poison James VI against them, then their best hope might be to oppose Scottish influence with Spanish. The interest in Span-

25. *Cal. Carew MSS*, 4:221; Handover, *The Second Cecil*, p. 244.
26. *Calendar of State Papers, Domestic Series, of the reigns of Elizabeth and James I, Addenda, 1582–1625* (London, 1872), p. 408.

ish claimants was a limited one tied to the factional struggles of the English Catholics, as Joel Hurstfield's article has indicated.[27] But it is interesting to note that in the correspondence Cecil undertook with the infanta's agents, even though great importance was placed on Nottingham's control of the fleet, Catholic spokesmen did not approach him directly. Father Persons explained to Philip III's representative in Rome that the English Catholics "do not wish that there should be any negotiations about this with the Admiral at the present time as he is a simple man and little able to guard a secret, but say that they will meantime keep on close terms of friendship with him by looking after his interests, so that they can always be sure of him."[28] This suggestion is highly damning if it can be believed. It is made more plausible by the fact that Nottingham took no direct part in intrigues with any of the contenders, although his "interests" were protected because of his alliance with Cecil. He wrote no letters to the infanta or her agents, so far as can be determined; he carried on no correspondence with James of Scotland. It was always assumed that his resources and influence were at the disposal of Cecil and whichever candidate Cecil chose.

Nottingham's letters from the period, however, do not altogether support a diagnosis of advancing senility. He was deeply involved with every phase of the management of the war in Ireland, including the recruitment and control of secret agents against the Irish rebels. He received frequent reports, often jointly with Cecil, from intelligence agents on the Continent, and they kept up a regular correspondence with Sir Francis Vere on the state of the Dutch war. Management of the navy was still as much in his hands as it had been in 1587 or 1591, and his attendance at the Privy Council was con-

27. Joel Hurstfield, "The Succession Struggle in Late Elizabethan England," in *Elizabethan Government and Society: Essays presented to Sir John Neale*, ed. S. T. Bindoff, J. Hurstfield, and C. H. Williams (London, 1961), pp. 369–96.

28. Leo Hicks, S.J., "Sir Robert Cecil, Father Persons and the Succession, 1600–1601," *Archivum Historicum Societatis Iesu*, 24 (1955):112–13, 125.

stant; there is no suggestion that he talked too freely about what was going on in the council or the admiralty, although much of the council's debates and some naval affairs were kept from the public. It must be admitted, though, that there is a difference between keeping secrets of state and successfully carrying on intrigues that would be technically illegal and certainly risky. Nottingham always thought of himself as a plain, blunt man who disclaimed any pretensions of eloquence and who lacked the sophistry to conceal his meaning in courtierlike language. He was willing, to everyone's satisfaction, to trust his friend with the safety of his fortunes in the succession while he busied himself with the ordinary affairs of state. He chose not to trust himself any more than the English Catholics would be willing to trust him in devious and compromising correspondences.

A similar situation came to exist concerning Cecil's intrigues with Scotland. After Essex died, it was in James's interest to cultivate the dominant group at court, just as it was in Cecil's interest to be on good terms with the likeliest heir. Correspondence between them was conducted through a third party selected by James, Lord Henry Howard, who had been an intermediary with Essex. It was an odd choice; Henry Howard had maintained no special connection with Cecil or most of Cecil's friends. He was a man notable both for his learning and for his treachery, a man of consuming hatreds and ambitions, a man of unlimited subtlety and highly refined corruption. He had thoroughly ingratiated himself with the elaborate flatteries that James VI enjoyed, and now he was designated as the instrument for securing the succession. The correspondence between Cecil and James lasted until Elizabeth's death, and it is universally given credit for preparing the way for a peaceful succession.

At first only Cecil and Henry Howard were privy to the Scottish letters, but in 1602 two others were told. These have been identified almost certainly as Nottingham and his cousin, Lord Thomas Howard, Henry Howard's nephew. Miss Handover believes that it was Thomas who was brought in first, the lord admiral a few months later.[29] In the absence of absolute proof, it would seem more likely that it was Nottingham—higher in office and prestige, closer to Elizabeth, the old friend and ally of Cecil, and the man whose control of the fleet would make him indispensable in case of foreign intervention—who would be the more valuable; it is also likely that he was brought in at Cecil's suggestion, and Lord Thomas, a rising man who was to become Cecil's close friend and the logical successor to the lord admiral, then completed the circle. But in whatever order they entered the intrigue, Nottingham left the negotiations to his colleagues; there are few identifiable references to him in James's secret letters, but his full support never seems to have been in any doubt.

Henry Howard shared some of the monopolistic tendencies of his earlier patron; he wanted to be the only tie between the English court and the Scottish king, the indispensable agent of a successful succession. But there were many others who felt the same needs as he and who were casting their bread upon the rising flood of Scottish expectations. Timely pledges of loyalty and service might bring rewards to more than one hungry courtier. Insofar as each one stood to gain James's trust, to that degree he threatened Howard's own position. Relentlessly he undermined all likely rivals. Against the most attractive, Sir Walter Raleigh, he directed a campaign of vituperation which was to have tragic consequences.

This campaign was one that left the lord admiral, as a confidant of Cecil and an ally of Henry Howard, in an irregular and uncomfortable position. His ties were far closer with Raleigh—a faithful friend throughout the Essex crisis and longer—than with Henry Howard, who had stayed with Essex as long as there was any chance he might succeed. More important, Raleigh's collaborator in succession intrigue was Henry Lord Cobham, brother of Cecil's late wife and still his protégé at court, but now married to the widowed countess of

29. Handover, *The Second Cecil*, p. 287; see also D. H. Willson, *King James VI and I* (New York, 1956), p. 152.

Kildare, Nottingham's somewhat tempestuous daughter. The marriage was not particularly successful, but both husband and wife were among the many who would have liked to have a hand in the succession decision. When he joined Raleigh and Northumberland in making approaches to King James, Cobham incurred Henry Howard's devastating enmity and complicated his own relationship with his father-in-law. Howard was so successful in poisoning James against the whole Raleigh group that when Cobham's brother became involved in Watson's conspiracy, James was ready to believe that Cobham and Raleigh were the true mainsprings of the treason.

The lively and strong-minded Lady Kildare was largely left out of her husband's involvements, but she was too restless and ambitious to keep her fingers out of the succession pie. She was feuding with Lady Raleigh, who blamed Lady Kildare for the fact that she had not received the queen's pardon after her secret marriage, and she was not on good terms with her husband. So she wrote to James independently and got a favorable answer. The possibility that she might become an alternative channel of communication with England was dim, but her correspondence made her a source of embarrassment to her husband and an additional source of danger to Henry Howard, who described her to James as indiscreet and violent.

James was easily persuaded to break off writing to Lady Kildare, but her efforts to find favor were not abandoned. After Elizabeth died, she got herself appointed as one of the two countesses to lead a delegation of court ladies to meet Queen Anne; they were to await her at Berwick, but Lady Kildare rushed on to Edinburgh—despite reports of plague—in hopes of being first in line for posts in the privy chamber. By that time her hapless husband was already in the Tower, accused of a treason he was probably incapable even of conceiving. It is perhaps surprising for that age that his ruin did not involve others, not even his wife, and certainly not his father-in-law. Nottingham was a man upon whom ties of blood exerted a powerful influence, but those ties did not encompass a dangerous son-in-law. The exclusion was made painless by the fact that he was not abandoning the daughter along with her husband. Indeed, parental indignation may have helped bring about Nottingham's rejection of the "Durham house crew." If Henry Howard can be trusted in the matter, by early 1602 the lord admiral had become so estranged from Cobham and his friends as to wish "from his soul that he had but the same commission to carry the cannon to Durham House that he had this time twelve months to carry it to Essex House, to prove what sport he could make in that fellowship."[30]

For personal reasons and for reasons of national interest, Nottingham was wholly faithful to his commitment, even though the commitment would involve him in his son-in-law's destruction and would throw his daughter on the mercy of the crown for support. His faithfulness cannot, however, be attributed to blood ties with other members of his faction. He was allied with Cecil and Henry Howard because it was in his interest, not because he was a Howard. Much is often made of the clannishness of the Howards, but with Henry Howard he never had been and never would be close. He was a first cousin, in half blood, of Lord Henry's father. Henry had been brought up as a Catholic, had intrigued with Mary Stuart, had been in and out of the Tower. Only once had the lord admiral shown himself to be conscious of a relationship, when in the years of the Spanish crisis he provided Henry with rooms and gave him a Spanish prisoner to interrogate. In this Henry managed merely to cast suspicion on his own loyalty, and he got no more patronage. There is nothing which indicates any common feeling or family loyalty between them until their alliances with Cecil brought them together. Nor, in fact, was there any warm feeling after both had gained high office under James I. The "Howard party" for the next several years seems to have been of Cecil's making and under Cecil's domination. Each of the three Howards who belonged to it had one thing principally in common—their ambitions—and Cecil was the leader able to bring them to fulfillment. These ambitions were enough to give them unity for the moment, and enough

30. Edwards, *Sir Walter Ralegh*, 1:311.

to insure their responsiveness to Cecil's initiative. "In my conscience," he wrote Lord Henry, "never treble strings were higher stretched than all the race of your kinsmen are, that have any participation of this matter."[31]

However, no matter how anxious the Howards were, they were almost as important to Cecil as he was to them. Henry was the vessel the Scottish king's capricious fancy had chosen; as long as he enjoyed James's confidence, he was automatically a key figure. Nottingham alone had authority to put the country in readiness in case Cecil's efforts were challenged from abroad. His friendship, therefore, meant a great deal to the success of the enterprise; perhaps even more important, his determined opposition could have killed it.

The pattern of the last phase of the succession crisis, then, was set. Cecil and his friends, secure in their secret knowledge of James's confidence, laid their plans; each was willing to give up personal relationships and former alliances if they seemed to interfere. Thus, when James came to England, he was ready to reward his faithful servants and to brand as flatterers and dissimulators those who had tried without success to become the channels through which the sovereignty would pass. The alliance between Cecil and the three Howards held firm through the early years of the new reign as well. Its members were able to entrench themselves so firmly that they came to constitute the nucleus of the council, a core of power in matters of policy and in the patronage for which the court clamored. As such the Howard-Cecil alliance did much to create the atmosphere of the Jacobean court.

The succession negotiations were, of course, strictly secret, and one of the most important aspects of Cecil's success was that he was able to serve both Elizabeth and James without conflict or, in a fundamental sense, even a division of loyalty. The correspondence had begun in good time to smooth the rough edges of the relationship between the two rulers, but it had begun none too soon for the safety of England. Later in 1601 the queen's health began to fail, and it deteriorated even

31. Handover, *The Second Cecil*, p. 274.

more seriously in 1602. At times Elizabeth seemed quite as vigorous as ever, dancing a galliard, riding, taking part in many activities, walking in her garden. But periods of indisposition became increasingly regular. Close observers could see that part of her heartiness was a pose and that she would not live years more.

During the same period, Nottingham must have wondered if he would long outlive his mistress. His health, like the queen's, had been good; he had survived long periods of sea duty with no serious effects, and even though he fell ill on his return from Cádiz, he certainly suffered no more infirmities than Essex. He was a few years younger than Elizabeth, but he too was now suffering from more frequent illnesses. When Essex made his foolhardy ride through London, Nottingham had just returned to court after an illness he described as severe, though he had missed the meetings of the Privy Council for only a week. It is likely that his sickness had been a cold or an ague; on January 26, 1601, he wrote Cecil that his wife was "extremely ill" with a cold, as bad as he had ever seen, and that nine in his house had fallen sick of agues within three days. Later that year and the next he apologized to Cecil in occasional letters that the unsteadiness of his hand made it necessary to use a secretary, and that at least once he had been compelled to write "from aboard my bed." But in April, 1602, he was still vigorous enough to meet Cecil for an afternoon of hawking.[32]

More distressing a sign of the passage of time was the growing infirmity of his wife. The illness of January, 1601, proved to be the beginning of a long decline which paralleled that of the queen. By mid-September, 1602, she was gravely ill; "God knoweth," Nottingham wrote Cecil, ". . . how long I shall have the comfort of my good wife, and therefore am, for the comfort of her and myself, desirous to be with her as much as I can, for I find it doth comfort her more than any physic can, and I am not yet out of hope of her recovery."[33]

32. *Cal. Hatfield MSS*, 11:19; 12:102.
33. *Ibid.*, 12:376–77.

She did recover sufficiently to allow her husband to return to court and to take an active part in entertaining the queen during the winter. But early in the new year her afflictions returned, this time in an aggravated fashion. On February 22, 1603, Nottingham added a postscript to a letter about the recovery of pirate goods: "My wife hath had an extreme fit of 38 hours and is not yet out of it. The Lord comfort her and me." Two days later she died at Arundel House.[34] Chamberlain, writing on the day of her burial, noticed that the lord admiral was affected "exceding grevously," but Philip Gawdy thought that "her Majestie tooke muche more heavyly than my Lorde."

Both reports might be near the truth. Lady Nottingham had lived in harmony with her husband for more than thirty years; during that time she had been a political and social asset of the greatest importance as well, presumably, as a devoted wife. Nottingham did not often express himself emotionally, and seldom mentioned his wife in letters, but the expressions of affection and concern during her illness were real. Regardless of what came later, he was genuinely grieved at her death.

However, during these same weeks it was the queen herself who was the center of all public concern, and she was visibly affected by Lady Nottingham's death. An intercepted letter written early in March suggested that she had remained ever since in "a deep melancholy, with conceit of her own death," complaining "of many infirmities suddenly to have overtaken her."[35] The death of almost the last of her female contemporaries seemed to be symbolic of her own hastening end.

Until shortly before Lady Nottingham's death, in fact, the queen had seemed in good spirits and had taken part in an active Christmas season, planned to keep her from moving the court to Richmond. The lord admiral's feast at Arundel House on December 23 was the last of many state and informal visits to an old friend, but Chamberlain reported that the affair was "nothing extraordinary." The court had somehow been led to

34. Thomas Faulkner, *An Historical and Geographical Description of Chelsea and its Environs*, 2 vols. (London, 1829), 2:128.
35. Devereux, *Lives and Letters of the Devereux*, 2:207.

expect that Nottingham would present Elizabeth with the great tapestries celebrating the victory over the Armada which he had ordered from the Netherlands, but his gift was "only a whole suit of apparel."[36] Perhaps he felt that the tapestries might be interpreted by the queen as a farewell offering, a recognition that there would probably be no more occasions on which to give them.

The banqueting did have the effect of keeping the court in the city through Christmas, but, nevertheless, Elizabeth went to Richmond at the end of January. On February 6, 1603, she was well enough to receive the Venetian ambassador, but after Lady Nottingham's fatal illness she went out no more. The French ambassador believed that the profession of grief given out at court was merely a device to cover her own illness; he heard that she had become almost unable to eat or sleep, and that she was distressed about Irish affairs, about Arabella Stuart's marriage to the earl of Hertford, and about her misgivings over Essex's death.[37]

The ambassador's suspicions were soon confirmed. Elizabeth had planned to attend services in the great chapel on March 21, but when the time came she was not able to go. She sent word that she would be in the small chapel, but finally gave that up and heard the sermon from her privy chamber, lying on cushions near the door. She remained there for three days and nights, refusing to go to bed. It became apparent to the court that she was dying. Nottingham, who had been away from the court since his wife's death, was sent for, and "what by fair means, what by force" he managed to get her to bed. She refused all remedies and continued to grow worse, as Sir Robert Carey said, "because she would do so."[38] During these last hours, Nottingham was one of the two or three who were almost constantly at her bedside, and, according to one account, it was he who finally insisted on knowing her meaning about the succession, she gasping in reply that the new king should be "our cousin of Scotland."[39] According

36. Nichols, *Progresses and public processions,* 3:601–2.
37. Devereux, *Lives and Letters of the Devereux,* 2:205.
38. Carey, *Memoirs of Robert Carey,* p. 119.
39. Cotton MSS, Titus 107/46, British Museum, London.

to Carey, however, she had by that time lost her speech and called the council to her by signs, "and by putting her hand to her head, when the King of Scots was named, . . . they all knew he was the man she desired should reign after her."[40] She was unconscious almost the rest of the day and died in the early hours of March 24.

This dramatic deathbed scene may or may not have taken place. Those present were, of course, vitally committed to the interests of the person she indicated, so it is entirely possible that she avoided the subject at death as successfully as she had in life, and that the story was created to help insure the peaceful acceptance of James of Scotland. However, once the queen recognized that she was dying, naming a successor would no longer endanger her position, and James was the logical candidate.

It is said that as soon as the councilors knew the queen was dead they retired to the secretary's room to prepare the proclamation of James I. Other steps had already been taken to insure the peace of the country—a watch was being maintained in London, guards and gentlemen pensioners had been alerted, lords lieutenants had been warned to prevent unusual assemblies, and the fleet under Sir Richard Leveson had been stationed to guard the Channel. But rather more significant was the fact that the council, thanks to the preparations that had been made by Cecil and his friends and to their presence in the key positions of government, was ready immediately to enforce the king's peace. Membership in the Privy Council and appointments in office had technically expired, but no lapse of authority which might breed civil disorder could be permitted; the council continued to meet almost daily, often at the house of the lord admiral, until its authority was formally renewed by James I. Because James was proclaimed immediately—to the satisfaction of a great part of the population—and because continuity in the powers of the crown was assured until he arrived, there was never any real danger of popular disturbance or disputed title, in spite of the inevitable disap-

40. Carey, *Memoirs of Robert Carey,* pp. 119–20.

pointment of other claimants, minority elements, and foreign powers. For this peaceful acceptance of the new order, Nottingham could take at least a share of the credit—as well as claim a share of the rewards.

Before James I came to claim his throne, Elizabeth was duly buried, with all suitable ceremonies. Her funeral at Westminster Abbey was observed just three days after Lady Nottingham was buried at Chelsea. Elizabeth's funeral was splendid, and in it the old lord admiral had a conspicuous place, walking directly behind the chief mourner, the old marchioness of Northampton. The sober panoply of the ceremony had been described often—the gentlemen pensioners marching solemnly with halberts pointed down; the earl of Worcester leading the riderless horse; the army of noble mourners and the crowd of poor ones; the great officeholders walking two by two; the leaden coffin surmounted by the wax image of the queen in her robes of state.

Nottingham had always taken pleasure in great public spectacles in the past, but as he followed the queen's coffin his reflections must have been sober indeed. He had buried his wife and his queen within the week, and now he surely felt a deep sense of isolation and loneliness. He was surrounded by men who were, for the most part, much younger, whose tenure in the service of the crown could not have matched his by half. It is difficult to see how Nottingham could have avoided wondering if his career, too, were not about over. No one could have anticipated that he would take a new wife within the year and begin a new career as a courtier under James I, a career that would last another fifteen years and end, not in death even then, but in retirement into years of obscurity. At the time of the funeral he must have faced the new reign with some serious misgivings. He had powerful friends and assurances of a kind reception by the king, but as an old man with weakening powers, he would be forced to compete for favors with younger and quicker individuals, to use the talents of the courtier, which he had never claimed to possess, not to gain new greatness but to hold onto what he had.

XIII: *An Old Man in a New Age*

By the time the late queen was buried, the court had begun to orient itself as rapidly as possible toward the north. Thanks to the precautions the council had taken in advance and to the general approval of James as the designated successor, there was no challenge and no unrest. But there was a general anxiousness at court—a recognition that what had been won or not won from the old ruler no longer held good, that all preferment would have to be confirmed anew, and that those who reached the king's ear first stood the best chance of having prayers answered. The new sovereign encouraged a deluge of subservience by the rash generosity with which he rewarded those who knelt before him to offer obedience as he made his triumphal entry from Scotland. It was a dangerous atmosphere that was being created; the king was posing as the careless dispenser of an everlasting bounty, feeding upon the egregious flatteries of job-seekers and showering his blessings on anyone who would parade his gratitude to receive them. The aura of unrestrained competitiveness which surrounded the king during these first weeks left its mark on the entire reign.

The principal councilors could not, of course, join in the stampede to the king's presence; their age, the dignity of the offices they had held, and the responsibilities essential to maintaining continuity in government demanded that they stay in London, even though James summoned Cecil to meet him at York. Those in Cecil's circle, including the lord admiral, had reason to believe that their places in the king's favor were safe, particularly since word had been sent from Scotland that all of Elizabeth's council members would be continued at their posts. But Nottingham, among others, felt that a few phrases of graceful flattery would do no harm; James's appetite for praise had already been demonstrated. So after Cecil left to join the king, the lord admiral sent him a draft of what he hoped to say, asking his friend to add those "curious words" which would keep his address from being too "barren."[1] Apparently what Nottingham said was well received; he met the king at Theobalds on May 3, along with much of the rest of the court, and the next morning James rode between him and Northumberland into Enfield Chace. At Theobalds, too, he was one of those specifically named to the commission to consider the needs of the king's household, and in London he and the most conspicuous of the other lords accompanied the king on his first inspection of the Tower and its defenses.

If Nottingham could rid himself of the lingering melancholy of recent losses—and there is no reason to think that he had any difficulty in doing so—he could take great pleasure in the ceremonials of the spring and summer. He had a far greater taste for matters of public show than did the king, and he could plunge himself with relish into plans for the displays that would introduce the king to his new realm. It was Nottingham as lieutenant of the Order of the Garter who had postponed the feast of St. George until July, and when that time came, it was he, with Buckhurst, who carried the saint's banner when Prince Henry was installed as a member. He was one of six given charge of coronation preparations, and he managed to get his appointment as lord steward renewed so that he could be the ritual master of the dignities of crowning the new king.[2] Along with Worcester, Thomas Howard (now lord chamberlain), and Lord Lumley, he received a significant patronage plum—a commission to designate the knights of the Bath who were to be created for "the more advauncement of the feast of his Coronac'on." But the vastly elaborated plans had to be cut short because of outbreaks of plague and the king's distaste for contact with crowds.

With these affairs and with regular attendance on the king

1. *Cal. Hatfield MSS*, 15:86.
2. Signet Office Docquets, James I, vol. 2, March–July, 1603, Public Records Office, London.

and the council Nottingham was busy and involved in useful activity, but he could scarcely fail to notice that he did not have the central place in the crown's confidence, despite his reconfirmed patents of office and his friendship with those upon whom the king most depended. There was a new power group forming, an inner circle of which he was at the most generous allowance on the fringe. It was primarily upon Cecil, Worcester, and Henry and Thomas Howard (now earls of Northampton and Suffolk) that the king depended for advice about English affairs—or, more properly, to whom he entrusted English affairs while he hunted. He had no need to fear for his place, since Cecil was his close associate and Suffolk almost his protégé. But he could not know what his new friend Northampton might be saying secretly, and Northampton was capable of saying much, as the lord admiral later learned. In addition, the admiral's place was subtly threatened by two events in that year of transition, the king's prosecution of Raleigh and Cobham and his efforts to come to peace with Spain.

Northampton's campaign against Raleigh, one of the several rivals he hated with an intensity that is difficult to explain, had converted the king to the belief that Raleigh and Cobham were dangerous radicals who threatened his security; even before the king had come to London, Raleigh had been deprived of his captaincy of the guard, and by mid-July both had been sent to the Tower on charges of plotting treason. There was no suspicion, of course, that the lord admiral might be directly or indirectly implicated in their assumed treason, but he was Cobham's father-in-law and had been Raleigh's friend. It was to him, primarily, that Raleigh had written the August defense of his role in the Spanish war.[3] And it was to him that Cobham turned for help; he instructed a servant to beg for the lord admiral's support and intercession with Cecil.

Although he had several times disclaimed any knowledge of courtly arts, Nottingham had by now become enough of a courtier to be circumspect in aiding one accused of ill will

3. Edwards, *Sir Walter Ralegh*, 2:271.

against the king and his heirs, no matter how shadowy the evidence of "Main Plots." He took some part in the investigation, at the end of July writing to Cecil and other commissioners the king's will that Raleigh be "well examined" in the company of a preacher who would let him know that "it is his soul that he must wound and not his body," so that at last "you will find out the bottom of this great ulcer." At Raleigh's trial Nottingham ventured so far as to suggest mildly that it would be reasonable to bring Raleigh and Cobham face to face to see whether Cobham would accuse him directly—thus giving indirect support to Raleigh's demand for two witnesses to treason. But the lawyers balked and Raleigh was condemned, mainly on Cobham's challenged note. Cobham was found guilty on evidence scarcely stronger.[4]

In the autumn Nottingham was again one of those appealed to as possible influences for mercy. Cobham in particular promised that if his father-in-law, Cecil, and Suffolk would visit him, he would tell the whole truth, presumably whatever would be necessary to get a pardon. His wife was also busy, frantically writing appeals to Cecil and others. But even though Lady Kildare had been accused by some of loving her husband too much for her own good, she was now mainly interested in saving his estate.[5] This was a cause in which her father also could become interested. If the forfeited lands were parceled out among the hungry suitors at court or re-granted to other heirs, Cobham's wife would be left without support, other than the remains of her spoiled Irish jointure. After diligent efforts on her behalf, she managed to get lands worth £1,000 a year, which was to be held in trust for her by Nottingham and two friends.[6]

4. *Cal. Hatfield MSS*, 15:212; for Raleigh's defense, see L. M. Hill, "The Two-Witness Rule in English Treason Trials: Some Comments on the Emergence of Procedural Law," *American Journal of Legal History*, 12 (1968):95–111.

5. *Cal. Hatfield MSS*, 15:380.

6. Signet Office Docquets, James I, vol. 2, January, 1603/4, and May, 1604; *Calendar of State Papers relating to Ireland, 1603–1670*, 13 vols. (London, 1872–1910), 1:157; *Cal. Hatfield MSS*, 16: 411–12.

Once the property settlement was reached, the unlucky Cobham was completely rejected by his wife and her family connections. The couple quarreled over chattel goods, including even the books in his study, and finally became so completely estranged that he wrote the following spring that "if her dearest friends did but truly know how scornfully she hath used me . . . I know they would detest her." Howard rejected what his daughter rejected. He wrote to Cranborne late in 1604 in shocked disbelief that Cobham would be allowed to leave the Tower and take a house near his wife's.[7]

There is no reason to think that James's opinion of his lord admiral was directly affected by the connection with Cobham. But Nottingham himself may well have felt some uneasiness, for in an entirely unrelated sequence of events the king was, with no apparent ill will, damaging him grievously. James came down from Scotland with a settled conviction that he had been divinely ordained to bring peace to this land of blood and turmoil. The war with Spain would be brought to an end, and he would live in harmony with all men. Actually, the war with Spain had for some time been in a state of relative suspension: the Spanish campaign in Ireland had finally failed; since Oostende there had been no major battles in the Netherlands; and since 1599 the Spanish had been unable to launch another great invasion fleet. So the most important hostile contact that remained was the scouring of Spanish seas by English ships in search of prizes, a kind of warfare the Spaniards had considered unworthy of a civilized nation, but out of which Englishmen still hoped to gain vast wealth. The level of privateering was no longer so high as it had been in the "good" years of the war, but that mattered little. Acts that were consistently interpreted as piracy were still being committed, and those acts constituted Spain's outstanding grievance against England. In fact, the administration of privateers had become so relaxed that the distinction between privateering and piracy had been largely lost; mer-

7. *Cal. Hatfield MSS,* 16:452; 17:82.

chants no longer had to present evidence of losses to get letters of reprisal, which were readily available by purchase,[8] and ships sailed without any form of license at all, depending on good luck and rich presents to legalize their catches when they returned. The admiralty court had lost all control over the authorization of voyages, and the privateering enterprise had deteriorated into an undignified scramble in which merchants, adventurers, and even royal officers and royal ships preyed on any traffic that might be liberally construed to be Spanish.

James had no understanding of the assumptions which underlay privateering and no sympathy for those who took part in it. To his eyes, as to the Spanish, it looked like piracy, and he very promptly stopped it. Even before his coronation he had issued orders forbidding any more of his new subjects from going to sea with an objective other than legitimate trade. His order was a clear declaration that he was ready to negotiate an end to the war; by this unilateral act he was anticipating and granting what the Spanish were sure to demand.

But the proclamation against privateering and piracy struck directly at the lord admiral's main source of income. His tenth of all enemy ships and goods brought into English ports had been worth many thousands of pounds every year. If his admiralty empire had been efficiently administered, it certainly would have made him the richest man in the country. Even as it was, with no one knowing how many adventurers went out or what prizes they brought back, with his dues frequently evaded and admiralty regulations dishonored, his prize tenths had been worth far more than all the rest of his incomes. And he had very quickly learned to adjust his scale of living to that princely standard which only sustained large-scale privateering could support. Of all Englishmen, there is no question but that the lord admiral had profited most from the Spanish war and the peculiar way it was fought. Other men may have

8. Andrews, *Elizabethan Privateering*, pp. 23–24.

hoped that the riches of the Indies would be theirs, but only he had seen the dream come true—and with very little effort on his own part.

The suspension of all letters of marque and reprisal, then, represented a financial disaster that was mitigated only by two considerations: his income from prizes had been declining anyway, and he might hope that a generous master would find him some alternative source of revenue. So he co-operated with the king's wish, although belatedly and with feet that were obviously dragging. Reports came to court throughout the next year that ships still went out to raid Spanish commerce, sometimes with the sufferance of the vice-admirals and port officers, sometimes by stealth. So in the summer of 1604 new orders were issued by the Privy Council, and letters were written to the lord admiral which implicitly suggested that he was not enforcing the king's will. He wrote back disclaiming responsibility; the king's order had been sent, he said, to the officers of the ports, which were outside his jurisdiction, as well as to his vice-admirals, so "if any be stolen out as they do write, there is great fault in them, for they are in all the ports and creeks, and the vice-admirals in few places." With evident resentment, he continued: "Yet I am sure the like proclamation never man did see before, but I was well content and am with anything that may do good; but I see it doth little good." Although it was fruitless to try to stop ships from slipping out, he had done what he could; even before getting the council's letters he had ordered a ship readied to "go along the coast." He well knew how much good a single ship could do, no matter how busily it plied the coastline, but more could not be expected of him. His men had served thirteen months without pay, so unless he could have money he could send no one else to sea. "So I hope you see that I have done what lieth in me; but I wish that there were fault found in them that had authority and would do nothing in it. Men will seek to have power to do all and then do nothing."[9] Not long before he would have hotly disputed any power other than his own to

9. *Cal. Hatfield MSS,* 16:202–3.

control seagoing traffic, but he was convinced that the present effort would fail, and he was anxious to shift the burden of responsibility to any convenient shoulders.

Eventually Nottingham found alternatives to his own prize incomes which would at least partly ease the hardships of peace,[10] but others who had learned to pin all their hopes of overnight riches on privateering did not. The bounty of the king could not supply a great class of restless and ambitious adventurers who lacked the patience or the capital to begin competing in legitimate commercial traffic. Many of these now crossed the nearly invisible line of legality into occasional or regular piracy. For decades piracy had been a serious problem. While the war lasted one of the lord admiral's most wearisome duties had been dealing with the complaints of foreigners who accused Englishmen of robbing their ships. Often foreigners trying to get their rights in English maritime courts had come away with little more than bruises; the lord admiral's administrative machinery had been geared to the need of finding prizes within the law. But when privateering stopped, these difficulties were compounded rather than eased. The number of active pirates multiplied, and admiralty bureaucrats at every level began to find it convenient and profitable to accept rewards from pirate captains and to connive in violation of the law rather than to suppress piracy and deny the country the profits and employment it might bring. Foreigners seeking justice now found themselves confronted by a wall of resistance which had been constructed out of piratical wealth. From these dealings with pirates the lord admiral himself was not exempt, and as a result, before the end of 1603 he found himself in serious disfavor at court.

In September a Captain Tompkins, who had plundered a Venetian ship, brought his spoil to the Isle of Wight; like another pirate earlier in the summer, he had a "golden key to open the doors of the great, especially of the High Admiral."[11] The Venetian secretary in London, Giovanni Carlo Scaramelli,

10. See below, pp. 274–75.
11. *Cal. S. P. Venetian,* 10:59.

wrote that after sending a messenger ashore "to learn how matters stand," Tompkins sent gifts—once described as four chests of money, another time as a cartload—to the lord admiral and similar gifts to Hunsdon, governor of Wight (and Nottingham's nephew). But robbing the Venetian republic was a greater indiscretion than attacking some private merchant, and immediate legal steps followed. Scaramelli got an order from the admiralty court which sequestered the ship and cargo and directed the arrest of the captain. Tompkins was warned of what was coming, so he disappeared, carrying everything he could from his ship. "This he succeeded in doing," said Scaramelli, "through bribes, which open every door in this country."[12] His crew had been disbanded and all the men escaped into the country, each one carrying what he could.

In late September Scaramelli confronted the lord admiral at Oxford with testimony that bribes had been offered and accepted. Nottingham admitted "at the very outset" that he had received "six sacks of silver money, which he did not believe to be worth four thousand ducats," swearing that he was "a rebel to his King if it were a penny more" and claiming that he believed it came from a Spanish prize. Tompkins' crime in Nottingham's view was that he had been privateering without a license, in which case his ship and goods should be forfeited to the admiral. But if Scaramelli could prove the ship to be Venetian, it would be consigned to him. He finally promised to do what he could to get Tompkins arrested, in return for the promise of a percentage of the value of the cargo, and he pointed out delicately that since "this was an affair belonging entirely to him I need not disturb his Majesty on the subject." They agreed to meet again at Winchester, near where an inquiry would be conducted into the matter, and parted in apparent harmony. "But I have little faith in his promises," Scaramelli wrote, "and far less in my own."[13]

In spite of any understanding Nottingham thought had been reached, Scaramelli lost no opportunity of telling the

12. *Ibid.*, pp. 91–94.
13. *Ibid.*, p. 96.

268

whole story to the king. In an audience at Woodstock, he sought James's intervention for the recovery of the booty, part of which, he did not neglect to mention, was in the hands of the lord admiral. The king was furious. He listened with "extreme impatience" and finally exclaimed, "By God, I'll hang the pirates with my own hands, and my Lord Admiral as well!" Secretary Cecil attempted to reprove Scaramelli for bringing before the king a matter that belonged in the jurisdiction of the admiralty and reminded him that since James's accession "not one privateer had set sail." But Scaramelli insisted, though "in a quiet voice," that he did not consider the admiralty competent to decide the matter since the lord admiral had part of the plunder. He was a minister of the Venetian republic, he said, accredited to the king and not to the admiral, "and while I could drink at the pure fountain of justice I need not go seeking turbid water in brooks." That fountain of justice promised to force Nottingham to return any Venetian money he had and said that there would be a full investigation made when the court returned to London.

Scaramelli was to remain in charge of Venetian affairs in England until the arrival of a regular ambassador to the new king. Before the affair of the Tompkins piracy had been settled, the envoy, Nicolo Molin, had come. But now there was a new embarrassment: Molin's goods had been seized by English pirates on his way from France, an incident "deeply regretted" by the king. James declared himself to have been insulted as much as the Venetians and announced that whatever Molin asked by way of restitution would be granted. When the king and his company came to dine with the ambassador, the lord admiral made "all sorts of apologies" and laid the blame on the Spanish war. He promised that the mischief would cease, but for the past, the Venetians noted, "we are aware that the whole question is full of difficulty, precisely on account of the Lord Admiral's interests."[14]

James was not at all comfortable as a king whose subjects harbored pirates and whose ministers shared in the spoil. He

14. *Ibid.*, pp. 100–101, 119–20.

told the Venetians that "none detested such actions more than he did." While he had been king of Scotland "his subjects had never committed deeds like this"—a fact which his lord admiral probably could have challenged—but as yet in England he had not been able to suppress the privateers. ". . . He was still new to the Government of England, and compelled to employ the old ministers, and, therefore, was unable to attend to everything at once, the more so that he feared his naval officers were somewhat interested in the matter; he added, in great confidence, that he had been obliged to give the Lord Admiral something out of his own purse, as the Admiral complained that he was unable to keep up his office, owing to the failure of revenues of this very nature."[15] The "something out of his own purse" was probably the grant of lands presented in October, 1603, one of several gifts to compensate for the admiral's loss of prizes.[16] James implied that if he were not bound by circumstances he would prefer to employ a lord admiral who would not accept money from pirates; if Nottingham felt that his position had been seriously shaken, his fears have left no record, but the incident did create a serious breach which was never entirely healed.

When it had been clearly shown that Tompkins had plundered a Venetian vessel and when it became widely known that Nottingham had been given part of the profits, at least a partial restitution was made. Just before Molin had his audience with the king, Scaramelli wrote that he had received from Nottingham 1,300 ducats in Venetian silver and 150 lengths of tabinet; he hoped to get more of both silver and stuffs, but he could not recover the Spanish gold that had been part of the payment, since enemy coin "the Admiral declares cannot be restored to Venetians."[17] He never got as much as he hoped for, and it is likely that the size of the gift had been exaggerated, but part of it might also have been in disposable goods that could not be proved to have come from pirates. From others, including some of the leading burgesses of South-

15. *Ibid.,* pp. 118–19.
16. See below, p. 274.
17. *Cal. S. P. Venetian,* 10:104–5.

ampton, one of them an alderman, Scaramelli recovered other goods, but not anything like what he said was lost, and Tompkins escaped into Wales.[18]

The lord admiral had claimed that he did not know the money was part of a pirate catch; he may have accepted it in good faith as his rightful tenth in a legitimate prize—except that there were no more legitimate prizes. It seems doubtful that he knew so little of what was going on in the area of his responsibility, and one can only conclude that he willingly and knowingly accepted illegal gifts with an at least implied promise of protection to the giver.

The Tompkins affair is the only clearly documented instance of bribery or direct dealings with pirates, but at no time was the lord admiral inclined to stir himself against the pirates when such steps might cause injury to friends, dependents, or ultimately himself. In the next years he preferred to ride along comfortably, believing that things were, after all, about as good as they could be expected to be, recognizing that whatever he did would not be enough to crush piracy— the next summer he wrote that he did not "look to live to see England and France free of pirates"[19]—and not choosing to question too closely the sources of his own income. And, not surprisingly, pirate activity continued to flourish, a major annoyance to English and foreign merchants and a source of humiliation to the king. The ability of the creaking admiralty machinery to hinder this traffic was as limited as its willingness. There were thousands of small ports and creeks where pirates could take cover out of sight of Nottingham's officers, and even the captains of the king's ships sometimes gave them shelter and took their goods on board. But a number of commissions were appointed to investigate the evils arising from piracy and to try to find a solution, such as that issued in 1608 to Sir Walter Covert, Sir George More, and others; another the next year was headed by Nottingham himself and Lord Zouche. Royal ships went out repeatedly, if intermit-

18. J. W. Horrocks, ed., *The Assembly Books of Southampton,* 2 vols. (Southampton, 1917), 1:xxviii–xxx.
19. *Cal. Hatfield MSS,* 16:202–3.

tently. On one occasion the commanders of Levantine ships were commissioned to seek and suppress pirates, and on another the mayor and alderman of Barnstaple and the earl of Bath were licensed to send out their own ships to help clear the seas. But throughout the Jacobean years the financial rights to pirate goods given to the lord admiral by his patent complicated the problem. In 1607 one of Nottingham's secretaries had been assigned his share of pirate spoil but had been given no special responsibilities for finding the spoilers, which brought him into strenuous conflict with vice-admirals claiming the rewards of their labors; in 1609 the lord admiral claimed that his patent allowed him to compound with pirates for their sins,[20] again underlining his view that the whole of the admiralty was a private domain to be milked for his profit and not one to be administered for the benefit of the country. The commission given to London merchants in 1616 to search out pirates was, in the circumstances, a confession of the government's inability to cope with a chronic problem.

Through the summer of 1603 Nottingham saw his privateering income dwindle away and his security in the power group threatened, if ever so slightly. He needed a new base of strength, some new ties with the crown like those which had so profited him under Elizabeth, some new justification for his claims. These he found—but not without paying a heavy price —in a new marriage. Beginning with Lord Kinloss, young Scotsmen were making their fortunes by marrying rich English heiresses; why could an Englishman not recoup his political fortunes by marrying a Scottish heiress who would insure his proximity to the Scottish king? It cannot be certain, of course, that such was Nottingham's reasoning, but it is the simplest explanation of an event which is hard to account for otherwise. Remarriage was a common thing, but not nearly so common for a sixty-eight-year-old widower as for younger men. And the choice of a partner, though it proved largely satisfactory to his needs, was one that "set his wisdom many

20. *Calendar of State Papers, Domestic Series, James I. 1603–1610* (London, 1857), p. 573.

degrees back in the repute of the world." In early September, 1603, before his first wife was six months in the grave, he met and married the nineteen-year-old sister of the earl of Moray, granddaughter of the late regent of Scotland. Apparently he saw the lady at Basing, where the queen was holding her court, admired her dancing, and arranged for a marriage almost on the spot. Inevitably, the court looked on the union as the act of a vain and foolish old man. Court wits heard with delight that Nottingham went straight to the king and "greatly bostethe" of his wedding-night exploits, but then fell sick the next day with an ague.[21] Such tales are what a man in Nottingham's situation might expect, as indeed were the persistent later rumors that the young and spirited countess was not entirely faithful to this husband old enough to be her grandfather.

Although the marriage may not have been quite as jumped-up an affair as the court chose to believe, Nottingham cannot have known his bride very well before the match was made—if he had, he might have had second thoughts. She was a pretty girl (although she developed a disfiguring nasal growth which was presumably removed by surgery in 1604), but she was also frivolous, indiscreet, and hot-headed. She made herself a conspicuous figure at court and was a frequent companion of Queen Anne, but she was not always in the good graces of her mistress and at least once got her husband into serious trouble. Also, she was not quite the link with the throne which would do her husband the most good. She was a cousin of the king—her grandfather was an illegitimate son of James V—and she had been brought up as a ward of the court. But if Nottingham had waited until he knew something of Scottish court gossip, he would have learned that his new lady's father, the "Bonnie Earl of Moray" of the folk song, was said to have been Queen Anne's lover, and that James was not free of suspicion in the bizarre episode in which Moray

21. John Nichols, *The progresses, processions and magnificent festivities of King James the First . . .* , 4 vols. (London, 1828), 1:274.

was killed.[22] The king had taken Moray's children into his own household and had treated them generously, but they were living reminders of past scandals, which meant that Lady Margaret Nottingham did not have anything approaching the intimate relationship with either king or queen that Lady Katherine had always maintained with Queen Elizabeth.

The marriage, however, did confer one immediate and supremely desirable benefit: it enabled Nottingham to shore up, for the moment at least, his collapsing finances. The king could not allow his pretty cousin to go undowered into marriage or to be maintained in unbecoming style, so the crown extended its support, despite James's views about the bridegroom's dealings with pirates. There was a clearly recognized relationship between the marriage and the grants that Nottingham received in October. As Sir Thomas Edmonds wrote, "My Lord Admiral hath made very good use of his marriage; having bemoaned himself that he is so much prejudiced by the ceasing of his accustomed profits of the Admiralty, as he hath not the means to defray the ordinary charges of his diet. . . ."[23] So Nottingham was given £600 a year for his diet at court, and lands worth £200 a year from the Exchequer and the duchy of Lancaster. More was to come; in June, 1604, the new Lady Nottingham succeeded the old as mistress of the mansion at Chelsea, and a month later her husband got an appointment as governor for Prince Henry with an allowance of £400 a year. In February, 1605, she was granted a pension of £200 a year from the Exchequer. These were compensations

22. John Heneage Jesse, *Memoirs of the Court of England During the Reign of the Stuarts, Including the Protectorate,* 2 vols. (London, 1857), 1:107. According to the legend, Moray, who had been involved with Bothwell, was promised a pardon in 1592; the king told his enemy, Huntly, to bring him to court, but Huntly attacked him, set his hair aflame, and killed him. The folk song suggests that the king had set a trap: "He was a braw gallant, / And he played at the glove; / And the bonny Earl of Murray, / He was the Queen's love."

23. [Sir Samuel Egerton Brydges], *Memoirs of the Peers of England during the Reign of James the First* (London, 1802), pp. 191–92.

which would certainly help Nottingham bear with patience the secret smiles of the court, but they would not yet replace the river of wealth that once flowed to Arundel House, Chelsea, and Reigate from the prize ships. Other members of the family shared in the bounty; one son received £1,000 from recusant lands and another son was given a pension of £200.

What must have been designed as the principal answer to the lord admiral's financial problem—and the principal testimonial to his and his bride's persuasive powers with the crown —was the patent given him in December, 1604, in succession to Sir Walter Raleigh's, to license sellers of wine. The wine monopoly was one of the great prizes of courtly favor-seeking. It had arisen out of a statute dating from Edward VI which was designed to curb the lawlessness of taverns: under its terms the right to keep a tavern or sell wines by retail would be conferred upon fit persons nominated by local officers through the purchase of a license. Enforcement of the law was entrusted to a figure at court, whose power and nearness to the throne would give weight to administration. The monopoly-holder would receive the license fees and collect fines for violations as his reward for seeing the statute duly obeyed. The theory was the same as that underlying the lord admiral's piracy franchise: the more vigorously the law was enforced, the greater would be the return. But as so frequently happened, the purpose of the law was gradually forgotten, and it survived as a private revenue device, a tax paid by tavern keepers to help maintain the standing of one of the royal favorites. By the end of the century the income from the grant had been frozen and bore only an indirect relation to the number of fines collected and licenses granted. The holder of the patent customarily appointed London men of affairs as his deputies for administering the law; from these farmers he received a fixed annual rental, and the farmers made their profits by selling licenses freely with little regard for the original goal of limiting the sale of wine.

In years just past, the wine patent had been one of the mainstays of the fortunes of Sir Walter Raleigh, to whom it brought £3,000 a year. So in succeeding him Nottingham became one of the principal beneficiaries of Raleigh's fall, which places his role in Raleigh's prosecution in a more ungenerous light. However, the income from the patent had been suspended before Raleigh's disgrace; it came under the scope of the proclamation of May 7, 1603, by which the king took Queen Elizabeth's remaining monopolies into his own hands. So for nearly two years the profits had gone to no patent-holder. Now both past and present holders claimed them. Lady Raleigh, deeply in debt and overwhelmed by the loss of her husband's entire estate, begged that "he would rather have given them something back again of this great portion" than take what she said the king had allowed for her relief; "the bread and food taken from her and her children will never augment his table."[24] Nottingham, however, was not impressed by her pleas for charity. The issue, he insisted, "concerns his Majesty, in whose right I hold it by my grant." The council was finally appealed to and it decided in Nottingham's favor, probably to the surprise of no one except Lady Raleigh, whose hangings, furniture, and even beds had gone to meet creditors' claims.

Overlooking any misgivings concerning Lady Raleigh, at the end of 1604 Nottingham could feel much more comfortable and optimistic. He sold the wine farm to a group of London speculators[25] for a rental of £3,000. With his pensions he was assured of nearly £4,000 a year plus what remained of his admiralty incomes, his rents, and the independent grants held by his wife and sons. In all it should have been enough to support even an earl's style of living, but this earl had learned to dance to a faster tune. Both he and his heir, Lord Effingham, who got very little settlement, remained critically short of ready cash. Again and again unable to meet immediate expenses, they were forced to sell part of their annuities to the farmers. The first installment on £1,500 was paid presum-

24. *Cal. Hatfield MSS*, 16:456.
25. The wine farmers included John Ferne, Arthur Ingram, James Cullimore, and later Lionel Cranfield, Samuel Hare, Richard Venn, and William Massam. Ferne retired in 1610 and was succeeded by George Low. See *Cranfield Papers*, pp. 68, 86, 95–97.

ably at the time the contract was made in December, 1604; the second was due the following Lady Day, but even before that Nottingham asked for an advance of £100 in return for his approval of Lionel Cranfield's admittance as a partner in the farm. Before the wine patent was nine months old, Nottingham had signed away to Cranfield £200 a year out of his £3,000 for an unspecified sum of cash. And within the next months, more of these indentures were signed by both the Howards: £100 a year to Samuel Hare in August, 1605; £200 a year to John Ferne in October, 1605; another £200 to Sir John Cullimore a year later; and £200 more to Hare and Richard Venn, £150 a year to Hare, and £300 a year to Cranfield in 1608. So in less than four years the lord admiral and his son had sold away annuities worth £1,150, more than a third of the value of the entire farm, to raise cash for immediate use. The merchants were able to force hard bargains on the noble concessionaires and turn a very good profit. Cranfield's records suggest that at least part of the time he paid three times face value to acquire a slice in the rental but that when he resold, as he sometimes did, he was able to get up to five times face value. So if Nottingham needed £300 right away, he had to reduce future incomes permanently by £100 a year. Cranfield could sell that same annuity at his leisure for as much as £500, or, if he kept it as long as the patent ran, he would earn up to £900. With each indenture, of course, the lord admiral and his son found it ever harder to live within what was left. The younger Howard, particularly, borrowed from the wine farmers on whatever collateral he could raise, thereby creating obligations he was unable to meet except by promising away more of his future revenues or by giving up lands.

It was to meet one of these debts that Donnington Castle, which Nottingham had won after so much ill feeling and litigation, was sold. The lord admiral had given the castle and park to his heir before March, 1608, when Lord Effingham leased it to Cranfield. The lease cost Cranfield £288 15s., paid on March 15, 1608; on July 9 of the same year he sold it to another London merchant, who was building a landed estate in Berkshire, for £1,700. So, because Effingham needed a quick source of cash and was already in Cranfield's debt, he had to give up the lease for far less than it was worth, and he enabled Cranfield to make a profit of £1,411 5s. in five months, "for which," Cranfield wrote in his account book, "Almighty God be praised."[26]

Within a few years Effingham was driven into even harder financial dilemmas and evidently mortgaged Donnington to Cranfield, since in May, 1612, he was obliged to write "upon a speedy occasion to try your friendship," asking to convert £500 that was due on the Donnington mortgage in two weeks into £1,000 due in five months. To the Donnington mortgage Effingham would add an obligation on the lands of Barnstaple Priory, also granted him by his father. The extra £500 in cash would enable him, he said, to make a better bargain for the sale of some other lands, "richly worth 14 or 15 hundred pounds, for the which I have a chapman now ready in London." Some kind of arrangement was worked out, but not what Effingham had in mind, for attached to his letter in the Cranfield papers was the counterpart of an indenture acknowledging receipt from Cranfield for the sale of the Donnington castle and park with neighboring lands.[27]

Bargaining away incomes from the wine farm was an expensive way of meeting present debts, and there was another device which worked more to the advantage of the patentees. The time of retribution could be postponed by selling annuities that would not begin until the death of one of the holders, presumably Nottingham, who turned seventy in 1606. The hitch was that the farmers would not pay as much for a reversion, usually only a two-year's purchase. In buying a postponed annuity, Cranfield and his colleagues were in effect gambling that the lord admiral would soon die. But as events fell out, reversions were a real bargain for the Howards—the grant was revoked before either died, so the reversions never took effect. The first of these bargains came

26. *Ibid.*, p. 152.
27. *Ibid.*, p. 262.

in August, 1605, with Samuel Hare; there were others in August, 1607, and April, 1608, with Cranfield, Venn, and William Duncombe, a London haberdasher, agreements which would have reduced Lord Effingham's income by another £800 a year upon his father's death.

In April, 1609, Nottingham summarized his obligations involving the wine rental in a document kept by Cranfield which reveals that it had been reduced further by other arrangements: he had given £100 a year to his nephew Edward Howard, £300 to "my son and Trevor," meaning probably his infant son Charles and Sir John Trevor, surveyor of the navy, £200 a year to one identified only as Jackson, and £100 a year to the two individuals who managed the Wine Office under the farmers. The last of these was probably a sale, although Nottingham may have been expected to pay salaries to the two functionaries, Harvey and Shelbury, out of his rental. Finally, £400 a year had been assigned to the lord treasurer, which may have been another sale, or perhaps the cost of Salisbury's influence at the time the patent was granted.[28] At any rate, by 1609 the lord admiral had only £900 a year left for his and Lord Effingham's purposes, a fraction of what the grant had been designed to produce. Rather than supply him with a comfortable capital reserve or a basis for a fortune, the wine monopoly had made him unable to meet current expenses, and he had to raid it again and again, each time making it more unlikely that he would ever recoup the losses.

Not only did the lord admiral have to sign away future incomes to meet present costs, but like his son he was obliged again and again to borrow on his wine money and to seek payment in advance of the due dates, Michaelmas and Lady Day. Advance payment, for which interest was usually charged, became so frequent that the wine farmers kept a running account of moneys drawn upon them. Often the entire salary and more had been paid out before it ever came due. This was the situation in September, 1609, when the creditors drew up a comprehensive state of Nottingham's

28. *Ibid.*, p. 90.

indebtedness. Between 1605 and 1608, they said, payments had been made totaling £11,602 9s. 8d. Within the last two years another £2,102 10s. had been paid out, "for which his lordship hath yet given no acquittance," or £13,704 19s. 8d. in all. The entire rent for the period would come to only £12,000, even before interest or annuities were figured. After they had been added, the total immediately due came to £2,998 18s. If the full £1,500 had been allowed Nottingham for his Michaelmas payment, he would still owe as much more, and he had already asked for an additional £300.[29] Once during the four-year period covered by the statement, he had borrowed an additional £1,680, using a "great diamond ring" —perhaps the one slipped on his finger by the king of Spain —as collateral, promising repayment out of future wine incomes. This debt had apparently been settled by September, 1609, since it does not figure in the company's statement.

In spite of the fact that he was not getting rich by it, the wine grant made Nottingham one of the principal monopolists at the Jacobean court and gave him a vested interest in one of the most sensitive political issues of the time. Complaints against monopolies had been growing for years as the commercial classes found themselves taxed to benefit court favorites. Parliament's noisy disapproval of monopolistic abuses in 1601 had persuaded Queen Elizabeth to promise to grant no more "but such as should first have a trial," to repeal the worst, and to suspend others. Her promise was more satisfactory than her performance, and resentment over monopolies was one of the legacies she left James I. James's Parliaments looked upon monopolies as crying grievances which turned loyal courtiers into "spaniels to the King, and wolves to the people."[30] When early in 1606 the House of Commons on the motion of Sir Robert Wingfield agreed to collect "all greavances wherewith the country is greaved,"

29. *Ibid.*, pp. 93–94.
30. Christopher Neville's speech in the Commons, quoted in Samuel R. Gardiner, *History of England from the Accession of James I to the Outbreak of the Civil War,* 10 vols. (London, 1883–86), 2:246.

monopolies immediately came to mind, and high on the list of monopolistic abuses was the lord admiral's patent for licensing sellers of wine. The Commons spent weeks denouncing the grants through which courtiers were fattening themselves by sucking the blood of the people, and when Nicholas Fuller formally presented the consensus of committee debates, the wine monopoly was preceded as a grievance only by the imposition on currants. It was solemnly agreed that "certaine Persons by force of some Statuts out of use, which are Impossible to be observed, and by Color of some Grant or Warrant from his Majesty" had increased the number of taverns, inhanced the price of wine, and "obtained from his Majestyes Subjects very great Summes of money for Fynes, besides that they doe receive . . . great yearly Rents, to the great Grief and Charge of the said Subject. . . ." Wine was now sold in the smallest villages "where no Wynes were usually sold in such sort before" and to "unruly Alehouse Keepers, who for their disorder have bene suppressed by Iustices of Peace to the great increase of Drunkennesse. . . ."[31]

The lord admiral's attitude toward these attacks can well be guessed. If Lady Raleigh's hope of a concession had concealed a thrust at the king's power, as he said, then this attack must have seemed little short of treasonable. But if Nottingham or his agents ever offered any genuine defense or rebuttal, it has not survived. The lord admiral remained a defender of prerogative, out of which everything he had and hoped to have was derived, but he was not a frequent or eloquent speaker and he may have reasoned that the Commons' criticism could best be answered by those who were.

Since the wine monopoly did not provide the sustaining support that Nottingham needed, he had to turn again to the king, and he did so at the same time that he was borrowing from Cranfield and his friends. The king's own finances were increasingly chaotic, and Cecil (now earl of Salisbury) despaired of ever bringing his extravagances within reason; but

31. D. H. Willson, ed., *The Parliamentary Diary of Robert Bowyer* (Minneapolis, 1931), pp. 109–10.

Nottingham, like other courtiers, continued to look upon the crown as the source of all bounty, an attitude which James did nothing to discourage. So he continued to touch the royal palm, and with considerable success in the light of services being rendered. Before the end of 1604 he had received grants of Ford Manor in Sussex and the castle and lands of Melbourne, Derbyshire, which was evidently sold as other land grants had been. Late in 1607 he won a grant of £3,000 a year for seven years, payable out of Irish tonnage and poundage, but he was to have some difficulty in obtaining this payment; six months later he wrote to the lord treasurer, pleading his pressing needs and begging him to give effect to the grant. Salisbury, who had the responsibility of trying somehow to cope with the king's mounting expenses, may have persuaded Nottingham to accept a smaller grant on a more permanent basis, for in 1611, when the subject came up again, there is record of a pension of £1,700, but no trace of the £3,000. On this occasion Nottingham again pleaded his needs successfully and received another £1,000 for life, with the promise of £300 a year to his young son Charles if he died.

During these years Nottingham was by no means a unique example of royal charity; his case is symptomatic of what was happening at the English court, where noblemen were encouraged and expected to become steadily more parasitic.[32] He still received his incomes and perquisites as lord admiral, diminished though they were in peacetime, and he still devoted his time and energies to the crown's service. But his value to the admiralty had diminished probably as much as his income from it, and by the end of 1605 he was becoming a less considerable figure at court, despite his gray hair, his august bearing, and the borrowed splendor of his style of living. With the accession of James he lost the primacy he had shared with Salisbury in the months after Essex's fall; he slipped back to secondary status and did not advance from it again, in

32. Lawrence Stone, *The Crisis of the Aristocracy 1558–1641* (Oxford, 1965), pp. 477–78.

spite of—or perhaps partly because of—a match with the
house of Stuart and in spite of the impressive evidences he
could collect of his sovereign's good will. He continued for a
while to have some part in most of the important political
events of the time—he was one of the first persons to whom
Suffolk presented evidence of the Gunpowder plot, and he sat
on the commission for the arraignment of the plotters; he was
one of the lords named to the commission for managing the
Scottish union, one of the examiners of the Jesuit Henry
Garnet, and one of the commissioners to hear ecclesiastical
causes in Winchester diocese. With Lennox, Suffolk, Northampton, and others, he helped to decide title and precedence
quarrels as a commissioner for the earl marshalcy. He still
acted as ceremonial lord steward as occasion demanded, and
as a justice in eyre there was much ado over preserving game
for the king's hunts and granting leases for timbering and
grazing in royal forests. He spent considerable time with the
Prince of Wales—he wrote Salisbury in June, 1606, that
he was "weary with waiting on the Prince, which was a
fishing at my house at Casholton and hunted afterward
in Bedington Park"[33]—and was much preoccupied with the
entertainments for the king of Denmark. He could by no
means complain of being passed over by the king, and his
influence was still worth cultivating. But though he continued
to fill court positions, it cannot be said that his opinion was
eagerly sought on difficult matters of state. And when his
advice was asked for, as it was in September, 1606, in a
question concerning treatment of some captured French
goods, he could only insist on his own rights and remember
that when the late queen had tried to negotiate with the
French they only "gave us a flap with a fox tail; and I think so
we shall be served again."[34] He could demand his right to
carry the infant Prince Charles when he was made duke of
York, but such honors did not signify closeness to the king;
James almost never referred to him in his jocular and gossipy

33. *Cal. Hatfield MSS,* 18:175.
34. *Ibid.,* pp. 290–91, 287–88.

letters to Salisbury, though there are allusions to Suffolk, Northampton, Worcester, Hume, and others again and again. Nottingham simply was not often in the king's thoughts except when some naval matter—usually unfortunate—broke in on the royal consciousness.

What he was, then, was a seconder and supporter of initiatives that were still supplied mostly by Salisbury. Especially in the early years of James's reign, Salisbury continued to be the focal point of political power, the center around which other luminaries grouped themselves. He was certainly the center of any "Howard faction" in the early Jacobean years; the three prominent Howards still had more reference to him than to each other. In Salisbury's last years, Suffolk and Northampton did develop a family compact that began to operate independently of him, but it had not done so as early as 1605 or 1606. Nottingham and Suffolk had ties that went back to Suffolk's childhood; by now, however, marriage connections and the pursuit of power had drawn Suffolk nearer to Salisbury, though his friendship with his cousin remained strong. Whatever closeness had existed between Northampton and Nottingham fast disappeared. Northampton, of course, was never really close to anyone, and it could finally be seen that he despised nearly everyone around him, including Salisbury.

Northampton's hostility toward Nottingham became quite active, although not open, at the time of the lord admiral's embassy to Spain, the only important manifestation of confidence he received from James. When the peace with Spain was negotiated—by a commission which included both Nottingham and Northampton but which was dominated by Salisbury—the Spanish crown sent to London the august figure of the duque de Frias, constable of Castile, to witness James's ratification. Diplomatic procedure required that when the treaty had been signed in England an ambassador be sent to Spain to witness Philip's acceptance. The embassy was not an office which would require a great measure of statesmanship, but the man chosen would be obliged to represent the dignity and honor of the English crown in a court which had seen no Englishmen but refugees and prisoners for twenty years.

James, in honor and courtesy, could send a man no less exalted in rank and office than Frias, which suggested, if not dictated, the choice of the lord admiral. He was a man of dignified presence and magnificent appearance—Francis Osborne recalled later that even when he had passed eighty there was not "a goodlier man for person in Europe."[35] He was the ranking earl and senior councilor, a man whose name would generate respect and deference in the memory of 1588 and 1596, member of a family that had suffered for the Catholic faith, and holder of one of the most pestigious offices around the king's person. The Nottingham embassy has been narrated in detail elsewhere,[36] but its result was that Northampton was able to undermine the value of his cousin's service. Nottingham believed that he had conducted himself with dignity and discretion, and he came home glowing with Spanish praises and warmed by Spanish gifts, but he also quarreled with the resident ambassador, Sir Charles Cornwallis, a follower of Northampton. In letters to the court, Cornwallis echoed the praises of the Spanish, but to Northampton he accused the lord admiral of accepting bribes, disgracing English religion, and committing English policy to the support of Spanish needs. None of the charges can now be substantiated, though it is not unlikely that he talked too much and too freely in responding to the flattery of his hosts. Northampton, however, pressed the stories successfully on the king, and when the "dull stone," as Nottingham had been called, returned, he was greeted so coldly that he withdrew from the court to "digest Melancholy."[37] He did not yet know that it was Northampton who had spoiled his triumph, but he soon learned that his cousin was ready to destroy him if he could.

The rupture between Nottingham and Northampton meant

35. Francis Osborne, *Historical Memoirs of the Reigns of Elizabeth and King James,* in *Secret History of the Court of James the First,* 2 vols. (Edinburgh, 1811), 1:79.

36. See my article, "The Earl of Nottingham's Embassy to Spain in 1605," *History Today,* March, 1970.

37. Sir Ralph Winwood, *Memorials of Affairs of State . . . ,* 3 vols. (London, 1725), 2:92.

either that from 1605 to 1614 there was no Howard party or that the Howard who was senior in experience and honor did not belong to it. Yet the three principal Howards and Salisbury still shared the same attitudes on fundamental public policy, including championship of the royal prerogative and the common need to be the agents through which the prerogative was turned into administrative act, the instinct to acquire and hold power. Individually they wielded great power and collectively they came near to monopolizing it, but there was no sense of unity which could be identified as a party, unless it is defined without Nottingham, the only one of the four who never really commanded the friendship of the king and was the particular target of the enmity of another of the same group.

XIV: *Years of Decline*

After his return from Spain, Nottingham became an increasingly remote figure—absent from court more frequently and for longer periods, burdened by the chronic disabilities of an old man, grasping at every chance to escape incipient decay and the desolation of his estates, haunted by private tragedies. But as he tended to turn inward, he was compelled to view the repudiation of his public role. His last years in office were preoccupied with the spreading rot which almost destroyed the English navy as an instrument of power, but almost miraculously the navy scandals never managed to touch Nottingham himself.

The old admiral probably would have been absent from court—and from his administrative duties—much more than he was had it not been for his spirited young countess, who enjoyed the frivolities of Queen Anne's court and took a leading place in them. She was one of the half-dozen ladies of the withdrawing room—which conveyed the coveted direct access to the queen—and she frequently had a part in the masques and dances with which the royal circle amused itself. This lively girl's relationship with her elderly husband can only be guessed at—and was guessed at with some relish by their contemporaries, the gossip adding no new luster to their reputations. In a court where sexual relationships were made and broken rather easily, it was assumed that a woman in her early twenties would cheat on an old man. Feeding on these rumors, Anne's tactless brother, Christian of Denmark, touched off a court tempest on his unprecedented visit in 1606. During a "remarkable debauch" the Danish king paid drunken and clumsy gallantries to the countess and offended her bitterly by "making horns in derision at her husband."

Later he supported his gesture with remarks that cast doubts on her virtue, repeating, no doubt, what was common currency at court. But Lady Nottingham had the misfortune to learn about it and dashed off a furious letter, its hot sincerity almost too much for her semi-literate style, to his resident ambassador. Once she had thought as highly of Christian as any prince, she said, but since learning of the "great wronge the kinge your Master hath done me, when I was not by to answere for my selfe," she perceived that "there is as much baseness in him as can be in any man." Although a prince by birth, "it seems not to me he harbours any Princely thought in his brest," for "it is the basest part that can be to wronge any woman of Honour." The name he called her she deserved no degree more than "eyther the Mother of him selfe or of his children." If she ever discovered who had been retailing gossip about her, she swore that she would do her best "to put him from doing the like to any other."[1]

As might be expected, this audacious production caused Lady Nottingham some little trouble. To teach her proper respect for a reigning monarch, Queen Anne expelled her from court. But the indignant lady was not so easily dealt with. Probably to justify herself, she persuaded her husband to take her "the privy way" to the queen's lodgings for a direct confrontation, which thus involved Nottingham in his wife's compounded indiscretion. Anne berated him sharply for abusing his privilege of access, and "he answered her in other sort than was meet, and with more haughty language than she expected." She did not choose to pursue a quarrel with him, "being an old man and a nobleman whom she respects," so the king intervened only to forbid Nottingham to bring his hot-blooded wife to court again until given permission.[2] But the issue of the lady's temerity completely eclipsed that of her virtue. The rupture finally healed and Lady Nottingham took her place again, but she remained one of that considerable

1. Harleian MSS, 787/62.
2. McClure, *Letters of John Chamberlain,* 1:217.

bevy of Jacobean ladies whose wifely chasteness was a matter of general interest.

Not long before this little court farce, the new countess of Nottingham had presented her husband with a son—it is tempting to speculate that it was the child's paternity which had given rise to speculations about the mother's marital honesty. It was not impossible for a man of seventy to become a father, but such an event was sufficiently rare that it would certainly provide food for a court that thrived on a diet of salacity. The child was named to honor his king and was given manors and livings, but in November, 1608, he died at Reigate. The lord admiral had already buried a wife, a daughter, and three sons-in-law, but now this melancholy duty of following to the grave the body of one of his family became almost regular. His second marriage produced other children, but all but one died after a few days, a few months, or a few years. After the death of this first son, another James was born who lived long enough to be endowed with a royal lease on properties at Chelsea in 1609, but he was buried in the parish church there in midsummer, 1610. Within scarcely more than twelve months in 1616–17, Nottingham lost three young children—a daughter, probably only a few days old, and two sons, Thomas, whose age is not now known, and William, an infant of two weeks. Two children were more fortunate: a son Charles, born at Haling House on Christmas Day, 1610, survived to become the third and last Howard of Nottingham, and a daughter, born in June, 1617, was receiving a pension as late as March, 1623, though she did not outlast her aged father. This last child was born after the lord admiral had passed his eighty-first birthday, and her birth no doubt produced smirking notice of the lady's favor to handsome pages.

Painful as infant deaths have always been to grieving parents, Jacobean parents were accustomed to a high rate of mortality; even when every available care was lavished on the newborn child, the chances were great that he would not live to see the end of his first year. Far more bitter was the death of an heir who had survived those precarious early years and had been expected to take over one of the great places of the state. Lord William Howard was perhaps not the most talented scion of a Jacobean house but neither was he the dullest. Although he had not always performed to advantage in court games—it was once remarked that of all the young men taking part in a joust, Lord Effingham did "absolutely worst"—he had won applause for his bravery at Cádiz while only a stripling, and he had accumulated respectable parliamentary and administrative experience. But he had always lived in relative obscurity and he had been slenderly supported. Steadily his position worsened. Nottingham had settled a few manors on him, including Reigate, but there was no great landed empire in which to share. For a while the grant of the wine patent was a godsend; while it lasted it was his principal means of support, although not as much support as his style of living required. More and more was borrowed from Cranfield, Ingram, and others, often at very high interest, and his remaining properties had to be mortgaged or sold until very little was left. He could continue to borrow, for his long-term prospects were good—his father and his rich mother-in-law, an heiress of the Dormer estates in Buckinghamshire, had both passed the normal life expectancy—but while he waited for one of them to die, he suffered an inevitable temptation to live as though these reversionary fortunes were already his.

Finally, in April, 1615, the old Lady St. John, a dowager for twenty years, died, and in his wife's right William Howard came into a large estate. After that, nothing is heard of his financial burdens, and he apparently was at last able to begin to build himself a place independent of his declining father. But he did not live long enough to make anything of his new prospects. Before the year was over, he suddenly died at the age of thirty-two. Whether or not he might have been the man to revive the flagging fortunes of the Howards and carry the greatness of his ancestors into the fifth generation is doubtful. But he probably had as much political skill as his father, and if the normal mortality had not been reversed, a young heir might have salvaged something from the collapsing estate. The old lord admiral was not writing many letters during these troubled times and no comment on this new tragedy survives in his unsteady hand, but there can be no doubt that the proud and family-conscious man felt the loss keenly.

Fate was showing its perversity in other ways during these unhappy years. For longer than most men at court could remember, Nottingham had ruled over what amounted to a private domain of ships and seas, a domain to be managed for the personal profit of himself and, increasingly, his friends. His rule, of course, was supported by royal and, indirectly, public funds, and in return he provided the crown and the public with their first protection against foreign enemies. His great semi-autonomous fief had brought him security, power, influence, and immense prestige; by right of his office he became one of the few indispensable men in the kingdom. And, generally speaking, he had given everything he could have given to earn his wealth and prestige. For long years he had been a prudent administrator and a wary and successful commander. He had never displayed any conspicuous daring or any striking creative imagination, but he had had enough common sense to give his unstinting loyalty to others who possessed those qualities. In 1605, had he looked back on a twenty-year tenure as lord admiral, he could have said in all modesty that despite his perquisites the country's debt to him was not an easy one to repay.

But since the advent of the new king, and particularly since his embassy to Spain, there were no foreign enemies against which the king and country had to be defended. Ships had to be maintained, for there was no way of predicting when they might be needed, and therefore money had to be spent. But it was money that would be spent in a way which was fundamentally reckless—the officers who used it knew with all the certainty that is possible in human affairs that they would not be forced to that final accounting which success in battle constitutes. So as the years of peace were spun out, it became progressively easier to make petty encroachments on the money, materials, time, and talents that properly belonged to the ships. And increasingly the lord admiral found his authority challenged and his prestige tarnished because of the way his private business (as it seemed to him) was being carried on.

It has frequently been pointed out that it was the admiralty's historical development as the private province of a single man that was its most serious weakness; the lord admiral was the holder of a royal patent which gave him near-complete authority over an important area of public affairs. To stimulate his zeal for serving the crown, he had been granted privileges out of which arose financial reward. But the reward did not necessarily increase when the law was stringently enforced; sometimes, as in the case of privateering, profits were greater when the rules were winked at. Since the officers of the admiralty were the lord admiral's servants, they acquired a natural interest in seeing that he got his monetary rights whether the law was obeyed or not. This was particularly true because the officers were paid with a share of the admiral's perquisites. The emphasis on perquisites was so great that it often must have seemed that money-collecting was the admiralty's most important function. And because of the lack of effective central control, it is not surprising that much of the money collected in the admiral's name and for the admiral's uses stuck to the fingers of the perquisite-gatherers at every level. From top to bottom, the admiralty was an enormous and complex structure of patronage offices, the holders of which had always been expected to pay for their appointments and had always dedicated themselves to profit-seeking off the body of the commonwealth. Nottingham had not created that structure, but neither had he tried to reform it—it was in the interest of the whole bureaucracy that it not be changed.

In what the Jacobean navy became, however, the lord admiral's direct responsibility was twofold. The trust he gave his subordinates became a major source of weakness. As long as his men were loyal to him, he repaid their loyalty with a fierce, feudal sense of obligation: he would defend them against their enemies and fight their battles for them; he would permit no questioning of their honesty or their motives. Such devotion to subordinates had had its place when he was being served by the likes of Francis Drake and John Hawkins; it had helped him to hold variegated personalities together in a common cause. But this personal loyalty stopped being an asset before the Spanish war ended. Howard was no judge of the abilities and honesty of other men, and those whom he raised to power in the navy did not deserve his confidence. The officers closest to him and most in his debt were systematically building empires of their own at the navy's expense.

As the lord admiral grew older, becoming increasingly preoccupied with family tragedy, shrinking fortunes, and waning reputation, he spared less time and energy for the administration of the navy. There had been years when hundreds of documents covering the whole range of the navy's activities had passed under his hand; at the height of the war he had been ceaselessly active, interfering almost routinely in the dealings of subordinates. Now that he was tired and old, he was willing to let the machine which had been so successful operate under its own steam with such direction as his officers, men who had served him long and dutifully, could provide. But he had misjudged his men, and they made the navy a fat, lifeless, supine organism which seemed to exist to be ravaged and robbed by its own personnel.

At the heart of the admiralty's power structure was the treasurer of the navy, who had more power to spend money than nearly anyone in the country except the lord treasurer and the chancellor of the Exchequer. It was as treasurer of the navy that Hawkins had engineered the reconstruction of the Elizabethan war fleet, and the office had given him all the power he needed. But there is much evidence that, even under his spirited and unquestionably high-minded administration, abuses had gone beyond his capacity to control. It was charged that the gunners were selling powder and shot "to maintain their idle lascivious expenses," that the captains sold the wine supplied for voyages and so filled their ranks with dead pays that ships left harbor critically undermanned, that boatswains and pursers connived with suppliers to accept short weight on beer and beef and hawsers and shrouds, and that the officers so exaggerated their losses of brass fixtures that it cost the queen hundreds of pounds a year to "replace" them.[3] Hawkins himself, in spite of his devotion to the navy's efficiency and effectiveness, was never entirely cleared of charges that he tried to enrich himself with the navy's funds; there was a full investigation of his conduct of navy business in 1583, and proposals for another investigation were made in 1591 but never materialized. Indeed, for him not to attempt to make personal gain out of the funds entrusted to him would have been accounted extraordinary. But in Hawkins' administration there was the essential saving quality that corruption never went so far as to render the navy altogether unfit for the service expected of it.

Hawkins' death, however, marked an important change in the ethical climate of the navy. The crisis of the Spanish war was past, and the principal effort to maintain the fight became the licensed robbery that was privateering. Even the Cádiz expedition had much of the character of a large-scale privateering venture. Every man was out for his own profit, and those in royal ships were not willing to let private adventurers outstrip them. If profits could be increased by cheating a little on the queen's accounts, what was to prevent it? Had the queen not grabbed more than her share of the really big prizes anyway? Such thoughts became all the more irresistible because for three years the vacant treasurership remained unfilled and there was no other officer with the kind of control Hawkins had possessed. The new treasurer, when finally appointed, was an ambitious opportunist who was more interested in proximity to the throne than in the maintenance of ships. Fulke Greville, "a silken courtier," was an accomplished and cultivated gentleman, an important royal favorite, and a young man, like most in his situation, of high martial hopes. But he knew more about constructing plays and sonnets than ships and dockyards, and he would have little basis for challenging the padded accounts and falsified bills submitted by

3. Oppenheim, *Sir William Monson,* 4:228–32.

the professionals. Greville no doubt did what he could to curb the worst grievances. John Coke, one of his officers, repeatedly investigated cases of theft, adulteration, forgery, false measurement, and other abuses, and won praise for his "honest and wise" overseeing eye.[4] It is interesting that when he compiled the notes of his inquiries Coke saw that the root of the problem lay in the admiralty's constitution as a private franchise and its operation as a patronage machine. Foremost among the "principal and original causes" of disorder was the fact that the lord admiral, into whose hands all appointments were drawn, preferred no man for his merit "but for means only"; since appointment came from on high, other officers had no power to reward the honest or censure the criminous. The officers all tried to escape any accountability for charges against the revenue, which almost came to mean that free disposition of the queen's treasure had drifted down to the level of clerks. It was a system of disorganized irresponsibility in which the only common cause that remained was self-help.

When Greville surrendered the office in 1604, it was to a completely different kind of individual but one even less able, had he been willing, to put the lord admiral's house in order. Nottingham had had nothing to do with the earlier appointments to the treasurership; Hawkins was in office before him, and Greville had risen through the favor of the queen. But Sir Robert Mansell was a man of Nottingham's own making, the creature of his choice. He had been Mansell's patron for years, had taken him on the Cádiz voyage, gotten him knighted, given him commands in the major voyages of the late nineties, and had finally made him admiral of the Narrow Seas. His rise in every way paralleled that of Sir Richard Leveson and, like Leveson's, was based on a family tie: the Mansells of Margam were cousins and political allies of the Gamages in Wales.

Mansell was an apt enough soldier; no one ever accused him of lack of bravery, and he was building a meritorious record at

4. Historical Manuscripts Commission, *Twelfth Report, Manuscripts of Earl Cowper*, vol. 1: *Coke Manuscripts*, pp. 27, 41–42; hereinafter cited as *Coke MSS*.

sea. But his talents were those of the field, not the counting house; he was swaggering, vain, and hot-tempered, with a penchant for abusive language and contempt for the arts of the courtier—almost the perfect stereotype of the soldier in Jacobean comedy. He had been provoked into a shipboard duel early in his naval career and, even though cleared by a commission of inquiry, he continued to use bluster and dash rather than eloquence and tact to make his way in the world. The story is told that during the Spanish embassy in 1605 he twice put the Spaniards to shame with his soldierly bravado. Once when returning to his lodging after "grande entertainment and revels," Sir Robert had a hat with a rich jewel snatched away; he and his friends followed with loud outcry and drawn swords into the house of a judge, which he insisted on searching "without form of law" until the thief was discovered hiding in a well. Again, when he discovered a Spaniard tucking silver plate into his clothing at a feast, he hauled the man to the head of the table and forced him to disgorge, to the amazement of the company. Such straightforward diplomacy may not have endeared him to his hosts, but it earned him among his compatriots the reputation of "a man born to vindicate the honor of his nation as his owne."[5] Even in Parliament Mansell had trouble holding his impetuous nature in check; Bishop Goodman recalled that when Mansell's valuable monopoly on glass-making was attacked, he responded in such heat that there was fear that he might be committed. Only the pleas of his friends that he spoke "like an openhearted Welshman and soldier" saved him. He got into trouble again and again for his rashness, but he was never at a loss for friends. Not only did he have Nottingham's full protection at his disposal, but he also attracted the favor of King James himself; Anthony Weldon called Mansell "the only valiant man" that the king ever loved, and loved so "intirely" that not even Buckingham was able to push him out.[6]

In a way it seems curious that a man who was so sharp-eyed

5. Anthony Weldon, *Court and Character of King James*, in *Secret History of the Court of James the First*, 1:354–56, 356–58.
6. *Ibid.*, 2:6–7.

in catching a Spaniard at petty theft would have been entirely blind to the enormously greater embezzlements that were going on in his own docks and yards. But Mansell was even less of an administrator than Fulke Greville had been, and his independent wealth was not nearly so great; he was a younger son of a Welsh family who needed to make his place pay. And though nothing was ever proved conclusively against him, there are many suggestions that he not only failed to check the squandering of naval funds but used the navy freely as the raw material for personal aggrandizement.

In Hawkins' time there had been a rivalry among navy officers which probably acted to keep them all reasonably honest. Sir William Winter, whose charges resulted in the commission of inquiry in 1583, was as surveyor of ships for a long time Hawkins' bitterest enemy. The surveyor had the burden, essentially, of seeing that the navy got full value for its money, which would enable him to cause endless trouble for a peculating treasurer. But at the time that Greville became treasurer, John Trevor, a man incapable of being an admiralty gadfly, was made surveyor. He, like Mansell, was a Welshman, one of a family of brothers that found preferment with the lord admiral. Although some of his brothers were notably factious, John was no swashbuckling soldier. After several years in lesser household offices, he became a personal secretary to the lord admiral.

The absence of any real distinction between the public and private business of a great officer can be no better illustrated than through Trevor's role as secretary. He was a private servant and privately paid, but he handled naval and family affairs indiscriminately; on one day he would represent Howard's interest in a prize claim, the next day he would work on a commission to suppress piracy, and the next he might supervise repairs on the house at Reigate. He was paid, characteristically, not at a fixed salary but with a slice of the admiral's perquisites—a share in prize incomes, which he helped to collect, and eventually a share in the receipts from the wine farm. The lord admiral got him a collection of minor offices, but appointment as surveyor was his highest preferment and marked his transition from private servant to officer of the crown. "Mild, wise, temperate"[7] Sir John was an experienced and probably able administrator, but he was not conspicuously honest and was certainly more disposed to co-operate with his fellow officers than to restrain them. He and fellow Welshman Mansell were firm friends who set out a number of joint ventures and worked closely together in managing their naval preserve. In time their private affairs and naval responsibilities became so inextricably tangled that with the greatest good will they could not themselves have distinguished one from the other.

Nor were the other principal officers willing to curb the enterprise of admiralty personnel—or even aware of the desirability of doing so. Sir Henry Palmer, the comptroller, Sir Peter Buck, clerk of the ships, Marmaduke Darell and Thomas Bludder, victualers, and scores of lesser figures had the same vested interest in the relaxed and comfortable status quo.

What had been created, then, was a progressive deterioration of standards of service which permeated every level and which became more flagrant as the peacetime navy fell into disuse. As long as active conflict lasted, it was with privateering that most financial expectations were bound up. Admiral, vice-admirals, judges, sergeants, and clerks all had their established claims on prizes and most were regular or occasional investors in prize ventures; victualers, ropemakers, and carpenters found their greatest markets in outfitting royal and private prize vessels; captains, boatswains, gunners, and crews lived in the hope of surprising that great carrack loaded with pearls and spices which would make them all rich. So the entire establishment concentrated on prize-seeking with single-minded enthusiasm. Sir William Monson, that energetic manager of the country's affairs, wrote to Cecil late in Elizabeth's lifetime that there was such an emphasis on privateering that the queen's proper service was being left undone.

7. Godfrey Goodman, *The Court of King James the First,* ed. John S. Brewer, 2 vols. (London, 1839), 1:57.

"And no man dares reprove it, because the Lord Admiral is interested. . . ."[8]

Privateering was an essentially immoral and illegal activity made permissible by the special requirements of war, and those who engaged in it gradually lost their appreciation for the fine distinctions that kept it inside the law. The lord admiral had no qualms about suspending the normal rules for his friends or pressing in his public capacity for something that would benefit his private estate. He made exceptions to admiralty procedures so casually that Caesar complained that his private warrants were "blunted and disgraced in the opinion of the people," who were taught to use them "rather as props to their disordered affections than as means for the futherance or execution of justice."[9] Ethical lines were further erased by the fact that the admiral and his officers were frequently promoters who naturally found any rulings against their own prizes very difficult to bear.

When the lord admiral set such an example, his inferiors learned not only to disregard the legal niceties but also to try to avoid paying what was due to him. His vice-admirals chronically failed to render their accounts, and when accounts were made, they were usually fragmentary. And there were many ways to evade the machinery of the vice-admirals—vessels were landed in isolated creeks and bays under cover of darkness, bulk was broken at sea, and ships' officers and crews smuggled ashore everything they could get their hands on. If caught, a share in the plunder would usually satisfy the local officeholder, and no one would be the wiser.

The kind of attitudes which had been nourished in the free-and-easy years of unrestricted Spaniard-chasing remained after King James ordered an end to privateering. For some figures on the fringes of the admiralty, outright piracy was a convenient substitute, particularly when carefully placed bribes would win protection at court. Those within the establishment presumably could have only peripheral dealings with

8. Oppenheim, *Sir William Monson,* 2:238.
9. Andrews, *Elizabethan Privateering,* p. 27.

pirates, but imagination and initiative could find ways of turning the penny that the privateers no longer brought in. Higher officers could still sell the places under them—at such rates that the underlings were driven into malpractices to realize their investments; clerks and officers could travel in great state and at great expense to view the works and take musters; worn-out ships could be kept in service so that inflated contracts could be let for repairing them; captains and pursers could league with suppliers to make a profit on stores and victuals; officers could use the crown's timber and stores to outfit their own ships; shipbuilders could capitalize on their minor perquisites so that, as Goodman remarked, great houses at Chatham could be built entirely of chips. Unnecessary appointments could be made to relatives and friends; wages to seamen could be cut and food adulterated; supplies could be shorted and surpluses spirited into private hands. There is ample evidence that all these practices, and others, occurred not occasionally but as a matter of habit; the atmosphere in the navy seemed to demand them.

The best single example of energetic milking of the navy by its own personnel might be the famous 1605 voyage of a little ship built by Phineas Pett, later the king's master ship-wright, in a private yard in Gillingham. Judging from evidence which came to light later on, it would seem that Pett used primarily the timber delivered to the naval stores at Chatham and equipment obtained by warrant from the principal officers, who later took shares in the voyage. The ship was fitted with rigging bought by the officers' favor from a royal ship for "bare 12£ only" and was furnished out of the king's stores with "cables, anchors, flags, pitch, and other stores and provisions, including 600 cwt. of biscuit" and 120 bolts of canvas. When Nottingham sailed for Spain in 1605, the vessel was set out as a transporter of provisions; it was paid wages and tonnage by the crown at twice its actual weight, but was entered on the customs book as a private merchantman carrying sixty tons of lead to Sanlúcar for a London merchant. Other goods aboard, including brass ordnance and ammunition, were sold in Lisbon to help meet the lord admiral's expenses, but the voyage cost the king "800£ or 1,000£, as appeareth by the accounts," and Pett, Mansell, and Trevor absorbed the profits.[10] As one captain had written late in 1603, "the whole body is so corrupted as there is no sound part almost from the head to the foot; the great ones feed on the less and enforce them to steal both for themselves and their commanders. . . ."[11] It is not possible to say that corruption began with any individual or was promoted or protected by any other; it had crept in unnoticed, "like rust into iron," as Monson put it, and had so permeated the structure that it had become an established way of life.

But it was a way of life that was out of keeping with the country's needs and with the king's resources, even though other areas of government were certainly not untouched by the same pattern. James's irresponsible openhandedness, the clamors of his courtiers for place and reward, and his growing estrangement from the Commons all severely limited the funds available to support a gluttonous and unproductive navy. When the Spanish war ended, of course, it was possible to make substantial reductions in total naval expenditures, mainly in sea charges, since there were no more large-scale expeditions to be equipped and the principal sea duty was that of patrolling the Channel and the Irish Sea. So in the first year of peace the money spent on the navy fell by nearly half— from more than £42,000 to just over £24,000. In 1605 the Spanish embassy increased the total artificially, but by 1607 the expenses had begun to rise again to wartime levels— £25,000 in 1607, more than £36,500 in 1608, and well above £43,000 in 1609—with no important actions which would justify them.[12]

Consciousness of increasing demands for funds and obviously deteriorating standards produced a royal commission early in 1608 to look into prevalent "abuses and discords" and make a report to the king. Interestingly enough, a commission

10. The episode is summarized in W. G. Perrin, ed., *The Autobiography of Phineas Pett* (London, 1918), pp. lviii–lxi.

11. *Coke MSS*, p. 45.

12. Oppenheim, *Administration of the Royal Navy*, 1:197.

was issued on March 30 with Nottingham at its head, but this was either altered or withdrawn, and a month later another one passed under the Great Seal in which Nottingham was superseded by the earl of Northampton. At any rate it was Northampton who was the driving force behind the commission and who probably secured its appointment. Why Northampton should have launched the inquiry is a problem in historical motivations: here is a man who in other contexts becomes almost a perfect specimen of cultivated aristocratic villainy; he is warped, deceitful, obsequious, devious. His life, said Willson, "was one long intrigue, as noisome and sinister as the ailment [a tumor which became gangrenous after surgery] that carried him off."[13] In the navy investigation, however, he may have been acting selflessly as the public-spirited agent of fiscal responsibility, the loyal subject inflamed by heedless waste of the country's substance. It is possible for a man wholly bad to undertake an action that is wholly good. But it should be remembered at the same time that Northampton had despised Nottingham since 1605 or before, and any attack on the navy undermined the admiral. Against Mansell, too, he nourished a hatred that burned hot and pure—he was once quoted as saying that he would be "content to be damned perpetually in hell to be revenged on that proud Welshman."[14] In addition, there may have been some relationship between his criticisms of naval waste and his hopes of becoming lord treasurer. Whatever Northampton's motives and hopes of personal gain and revenge, a systematic inquiry into naval conditions could benefit the crown enormously—and, of course, destroy nearly everyone in the lord admiral's fiefdom. The commission was large and sufficiently prestigious; it included, besides Northampton and Nottingham, Lords Zouche and Wotton, Sir Julius Caesar—for many years admiralty judge and probably the most learned man in the country on admiralty affairs—Sir Robert Cotton, Sir Francis Bacon, the king's solicitor general, the attorney

13. Willson, *King James VI and I*, p. 349.
14. Weldon, *Court and Character of King James*, 1:333–35.

general, the lieutenant of the Tower, the chancellor of the duchy, and others, fifteen in all. But of the fifteen, only Northampton and Cotton, who worked closely together, attended all sessions and signed all depositions. The commission was Northampton's vehicle, and he dominated it from beginning to end. When it first met on May 5, 1608, it was only to hear him make an "Eligant" speech affirming the king's "princely purpose," appoint Cotton secretary, and hear a single examination, "for forms sake."[15]

The commission continued to sit—once, twice, three times a week—through the spring and summer and, with a recess in August, into the fall. There were fifty-three meetings, including meetings of a subcommission at Rochester, before the end of the year, meetings at which "many were brought into great question and tossed to and fro before the commissioners . . . to their no small charge and vexation," as Phineas Pett, one of those principally tossed, put it. Apart from these personal traumas, Pett thought that the only result was that the "government itself of that Royal Office was so shaken and disjointed as brought almost imminent ruin upon the whole Navy, and a far greater charge to his Majesty . . . than was ever known before." His view was not entirely impartial, but it may be that the transportation of witnesses and the collection of evidence and depositions had something to do with the inflated naval accounts for that year.

What was brought to light, however, was a vast and labyrinthine system of malpractice in which everyone seemed to have a profitable part. Depositions were taken from scores of individuals who again and again admitted taking their modest profits from the navy's ships, men, and goods, but who swore that there were many others far worse than they. William Pope, examined late in July, testified that he had seen the lord admiral's signature on blank pages which could then be used for whatever purpose the officers' greed might fancy. He did not know how such a situation came to be, but he "hath heard that some of those passes that have bene signed by my l.

15. Cotton MSS, Julius F:III/1.

Admiral have bene otherwise disposed of then he intendeth."
John Ackworth, clerk to the keeper of the king's stores in
London, admitted that "at sundry tymes bills passed wt increase upon certeyne provisions," creating surplus funds which
were shared between himself and others. With various partners he had profited from £7 to £8 on deliveries of flags, £15
on resins, and £10 on cables. He had had his share of the
remnants of canvas left from cutting sails, and he and others,
including Sir John Trevor, had made away with hundreds of
pounds of rope. John Rockwell, a purser, gave instances in
which the king's foodstuffs, amounting once to 15 days' victuals for 250 men, were loaded into private vessels on Trev-
or's warrant. Twice he had been employed as a factor by
Mansell and Trevor to sell corn in Spain, but had had his
wages and allowances paid by the king. Another witness, who
for seventeen years had been delivering timber to the king's
storehouses, admitted that he had had "increase upon all his
bills more or less" and that he had falsified amounts delivered,
splitting the profits with the clerks. Others testified to habitual
deliveries of short measures of oil that was so "drossy and
unserviceable" that only one hogshead in twelve would be
usable at all, to carelessness in record-keeping so pervasive as
to make it impossible to tell what was on hand at any time, to
private sales by ropemakers from the royal supplies, and to
outright embezzlement on a grand scale. Mansell was accused
of entering whatever "summe he thinketh good" for oil, tar,
oakum, pitch, and other commodities on his accounts, often
from £200 to £300 more per month than actually delivered,
transferring the surpluses to accounts for past years, and then
splitting the proceeds, as much as £3,000 a year, with Trevor.[16] The chronicle fills a thick volume in Cotton's neat hand
and implicates the whole admiralty hierarchy—the lord admiral himself stood accused of a negligence so gross as to be
intolerable even in Jacobean society and certainly serious
enough to warrant the talk that he had turned himself over
completely to Mansell, who was without doubt the procurer

16. *Ibid.*, fols. 116–19, 154, 168–70, 183–84, 206–7.

of blank warrants. Both Mansell and Trevor, if their accusers are to be taken at face value, did not hesitate to countermand such directions as Nottingham did give which might inconvenience their business arrangements. The lord admiral's neglect of duty had opened the way for an abuse of power on the part of his subordinates which was so flagrantly subversive of the king's service that it could scarcely be said that the navy was an instrument of service at all; it is difficult to say whether Nottingham's carelessness or his officers' criminality was more reprehensible.

Some of the witnesses, of course, might themselves be impeached for standing to gain from a wholesale turnover within the bureaucracy. The principal accusers, who may have incited Northampton at the beginning, were officeholders or office-seekers: Sir Peter and Thomas Buck, clerk and under-clerk of the ships, Matthew Baker and William Bright, master shipwrights, other masters, clerks, and pursers, most of whom did have long experience and established reputations as craftsmen, and office-seekers like George Waymouth, an unemployed master and self-appointed expert on nautical construction. But as the inquiry progressed, there were more and more boatswains, ropemakers, carpenters, clerks, and workmen and contractors of every degree who admitted a formidable array of misdeeds of their own, who could hope for reward on no basis except frankness. Their evidence, it seemed, would have to be accepted substantially as presented, and it should have been sufficient to convict the principal officers of any charge the king might bring.

One of the principal complaints had been directed against Phineas Pett, the master shipwright who designed and built the *Royal Prince* for Prince Henry. On this special inquiry, as on the commission as a whole, Northampton staked his credit with the king only to find himself thwarted and ridiculed. It was a prolonged and intricate affair. Pett had first of all been authorized to make repairs on the *Victory,* which James had given to his son. But he finally persuaded the lord admiral to let him draw up plans for an entirely new ship, new in concept and bigger than any previously built. He made a scale model from his design which so charmed the king that he agreed to the new proposal (and set a precedent which later shipwrights found useful when they wanted to make innovations). Construction was still under way when the commission met in December, 1608; before it Pett's rival Matthew Baker raised questions of the appropriateness of the new design, Pett's competence as a builder, and the cost and suitability of the material used. He said that Pett, who through the lord admiral had gained the favor of Prince Henry, was a "man most simple for such a purpose," who in the past had been entrusted with repairs which had only turned out badly, that the timber was chosen not for its suitability but for the builders' profits and would not prove seaworthy, that the design was unjustified by past experience, and that Pett's estimates of costs were unreasonably inflated. Baker was reinforced by the testimony of Waymouth, who had visited the yards at Woolwich on a warrant from Northampton, and other experts. Pett himself believed or claimed to believe that they were motivated by jealousy of his commission and by the personal malice of Northampton, "my most implacable enemy." He sounded the alarm to Trevor and Mansell, who rode the next day down to Woolwich to survey the work. Apparently on their advice he wrote to Nottingham himself that there was a plot afoot to destroy him, "earnestly beseeching [him] . . . since the matter so nearly concerned his Majesty's profit, the honour of the state, his Lordship's own safety, and the reputation of his Office," to head off his enemies and have a new survey made by "judicious and impartial persons." The lord admiral, "not a little troubled to observe their malicious practices," summoned Pett for conference the same night, and by four the next morning Nottingham was at the king's door begging for audience about "some business of great consequence." The king, whose sympathies were entirely with Pett because of his pleasure in the project, "seemed greatly to pity the wrong and injury done" and immediately appointed a "judicious and impartial" panel consisting of the lord admiral, Suffolk, and the earl of Worcester to hear the accusers and make trial of the work.

Not surprisingly, they found the workmanship sound and discovered that Baker was acting "more out of an envious malicious humour against me than upon any certain ground of error." Waymouth was found to be so tedious in his "infinite rabble of idle and unprofitable speeches" about proportions, measures, and lines that he was finally commanded into silence. Sitting in Pett's own dining room, they told him that he "had no cause to be discouraged" in his service and they promised not only a favorable report to the king but defense against any future charges.[17] Nottingham might have been negligent, but no charges could be brought against him for disloyalty to his followers.

His opponents returned to their own patron, Northampton, who was now so "vehemently incensed" over the partiality of the panel that he begged the king to require a second hearing. James defended his choice of "three principal peers of the realm, of whose faithful fidelity he was so confidently assured," but finally agreed to preside over a second hearing himself, in the role of Solomon he so much enjoyed.

The new hearing was set for May 8, 1609, and was preceded by a period of frantic activity. Both parties summoned together a corps of builders and designers who would support their case, and there were many inspections of the work, which was suspended lest Pett "reform" those things which had been found defective. Baker and his "malicious associates" met almost daily to "deface the work by striking aside the shores, and condemning the materials, aggravating continual disgraces upon me, and railing despitefully to my face," which he endured, Pett said, patiently, "flying to God, on whose mercy I wholly depended in these extremities." But if he depended wholly on God, he might also have found solace in the activities of friends at court. The lord admiral was busy with Trevor and Mansell preparing a defense against every objection that might be raised, and Prince Henry almost every day sent "a comfortable encouragement," promising that, even if he were altogether overthrown in the present affair, he

17. Perrin, *Phineas Pett*, pp. 38–46.

would be taken into the prince's own household. Such support —with the known disposition of the royal judge—forecast the outcome of the hearing.

The day of trial was a complete victory for the defenders of the establishment. No later than his arrival, the king let his inclinations be known when he refused to enter the yards on Northampton's invitation and go to his headquarters at the house of the clerk of the cheque, but insisted on being taken by the lord admiral through the gates to Pett's own house, which had been decorated to receive him. He then opened the proceedings with a little speech on the king's function as giver of laws: neither side, he said, should act out of malice or other "pretence" or seek excuse in favor, "for that his Majesty in the seat of justice [re]presenting God's person, would not be deluded, nor led by any coloured pretences from understanding the very plain truth of that business which was to be handled." Having assumed ex-cathedra infallibility, the king adopted a severe look and commanded Pett to kneel before him as the charges, which were many and technical, were read. James was able to group the charges as relating to "art" or design, materials, and cost.

As to design, both sides summoned their experts and debated "with much violence and eagerness" but reached no decision. The king, of course, was no judge of such matters of shipbuilding theory and could find no basis for deciding. Finally, as a symbolic test of Pett's innovations, he settled on one point that could be determined: the accusers insisted that the square of the ship's flat at midships was a full thirteen feet, which was felt to be unwieldy; Pett claimed that it was but eleven feet eight inches. The king appointed his own experts to determine the flat; when after prolonged calculations they pronounced in Pett's favor "the whole multitude heaved up their hats, and gave a great and loud shout."[18] Later students have generally agreed and have found that the changes Pett introduced, including a deeper draught, were entirely justifiable.

18. *Ibid.*, p. 62.

The question of cost was easily disposed of; the king simply accepted Pett's contention that, ton for ton, the *Prince Royal* would not be more expensive than ships built in Elizabeth's time. Northampton and his "bandogs" were not able to refute him, but they were right; by the time it was finished, this was the most expensive ship England had ever launched. Baker, the rival shipwright, had charged that the total cost would come to £7,000, nearly twice what he had been paid for a somewhat smaller ship, the *Merhonour.* Pett disputed the figure indignantly, but the final cost of the *Prince Royal* was just under £20,000, including more than £1,300 in decorations.

To test the suitability of materials, James had workmen plane those spots which had been judged green, rotten, or cross-grained and found them sound and serviceable; he immediately pronounced that "the cross-grain was in the men and not in the timber" and that the ship would "be too strong if one third of the timber were left out." Pett's narrative does not indicate whose advice the king took in deciding; certainly he would scarcely have been able to judge for himself. But once again his decision was refuted by time; the navy commissioners in 1621 supported every charge that had been made in 1609.[19]

In conclusion, the king again commended Pett, "bitterly reprehending" his accusers, but he encouraged Northampton to continue in his search for errors and abuses. As James rose to leave, Nottingham offered a speech of his own "to admire and extol his Majesty's justice, great wisdom, and princely care of the good of the commonwealth, in that he had refused no pains . . . to provide to rectify and set straight, to the wonder and admiration of them all, a work of so great a consequence, and of such a kind of intricacy as his Majesty had never been accustomed to before, and yet so clearly to examine and try in so short a space, as he had only [been] bred and accustomed to such elements, with many other honourable speeches tending to that purpose." Placing his hand on Pett's head, he staked

19. *Ibid.*, p. lxxxii; *Coke MSS*, p. 114.

his life, lands, and honor on the work undertaken and swore that when the ship was finished he would assume all charges himself if the king did not like it. So the day ended happily for the navy, Nottingham attended the king to Whitehall, "being never better contented in all his life," and Northampton slipped out the back way "railing bitterly."[20] Pett never once admitted that anything might be involved in the inquiry other than the envy of his enemies, so his victory was their comeuppance: "God put a hook into their nostrils and by the justice of the King caused themselves to fall into the pit they digged for another." But if the justice of the king had been more carefully considered or less prejudiced, the outcome might have been far different for the pious Pett.

The controversy over the *Prince Royal* had been but a part of the naval investigation, but with the intervention of the king it became such a *cause célèbre* that its outcome tended to undermine the larger findings of the commission. By May, 1609, the investigations were about complete; with all the concentration on Pett's ship, there had been very few hearings since December. In early June the king asked his commissioners to account for their labors, so Cotton drew up and submitted abstracts of all the depositions received. For three whole days during Whitsun week he listened to the allegations and heard what defense could be offered, but the fire had gone out of the investigation. At the beginning, Northampton made the tactical blunder of complaining against the outcome at Woolwich and "alleging the confidence of the informers who were ready to maintain the truth of their former informations with their lives." James was naturally offended that his justice should be challenged and cut Northampton short; in all probability, the insult made him more disposed to leniency. By the end of the week he had had his fill of naval controversies and postponed the final disposition until mid-September, after the summer hunting was done and before the term's business began. When the hearings ended, Northampton was still optimistic. The king had promised him that everyone charged

20. Perrin, *Phineas Pett,* pp. 64–67.

would be referred to the courts, "according to the Quallity of every Man's Offence to be condignely censured and chastized." If his present resolution held, "if those Humours which are stirred may be purged . . . there will be a mighty saving of the King's Treasure, as great a Satisfaction to the Subject, and a Preservation to this Island equal if not superior to any other whatsoever kind that may be devised." Their labors "hath been Paynfull, the Pursuit Industrious; but above both, Oppositions out of the Guiltiness of corrupt Affections have been desperate." But "I learned of my Father *droict & devant* and in the end, *vincit veritas. . . .*"[21]

Northampton's great hopes, however, bore little fruit. There was no referral of naval officers to ordinary courses at law; the king allowed the offenders to throw themselves on his mercy and contented himself to forgive them if they "would every on of them in ther places respectively perform their dutyes Justly and carfully." Northampton was asked to draw up a book of ordinances for naval government, over which he labored so painstakingly that it "put you in minde of the question at Athenes whether Minervas shippe that had bene so often peeced and repaered as it was made wholly of newe wood was the same or another." "And this," Cotton wrote laconically in his own report, "is a sum of the wholl years service."[22]

In the whole year's service, one commission member had been conspicuously absent. Several appointees, including Caesar, attended only occasionally, but Nottingham sat through none of the hearings and signed none of the depositions—which suggests what would have happened if he had remained the head of the commission. Although there is nothing which says so explicitly, the implication is strong that he resented the investigation as a derogation of his administration—which it was—and chose to dissociate himself entirely from it. His energies were no doubt being spent on behalf of other followers, as well as on Pett, in an effort to subvert and undermine

21. Winwood, *Memorials of Affairs of State,* 3:54.
22. Cotton MSS, Julius F:III–1.

the inquiry. It is debatable whether or not the final outcome owed something to his influence and efforts. The king was by nature a man of easy forgiveness, and two of the defendants, Pett and Mansell, were high in his favor anyway, but one may be sure that whatever influence Nottingham still possessed was exerted in the cause. Northampton and Cotton were far from contented, but the king's decision had been made and for the time being they had no choice but to swallow it. They could, however, take some solace in the "most gratious acceptance" of Northampton's rules for naval government; Nottingham "fled in distresse" from the presentation but was compelled by the king "to look on rather with an approving then an opposing view which is more then half a miracle."[23]

Until enough time had elapsed for a new investigation to be called, the lord admiral's free-wheeling and unregulated province was safe. For him, the quashing of the naval inquiry marked the beginning of a quieter and less controversial period. As Prince Henry's governor, he was enmeshed in the feastings and games that celebrated Henry's investiture as Prince of Wales. And with the prince again, he looked forward with keen pleasure to the completion and launching of the *Prince Royal.* This was made a great state occasion, with not only the ship itself but the houses around it decorated, the king and queen with their courts in attendance, and Nottingham and the principal officers of the navy hovering about. But if God had favored Phineas Pett before, he did not now. The ship stuck fast in the dock gates and then settled hard on the ground, to the discomfiture of the king, who was suffering from diarrhea and found waiting difficult, and the great lords on the poop, standing by the gilt cup filled with wine. The king waited most of the day, but there was no possibility of launching until the next flood tide, after midnight, so the crowd finally dispersed. That night Nottingham sat up in his chair until the flood came; Prince Henry had ridden off to Greenwich but returned in a heavy storm in the middle of the night, and, at two o'clock in the morning, the great, costly,

23. *Ibid.*, Titus C: VI/154–55.

and elaborate ship was finally floated, although not to the applause of the court.

Nottingham's relation to Prince Henry had always seemed cordial; Henry had a strong (though rather uncritical) interest in the navy, which was best exemplified in the construction of the *Prince Royal,* and the lord admiral took pleasure in leading him through ritual inspections of ships and storehouses. Their apparent intimacy makes another distinction between Nottingham and what has been called the "Howard party," to which the Prince of Wales tended to be opposed. Weldon would have it that Henry disliked the Howards uniformly: "being a prince of open heart, hating all basenesse, [he] would often say, if ever he were king, he would not leave one of that family to piss against a wall."[24] But there is no suggestion that he included Nottingham in that category of abuse. The prince's support had been important to the admiral throughout the investigations and could be again. So Henry's unexpected death in 1612 was cause for shock and sorrow. At his funeral Nottingham was among the dozen assistants to the chief mourner—marking again the many times in recent years that he had appeared in such a role.

A few months earlier, another death had brought Nottingham personal dismay: the earl of Salisbury had died on his way from the waters at Bath. In a way it seems curious that he made no mention of his old colleague in his will when there were bequests to Suffolk, Worcester, and others at court.[25] Nor was Nottingham an official mourner at Salisbury's funeral, although he did stand as godfather to the granddaughter born the next winter. The simplest explanation, of course, is that Salisbury could not, when writing his will, have expected Nottingham to outlive him, and there is reasonable probability that poor health prevented the admiral from appearing at the funeral. But Salisbury's death also accentuated Nottingham's increasing isolation at court. Salisbury had kept him within the "Howard" group as much as he was, and now that

24. Weldon, *Court and Character of King James,* 1:393–94.
25. Additional MSS, 34,218/138.

Salisbury was gone, the lord admiral was really in no group at all. Suffolk had been wholly drawn into the whirlpool of the Carr alliance, and that alliance, with Northampton as its architect and engineer, was now the center of the "Howard," or "Spanish," party. Nottingham still had in common with that group the sympathy toward Spain entertained since 1605, and he still held the same exalted view of a royal power that would support his own needs, but it was not his views on either Spain or the prerogative that really mattered any more. Northampton knew that as well as anyone did, and he, the guiding spirit of the "Howard" party, continued to treat this Howard with scarcely concealed contempt. Nottingham could still busy himself with the petty responsibilities of keeping the castles, parks, and forests he held from the king, with court ceremonial, and with an occasional dabble in the business of the navy, which was again beginning quietly and profitably to decay after the trauma of 1608–9 had passed. But he was an isolated figure nevertheless. It was not that he stood apart from the luxury, intrigue, and vice of his day by any self-conscious act—his world was as steeped in corruption as any other—but he was old and remote, and the court was taking less notice of him. His finances were as shaky as ever; with most of the income from the wine farm granted away before he ever got it, with his debts to the crown and to private lenders steadily accumulating, he had no recourse but to sell off capital assets. Eastbrooke Manor in Sussex had been sold in 1607, and Lymington, Hampshire, was disposed to Abraham Campion by 1609. Early in 1612 Nottingham made an important symbolic gesture in the direction of a more modest scale of living: the great tapestries woven in Holland to celebrate the victory over the Armada, the tapestries he had been expected to give Queen Elizabeth on her last visit, the tapestries which had been the chief ornament of Arundel House and the principal symbol of Nottingham's public stature, were sold to the king. James's payment was no mere token—£1,628 8s. for 708 Flemish ells of cloth "in full satisfaction and payment"—but it seems doubtful that the money to redeem a few debts could give the old commander nearly as much satisfaction as the tangible reminder of his great exploit.[26]

At state functions, however, Nottingham emerged in his former glory—taking the arm of the newlywed Princess Elizabeth to escort her from the royal chapel, placing the Garter on the leg of the Prince Palatine, and helping to garb Rochester in the splendor of his new earldom.[27] When Elizabeth married, Nottingham announced that he meant to make it his last service at sea to "wafte her over" to her new domain, and it was done in a style suitable to the closing of his public life and the beginning of hers. Six of the king's ships—including the magnificent *Prince Royal,* the royal barge, and the lord admiral's barge—and five merchant ships were equipped at the king's expense to carry the cumbersome retinue across the Channel and were escorted by the admiral of the Narrow Seas with his squadron. The short crossing to Flushing cost James £5,555, not including £4,800 for the mock naval battle on the Thames which wounded several of the participants or the £2,800 spent for fireworks at the river before departure. The sum, however, did presumably include the £4 a day Nottingham allowed himself for personal expenses, which set a new standard for officers' sea pay and became a troublesome precedent for later navy commissioners. When the fleet landed, the lord admiral caused heaven and earth to respond to the glory of the union with a great volley of four hundred shot, to which the town responded suitably. After a few days of civic celebrations he returned to his ship to find that such multitudes had come to gape at its size and decorations that he had to take his leave at night.[28] The brief voyage, which lasted a week, was a pleasant interlude and an apt enough parting gesture for an old warrior.

When Nottingham viewed the voyage as his last service to the state, he did so correctly, but that does not mean that he

26. Frederick Devon, ed., *Issues of the Exchequer: Being payments made out of his Majesty's revenue during the reign of King James I* (London, 1836), p. 146.

27. McClure, *Letters of John Chamberlain,* 1:485.

28. Nichols, *Progresses of King James the First,* 2:611–14.

retired from naval life. His decision reflected a continuing attitude: the command of ships was the service he had rendered to the crown; the administration of ships was the reward he would continue to receive from it. For he did not yet intend to give up the stature that his naval princedom automatically conferred. Neither did he have plans for changing anything very dramatically in the admiralty as long as he lived, although in 1611 he did order a complete survey made of the serviceability of the ships in the king's possession so that at least that elementary information as to the country's preparedness would be available.[29] The fact that such a survey was thought necessary is a commentary on the state of record-keeping by the naval officers. But there were others who were more restless about the admiral's business than he. Northampton had not forgotten his humiliation at Woolwich or the abortive justice that had come of his year's labors. Early in 1613 he and Sir Robert Cotton pleaded with the king for a renewal of their commission to redress naval abuses. Eventually they, with Nottingham, Suffolk, Ellesmere, and others, received a generous grant not only to investigate but to punish those who were responsible for the navy's pitiable weakness.

But once again the establishment was able to turn aside a frontal attack, this time more easily because of earlier victories. Sir Robert Mansell, that doughty defender of illicit wealth, now without the pacifying influence of Trevor, who had retired to his Welsh estates, plunged into the fight in an effort to turn a challenge to his own misadministration into an attack on his constitutional rights as a subject. He did not quite succeed, but so diverted the inquiry that it came to nothing. He went to James Whitelocke, whose stinging speech on impositions had made him a notable parliamentary critic of royal prerogative, to see if the commission could not be found illegal.[30] Whitelocke obligingly found objections on

29. *Cal S. P. Dom., James I, 1611–1618* (London, 1858), p. 50.
30. Gardiner (*History of England,* 2:187) believed that Nottingham was the responsible agent and that Mansell simply covered his patron's role. But even though there can be no doubt that Nottingham took serious exception to the new commission and would

many counts and couched them in tactless language that was certain to cause offense in the council. He discovered that the commission was "irregular, without president, strainge, of a newe moulde" which would use inquisitorial techniques to achieve unconstitutional ends. The king, he claimed, could not meddle with the lands, bodies, or goods of his subjects without the due process of arraignment and trial; thus the power to punish miscreants in the navy was illegal and voided the whole commission. When Mansell began to circulate the objections, he was promptly jailed in the Marshalsea; White-locke, who was at this point only presumed to be the author, was sent to the Fleet for his attack on the legitimacy of the Earl Marshal's court. After some days, both were hauled before the council to answer for their contumacy. The king's counsel pressed them to give up—which they did with becoming humility—the "grossely erroneous" and "daingerous" view that the king could not punish his own servants without trial, a view which denied martial and proclamation law and the authority of the council, and which tended "to the dissolvinge of government." The pair admitted that their offenses deserved sharp punishment but threw themselves on the king's mercy and begged that they not be punished except by the imprisonment they had already endured. One by one their judges condemned their offenses but declared themselves inclined toward clemency, and both were restored to the king's favor after making their submissions in writing.[31] The fact that they were not fined and dismissed from office again bespeaks the enduring influence of the naval establishment—but even more the king's unaccountable fondness for his pet

---

have liked to see it quashed, he was too consistently the defender of the prerogative to sponsor a constitutional challenge to the crown. He also lacked the temperament which would lead to such a step—in more than forty years of employment by willful sovereigns, only once had he acted in reckless defiance, when he wrote his impetuous protest to Elizabeth against being left out of the commission to relieve Calais in 1596, and he was not likely to do so again as an old man. But the hotheaded Mansell would not hesitate.

31. Dasent, *Acts of the Privy Council,* 33:211–19.

soldier. Mansell would seem to have been humiliated by this prostration before the awesome authority of the council, but though he had lost the battle, he had won the war. It was clear that no matter how foul the navy might be shown to be, Mansell was not going to be punished for it, so the investigation never really got off the ground, for which the machinations of one commission member may be assumed partly responsible. Later in the year, however, a few feeble thrusts were made at some of the most conspicuous abuses. A council order in July directed the shipwrights' company to maintain better discipline and control over its members, there was another effort to commission pirate-hunters, orders went out to repair the most evidently faulty vessels, and some of the back pay of the Channel-fleet mariners was produced after long delays. But in November Northampton wrote in discouragement to Sir Thomas Lake that the king had lost £100,000 through pilfering since he had begun investigating naval frauds and that it was impossible to set things right, particularly while the pay remained so much in arrears "that the wives and children of the sailors are hardly kept from making outcries at the gate."[32] But Northampton had failed to make the navy honest, and, though he kept a keen and critical interest in naval abuses, he did not have another chance to do more than annoy his cousin with vengeful stories; by the time the next investigation into naval abuses came, he was dead.

With his privileges in one quarter secured for the time being upon the death of the 1613 commission, Nottingham soon found other privileges attracting attention as public outrages. The patent for licensing wine-sellers had drawn irregular fire throughout James's long Parliament; when Parliament was summoned in April, 1614, the air was again heavy with resentment over abuses of prerogative, one of the most important still being the granting of private-revenue monopolies, and one of the most troublesome of these still being that of wine licensing. The patent carried—though unsuccessfully—the principal burden of supporting one of the

32. *Cal. S. P. Dom., James I, 1611–1618*, p. 208.

most conspicuous noble households in the country and it provided a profitable venture for a group of hard-driving merchant entrepreneurs, but to the rest of the country it was a cause of disorderly drinking and breaches of the peace, an endemic threat to the security of the countryside. So once again it was high on the list of the grievances which the House of Commons insisted upon debating.[33]

In the House of Lords, Nottingham followed precisely the pattern that could be expected of a principal councilor. He made no direct defense of monopolies but defended the prerogative, thereby implicitly supporting the king's right to grant them. When the Commons requested a conference to consider impositions, Nottingham rose to express shock and horror; he trembled to think that "such a flower of the Crowne" could be called into question without the king's prior consent and said that at this time it would "not [be] fitt eyther to meete or conferre with them."[34] When impositions became subordinate to the slur on the Commons voiced by Bishop Neile in the same debate, Nottingham again took a high, if rather irrelevant, tone; he was one of those who had heard Neile speak but he insisted, despite all the arguments of common sense, that "I never sawe that it stoode with the iustice and equity of this house to punish or condemne a noble man of this house by common fame." This was the line taken in the answer of the Lords which ignored the obvious fact that what might be common fame when reported in the Commons was something more when the Lords had heard it with their own ears. But when the Commons persisted in demanding an explanation, the lord admiral was the first to agree—presumably in the hope that the work of Parliament could then be taken up in earnest—that Neile should be allowed to "interpritt his owne meaninge."[35] Others followed suit, but Neile's abject and self-deprecating speech failed to mollify the Com-

33. *Ibid.* p. 232.
34. Historical Manuscripts Commission, *The Manuscripts of the late Reginald Rawdon Hastings, Esq. of the Manor House, Ashby de la Zouch,* 4 vols. (London, 1928–47), 4:260.
35. *Ibid.,* p. 274.

mons, and, when that house persisted in intemperate debate, the king brought it to its altogether fruitless end.

The end of the Addled Parliament marked another turning point in Nottingham's relations with the crown and the country. Within a few days after the Commons disbanded, Northampton, who is given general credit for the final alienation between the king and his subjects which would force James more directly into the arms of Spain, was dead. In spite of his own sympathy for the Spanish alliance, Nottingham's sorrow was no doubt easy to contain; for years his cousin had been the chief threat to his security. Now that he was gone, a lazy and peace-loving sovereign could be more easily persuaded to forget uncomfortable probings into the state of the navy. Had Northampton lived, it seemed likely that he would have been made lord treasurer, which would have meant tedious times ahead for the naval establishment. But now the easy-going Suffolk, who had risen to greatness through his own naval achievements, got the place, and Suffolk, though certainly sincere in his loyalty to the king's service, had no reason to pry into corruption in departments other than his own.

After the fiasco of the Addled Parliament, Suffolk and the council did what they could to begin getting along without Parliament. A few pounds were raised in gifts from the clergy and from courtiers to meet the most pressing royal debts, a few steps were taken to try to reduce expenses, and some attempts were made to undercut the opposition of the parliamentary class by relieving a few of the grievances most loudly complained of. Among these were the monopoly grants, including the lord admiral's. There are undated documents in the State Papers, drafted as the king's answers to complaints, which uphold the legality of monopoly supervision of wine licenses but which indicate that no further grants will be made after the current one expires. These papers, like some of the arrangements within the wine farm, seem to have been worked out on the assumption that Nottingham's grant would not last many more years; the lord admiral, however, had displayed a remarkable durability. So on October 30, 1614, a further step was taken: his grant was annulled, and he and his son were awarded a payment of £11,072 6s. 8d. in compensation.[36] Just why that particular figure was set it is impossible to guess, but the sum represents just short of four years' purchase of the rental. It was, of course, far more than four years' purchase of the lord admiral's remainder after the several annuities had been subtracted.

It is interesting that the sum spent for the repurchase of the wine monopoly, which came out of the king's purse, represented about half of the £23,000 that had been collected in free-will gifts after Parliament was disbanded. James was more than half a million pounds in debt, but Nottingham, preoccupied with his own problems, could only continue to think of himself as constituting an important royal financial obligation. It might be argued that a man like Nottingham, old in years and in service, could be expected to take a more responsible attitude in the financial crisis, to urge moderation on the king and to practice it himself, reducing, if possible, his dependency on royal generosity. But the lord admiral apparently saw no relationship between his own needs and the king's debts; he was acutely conscious of his own obligations and he believed that his long and uninterrupted service gave him a right to claim a reward. After all, should the man who defeated the Spanish Armada be allowed to spend his declining years in penury? The recall of the wine grant made the lord admiral more than ever dependent on the careless liberality of his master, and, since Parliament did not meet again for nearly a decade, the political advantage in canceling the monopoly was soon lost. But the money received did allow Nottingham a few months of ease before the next and last crisis of his stewardship in the affairs of state.

By 1617 the long relationship between Nottingham and the admiralty was drawing toward the end made inevitable by his temperament, his age, his friends, and the climate of the time. Early that year his tempestuous lieutenant, Robert Mansell, took a wife, a lady who had been one of Queen Anne's maids of honor. It is nearly incredible that, in spite of Man-

36. Patent Rolls, 12 James I, p. 8, Public Records Office, London.

sell's imprisonments, his public outbursts, his well-known peculations, and his outright defiance of the prerogative, he was still firmly in favor. The king gave him £10,000, a generous reward, certainly, for one who had made away with far larger sums without his leave, and the festival was held at Denmark House at the charge of the queen.[37] It was not quite so excessive an affair as Rochester's union with Lady Essex, but it was nevertheless a gaudy show for a man who had every reason to want to live inconspicuously. Mansell's wedding was the last anachronistic display of the wealth and security of the old establishment in the admiralty, however. Rumors of reformations in the navy were again adrift, this time as part of a major royal house cleaning which would systematize the king's revenues and reduce his costs. And this time the issue was not clouded by the personal antipathies of Nottingham and Northampton.

There is an element of irony in the fact that the driving force behind fiscal revitalization was Sir Lionel Cranfield, who had risen as a farmer of revenues to members of the Howard family. He had received none of the public disapproval over management of wine licenses, for which he had been one of those directly responsible—the gentlemen who resented the existence of the patent recognized that the farmer was not to blame for the system which brought him a profit. But he had become the advocate of efficiency and economy against those interests and personalities which had been the avenue of his own advancement. This situation did not make him more widely beloved at court, but there is no suggestion that Nottingham resented him or what he was doing. There were even rumors for a time that Cranfield would be brought almost into the family as the second husband of the newly widowed Lady Effingham.

Cranfield's task was made easier by the apparent fact that Nottingham was finally ready to give up the admiralty in 1617, if only some way could be found to provide for his family. There is no suggestion whatsoever that he had been

37. Nichols, *Progresses of King James the First,* 3:254.

persuaded that the crown deserved better service or that he now admitted that he was a hindrance to reform of the abuses which had not diminished since 1608. The admiralty was still his property by patent, and its functioning was his concern and his officers'; no new investigations, by however highly placed critics, would ever change that. But what he recognized was that he was feeble, old, and sick, that he would not likely live much longer, and that unless something was done his family would be left in want when he died. Even with what income the admiralty still brought in, the main support of his house was clearly royal charity. Nottingham himself had two pensions totaling £2,700 from impositions, and these were augmented by separate allowances for his wife and young children. It was well known at court that each of the several infants his wife was still producing had to be provided for at public expense; at the end of the year Chamberlain wrote laconically that "the Lord Admirall had a young sonne about a fortnight since but yt lasted not above a weeke and so a pension is saved."[38] The pensions were never enough; in both 1616 and 1617 Nottingham had received £1,500 as the king's "free gift" from the Exchequer. It can hardly be said in these circumstances that he was providing for his family while he lived, but with his death there would be much less. He had never possessed a great deal of landed property and most of that was now gone; no doubt he had scraped together some kind of a jointure for his young wife, but it cannot have amounted to much. The loss of his own pensions and admiralty fees would be a devastating blow.

The prospect of death must have seemed more real to Nottingham in the early months of 1617. In the past few years, to judge from surviving references, his health had declined steadily, and he now seemed to spend about as many days in bed as out. He rarely ever attended the council any more; he signed council letters on only four occasions during 1617. When Mansell married, Nottingham was "dangerously ill" and may indeed have despaired of recovery, since during

38. McClure, *Letters of John Chamberlain*, 2:122.

his illness his wife was granted two new pensions for child support to take effect on his death. He survived this crisis but continued to be weak; Sanderson described him as "almost bed ridd."[39] It is strongly probable that his unhappy state and his family's gloomy future finally persuaded him to think about yielding up his place. At eighty-one he could scarcely expect to enjoy it for long anyway, so if he could somehow convert it into an endowment for his survivors his obligation to do so was clear.

The lord admiral's new interest in a personal settlement can be cited as one of the distinctions between the reorganization of the admiralty and that of the treasury, both of which were undertaken at the same time. Cranfield's commission from the king had not been directed toward a single department; he was to do what he could to save the king money and make his service more effective. By what certainly may be more than coincidence, those areas of administration most evidently abused were presided over by the Howard earls, Nottingham and Suffolk, and the court was overburdened with their rapacious connections. Both Howards were genial, loyal to their own, and sensitive on points of honor, and each as years passed had allowed the essential direction of his own business to slip out of his hands. The lord admiral was not, however, an object of suspicion himself, as Suffolk became. He had so obviously not enriched himself from his office in recent years that his own honesty was never questioned, and this gave him bargaining power that Suffolk or Sir Thomas Lake or even Lord Knollys did not possess; he was still the "good and gallant old lord"[40] who deserved well of the country. His own situation placed the newest investigation of the navy on a different if not necessarily nobler plane; there was no serious threat of scandalous and tawdry public prosecution, as in the cases of Suffolk and Lake, even though the sins committed in

39. [William Sanderson?], *Aulicus Coquinariae, or a Vindication in Answer to a Pamphlet, entituled The Court and Character of King James*, in *Secret History of the Court of James the First*, 2:263–64.

40. *Ibid*.

the navy were probably as grievous as those anywhere else. Property rights would be respected, prestige and precedence would be safeguarded, and futures would be protected.

The investigation into and reorganization of the navy proceeded decently, decorously, and quietly; there was little, in fact, to link them to proceedings elsewhere or to give rise to speculation that a campaign for the overthrow of the Howard faction was underway except the fact that Buckingham needed to overturn any organization independent of himself. Certainly Nottingham as well as Suffolk dabbled in intrigues to block Buckingham's rise: the young man whose face Lady Suffolk washed every day with posset curd in the hope of making him a rival was Nottingham's protégé, his wife's former page, a boy who had grown up in his house.[41] But the two men were not able to join together to prevent common downfall; there is even a suggestion, as late as April, 1618, that Suffolk was trying to block part of Nottingham's program for his own and his subordinates' insurance. Although each one's fate was worked out without much reference to the other, their eventual departure from office represented a significant change in the character of the court.

In Nottingham's case it is evident that there was some talk of a shift in personnel even before Cranfield's commission began its work—which reinforces the view that the lord admiral had begun to think about trading the power he could no longer exercise for financial support he sorely needed. At the time of his illness in March, 1617, there was "much speach" that he would resign his office to the earl of Pembroke, the richest nobleman in the country, who would presumably make it worth his while to do so. Six months later it was being said that he would "compound" with Buckingham for his place.[42]

But it was no longer Nottingham who was the principal obstruction to naval reform. Mansell, who controlled the records of expenditure, had so deeply rooted himself in the decayed body of the admiralty that he could still thwart any

41. Oppenheim, *Sir William Monson*, 1:xli.
42. McClure, *Letters of John Chamberlain*, 2:118.

investigation, which would, after all, concern itself largely with his own peculations. He would have to be removed from the treasurership before any substantial improvement could be made. He had been more discreet than Lady Suffolk, however, for no charges against him had been proved, and the king and the lord admiral were still his friends. What continues to excite wonder, though, is the contrast between Mansell and the even more exalted figures, Suffolk and Lake, who were guilty of sins no worse than his and who had also warmed themselves in the king's favor. They fell, ruined and disgraced, but Mansell did not. His office was removed, but this bluff soldier suffered no personal affront. In April, 1618, it was reported that the newly knighted Sir William Russell, a merchant in the Muscovy Company, was "in speech with Sir Robert Mansfield to buy his place. . . ."[43] Within a few weeks the negotiations had been worked out: Mansell would surrender his office to Russell for a cash sum and would be given a more prestigious and lifelong position, that of lieutenant of the admiralty, an office which had been vacant since the death of Sir Richard Leveson. Most extraordinary of all, Mansell would receive indemnity for any past errors; his grant of office was accompanied by the legal opinion that he could not be deprived of his new place for "any misdemeanors but such as belong to the execution of it." The sins of the treasurer, then, whatever investigation might show them to be, would not be visited upon the lieutenant. All in all, it was a remarkable bargain for a man in Mansell's position to have struck; his records had already been called for and it could not have been unknown to Cranfield or the king what they reflected. Presumably, however, he was able to demand and was granted the entire handsome settlement as his price for permitting the king's service to continue. Presumably, also, he had the lord admiral's full encouragement; Weldon believed that the favor to Mansell was made one of Nottingham's conditions for giving up the admiralty to Buckingham.

Mansell's promotion did not necessarily demonstrate the

43. Nichols, *Progresses of King James the First*, 3:478.

lord admiral's "care to the state, that his experience and abilities might support the others [Buckingham's] inabilities,"[44] as Weldon thought, and it was surely a strange precedent, but at least it did allow investigation to proceed without impediment.

The new commission, of which Cranfield was the nominal head, worked most of the year. Cranfield was giving most of his attention to the king's household, but at least three of the members—Sir John Coke, Thomas Norreys, and William Burrell—were experienced administrators who knew the navy well and could function with considerable independence. Both Burrell and Norreys had been involved in the 1608 investigations—Burrell then had been one of the admiralty's expert witnesses—and Coke had made investigations of his own during Fulke Greville's treasurership. By April, 1618, principally on Coke's initiative, they were reviewing such records as Mansell would make available—his ledgers and vouchers, however, had been conveniently lost and he was able to produce only an uncertified abstract of his payments for the last five years—and through the summer their labors continued. They found what everyone expected them to find: the disorder which had robbed the navy of its effectiveness had proceeded without check since the beginning of James's reign and earlier; conditions were shocking even to a court nurtured on laxity and luxury. In early September Cranfield offered Villiers some examples of "the abuses which we every day discover." So much money was paid to bring disabled ships from Chatham to Woolwich or Deptford for repairs that "it had been better for his Majesty to have given them away at Chatham, and £300 or £400 in money, to any that would have taken them." More was spent to transport timber from the king's own forests than it ought to have cost to buy it outright at the yards. The commissioners, he wrote, would gladly supply the navy with timbers for the money now being paid for carriage alone, "but we will make no such ill match for his Highness." No less than a quarter of the king's ships,

44. Weldon, *Court and Character of King James*, 1:429–32.

they found, were "wholly decayed and fit for fire-wood," in spite of the sums spent for repairing them which would have provided new ships. Officers still sold appointments at such high prices that the buyers "profess openly that they cannot live unless they may steal." Money was still being paid to maintain ships that had been broken up years ago, and excessive amounts were being paid for insufficient and faulty supplies.[45] For all these conditions and more, the final responsibility lay where it had always rested, with the lord admiral and his principal officer, the treasurer. Both were now in effect immune from prosecution, one because of his age and personal guilelessness, the other by fiat of the king. Other officers, however, fought the investigation step by step—Coke later reminded Buckingham of the "oppositions we endured" and the "envy . . . cast upon us"—and some, including Richard Bingley and Sir Guildford Slyngsbie, who had bought Trevor's place, were suspended from their offices, feeling, no doubt, that they had been unjustly singled out.

In place of the superseded officers, the investigating commission was reconstituted as an executive commission, which promised to reduce naval expenses by £20,000 a year and at the same time to build two new ships a year for the next five years. It is the final verdict on the Nottingham-Mansell administration that, even though there was still a degree of corruption, the commission made good its promise.

There remained only the question of the lord admiral himself. It was, however, no longer a matter of what would happen but of how it would be done. The possibilities were several: Nottingham might keep his office but yield the active administration to Buckingham or some other figure, Buckingham might be given joint authority as a co-admiral, or Nottingham might be persuaded to resign his patent completely for emoluments from the crown or the new admiral or both. All these solutions seem to have been considered in negotiations which continued through the rest of the year. As a first step, Prince Charles gave up to Buckingham his rever-

45. Oppenheim, *Administration of the Royal Navy*, 1:195–96.

sion to the office, but a reversion would convey no present powers. Very shortly it was given out that Buckingham and Nottingham would be made co-admirals; by late October the price had been worked out—Buckingham would pay "a goode round summe of redy monie," later revealed to be £3,000, and the crown would supply a pension, £1,000 a year for the rest of his life and the lives of his young wife and their eldest son (who continued to collect it until 1642), with £500 a year for support of the son while his parents lived. This much, apparently, was worked out amicably enough; Sanderson said the settlement was reached "with so much love and liking, that I have often observed Villiers his great civility to him ever after, at each meeting to call him father, and bend his knee. . . ."[46]

This much, too, allowed Buckingham to proceed with the reconstitution of the navy. During the fall and winter of 1618 he wrote often to John Coke and other commissioners, who busied themselves with the docks, yards, and ships. Unserviceable vessels were sold or destroyed, with some of their timbers going into a new dock at Chatham, the "rabble of loose people" that had encumbered naval payrolls was cleared away, and, most important, plans were made for rendering the service both more efficient and more honest. Coke's recommendations to that end reflected a change of view since the days when he had been a private agent for Fulke Greville. At that time he had damned the engrossment of all appointive powers into the hands of the lord admiral—now he believed that entrepreneurs like Mansell, holding patents for life, were a far greater source of danger. Since there was a new admiral, Coke would now recommend that even those whose offices came from the king "may notwithstanding depend upon the Lord Admiral for the recommendation of their ability and worth" and that the lesser officers, who customarily held patents for life, be reduced to tenure at the admiral's pleasure. To avoid the quagmires of "senates and synods," even the present commission, whose powers preceded Buckingham's,

46. [Sanderson?], *Aulicus Coquinariae,* 2:264.

should "wholly depend" on the admiral's authority and protection.[47] The presence of a new broom would sweep the admiralty clean, he thought, no longer appreciating as he once had that the most fundamental problem of the naval service was the quality which he would accentuate—its character as a private franchise of the admiral. But the commission (of which Coke remained the leading member) did represent something of a shift away from that character: in the next months Buckingham, always preoccupied with his manipulations of the king, dabbled only occasionally in admiralty business, and the commission, the nearest thing to a board of disinterested supervisors that the Jacobean age could provide, ran the navy. The frequency with which naval affairs were committed to a board of commissioners in the seventeenth century does suggest a groping toward professionalization and a rejection of the late medieval concept of private sovereignty.

During the winter both Nottingham and Buckingham continued as co-admirals, which may be one of the reasons why it was said that the commission system of administration was proving "inconvenient." The position of shared authority must have been galling to the old man who had had exclusive use of title and privileges for such a long time, but when he finally surrendered the office in January, 1619, it became evident why he had held onto an adulterated dignity: not all his conditions had been met. Financial security was one thing; the deference he had lived with was something that could not be paid for with a pension. As a former lord admiral he would have to take his place with other first-generation earls without regard to the glories of the past. Perhaps more to the point, Lady Nottingham would be nothing more than the young wife of an old, sick, and penurious earl. It was rare for an officer, no matter what his age or previous effectiveness, to give up a patent except through death or disgrace. To avoid the appearance that what was happening to him was only a degree less shameful than what had befallen Suffolk, Nottingham asked to be made Constable of England, which

47. *Coke MSS,* pp. 99–100.

would preserve his ceremonial precedence.[48] That request was refused, but the king did issue a new patent allowing him and his lady to precede all earls who had no offices of state. The patent would allow him to behave as though his title had not been created for him but inherited from his Mowbray ancestor, earl of Nottingham in the time of Richard II. This was a cheap enough honor, but the rules of precedence had rarely been tampered with; the step was apparently resented in other quarters, for Lady Nottingham later became involved in an acrimonious quarrel with Lady Arundel over their relative status as mourners for Queen Anne.

48. *Cal. S. P. Dom., James I, 1619–1623* (London, 1858), p. 40.

Epilogue

Queen Anne's funeral marked Nottingham's final disappearance from public life in England. When he gave up the admiralty he also gave up, so it seems, his seat on the Privy Council and retired almost completely from court life. He still held, for a time, an assortment of minor offices from which he would get a trickle of revenue and perquisites and with which he could busy himself if he chose. He was lieutenant and warden of the Windsor castle and parks, chief justice in eyre for the forests south of Trent, and lord lieutenant in Surrey and Sussex, offices which would not, in time of domestic peace, strain the capacities of even an old and tired grandee. Before the end of 1619, word spread that the engrossing Buckingham was buying the justiceship; Chamberlain understood that in November Buckingham had yielded to Rutland his own justiceship north of Trent and had arranged to take Nottingham's place in the south, but the agreement must have fallen through, for he did not actually take possession by grant until Nottingham's death. In all probability, price was the sticking point, since Nottingham now had no reason to hold the position except for its monetary value.

Physically, Nottingham seemed stronger after his retirement than he had for some years before. Even though he begged off attending the meeting of the Order of the Garter in June, 1619, because of a cold, he was no longer bedridden and could even venture out occasionally to hunt. As late as 1622 he was begging the king for a gift of sixteen or twenty stags for his park at Reigate, the pursuit of which would comfort his old age. He had always loved hunting and it was with game that these last years were preoccupied. His functions as an officer of the state seemed to devolve into the management of the king's deer around Windsor, Hampton Court, and Oatlands, though occasionally he did have to forward an order about beacons or musters in the areas of his lieutenancy. The old man made some little bustle over the distribution of gift deer to ambassadors and favorites, over restocking the forest walks, and over the capture of a ring of poachers.

But in the end not even this petty domain was managed to the satisfaction of its overlord. The king in his own declining months felt himself shut out of his government and tried to solace himself with the country life he had always enjoyed so much; he was no longer able to hunt, but he became upset over the shortage of deer. In August, 1620, he had to warn Nottingham to "take special care" of the Hampton Court game. It was not easy to replenish the herds, particularly when Secretary Conway and others sent long lists of people who were to be supplied with the bucks of the season. In 1623 a royal order countermanded all warrants for venison within thirty miles of London, but deer continued to be scarce, and in the summer of 1623 Nottingham feared that he would be punished by having what little public role he had left stripped away. Conway reassured him that the king had no wish to suspend him from any offices, but that he would need to "qualify" his authority "for the preservation of the game"—which seems to have meant that he could keep the offices while he lived but that others, mainly Buckingham, would shoulder his trivial bundle of responsibilities.

By the time Conway's letter was written, the man who was to receive it bore little resemblance indeed to the magnanimous conqueror of Cádiz who had been saturated with the accumulating gratitude of the crown. His mind had not dimmed appreciably—he had kept his faculties beyond the deaths of most of those who twenty years earlier had thought he was turning senile. But his confidence had evaporated with his wealth, leaving a consciousness of personal failure. Tatters of dignity had survived his withdrawal from office, but long commitment to public life and lavish rewards from it had not preserved a decent estate to pass on to his heirs. His successor as earl would be a man low in worldly esteem and probably lacking even in Nottingham's perception; to him Nottingham would be handing over a pitiful remnant of a patrimony, the scanty handful of manors that had not been sold off for debts or set aside as jointure. Besides the heir, there were the small, frail children whose main support would have to be the crown's fading memory of services performed a generation ago for another royal line—if, indeed, those small children were his own; a proud man might still remember the stories of infidelity that had amused the court not so many years before. One child, born late in 1617, and dead within a few weeks, must have been conceived somewhere near the time when Nottingham was believed to be on the edge of death. At any rate his widow and offspring would get little but the pensions that had been his most important support for more than a decade. In March of 1623 the king estimated Nottingham's pensions to be worth £3,700 a year; when he died, that sum would be reduced to £2,016 13s. 4d. for his survivors. Ironically, the king calculated the totals only in looking forward to Nottingham's death—the difference could make up the greater part of an annuity already promised to the earl of Carlisle. Given the wreckage of the king's finances, no poor nobleman could be sure that the royal liberality would not be shut off. When Cranfield temporarily stayed pensions in 1621 while he surveyed the range of the king's obligations, Nottingham wrote to him in panic, pleading his needs, his age, his past services, and the great sums he recalled spending in the Elizabethan wars; the same dread prospect arose again in 1623, and he wrote to Cranfield to swear his poverty and his gratitude in equally fervent terms.

These pleas for continued support are among his last surviving correspondences. In 1623 he wrote to Archbishop Abbott to inform against the son of his old naval associate Sir William Monson, a member of his own household, as a dangerous papist; the young man's imprisonment in the Gatehouse was the natural result of what was probably Nottingham's last public act. In early November, 1624, Conway intercepted a petition to the crown from one of the old earl's creditors, who had grown desperate of repayment; he for-

334

warded the petition to Nottingham with a respectful note that he would "not meddle any further" in the affair. If the creditor got anything, even the £100 for which he said he was willing to settle, he probably felt himself lucky. Time for collection was running out, and claims against an overburdened estate would be many.

Nottingham may never have read that note or seen the petition. His last days and the circumstances of his death are clouded by the same mist that envelops so many of the personal aspects of his life. For some years he had been living at Haling House, one of the few remaining residual profits of the Spanish war, and it was there that he died on December 14, 1624. By the time of his death he had already been forgotten outside his own family. He had been for so long a lingering anachronism that the nation no longer knew or cared whether he was still there or not. He was buried in the parish church at Reigate on December 18, the lead coffin being placed in the vault beneath the chancel where his father lay. His death was so little noticed that on the day his funeral was celebrated John Chamberlain, the ubiquitous court gossip, observed with astonishment the number of ex-officers of state still about the court; he counted four lord treasurers, four chamberlains, four secretaries, three masters of the wards, two chancellors, and two admirals, "unless the report of the Earl of Nottingham's death be true."

Even within Nottingham's family the sense of loss was not insuperable. His heir had complained years before of the burden of poverty which his father's long life implied, and his widow was soon able to comfort herself. Not quite a year later she married young William Monson, who, like others of his family, had been brought up in Nottingham's household and had once been her page; the next day, it is said, "she rid through the market" at Reigate and "hath since made more than ordinary visits to her neighbours to show her new husband." Just as Nottingham had made a surprising second match, so did his countess; Monson, the future viscount Castlemaine, was fourteen or fifteen years younger than she and well beneath her social plane. His rise in status from page to husband might have refueled the old rumors of flirtations under the earl's nose, but there is nothing now which can either prove or disprove them.

It is not recorded just how the citizens of Reigate welcomed the new lord of the manor; no doubt they were able to conceal any nostalgia or remorse they felt. But the fact was that it had been a long time since Reigate had known any lord but a Howard, and the Howards who lived there had been greater men than the place would know for many years to come. The first Howard of Nottingham and his father before him had had a quality of grandness—from their name, their ambition, their scale of life, and the reach of their power—which was now forever dead.

Reigate had been a prominent part of the patrimony of the barons of Effingham; it is perhaps symbolic of the decline of the family that it fell into new hands in 1624. The Howards of Effingham had for the better part of seventy-five years been as great or greater than the Howards of Norfolk, but now the vitality of the line was as weak as the estate was small. The second earl of Nottingham was a reasonably good argument in support of the Commonwealth's drive toward abolition of hereditary titles. Dim and dull, about all that can be said for him is that he performed minor services as lord lieutenant and continued to live off the overburdened royal bounty. When he died, his much younger half-brother took his title and his decayed claims on the nation's generosity. None of the first earl's sons had male heirs, so on the third earl's death the title expired—temporarily. Within a few months a rich and ambitious judge, whose ancestry could by no means be traced to the friends of Richard II, carried the dignity of the earldom of Nottingham. If he could have known about it, it would no doubt have wounded Charles Howard that the title he cherished had been given to a lawyer. The barony of Effingham still had heirs, the descendants of Sir William Howard of Lingfield, the faintly remembered son and brother of two lord admirals. In due time they were elevated to the earldom of Effingham, ancestors of the twentieth-century earls.

The first earl of Nottingham, in the generous characterization of Sir Robert Naunton, had been "as goodly a gentleman as the times had any." To Naunton, "it is out of doubt . . . that the admiral was a good, honest, and a brave man, and a faithful servant to his mistress." As his comment betrays, Naunton was remembering the vigorous Elizabethan Nottingham and not the venal Jacobean one. Indeed, it has been difficult for later generations to recall that the two men were the same, but in the spirit of charity the older man has much the lesser place in his country's memory. Even the spirit of charity, however, would tolerate some modification of Naunton's obituary: good, honest, and brave he was, as he knew those terms; faithful and diligent he was, and earnest in maintaining the dignity of his name and his place. But he lacked the perception and the skill to do more than what was expected of him, and he lacked the strength and the vision to separate himself from the worst aspects of the government of which he was for so long a part.

Index

Abbott, George, Archbishop, 334

Admiral, lord: appointment of, 33–34, 96, 102; complaints to, 60–62; interest in piracy, 75–76, 267–72; judicial functions of, 39, 41–42; legal jurisdiction of, 49–50; powers of, 37–39, 50–62, 98, 108–10; punitive powers of, 65–67; rights and perquisites of, 39, 44, 47–48, 58, 63–87, 271, 292, 329–30; warrants of, 48–49, 60, 67, 299, 303–4. *See also* Howard, Sir Charles

Admiralty: administration of, 265–66; as private franchise, 37, 63–87, 272, 291–93, 302, 322–23, 329–30; growth of, 37; judges of, 41–49; machinery of, 69–70; officers of, 39–42. *See also* Caesar, Sir Julius; Howard, Sir Charles; Navy

Admiralty, High Court of, 41–42; administration of, 64–65; cases in, 42–49, 68, 164, 265; fees in, 49; orders and warrants of, 43, 268; procedures in, 109–10. *See also* Caesar, Sir Julius; Privateering

Allyn, Edward, 31–32

Andrews, K. R., 64, 86–87, 163

Anjou and Alencon, duc d', 23–24

Anne, Queen, 252, 273, 274*n*, 287–88, 321–22, 331–32

Antônio, Dom, Portugese pretender, 116, 139

Antwerp, 22*n*, 24, 103

Appledram, Sussex, 20

Armada of 1588: attempt to prevent sailing of, 132–33; battle with, 146–60; coming of, 145; defeat of, 150–52; fears of new sailings, 161–62, 166, 182, 207, 209, 231–32; preparations for, 41, 111–14, 116, 118, 123–28, 131–32, 133–34, 138, 146, 167; retreat of, 150–54; rumored dismissal of, 130–31; rumor of return of, 153; sailing postponed, 127; size of, 146; tapestries commemorating, 160, 215, 257, 314–15; tradition of, 121–22; other references, 38, 59, 90*n*, 99, 184, 208

Armada of 1599, 222–32

Arundel House, London, 215, 256, 275, 314

Ashley, Sir Anthony, 174, 188, 195, 201

Azores, 50–54, 163–64, 207, 195, 198, 200–201, 210, 230

Babington plot, 104, 108

Bacon, Sir Francis, 214, 219, 235, 302

Bacon, Sir Nicholas, 97

Baeshe, Edward, 39–41

339

Baker, Christopher, 35, 113
Baker, Matthew, 113, 305–7, 309
Ballard, John, 104
Barnham, Sussex, 20
Barnstaple, 272
Barnstaple Priory, 20, 278
Baskerville, Sir Nicholas, 181
Bath, Knights of the, 261
Bath and Wells, bishop of, 215
Bedford, earl of. *See* Russell, Francis
Beeston, Sir George, 148
Bell, Philip, 84
Bergen op Zoom, 98
Berkshire, Howard property in, 12, 214, 277–78
Berwick, 26, 252
Beza, Theodore, 121
Billeshurst, Surrey, 18, 20
Billing, Northamptonshire, 12
Bingley, Sir Richard, 328
Blechingley, Surrey, 18, 20, 213, 215, 245
Blount, Charles, Lord Mountjoy, 219, 224
Blount, Sir Christopher, 174
Bludder, Thomas, 298
Bonds, for control of ships, 49, 56, 61, 68–69, 71, 73
Borough, William, 39, 41, 55–57, 113–14, 117, 133, 142
Bourbourg, negotiations at, 132–33, 135, 139
Bourchier, William, earl of Bath, 225–26, 272
Bourne, William, 35
Brest, 166, 227
Bridgwater, 53, 81, 86
Bristol, 72–73, 81, 86–87
Bromley, Sir Thomas, 23, 30, 97
Brooke, Frances Fitzgerald, nee Howard, countess of Kildare, 94, 204, 251–52, 263–64

Brooke, Henry, 8th Lord Cobham, 56, 203, 204, 237–38, 241, 251–52, 262–64
Brooke, William, 7th Lord Cobham, 22*n*, 104
Browne, Sir Thomas, 23, 89
Buck, Sir Peter, 298, 305
Buck, Thomas, 305
Buckhurst, Lord. *See* Sackville, Thomas
Burbage, Richard, 31
Burghley, Lord. *See* Cecil, Sir William
Burnell, Francis, 79
Burrell, William, 327

Cádiz, expedition to, 1596: anticipated, 167; arrival at city, 185–86; capture of city, 189–90; commission for voyage, 172–73; declaration justifying, 180–81; defenses of city, 186; departure for, 170–71, 184; evacuation of city, 197; fleets destroyed by, 118; honor of, 198, 202–3, 208; knighthoods conferred during, 148, 194; plunder taken on, 190–93, 199–202; preparations for, 166–74, 179; proposal to garrison city, 195–97; return from, 207; rivalries among commanders of, 183–88, 190, 203; size of, 173; other references, 52, 59, 85, 164
Caesar, Sir Julius: judge of High Court of Admiralty, 36, 41, 70; and Sir Charles Howard, 41–49, 63–65, 299, 243; correspondence of, 37–38, 41–42, 47–49, 74–76, 78, 111, 128; on commission for naval abuses, 302; perquisites of, 49, 68, 71, 73–74, 78–85; suits of, 45, 63–64

Calais: captured by Spain, 169, 178–79; fight in harbor of (1588), 149–50, 159; governorship of, 5, 10; siege of (1596), 174–77
Cambridge, University, 13
Campion, Abraham, 314
Carew, Sir George, 173–74, 182–83, 246
Carey, George, of Cockington, 199
Carey, Henry, 1st Lord Hunsdon: and Sir Charles Howard, 13, 16, 21, 24, 99, 129; as commissioner for earl marshal, 166; as lord chamberlain, 26, 28, 56, 97; as member of Privy Council, 30, 103–4; as patron of players, 32
Carey, Sir George, 2nd Lord Hunsdon, 68, 205, 268
Carey, Sir Robert, 118–19, 257
Carey family, 35, 75, 118
Carmarthen, Richard, 54, 199
Carr, Frances (Devereux, nee Howard), countess of Somerset, 322
Carr, Robert, earl of Somerset, 314–15, 322
Carsholton, Surrey, 215, 283
Castile, *adelantado* of, 222, 230–31
Cateau-Cambrésis, peace conference at, 10–11
Catholic League, 52, 61, 102, 110
Catholics, English, 139, 240, 249
Cecil, Sir Robert, Viscount Cranborne and earl of Salisbury: and Cádiz expedition, 168–69, 172–73, 182–83, 202–3; and Cobham, 251, 263; and Essex, 203, 206, 219–20, 225, 236, 240, 242; and "Howard party," 253–54,

284; and James I, 260, 262, 281–82; and Northampton, 284; and Scaramelli affair, 269; and Sir Charles Howard, 164, 204–6, 212, 246–47; and Spanish peace treaty, 284; and the succession problem, 247–54; correspondence of, 78, 168, 172, 176–77, 179, 180, 182–83, 199, 205, 214, 220, 221, 226, 228–29, 243, 254, 264, 284; death of, 313; intelligence agents of, 164; marriage of, suggested, 248
Cecil, Thomas, 2nd Lord Burghley, 237–38, 241
Cecil, Sir William, Lord Burghley: and Cádiz expedition, 168, 173, 179–81, 199; and Calais siege, 175; and Dutch treaty, 103; and Elizabeth I, 218; and naval affairs, 28–29, 40, 50, 58–60, 108, 112–13, 125, 128, 138, 154–57; and Mary Stuart, 104–6; and Sir Charles Howard, 52, 100, 129, 179–80, 204, 206; correspondence of, 56, 89–90, 119–20, 138, 145, 156; as court factionalist, 96
Chamberlain, John, letters of, 218–19, 221, 225–27, 256, 323, 332, 335
Chamberlain of the Household, 20, 25–30, 33, 97. *See also* Carey, Henry; Howard, Sir Charles; Radcliffe
"Chamberlain's survey" of the navy, 28–29, 113
Champernowne, Sir Arthur, 35
Channel, fleets in, 10, 14, 24, 38, 51–52, 112, 118–19, 126, 131–32, 137, 138, 141, 147, 149, 154, 162, 222, 258, 301, 315
Chapman, Richard, 56, 113

Charles, Prince (Charles I), 283, 328
Chatfield, Stephen, 92
Chatham, naval installations at, 41, 57, 119, 126, 205, 226, 300, 327, 329
Chelsea, Howard property at, 84, 92, 212, 213, 215, 274–75, 289
Chichester, militia captain for, 91
Chieveley, Berkshire, 12
Christian IV, king of Denmark, 226, 283, 287–88
Cinque Ports, 72, 85–86, 125, 206
Clifford, Sir Alexander, 185
Clifford, Sir Conyers, 174, 188
Clifford, Sir George, earl of Cumberland, 35, 51, 77, 151, 162, 166, 174, 178, 208, 238
Clinton, Edward Feinnes de, Lord Clinton and Saye, earl of Lincoln: as lord admiral, 13–14, 23, 25, 28, 35; death of 26, 28, 33, 96–97
Clinton, Henry Feinnes de, 2nd earl of Lincoln, 238
Cobham. See Brooke
Coke, Sir Edward, 235
Coke, Sir John, 295, 327, 329–30
Collectors of tenths, 70–71, 79, 81–86
Commons, House of, 12–13, 93, 245–46, 280–81, 296, 318–19
Constable of England, Howard as, 330–31
Conway, Sir Edward, 333–35
Cornwall, 69, 85–87
Cornwallis, Sir Charles, 285
Cotton, Sir Robert, 302–4, 310–12
Covert, Sir Walter, 89, 271

Cranborne, Lord. See Cecil, Sir Robert
Cranfield, Sir Lionel, 215, 276n, 277–79, 290, 322, 324–25, 334
Croft, Sir James, 132
Cross, Captain Robert, 53, 189
Cullimore, James, 276n, 277

Darrell, Marmaduke, 54, 170, 298
Dartmouth, 79, 81, 226
Davison, William, 104–6
Deptford, Kent, 41, 119, 129, 216, 327
Derby, earl of, 33, 69, 97
Derbyshire, Howard property in, 282
Devereux, Sir Robert, earl of Essex: and Cádiz expedition, 85, 167–68, 169, 173, 180–81, 185, 188–91, 195–97; and Calais siege, 175–79; and Henry IV, 169, 179; and Irish command, 217–223; and islands voyage, 207; and the succession problem, 247–48; as commander, 161, 198, 221–22; as factionalist at court, 206–7, 209–13, 218–20, 233, 243; debts and expenses of, 172, 174, 179, 181–82, 194, 200, 235–36, 243; disgrace of, 233–36; rebellion of, 235–39; relations with Cecil, 172, 236; relations with Elizabeth, 210–13, 217–18, 221–22, 233; relations with Howard, 93, 158–59, 170, 176–78, 183, 187–88, 194, 196–98, 203–4, 206, 208, 209-13, 221, 227, 236; relations with Raleigh, 207, 209; temperament of, 196; trial and execution of, 240–42; widow of, 239, 243

Devereux, Walter, 196, 207
Devonshire, 17, 69, 85–87, 225–26
Dieppe, 153, 169
Dockyards, supervision of, 40–41, 56
Donnington Castle, 214–15, 277–78
Dorset, earl of. *See* Sackville
Dorsetshire, 81, 83, 86–87
Dover, 24, 30, 130, 133, 153, 162, 175–76, 179
Drake, Richard, 159
Drake, Sir Francis: and the Armada, 122, 125–27, 132, 135, 138–39, 141–42, 147–48, 150, 153–54, 156; death of, 167, 181; voyages of, 77, 102–3, 115–18, 123, 162, 164, 168; other references, 35, 54, 60, 113, 119, 161, 167, 293
Drury, Sir Drue, 72
Dudley, Ambrose, earl of Warwick, 13, 26, 99
Dudley, Robert (son of Sir Robert D.), 93*n*
Dudley, Sir Robert, earl of Leicester: and court factions, 96–98; death of, 101; in the Netherlands, 99–100, 118–20, 123, 127, 135–36; political attitudes of, 100; relations with Howard, 69, 96–100, 204; other references, 21, 23–25, 30, 74, 99, 103, 235
Dudson, William, 79, 81
Duncombe, William, 279
Dunkirk, 68, 149, 152

Earl marshal, court of the, 166, 283, 317
Eastbrooke, Sussex, 17, 20, 314
East Indies, 80–81, 115
Eccles, Norfolk, 72

Edmonds, Sir Thomas, 274
Edward IV, king of England, 3, 73
Edward VI, king of England, 5, 17, 100, 275
Effingham, earls of, 336
Effingham, Lord. *See* Howard, Sir Charles
Effingham, Surrey, 17, 20
Egerton, Sir Thomas, Lord Ellesmere, 240, 242, 316
El Ferrol, 52, 209
Elizabeth I, queen of England: accession of, 10; and Cádiz expedition, 168, 173, 174, 181–83, 184, 193, 199–200; and Essex, 210–13, 217, 242; and France, 11, 176; and Katherine Howard, 16–17, 256; and naval affairs, 39–40, 51, 60, 77, 122, 125, 137, 139–40, 162; and Sir Charles Howard, 10, 12, 16, 177–80; and Spain, 14–15, 127, 132; and the Netherlands, 103, 119–20, 132, 136; and William Howard, 5*n*, 6, 17–18; decline and death of, 218, 246, 252, 254–55, 257–59; marriage negotiations of, 12, 23–24; plots concerning, 5–6, 104–5, 236; progresses of, 20–21, 30; succession problem and, 246–54, 257–58; other references, 12, 95, 226–27, 280
Elizabeth, Princess Palatine, 315
Esher, Surrey, 129, 213, 215
Essex, earl of. *See* Devereux, Sir Robert
Essex, 48, 72, 176
Essex House, London, 215, 239, 241, 253
Eversholt, Northamptonshire, 12
Exchequer, chancellor of, 28, 41

Farnese, Alexander, duca di Parma, 101, 103, 119, 131–34, 141, 146, 149, 151, 160
Fenner, Edward, 81
Fenner, George, 230
Fenner, Thomas, 35, 142, 153
Ferne, John, 276n, 277
Finch, Heneage, earl of Nottingham, 336
Fines, paid to lord admiral, 65–66
Fitzalan, Henry, earl of Arundel, 23, 215
Fitzgerald, Henry, earl of Kildare, 94, 289
Flemyng, Captain Thomas, 145
Flicke, Captain Robert, 53–54
Flushing, 38, 98, 119, 135–36, 315
Ford, Sussex, 282
Fortescue, Sir John, 56
Forts, admiralty jurisdiction over, 38–39, 162
France: ambassadors of, 24, 33, 62, 105, 109, 111, 211, 234, 257; and Mary Stuart, 105–6; pirates of, 70–71; privateering against, 34, 109–11; troops sent to, 54, 90, 161, 175–78; other references, 11, 58, 61–62, 101, 134, 283
Francis II, king of France, 11
Frederick, Prince Palatine, 315
Frias, duque de, constable of Castile, 284–85
Frobisher, Sir Martin, 50, 57, 139, 142, 147–48, 161–62
Froude, J. A., 159
Fuller, Nicholas, 281
Fuller, Thomas, 216

Gage family, 213
Gamage, Sir Thomas, 9
Gamage family, 9, 295
Garnet, Henry, 283

Garter, Order of the, 21, 261, 332
Gawdy, Philip, 256
Gerard, Sir Thomas, 174
Gillingham, shipyards at, 300
Gloucestershire, 20, 83
Gonson, Benjamin, 55
Goodman, Godfrey, 296, 300
Gorges, Sir Ferdinando, 199, 201, 230, 238, 241
Gorges, Nicholas, 35, 143
Gorges, Sir Thomas, 54, 158
Gravesend, 225
Gray's Inn, London, 13
Great Bookham, Surrey, 17, 20
Grenville, Sir Richard, 35, 50–51, 165, 188, 199
Gresham College, London, 245
Greville, Sir Fulke, Lord Brooke, 183, 238, 294–95, 297, 327, 329
Grey, Thomas, Lord, 241
Guiana, voyage to, 163–64, 165n

Hackstal, Surrey, 18, 20
Hakluyt, Richard, 14, 92, 245
Haling House, Croydon, 213, 215, 289, 335
Hampshire, 30, 70–71, 81, 83, 86, 214, 314
Hampton Court, 166, 333
Handover, P. M., 233
Hare, Samuel, 276n, 277, 279
Harington, Sir John, 235
Harwich, 86, 130
Hastings, Henry, earl of Huntingdon, 72
Hatton, Sir Christopher, 26, 31–32, 74, 99, 103, 106
Hawkins, Sir John: and the Armada, 41, 122, 133, 139, 142, 148, 153; as treasurer of the navy, 39–41, 50–51, 112–15, 124, 126, 133, 155–56, 159, 162, 163, 170–71,

293–94, 297; charges against, 28–29, 112–14, 293–94; correspondence of, 51, 55–57; death of, 167, 170, 181, 294; voyages of, 50, 104, 115, 119, 162, 168; other references, 77, 79–80, 116, 161, 167
Heneage, Sir Thomas, 154
Henry II, king of France, 11
Henry III, king of France, 33, 134
Henry IV, king of France, 102, 168–69, 176, 179, 234
Henry VI, king of England, 72
Henry VIII, king of England, 17, 39, 212, 213
Henry, Prince of Wales, 31, 216, 261, 274, 283, 306–7, 312–13
Henslowe, Philip, 31
Heralds, College of, 208
Herbert, Henry, 2nd earl of Pembroke, 69, 208, 225
Herbert, William, 3rd earl of Pembroke, 325
Heton, Thomas, 82
Hicks, Leo, 248–49
Hoby, Sir Edward, 143, 151, 166
Holstock, William, 35, 39
Holy League. See Catholic League
Howard, Anne (St. John), Lady Effingham, 322
Howard, Catherine (Knyvet), countess of Suffolk, 325–26
Howard, Charles, 2nd earl of Nottingham, 92–93, 245, 335–36
Howard, Charles, 3rd earl of Nottingham, 279, 282, 289, 336
Howard, Edward, 270
Howard, Henry, earl of Northampton: and Cecil, 250, 284;

and earl marshalcy, 283; and Essex, 251; and James I, 250–54, 262, 284; and naval inquiries, 302–12, 316, 318; and Raleigh, 251, 262; and Sir Charles Howard, 250, 284–86, 302, 322; and Spanish peace, 284–85; and Suffolk, 284; and the succession question, 250–54; character and motives of, 250, 302; correspondence of, 250, 253–54; death of, 318, 320
Howard, John, 1st duke of Norfolk, 3, 34
Howard, Katherine (Carey), countess of Nottingham, 16, 27, 118, 129, 205, 213, 255–56, 259, 289
Howard, Margaret (Gamage), Lady Effingham, 9, 20
Howard, Margaret (Stuart), countess of Nottingham, 273–74, 287–89, 330–31, 334–36
Howard, Philip, earl of Arundel, 215
Howard, Robert, 3
Howard, Sir Charles, 2nd Lord Howard of Effingham and 1st earl of Nottingham:
BIOGRAPHY
early life of, 7–10; early naval experience of, 10, 14, 22n, 24–25, 34–35, 118–19; in Northern Rebellion, 13–14; knighthood, 15; first marriage of, 16; Order of the Garter, 21; in Mary Stuart crisis, 104–6; as lord chamberlain, 20–21, 26–30, 96; as lord lieutenant, 88–92, 123, 125, 332–33
As lord admiral: appointment, 26, 33–35, 96, 102; administrative role of, 113–14,

271, 291–93, 305; rights and perquisites of, 63–87; ethical standards of, 42, 44, 46, 164, 267–72, 325–28
Armada command: 121–60; Armada instructions, 127–28, 140–41; in command of fleet, 128, 130, 137, 139–43, 145–60; exercise of responsibility, 144–60; tactics of, 146–47, 158–60; criticisms of, 158–59; war council, 128, 142–43; return to court after battle, 145; rewards of victory, 157–60
Cádiz command: appointment to lead, 169; plans made, 167–69; in attack on harbor, 188–89; attack on city, 190; knighthoods given, 194; plundering of city, 192–93, 194–95; return to England, 200–201
Earldom: 208–13; as lord general (1599), 222–32; and the Essex rebellion, 233–42; in succession intrigues, 246–54; second marriage of, 272–74; embassy to Spain, 291, 296, 300; inquiry into naval abuses (1608), 302, 306, 309–12; inquiry of 1613, 316, 316–17*n;* last command of, 313–16; retirement of, 321–30, 332; death of, 335; will of, 129
GENERAL CHARACTERISTICS attitudes toward Spain, 284–85, 314; character and appearance of, 6–7, 10, 36, 101, 176–77, 243–44, 282, 285, 336–37; debts and expenses of, 130, 156–57, 160, 171–72, 174, 179, 181–82, 194, 276–79, 287, 314, 321, 323–24; garrulity of, 7, 117,

249–50; health of, 196–97, 205, 207, 212, 255, 287, 323–24, 332; incomes of, 17, 27, 36, 63–87, 93, 111, 213, 215–16, 244, 264–67, 270, 274–82, 314, 323–24, 332–35; interest in sports and games, 6–7, 9, 12, 15*n*, 205, 244, 255, 332–33, membership in Parliament, 11–13, 22, 319; membership on Privy Council, 27, 29–30, 53, 55–56, 94–96, 104, 119, 255, 323, 332; offices and grants of, 12–13, 18, 21, 23, 25, 78, 96, 116, 157–58, 208, 214, 222–24, 238, 244, 282, 332–33; patronage, 91–93, 245–46, 246*n;* political attitudes of, 100–101, 132–35, 137, 281, 285–86, 314, 319–20, 337; precedence, 330–31; protection of players, 30–32, 244; rumored commands of, 116, 161, 165–66; ties with pirates, 75–76, 267–71; ties with Wales, 9, 297–98
RELATIONS
with Anne of Denmark, 288; Buckhurst, 123; Burghley, 40, 52, 100, 128–29, 179–80, 204, 206, 218; Caesar, 41–42, 43–46, 48–49, 63–65, 74–76, 111; Cecil (Robert), 128, 164, 204–6, 212, 243, 246, 251, 255, 261–63, 279, 282, 284, 313; Cobham, 204, 251–53, 262–64; Drake, 117, 141–42; Elizabeth I, 7, 10, 12, 25, 105, 130–31, 139–40, 177–78, 180, 200–202, 208, 212, 256–58; Essex, 93, 158–59, 170, 176–78, 183, 187–88, 191–92, 194, 196–98, 203–4, 206, 209–13, 211, 217,

219–21, 227, 233–42;
France, 9, 11–12, 111;
Henry, Prince of Wales, 313;
James I, 6–7, 134, 160, 260–
62, 264–65, 269–71, 273,
282–84, 314–15, 323; Lei-
cester, 96–100, 119, 123,
143, 204; Mansell, 304–5,
326; Northampton, 253, 262,
284–85, 302, 322; Raleigh,
159, 162–63, 165, 204,
212, 251, 275–76; Suffolk,
165, 262, 325; the Netherlands, 103, 119, 121, 135–
36
Howard, Sir Edward, 34
Howard, Thomas, earl of
Arundel, 215
Howard, Thomas, 2nd duke of
Norfolk, 3, 5
Howard, Thomas, 3rd duke of
Norfolk, 9, 34
Howard, Thomas, 4th duke of
Norfolk, 9, 21
Howard, Thomas, Lord Howard
of Walden and earl of Suffolk: and Cecil, 284, 313;
and Cobham, 263; and
James I, 250–51, 261–62,
284, 320; and naval inquiries,
306–7, 316; and Northamp-
ton, 284; and the Armada,
battle, 142–43, 148; and the
Azores expedition, 50–54,
162–63, 165–66, 199; and
the Cádiz expedition, 171,
173–74, 179, 182, 184, 188,
195, 198; and the crisis of
1599, 224, 228–31; and the
Essex rebellion, 238, 241–
42; as lord treasurer, 320,
324–26; disgrace of, 330;
other references, 35, 60, 161,
283
Howard, William, 1st Lord
Howard of Effingham: as

governor of Calais, 10; as lord
admiral, 5–6, 10, 33, as lord
chamberlain, 6; as lord privy
seal, 19; other references, 12–
13, 17–19, 213
Howard, William, 3rd Lord
Howard of Effingham, 92–93,
143, 189, 194, 215, 238, 245,
276–79, 289–91
Howard, William, of Lingfield,
89, 336
Howard family, 2–6, 25, 34,
93–94, 101, 129, 205, 285,
289, 323, 334–36
"Howard party," 253–54, 284,
286, 313–14
Hurstfield, Joel, 249

Impositions, debate on, 319
Infanta, Spanish, 248–49
Ingram, Arthur, 276n, 290
Inquiries into naval abuses: in
1608–9, 301–12; in 1613,
316–18; in 1618–19, 309,
325, 327–29
Ireland: lord deputyship of,
217–19; ships of, 185;
troops sent to, 54, 90, 161,
220–21; war in, 141, 205,
218–22, 233, 234–35, 264
Irish Sea, fleets in, 301

James V, king of Scotland, 273
James VI and I, king of Scotland and England: accession
of, 260–62; and Cobham,
252, 262; and Essex, 236;
and Mansell, 296, 312, 317–
18, 322; and monopolies,
277, 280–81; and naval affairs, 264–66, 267–71, 299,
306–10, 316–18; and Par-
liament, 318–21; and Ra-
leigh, 252, 262; and Sir
Charles Howard, 6–7, 213,
262, 269–71, 284, 314–15,

323; and the Armada, 134, 153; and the Spanish peace, 75, 284–85; and the succession question, 248–54, 257–60; character of, 260; extravagance of, 260, 281–82; other references, 202, 214, 252, 273–74

Jenkinson, Anthony, 35

Jesuits, in England, 91, 99, 194, 283

Jobson, Humphrey, 70–71, 76

Joinville, Treaty of, 102

Justice in eyre, 98, 283, 332

Kent, 162, 224–25; Howard property in, 129, 213, 215

Kildare, countess of. *See* Brooke, Frances

Kildare, earl of. *See* Fitzgerald

Killigrew, William, 199

Killigrew family, 69, 75

King's Bench, Court of the, 38, 48

King Street, London, 92, 215

Kingswood Liberty, Surrey, 18, 20

Knollys, Sir Francis, 103

Knollys, William, Lord, 324

Knyvet, Thomas, 143, 144*n*

La Coruña, 170, 228

Lagos, 197–98

Lake, Sir Thomas, 318, 324, 326

Lancaster, duchy of, 206, 210, 274, 303

Laughton, Sir J. K., 146

Lea, Thomas, 240

Leckhamstead, Berkshire, 214

Leicester, earl of. *See* Dudley, Sir Robert

Lepanto, Battle of, 153

Leveson, Margaret (Howard), 94, 289

Leveson, Sir Richard, 94, 143, 194, 258, 289, 295, 326

Leveson, Sir Walter, 94

Lieutenant, lord, 88–89, 104, 123, 125, 170, 258, 332

Lingfield, Surrey, 18, 20

Lisbon, 116, 118, 138, 300

Little Bookham, Surrey, 17, 20

London: and the crisis of 1599, 223, 225, 232; and the Essex rebellion, 237–39; Howard property in, 92, 215; merchants of, 77–78, 98, 272, 275–77, 300; piracy and privateering involving, 75–77, 78, 85–87, 162; ships of, 74, 123, 144, 164, 169, 173, 184, 223, 225; Tower of, 237–39, 252–53, 261; troops levied in, 176, 225, 230, 237–38

Lords, House of, 160, 208, 319

Low, George, 76*n*

Lubeck, ships of, 53, 110

Lymington, Hampshire, 214, 314

Lynn, 48, 86, 245

"Main Plots," 263

Manners, Edward, 3rd earl of Rutland, 25

Manners, Francis, 6th earl of Rutland, 332

Manners, Roger, 5th earl of Rutland, 25–26, 239

Manners family, 35

Mansell, Sir Robert: and James I, 296, 312, 317–18, 322; and Sir Charles Howard, 304–5; as lieutenant of admiralty, 325–26; as treasurer of the navy, 295–96, 325–28; at Cádiz, 295; in the Commons, 245–46; marriage of, 321–22; on the Spanish

embassy, 296; role in naval abuses, 301, 304–7, 316–18
Margate, 136, 152–55
Mariners: conditions among, 154–56, 318; levy and recruitment of, 55, 169–70
Marlowe, Christopher, 31
Marque and reprisal, letters of, 53, 58, 60, 67–68, 75, 266. *See also* Privateering
Marsden, R. G., 65, 71
Martial law, at sea, 37
Mary, queen of England, 5, 10, 17, 100
Mary Stuart, queen of Scotland, 11–14, 101–2, 104–6, 253
Massam, William, 276*n*
Mattingly, Garrett, 106, 122, 149
Maurice, prince of Orange, 135
Medina Sidonia, duque de, 138, 147, 149, 192, 194–95
Medway, the, ships at, 118, 123, 126, 176
Melbourne Castle, Derbyshire, 282
Mendoza, Bernardino de, ambassador of Spain, 30, 96–97, 115–17, 123
Merrick, Sir Gelley, 194, 201
Merton Priory, Surrey, 214
Middlesex, 23, 32, 176, 240
Molin, Nicolo, 269–70
Monopoly: on glassmaking, 296; on licensing sellers of wine, 275–82, 318–21
Monson, Sir William, 53, 334–36; in the Cádiz expedition, 186–88, 191–92, 197–98; on naval abuses, 298, 301
Monson, William, Viscount Castlemaine, 335–36
More, Sir George, 271
More, Sir William, 13, 23, 69, 89–90, 123
Mowbray, Margaret de, 3

Mowbray family, 3, 331
Myddelton, Thomas, 78

Naunton, Sir Robert, 36, 337
Navigation, books on, 36, 244
Navy: abuses in, 28–29, 163–64, 200–201, 267–72, 287, 291–313, 314, 316, 322, 325–28; officers of, 42, 55, 56–57, 124, 126, 162–63, 303–12, 328, 330; rules for government of, 312; size of in 1588, 146; treasurer of, 39–41, 59, 170 (*see also* Hawkins; Mansell)
Neile, Richard, bishop of Lincoln, 319
Netherlands, the: ambassadors of, 47, 109; news from, 227–28; privateering against, 34, 62, 109; ships of, 47, 61, 169, 173, 184–85, 189, 230; trade of, 108–9, 217; troops in, 54–55, 90, 98, 119, 161, 170, 173, 221, 223, 228–30; war in, 98, 101–4, 119–20, 124, 135, 264
Newfoundland, 52–53, 61
Nichols, John, 24
Norfolk, 69, 93, 229
Norfolk, duke of. *See* Howard, Thomas
Norreys, Thomas, 327
Norris, Sir Edward, 169, 174
Norris, Sir John, 55, 103, 162
Northampton, earl of. *See* Howard, Henry
Northamptonshire, 12, 20
Northern rebellion (1569), 13–14
Northumberland, earl of. *See* Percy
Nottingham, earl of. *See* Finch; Howard, Sir Charles

O'Neill, Hugh, earl of Tyrone, 94, 218–19, 242
Oostende, 118, 264
Oppenheim, M., 50, 75
Ordnance, manufacture of, 91
Osborne, Francis, 285
Oxford, earls of, 27

Palmer, Sir Henry, 35, 51–52, 57, 60, 89, 132, 142, 153–54, 220
Palmer, Sir Henry II, 298
Parliament, 104–5, 124, 208, 210–12, 245–46, 280–81, 296, 318–21
Parma, duca di. See Farnese
Passports, the issuing of, 38, 49, 67, 71
Paul's Cross, London, 227, 232, 237–38
Payton, Sir John, 241
Pembroke, earl of. See Herbert
Percy, Henry, 9th earl of Northumberland, 225, 252, 261
Percy, Thomas, 7th earl of Northumberland, 13–14
Perez, Antonio, 167
Pett, Phineas, 300–301, 303, 305–12
Petworth Castle, Sussex, 14
Philip II, king of Spain, 10–11, 50, 52, 102, 106, 115, 130–31, 133–34, 152, 161
Philip III, king of Spain, 249, 280, 284–85
Piracy, 94, 108, 266–67; and privateering, 67–68, 102, 264–66, 299–300; attempts to control, 38, 271–72, 318
Pirate goods, 44, 69–70, 73, 268–71
Pirates, 14, 44, 61, 70–71, 75–76, 112, 268–71
Plague, precautions against, 24, 91, 166
Players, at court, 30–32

Plymouth, 86, 145, 205, 226, 240; ships at, 51–52, 54, 57, 116, 118, 126, 133, 138, 140, 142, 155–56, 180–81, 200, 209
Portsmouth, 41, 57, 70–71, 81, 91, 118, 132, 142, 179
Portugal, 53, 58, 86, 101, 116, 139, 173
Preston, Amyas, 150
Privateering, 14, 24, 34, 48, 108–10, 217; and piracy, 61, 102, 264–67, 299–300; connection with naval abuses, 298–99; control of, 67–70; ended by James I, 264–65; income from, 67, 76–87
Privy Council: and military affairs, 90–91, 124–25, 132, 221–22; and naval affairs, 38, 50, 52–56, 58, 60–61, 75–76, 110–11, 122–23, 127, 134, 155, 168, 200–201, 207, 266, 318; and the crisis of 1599, 223, 225, 230; and the Essex rebellion, 236–39, 240–41; and the succession question, 258–59; politics within, 94–97
Prize goods, disputes over, 45, 47, 67–70, 110. See also Privateering
Puritans, 100–101, 235

Quarles, James, 41, 50, 124, 170–71
Queenborough, ships at, 126, 132

Radcliffe, Robert, 5th earl of Sussex, 208
Radcliffe, Thomas, 4th earl of Sussex, 13, 20–21, 23, 25–26, 97, 99
Raleigh, Elizabeth (Throgmorton), 276, 281

Raleigh, Sir Walter: and Essex, 203–4, 206–7, 209, 237; and Howard, 44, 159, 165, 165*n*, 204, 212; and James I, 247, 251–52, 262; and Northampton, 262; and the Cádiz expedition, 171, 173–74, 179, 183, 185–86, 188–89, 192, 195, 198; and the crisis of 1599, 229; finances of, 275–76; naval ventures of, 51, 54, 162–64, 166, 207; trial of, 262–63; other references, 77, 79, 123
Read, Conyers, 96, 100, 103
Read, Sir William, 119
Reigate, Surrey, 17–18, 20, 92, 213, 215, 245, 275, 289–90, 297, 332, 335–37
Rich, Penelope (Devereux), 242
Rich, Robert, Lord, 48, 72
Richard II, king of England, 331, 336
Richard III, king of England, 3
Richmond, duke of, 34, 39
Rochester, 119, 303
Russell, Elizabeth, Lady, 214–15
Russell, Francis, earl of Bedford, 26
Russell, Sir William, 136
Rutland, earl of. *See* Manners
Ryther, Augustine, 160

Sackville, Thomas, Lord Buckhurst and earl of Dorset, 78, 89–91, 104, 120*n*, 123, 217, 234, 242, 247, 261
St. John, Elizabeth (Chambers), 290
Salisbury, earl of. *See* Cecil, Sir Robert
Sanderson, William, 324, 329
Sanlúcar, 199–200
Santa Cruz, marquis de, 127, 183

Scaramelli, Giovanni Carlo, 267–71
Scarborough, 244
Scotland: fear of Spanish landing in, 131, 134–35, 141, 152; merchants of, 134; privateering against, 62; other references, 12, 58, 105–6
Seymour, Edward, earl of Hertford, 248
Seymour, Edward, Lord Beauchamp, 248
Seymour, Frances (Howard), countess of Hertford, 143, 248
Seymour, Henry, Lord, 35, 122, 141, 143, 149, 151, 153
Seymour, Thomas, lord admiral, 215
Sheffield, Edmund, Lord, earl of Mulgrave, 31, 142–43, 148, 205
Shipping: confiscation of, 102; damages to, 101–2, embargo on, 55–56, 60, 126, 169, 226
Ships: construction and maintenance of, 40–41, 50, 56–57, 59, 111–14, 119, 126, 133, 159, 181, 291, 300, 305–10, 318; sale of, overseas, 56; seizure of, 38, 73; individually mentioned: *Amity*, 44; *Antelope*, 220; *Ark Royal*, 113, 135, 143, 148, 150, 184–86; *Band*, 84; *Bonaventure*, 51, 53; *Concord*, 44; *Charles*, 163; *Cygnet*, 77; *Dainty*, 56; *Delight*, 163; *Disdain*, 146, 163–64; *Dragon*, 44; *Dreadnought*, 148, 220; *Elizabeth Jonas*, 143, 155; *Exchange*, 84; *Foresight*, 113; *Garland*, 51; *Golden Lion*, 148; *Katherine*, 42; *Lion's Whelp*, 77, 163–64; *Little Katherine*, 84;

Madre de Dios, 162; *Merhonour,* 309; *Minion,* 73; *Prince Royal,* 305–10, 312–13, 315; *Rainbow,* 178; *Randall,* 81; *Revenge,* 50–52, 113, 165; *St. Andrew,* 188; *San Felipe,* 77, 118; *Triumph,* 148; *Truelove,* 164; *Uggera Salvagnia,* 166; *Victory,* 305; *White Bear,* 126, 129, 135; *White Lion,* 77, 143

Shirley, Sir Thomas, 47, 89

Sidney, Sir Henry, 21

Sidney, Sir Robert, 238

Skynner's Place, Greenwich, 213, 215

Sluis, siege of, 119–20, 120n

Slyngsbie, Sir Guildford, 328

Soame, Stephen, 225, 227

Somerset, Edward, earl of Worcester, 208, 225, 261–62, 284, 306, 313

Somerset, 17, 69

Sonoy, General, 135–36

Southampton, earl of. *See* Wriothesley

Southampton, 72, 81–82, 164, 226, 270–71

Southwell, Elizabeth (Howard), 93

Southwell, Sir Robert, 69, 93, 143, 148, 155, 173–74, 179, 289

Southwick, Sussex, 17, 20

Spain: and the succession question, 248–49; armies of, 24, 169, 179, 226; embassy to, 284–85, 291, 296, 300; finances of, 50, 162; fleets of, 14–15, 50–52, 179, 185, 191–92, 194, 202, 208, 222, 224, 226, 228–31, 264 (*see also* Armada); peace with, 75, 132–33, 265, 284–85, 301; privateering against, 58, 61, 67–68, 73, 79, 86–87 (*see also* Privateering); war with, 30, 34, 61, 63, 85, 88–91, 100–104, 108, 111–16, 121–60, 161–62, 166–202, 207, 219, 222–32, 264, 269

Spenser, Edmund, 121–22

Stafford, Douglas (Howard), 38

Stafford, Sir Edward, 61, 99, 116

Standing army, need for, 231

Stanhope, Sir John, 213, 225, 238, 248

Star Chamber, 178, 234, 240

Steward, lord, Howard as, 208, 212, 283

Stokeham, Devonshire, 72

Stuart, Arabella, 96–97

Stuart, James, 1st earl of Moray, 273

Stuart, James, 2nd earl of Moray, 273, 274n

Stuart, James, 3rd earl of Moray, 273

Stuart, Ludovick, duke of Lennox, 283

Suffolk, earl of. *See* Howard, Thomas

Suffolk, 93, 125, 229

Surrey: elections in, 12–13, 22, 245; Howard property in, 17–18, 20, 92, 129, 213–15; lord lieutenancy for, 22, 88–92, 123, 225; other references, 30, 32, 91–92

Sussex, earl of. *See* Radcliffe

Sussex: elections in, 245; Howard property in, 17, 20, 282, 314; lord lieutenancy for, 88–92, 123, 224–25; other references, 14, 69

Swift, Garrett, 166

Talbot, George, 9th earl of Shrewsbury, 106

Talbot, Gilbert, 10th earl of Shrewsbury, 35, 208, 225
Thames, shipping in the, 55–56, 71, 130, 133, 153, 225
Theaters, 31–32
Theobalds, 20, 119, 261
Tompkins, Captain, 268–71
Townshend, Sir Roger, 148
Treasure fleets, from the Americas, 50, 52, 115, 162, 195–96, 198, 200
Trevor, Sir John, 279, 297–98, 301, 304–7, 316, 328
Trevor, Sir Richard, 245–46
Trinity House, London, 42–43, 71
Troops: discharge of, 228–30; levy of, 90–91, 104, 125, 169–70, 175–76, 223–25, 229–31, 237–38; transport of, 54–56

Ubaldini, Petruccio, 148, 160
Unton, Sir Henry, 169

Venice, 166, 229, 257, 267–71. *See also* Scaramelli; Molin
Venn, Richard, 276*n*, 277, 279
Vere, Sir Francis, 169–70, 173–74, 183, 190, 205, 209, 224, 228–30
Vice-admirals, 41, 53, 69–70, 126; accounts of, 74, 80; perquisites of, 70, 72
Victualing, 40–41, 52, 54, 57, 124, 221, 304; problems of, 137–38, 154–56, 170–71
Villiers, Sir George, duke of Buckingham, 72, 296, 325–30, 332–33
Vroom, Cornelius, 160

Wales, 9, 271, 295
Walsingham, Sir Francis, 22*n*, 25, 28–30, 100–101, 103–6,

108–9, 128–29; correspondence of, 24, 33, 62, 98–99, 130–35, 139, 142, 145, 150–52, 157
Wards, Court of, 41, 218
Warwick, earl of. *See* Dudley, Ambrose
Warwickshire, 20–21
"Watson's Conspiracy," 252
Waymouth, George, 305–7
Webster, Richard, 93
Weldon, Anthony, 326
West Humble, Surrey, 17, 20
West Indies, 115, 164, 168. *See also* Treasure fleets
Weymouth, 81, 84, 86
Whitelocke, James, 316–17
Whitgift, John, Archbishop, 104, 218, 225
Wight, Isle of, 24, 57, 140, 148, 226, 267
William of Orange, 24, 103
Williams, Sir Roger, 120*n*, 142
Williamson, J. A., 28, 114, 122, 141
Willson, D. H., 302
Wilson, Thomas, 247
Winchester, 92, 268, 283
Wine monopoly, 275–82
Windsor, 21, 244–45
Windsor Castle, 166, 214, 332–33
Wingfield, Sir John, 174, 190
Winter, Sir William: as surveyor of ships, 29, 39, 41, 112–14, 297; as vice-admiral, 69; naval commands of, 14–15, 35, 41, 104, 119, 122, 133, 149, 153
Wisshanger, Gloucestershire, 20
Woodhouse, Sir William, 221
Woodstock, 20, 269
Woolwich, 41, 306, 316, 327
Worcester, earl of. *See* Somerset, Edward

Wreck, rights concerning, 45, 48, 65–66, 70–74
Wriothesley, Henry, earl of Southampton, 70–71, 236, 239, 242

Yelverton, Sir Christopher, 235

Zouche, Edward, Lord, 72, 271, 302
Zouche, Nicholas, 82–83, 214

THE JOHNS HOPKINS PRESS

Designed by James C. Wageman

Composed in Linotype Garamond text with Monotype Garamond display

Printed on 60-lb. Lockhaven and

bound in Interlaken ARCO Vellum

by The Kingsport Press, Inc.